6. The party

Our relationship took off like a rocket launch. Ade and I saw each other at work and spent most evenings at home, cuddled up listening to music, watching a movie or talking about our hopes and dreams for the future. Occasionally we went out to the cinema but stayed well away from the gay scene in London. It didn't bother me, because I was in love and had everything I needed right at home.

On the few occasions we were apart, I used the opportunity to catch up with my friends. I didn't want to turn into one of 'those men' who dropped his friends the minute he found himself a partner.

I'd always taken pride in my ability to prioritise my time to allow for working at relationships, be they platonic or romantic. I viewed friendships as entities that required effort. After all, I worked at other things in my life that were important to me, such as my career, or hobbies and, since my friendships were important to me, I was prepared to work at maintaining them.

Working alongside Ade did wonders for my self-discipline. It took every effort to stop myself from dragging him off to a secluded area of the ward every five minutes to kiss those full, sexy, lips of his.

We were both quite clear that we wanted to keep our private life private, so we kept it under wraps at work. We only needed to continue like this for a short time because Ade was going to be moving to another job in a couple of months. Keeping our relationship a secret from our colleagues was one thing, but keeping it from my friends was a different kettle of fish.

I decided to break the news about dating Ade gently to Kunle.

"Kunle, how would you feel about me dating Ade?" I asked casually.

"You're an adult Chris and it's your business. You don't need my approval to date him. You know how I feel about him, but at the end of the day it's your call."

"I just asked for your opinion, that's all. No need to get your knickers in a twist about it," I said, a little too defensively.

"Whatever Chris, just don't come running to me when it falls apart."

"What do you mean?" I asked.

"Don't play games Chris; you know exactly what I mean. I told you about him approaching me for a date after my separation from his cousin, Aduni."

"Don't you think that people can change? Doesn't everyone deserve a second chance?" I asked.

"Chris, how many leopards do you know that changed their spots?"

"Well, I was just considering dating him, I haven't done anything about it as yet," I lied.

"Looks to me like you've made your mind up already," he said.

"Are you upset about my decision?" I asked.

"Chris I care about you too much to get angry over this. If going out with this asshole means so much to you, then you have my blessing-but you will need more than my blessing-Baby you'll need a miracle, the walking on water kind at that too," he said.

After talking with Kunle I felt a sense of relief, not dissimilar to the kind I'd felt in the past after confession. I reflected on our conversation and wondered if his warnings about Ade were purely platonic. He sounded like an ex-boyfriend who wasn't happy seeing me date anyone, let alone someone he didn't particularly get along with. I once thought that Kunle was my soul mate, but our lives had changed course and we were now best friends; so I shouldn't have been surprised when some of the closeness we shared as lovers infiltrated our friendship.

Whenever I spoke with Kunle I felt listened to. He had a way of making me believe that I had his full attention as well as his loyalty. I hoped that I could be as good a friend to him as he was to me. I wanted him to find someone special; someone who would treat him the way he deserved to be treated. He was too beautiful a person to be on his own and would be a prize catch for some lucky man.

Ade was planning to visit his parents in Nigeria over the Christmas holidays. He was due to leave for Lagos on December 21st for two weeks. It would be our first Christmas as a couple and I knew I would miss him terribly.

He stopped momentarily, to ask if I was sure that this was what I wanted. A voice in my head screamed, 'Don't stop, for fuck sake don't stop.'

I motioned for Ade to lie down, before gently pulling down his underwear. I wanted to feel his naked body against mines. Everything seemed to be happening in slow motion. With my eyes closed, I used my hands to create a mental image of his body. I covered his body with little kisses, to his delight. His breath seemed to quicken, as I kissed the insides of his legs. He pulled me onto him, and we were locked in an embrace for what seemed like forever.

The falling rain created an ideal backdrop for our passion. We took turns satisfying each other. Making love to Ade felt right. I had been worried that sex with him, might not have lived up to the fantasy in my head. Thankfully, I was wrong. The connection I felt, made the experience even more special to me, and took me to a place I hadn't expected to visit. Our lovemaking was passionate and deliberate, stopping only when we were both spent of energy.

Lying next to Ade, listening to his gentle snoring, I couldn't help feeling that I'd found him-the one I'd been searching for. It was early days, but I wanted to hold on to the dream for as long as I could. As if on cue, Ade pulled me closer to him, like a child clutching his favourite blanket. I smiled to myself, before drifting into a peaceful sleep.

I woke up early the next morning. It took me a few seconds to realise that the memory of the previous night had not come from a dream. Ade was lying next to me snoring lightly. I smiled as a warm feeling engulfed me. I felt happy as I drifted back off to sleep, holding my man.

The next time I woke up, Ade's arms were embracing me. I liked how they felt. He also had a morning erection; but, after the night we'd had, I didn't have the energy to do anything about it. Although my heart was willing, physically I wasn't up for another session. Neither of us made a move to get out of bed.

We spent most of the morning in bed talking and sometimes just holding on to each other. Secretly I hoped this would be the start of a relationship, but I couldn't rule out the possibility that it could just be a hook up. I didn't want to misread the situation. I'd seen the movie 'Fatal Attraction' too many times to know that 'bunny boiling' wasn't my style.

I would not be able to bear it if, after that wonderful preview, I had to miss the main attraction. I wasn't sure that my heart would be able to withstand further disappointment. I also didn't want Ade to feel pressured into anything he wasn't ready for. If he needed time to be sure, then that was fine by me. I was prepared to be patient.

I made Ade brunch in bed. He left to get a change of clothing from his flat, and promised to see me later that evening. He thought it would be fun to rent a movie and stay in. I suggested he get the movie 'Bringing down the House' starring Queen Latifah. I had a few errands to run while he was gone.

We kissed before he left. I did offer to drive him to his flat but he wanted to make his own way there. He said he didn't want to impose, although in my estimation it was no imposition at all. I was happy to assist my man in any way I could.

The radio played loudly in the background as I tidied the flat. A song came on, which encapsulated what was going through my mind. I felt on top of the world, and wondered if indeed Ade was just too good to be true. All I wanted was someone I could love and who would love me back. With my luck in choosing men, my 'prince' would probably turn out to be Satan's long lost son, who was an emotionally crippled, crack-head, and devoid of a soul.

ETHICS AND ENJOYMENT IN LATE MEDIEVAL POETRY

Jessica Rosenfeld provides a history of the ethics of medieval vernacular love poetry by tracing its engagement with the late medieval reception of Aristotle. Beginning with a history of the idea of enjoyment from Plato to Peter Abelard and the troubadours, the book then presents a literary and philosophical history of the medieval ethics of love, centered on the legacy of the *Roman de la Rose*. The chapters reveal that "courtly love" was scarcely confined to what is often characterized as an ethic of sacrifice and deferral, but also engaged with Aristotelian ideas about pleasure and earthly happiness. Readings of Machaut, Froissart, Chaucer, Dante, Deguileville, and Langland show that poets were often markedly aware of the overlapping ethical languages of philosophy and erotic poetry. The study's conclusion places medieval poetry and philosophy in the context of psychoanalytic ethics, and argues for a re-evaluation of Lacan's ideas about courtly love.

JESSICA ROSENFELD is Assistant Professor of English at Washington University in St. Louis.

CAMBRIDGE STUDIES IN MEDIEVAL LITERATURE

This series of critical books seeks to cover the whole area of literature written in the major medieval languages – the main European vernaculars, and medieval Latin and Greek – during the period *c.*1100–1500. Its chief aim is to publish and stimulate fresh scholarship and criticism on medieval literature, special emphasis being placed on understanding major works of poetry, prose, and drama in relation to the contemporary culture and learning which fostered them.

RECENT TITLES IN THE SERIES

Edwin D. Craun *Ethics and Power in Medieval English Reformist Writing*
David Matthews *Writing to the King: Nation, Kingship, and Literature in England, 1250–1350*
Mary Carruthers (ed.) *Rhetoric Beyond Words: Delight and Persuasion in the Arts of the Middle Ages*
Katharine Breen *Imagining an English Reading Public, 1150–1400*
Antony J. Hasler *Court Poetry in Late Medieval England and Scotland: Allegories of Authority*
Shannon Gayk *Image, Text, and Religious Reform in Fifteenth-Century England*
Lisa H. Cooper *Artisans and Narrative Craft in Late-Medieval England*
Alison Cornish *Vernacular Translation in Dante's Italy: Illiterate Literature*
Jane Gilbert *Living Death in Medieval French and English Literature*
Jessica Rosenfeld *Ethics and Enjoyment in Late Medieval Poetry: Love after Aristotle*

A complete list of titles in the series can be found at the end of the volume.

ETHICS AND ENJOYMENT IN LATE MEDIEVAL POETRY

Love after Aristotle

JESSICA ROSENFELD

CAMBRIDGE UNIVERSITY PRESS
Cambridge, New York, Melbourne, Madrid, Cape Town, Singapore,
São Paulo, Delhi, Dubai, Tokyo, Mexico City

Cambridge University Press
The Edinburgh Building, Cambridge CB2 8RU, UK

Published in the United States of America by Cambridge University Press, New York

www.cambridge.org
Information on this title: www.cambridge.org/9781107000117

First published 2011

Printed in the United Kingdom at the University Press, Cambridge

A catalogue record for this publication is available from the British Library

Library of Congress Cataloguing in Publication data
Rosenfeld, Jessica, 1976–
Ethics and enjoyment in late medieval poetry : love after Aristotle / Jessica Rosenfeld.
p. cm. – (Cambridge studies in medieval literature)
Includes bibliographical references and index.
ISBN 978-1-107-00011-7 (hardback)
1. Poetry, Medieval–History and criticism. 2. Pleasure in literature.
3. Ethics in literature. I. Title.
PN688.R67 2010
809.1′9353–dc22
2010038968

ISBN 978-1-107-00011-7 Hardback

Contents

Acknowledgments

This book had its beginnings in a conversation about Aristotle with Rita Copeland, in a cafe on Rittenhouse Square. My work has been indelibly shaped by her ideas and exemplary scholarship, and I remain indebted in countless ways to her generosity and inspiration as my teacher, advisor, and friend. I am also incredibly lucky to have been a student of David Wallace; I am grateful to him for his knowledge and imagination, and for making me an avowed comparatist and a confident scholar. Emily Steiner and Kevin Brownlee were essential advisors, and I am enormously thankful for their instruction, expertise, and faith in this project. I would like to thank Simon Gaunt for being a welcoming teacher and valuable reader during a year spent at King's College London and beyond. I continue to be grateful to Denise Despres, who taught an undergraduate course on medieval literature that showed me what an intellectually rewarding and exciting field of study it could be.

I would like to thank the two anonymous readers for Cambridge University Press for their eminently sound suggestions, which markedly improved the book. Frank Grady gamely read just about the whole thing in various stages and dispensed a great amount of thoughtful criticism with humor. Bruce Holsinger gave incisive comments on an early chapter and later gave me tough but welcome advice about the framing of the book. Holly Barbaccia, Jane Degenhardt, Jennifer Higginbotham, and Elizabeth Williamson were excellent writing companions during the dissertation years. Shane Duarte was and is an indispensable source of knowledge about ancient and medieval philosophy. Many others near and far have given exceedingly helpful feedback on various portions of the manuscript and provided other important support; I especially want to thank Jennifer Arch, Guinn Batten, Hans Bork, Lara Bovilsky, Kim Haddix, Sean Keilen, Irit Kleiman, David Lawton, Robert Lerner, Mark Miller, Allan Mitchell, Anca Parvulescu, Jean-Michel Rabaté, Melissa Sanchez, Julie Singer, and Alicia Walker.

Without Michelle Karnes as my cheerleader, critic, interlocutor, and friend, my life as a medievalist would have far less enjoyment in it. I'm grateful to my family for their unwavering support, excitement, and constant nudging about when the book would be done already. And I am thankful beyond measure to have Dillon Brown as my first, last, and sharpest reader and strict advocate of the happy life.

A slightly earlier version of Chapter 2 was published as "Narcissus after Aristotle: Love and Ethics in *Le Roman de la Rose*" in *New Medieval Literatures* 9 (2007): 1–39. Part of Chapter 5 appeared in an earlier form as "The Doubled Joys of *Troilus and Criseyde*," in *The Erotics of Consolation: Desire and Distance in the Late Middle Ages*, ed. Steven Milner and Catherine Leglu (New York and Basingstoke: Palgrave Macmillan, 2008), pp. 39–59, reproduced with permission of Palgrave Macmillan. I thank the publishers for permission to reprint.

Introduction: love after Aristotle

The story of the impact of the late medieval Latin translation of Aristotle has been told and retold for the fields of medieval philosophy and theology.[1] This book tells the story for the medieval English literature of love. The existence of such a narrative might seem unlikely, given the distance between the discourses of a highly specialized, university-centered, Latinate medieval philosophy and an entertainment-oriented, court-centered, vernacular poetry, but it is the late medieval configuration of ethics that brings these two worlds together. Medieval commentators considered poetry to be an ethical genre, typically referring to poetry's interest in human behavior and moral choices to justify this classification. As the field of philosophy constituted by both practical and abstract considerations of virtuous action, desire, and relationships, it is even now not terribly controversial to claim that moral philosophy is involved with the same kinds of human experience as poetry. Yet the medieval emphasis on love as a central ethical concern meant that – from the moment of the "birth" of the vernacular literature of love – philosophy and poetry were yoked together in often surprising ways by a shared language of longing, despair, pleasure, and union. Vernacular poetry constituted a site for thinking through ethical problems such as conflicting loyalties, conflicting emotions, and the necessity for self-sacrifice within the larger context of the pursuit of erotic enjoyment; clerkly ethical concerns with spiritual culpability and love of God were transformed and given voice in a context of pursuits of human justice, love, and happiness. Yet with the sudden availability of Aristotle's ethical writings in the mid thirteenth century – including the entirety of the *Nicomachean Ethics* – vernacular love poetry no longer offered the only space for the consideration of earthly happiness, and central ethical concepts of pleasure, love, and happiness were subjected to reconsideration and redefinition.

The full translation of Aristotle's *Nicomachean Ethics* in particular opened up a new framework for philosophical speculation about the nature of and path toward the sovereign good, a framework that had immediate and widespread effects owing to the centrality of Aristotle in the arts curriculum of the medieval university.[2] Aristotle was already an authority on moral philosophy, with his ideas about moderation, virtue, and *habitus* known through early, partial translations of the *Ethics* and the writings of Boethius and Cicero.[3] But his idea of happiness was typically understood to pertain solely to practical, political happiness. With the full translation of the *Ethics* by Robert Grosseteste (*c.*1246–7; revised by William of Moerbeke *c.*1250–60), the confinement of Aristotelian felicity to the practical was difficult to sustain.[4] The *Ethics* in its full form introduced a definition of felicity that would prove challenging to assimilate to a Christian worldview, for its previously unavailable final book describes a life of perfect contemplative happiness that is theoretically attainable in the mundane world. Early Christian theologians had certainly treated happiness as a spiritual goal, but this happiness was typically only accessible in the afterlife or through experiences bestowed by God's intervention. Absorbing a notion of self-reflection and intellectual contemplation as the highest *human* happiness would require a re-examination of central concepts in medieval ethics: action, love, pleasure, felicity, the good. Human happiness thus became a valid starting point for ethical inquiry, and earthly "imperfect" felicity a suitable moral goal. The new translation of Aristotle's *Ethics* offered an ethical goal imaginable within the space of the narrative of a human life.[5]

It was this earthly location of happiness that changed the way both philosophers and poets thought about love. For beyond the difficulty of assimilating Aristotle's notion of happiness as an earthly activity lay the problem that this theory did not appear to include love. Aristotle's definition of happiness as the most excellent activity of the most virtuous person upon the best object recognizes pleasure as an integral aspect of such action, but this pleasure accompanies, as a "supervening end," the activity of contemplation, not joy in the beloved object.[6] Not only could Aristotelian happiness no longer be explained away as purely active or practical, his contemplative ideal could not easily be assimilated to Christian contemplation, or loving reflection upon God. Medieval readers were left to account for and justify what they understood as an omission in a variety of ways, a project that began with the first complete Latin commentary on the *Ethics*, written by Albert the Great. Albert introduced the problem of Aristotelian contemplation's relationship to love, and proposed that, even in Aristotle, contemplation must be oriented ultimately toward love of God; his student Thomas Aquinas resolved that Aristotle must be speaking about "imperfect" rather than perfect happiness. While this attribution of imperfection to Aristotelian happiness may seem to be a willful misreading of Aristotle, it had the effect of rendering human imperfection and incompleteness, not to mention unfulfilled desire, valid topics for philosophical speculation and ethical consideration. Such shifts were deeply influential, for the relationship between happiness and love of God were hardly peripheral considerations, even outside Aristotelian science. Moral philosophy of this period was already gripped with the challenges of defining pleasure and love, usefulness and enjoyment, need and desire, lack and fulfillment, largely in the wake of Peter Lombard's *Sentences* (required theological reading for university students). Medieval philosophers debated whether enjoyment (*fruitio*) – defined as love of an object for its own sake, and the highest good – was a function of the intellect or of the will, whether pleasure (*delectatio*) always accompanied enjoyment, and whether it was ever appropriate to talk about happiness in this world, and in what terms. They asked questions about the proper object of love (*dilectio*), the relationship between love and pleasure, and the possibility that love might be accompanied by despair (*tristitia*). They wondered about the relationship between the intellect (*intellectus*) and the will (*voluntas*) as well as which faculty was the seat of love and the noblest pleasure. Aristotle – referred to typically as "the Philosopher" (as Augustine was "the Theologian") – was an important and constant reference point in these discussions.

Although I will focus largely on the *Ethics* in this study, Aristotle's ideas about the good, pleasure, happiness, friendship, and community were also newly available in the *Politics*, *Rhetoric*, *De Anima*, and the pseudo-Aristotelian *Economics*.[7] The *Politics* offered a way of thinking about communities that were oriented toward secular ends, as well as a notion of a "common good" that was not defined solely in terms of Christian morality.[8] Like the *Nicomachean Ethics*, the *Politics* treated life as an end in itself, finding solace and natural sweetness (*solatio … et dulcedine naturali*) in living for its own sake – even despite hardship and pain.[9] Similarly, Aristotle observes that people form friendships and communities because of an innate desire for company, not necessarily or only because other people provide for specific needs.[10] The *Economics* describes marriage as a moral community; in an ideal partnership a husband and wife are agreed "about the best things in life" and their friends follow suit.[11] Unlike animals, the human male and female couple aims not only at continued existence (*esse*), but a moral, happy life (*bene esse*).[12] The *Ethics* was not understood in isolation, but in the larger context of other Aristotelian writings on the psychology of happiness and free will, the role of the state, the nature of marriage, and the nature of pleasure, pain, and the emotions. Jean Buridan exemplifies this context in his commentary on the tenth book of the *Ethics*, which references the *Politics*, *Metaphysics*, *Posterior Analytics*, *Rhetoric*, and *De Anima* alongside the writings of Cicero, Seneca, and others. In addition, as Matthew Kempshall shows with respect to Giles of Rome's *De Regimine Principum*, a treatise largely on ethics and politics may be influenced not only by Aristotle's *Ethics* and *Politics*, but by a text like the *Rhetoric*, which often circulated with the latter works in the same manuscripts.[13]

The new Aristotelian moral science did not confine itself to learned Latin discourse; the philosophical debates and questions described above are recognizable in the transformed contexts of vernacular literature, and give new dimensions to what scholars have long recognized as the ethical contexts and content of medieval poetry. As Judson Allen has illustrated, the lines between ethics and poetry in the medieval period are indistinct at best. In the introduction to *The Ethical Poetic of the Later Middle Ages*, Allen describes his search for the medieval category of the "literary," only to find the ethical. In a common medieval classification system that divided knowledge into three branches – logic, ethics, and physics – poetry was quite consistently placed in the category of ethics.[14] His cataloguing of dozens of medieval commentaries on classical and medieval literature (Ovid, Statius, Boethius) led Allen to the conclusion that poetry constituted a significant part of ethical knowledge in this period, and that ethics is itself "enacted poetry."[15] Allen argues that the ethical aspect of poetry is revealed not only in commentaries, but in the way medieval poetry itself functions. For the medieval subject to think ethically, he or she "must behave as if in a story."[16] One often finds characters in medieval narratives comparing themselves to other literary figures – as ideals, or as dangerous examples to avoid. They embody and make explicit the notion that literature offers models and possibilities to embrace, re-enact, or ward off. As John Dagenais describes the medieval practice of "ethical reading," texts "reached out and grabbed the reader, involved him or her in praise and blame, in judgments about effective and ineffective human behavior" and invited readers to confront "basic questions about how one should behave with a view to greater happiness in this world and the next."[17] Of course, such thinking does not guarantee ethical behavior or success. To call medieval poetry ethical is not to lose the subversive or excessive, the rebellious or the strange; it is simply to acknowledge an interest in "telling stories about what we think we are like, what we think we want, and what we think we are capable of."[18]

Perhaps surprisingly, fourteenth-century moral philosophers similarly acknowledged the literary dimensions of even academic ethical discourse. By the same reasoning with which commentators determined poetry to be part of the science of ethics, ethics was understood to have a poetic logic. In the prologue to his commentary on Aristotle's *Nicomachean Ethics*, Jean Buridan explains that while the principal content of moral philosophy is conveyed in the *Ethics* and *Politics*, the way of teaching ethics is communicated in the *Rhetoric* and *Poetics*. In fact, he claims, moral philosophy requires its own special logic:

> Since it is only in moral matters that appetite is inherently supposed to take away the judgment of reason, and thus in other arts and sciences an unqualified logic suffices for us, in moral matters we require a special logic. However there are two parts of this moral logic, namely rhetoric and poetry, which differ in this way: because rhetoric desires clear knowledge, it uses words retained in their proper signification. Poetry endeavors to obscure knowledge delightfully through metalepsis or by other means.[19]

Rhetoric and poetry are necessary to the transmission of ethical knowledge because the audience for such teaching is the human subject conceived of as appetitive and emotional. As Buridan observes, a thing does not seem the same to those who love as to those who hate (*amantibus et odientibus*), and it is these affect-driven people with whom moral philosophy is concerned. Poetry, as a part of "moral logic," is a means of conveying ethical knowledge by first obscuring it "delightfully." In addressing the pleasures, desires, prejudices, and passions of the ethical subject through rhetorical and poetic language, moral philosophy turns the frailties of reason to its advantage. Thus Buridan, in his discussion of certain thorny questions concerning happiness in Book x of Aristotle's *Ethics*, advises that if he has not offered "real solutions" to these questions, they should "nevertheless be received as dialectical and playful (*logice et lusive*)."[20] He is not here giving up on the possibility of arriving at ethical truths, and avers that it is clear that happiness consists in one act toward which we must order all of our other actions. Yet the subject of happiness admits of playfulness, and it is appropriate that Buridan offers this mode of ludic argument when speaking about the way happiness might be thought of in the context of lived experience – whether happiness is compatible with old age, misery, ill fortune, or even sleep. These narrative, experiential possibilities complicate the logical definitions of happiness, and thus open questions that can only rightfully be answered dialectically, playfully, perhaps poetically.

The desiring, pleasure-seeking, loving, pain-experiencing ethical subject described above shapes both vernacular poetry and scholastic moral philosophy.[21] Nevertheless, while a great deal of scholarship has engaged with medieval literature as an ethical discourse, there has been much less attention given to the relationship between this literature and the ethical conversations taking place in the context of the moral philosophy produced at the universities.[22] Gestures toward such work have been made more often by intellectual historians than by literary critics. In an essay on late medieval theories of enjoyment, William Courtenay notes that in the twelfth century both theologians and courtly poets were interested in seemingly parallel notions of pure love, a juncture that might encourage one to seek other "cross influences between theological and poetic discourse on desire and longing (*cupiditas* and *desiderium*), on doubt, sadness, and despair (*tristitia*), and pleasure or joy of possession (*delectatio*)."[23] Arthur Stephen McGrade proposes that, for the fourteenth century, "Ockham and his successors provided a framework for human understanding which poets and others could have utilized in many concrete ways, both in understanding, for example, how poetry itself affects us and in understanding or depicting the behavior of actual fictional characters."[24] Despite the acknowledgment of the ethical content of medieval literature, the question of the relationship between poetry and the moral philosophy of Augustine, Abelard, or the scholastic philosophers of later centuries remains largely open.[25] My readings of vernacular poetry in the chapters below show that poets were often markedly aware of the overlapping ethical languages of clerkly philosophy and poetic depictions of love.[26] There is no question that ethical debates about the nature of culpability, intention, virtue, desire, and pleasure suffused the world of courtly poetry, and it is the guiding thesis of this project that the philosophy and poetry of the later Middle Ages together formed a thriving ethical discourse, particularly in response to the challenges of defining pleasure and love, usefulness and enjoyment, need and desire, lack and fulfillment. These terms, in Latin as well as in the vernacular, are weighted after the twelfth century with the burden of secular love poetry. With the influence of Peter Lombard's *Sentences* and the assimilation of Aristotle's philosophy, enjoyment as an ethical, psychological, and theological phenomenon took on an increasingly central role in philosophical discourse.

Enjoyment thus emerges as the key term of this book, precisely because it functions as a focal point and ethical goal for medieval moral philosophy and medieval poetry. It is a useful umbrella term because it conveys the fundamental qualities shared by Aristotelian *eudaimonia*, vernacular "joy," Christian *fruitio*, and even Lacanian *jouissance*: it is desirable for its own sake as an end goal, it is "complete," and it includes pleasure.[27] Aristotle's *eudaimonia*, usually translated as "happiness," literally means "having a good genius (*daimōn*)," suggesting good fortune.[28] For Aristotle, happiness is the self-sufficient and complete telos of life – the "best possible life"; at the end of the *Nicomachean Ethics* he defines it as the most excellent faculty of the human mind engaged in the most virtuous activity, with the best object.[29] In discussing Aristotle's concept of *eudaimonia*, Latin writers such as Cicero and Seneca most often translate it as *beata vita*, a phrase used also by Augustine to speak about the happiness of life after death. For medieval Latin writers, *beata vita* or *beatitudo* are used to talk about happiness as the goal of life, along with *felicitas* – a word used to translate *eudaimonia* in Aristotle's treatises. Occasionally, these terms are differentiated, as Boethius uses *felicitas* to speak about earthly (false) happiness, and *beatitudo* to speak about true happiness outside the realm of fortune.[30] In later scholastic writings, *felicitas* and *beatitudo* are often used interchangeably.[31] Latin *gaudium* – the inner joy that Thomas Aquinas and others speak about as the inner joy infused by God – is recognizable as the root of vernacular *joi*.[32] And yet the Latin term *fruitio* – typically translated as enjoyment – is perhaps the location of the most difficult terminological, theological, and ethical assimilation of Aristotle's ideas about pleasure and happiness. Augustine defines *fruitio* in *De Doctrina Christiana* as "inhering with love in something for its own sake" – a definition that persists throughout the Middle Ages.[33] Enjoyment, in this view, is a self-sufficient act of love, and the enjoyment of the beatific vision was understood to be the *summum bonum* of Christian life. One might understand an Aristotelian life of flourishing (*eudaimonia*) to be oriented toward a life of virtuous political or contemplative activity, while the Christian life of flourishing (*beata vita*, *beatitudo*, or *felicitas*) was oriented toward the enjoyment of God. The medieval reception of Aristotelian ethics led to questions about how to understand an act of *fruitio* that could be oriented toward felicity as an ethical goal for human experience in this world. But Aristotle was also marshaled as an authority regarding questions about the beatific enjoyment of God. The Aristotle of medieval philosophy is both a source of knowledge about the possibilities for ethical earthly pleasures and an authority on the relationship between these pleasures and the love of and imitation of the divine. As Jacques Lacan would observe in the twentieth century, Aquinas and other medieval theologians created an Aristotle who had a privileged understanding of the obstacles to human desire, a philosopher who was – above all – a theorist of love and pleasure. Lacan's Aristotle seeks after the "*jouissance* of being" itself, recognizing the way that we model the enjoyment of God on our own enjoyment, and acknowledging that philosophical "thought" is not only pleasurable, but a form of loving God.[34] This Aristotle emerges from the Latin authors who tried to reconcile an ethics oriented toward human happiness in this life with a Christian ethics, largely Augustinian, which tells us that the only object rightfully to be enjoyed is God.

Vernacular love poetry, with its simultaneous commitment to a sacrificial ethics and a working out of happiness in a world of conflicting desires, was as shaken as theology by the advent of an ethical system that located felicity and love in this world. Late medieval love poetry is interested in what it might mean to love someone as another subject who is pursuing his or her own happiness in the world, and especially what it might mean to pursue such a love toward an enjoyment that acknowledges the overlap between the philosophical pursuit of happiness and the happiness pursued by lovers. The post-Aristotelian courtly lover acknowledges his narcissism, worries about her free will, talks about clerkly happiness, and pursues his love not just to its ineffable conclusion, but beyond. The scholarly Aristotelian discourse of happiness is both compelling and inadequate for the subject of courtly love. As the narrator of Chaucer's *Troilus and Criseyde* comments, speaking about the bliss of the two lovers, "Felicite, which that thise clerkes wise / Comenden so ne may nought here suffise" (III.1691–2).[35] Chaucer's romance is a poem that is at least in part about taking this clerkly intrusion into the bedroom seriously, asking what it means for felicity to "suffice," and moreover what these clerks might have to say about the pursuits of thirteenth- and fourteenth-century lovers, or perhaps what lovers might be able to reveal to the clerks.

Many late medieval poets recognized that what was most radical in Aristotle was not only that happiness is worth striving for on earth rather than being deferred to the afterlife, but also the corollary insistence on contingency as a component of love and happiness – what the Middle Ages refer to as fortune, and often personify and deify as Lady Fortuna.[36] This orientation toward earthliness and fortune ensured that the medieval reception of Aristotle begat a number of ongoing ethical discussions and debates as to the ontological and ethical relationships between love and pleasure, the propriety of loving earthly objects, the psychological experience of love, and what, if any, happiness may be had on earth. These debates, though necessarily in less formal terms, were equally the stuff of medieval love poetry. A fuller literary account of the reception of Aristotelian ethics in the late medieval period, an age when poetry itself was considered part of moral science, can help us to understand the ethical history of European medieval poetry, and to gain a richer and more nuanced understanding of psychoanalytic and other modern ethical theories about love that root themselves in the "birth" of love as we know it in the Western world.

This book examines the medieval history of enjoyment, the intellectual context for the production of poetry in the thirteenth century, particularly the vastly influential *Roman de la Rose*, and the resultant "intellectual-erotic" tradition. As moral philosophy and poetry moved closer together in their central concern with love as an ethical problem, philosophy and poetry were brought geographically closer as Paris became a center of university life and literary production. With its wide readership and explicit intertwining of romance narrative and philosophical debate, the thirteenth-century poem the *Roman de la Rose* played an influential role in the unification of intellectual and poetic discourses. In its unique circumstance of a double authorship which took place on either side of the reception of the full *Nicomachean Ethics*, the *Rose* offers remarkable insight into the changing discourse of love and ethics. The philosophical and literary history that follows after the *Rose* allows for a clearer picture of the questions at stake in late medieval ethical discourse: What is the relationship between love and pleasure? Is human happiness possible or desirable? Is love an activity or a state of rest? Can one love without objectification? What are the dangers of deferred desire? Tracing the asking, answering, and revising of these questions offers another way of thinking about the intellectual and poetic history of medieval love and the roots of modern "amorous subjectivity."[37]

The following chapters tell a story of enjoyment that traces the efforts of both philosophers and poets to grapple with the new possibilities and challenges wrought by the reception of Aristotelian ethics in a Christian world. The first chapter provides an intellectual history of enjoyment, considering its meanings in the frameworks that existed before the Latin translation of Aristotle's writings on ethics. It traces the transformations of pagan philosophical virtue into Christian love, followed by the development of Christian enjoyment as it breaks down into the various components – intellect, pleasure, labor, and happiness – that would become particularly controversial in the wake of the full translation of Aristotle's ethical writings. Following these aspects of enjoyment from antiquity through the twelfth century illustrates the way in which already-existing tensions in the philosophical tradition were poised to emerge more forcefully with the Latin reception of Aristotle. The chapter further shows that questions about enjoyment animated both philosophical discourse and vernacular poetry in the period just prior to the full translation of the *Ethics*, in texts such as Peter Abelard's *Dialogue between a Philosopher, a Jew, and a Christian* and the troubadour poetry of Guilhem IX, Bernart de Ventadorn, and Jaufré Rudel. While providing a history of a key set of terms associated with enjoyment, I argue that vernacular poetry – with its concerns about love, loss, and satisfaction – was a natural, if not inevitable, space for the emergence of earthly enjoyment as an ethical problem.

Chapter 2 explores the way in which the "new Aristotle," the flood of translation into Latin from Greek and Arabic in the twelfth and thirteenth centuries, affected courtly poetry, by examining the famously bifurcated *Roman de la Rose*. I argue that the poem is divided not only by a temporal gap and a shift in authorship, but by the impact of the full translation of Aristotle's *Nicomachean Ethics* that takes place during that gap. Where Guillaume de Lorris writes within an ideological framework in which neither the political nor contemplative lives are thought to offer any hope of earthly perfection, Jean de Meun writes within a new, controversial context of Aristotelian contemplation, where contemplation provides the best life for man on earth and therefore confers human happiness. I argue that Jean was attracted to Guillaume's poem for its ethical exploration and linking of the Narcissus myth, poetic activity, intellectual self-reflection, and physical labor. Jean thus asks what Guillaume's Narcissus might look like in the new Aristotelian context, a context where self-reflection might inhabit a continuum including erotic love, intellectual contemplation, and the beatific vision. Exploring the potential of self-reflection through art to bring happiness, madness, love, and hate, Jean's portion of the *Rose* experiments with the assumption of Aristotle's narrative ethical system, where rational activity precedes love, self-knowledge determines love, and happiness consists in labor rather than rest. The *Rose* in its widespread influence bequeathed vernacular poetry a distinctly intellectual erotics, a discourse that would have lasting implications for the ethical engagements of late medieval poetry.

The following three chapters take stock of the repercussions of both the "new Aristotle" and the Aristotelian aspects of the *Roman de la Rose*. Chapter 3 focuses on the way that Aristotelian definitions of pleasure are disturbingly silent on one of the most pressing issues for Christian theologians: the motivation for pursuits of contemplative happiness. Do we seek to know and love an object (God, in this context) because of the promise of pleasure experienced when that object is possessed or loves us in return? Or is pleasure somehow inextricable from the act of love, rendering questions of causation ontologically if not ethically irrelevant? The chapter examines scholars including William of Ockham, who imagined the possibility that God might withhold pleasure from the experience of enjoyment, thus preserving God's freedom, and the Aristotelian commentator Jean Buridan, who denied that true enjoyment could ever exist without delight. Placing these philosophers in conversation with vernacular poetry brings a flourishing, hitherto unexamined fourteenth-century ethical discourse of pleasure into view. Froissart and Chaucer, in their simultaneous reception of Guillaume de Machaut, each address love's pleasure through the staging of ethical crises – and the depiction of ethical lovesickness – that bring clerkly and erotic discourses together. I conclude with a reading of Chaucer's *Book of the Duchess* as an overtly ethical commentary upon the poetry of his French contemporaries, addressing precisely the moral ramifications of an experience of love that elides the differences between pleasure and pain, joy and sorrow. In doing so, Chaucer ultimately offers an ideal of love that places this elision not in the confused, lovesick subject, but in the space of shared desire between two lovers in the contingent world. Chaucer's earthly "solution" to the problem of the relationship between love and pleasure puts fortune in the place of God, and allies his ethics with an Aristotelian-inflected ideal of love as courage in the face of destiny, happiness in the midst of contingency. All of these poets' engagement with Ovid's *Metamorphoses*, and particularly the figure of Morpheus, allows them to imagine love in the context of an Aristotelian "whole life" of flourishing.

Another key controversy in the reception of Aristotle concerned the location of enjoyment: scholars debated as to whether, following Augustine, enjoyment was seated in the faculty of the will, or whether, following Aristotle, it was located in the intellect. Chapter 4 argues that even the influential strand of voluntarism in the fourteenth century operates within the tradition of courtly Aristotelian intellectualism. An examination of the "mounted Aristotle" topos in sermons, fabliaux, and visual art shows that this voluntarism was not solely invested in a return to Augustine after the excesses of thirteenth-century intellectualism, but also in an exploration of the erotics of intellectual inquiry. The chapter uses the logics of both fabliaux and philosophical commentaries to reread two poems often placed in an anti-intellectualist tradition: Guillaume de Deguileville's *Pèlerinage de Vie Humaine* and William Langland's *Piers Plowman*. While both poems reject Aristotelian intellectualism as a means to full knowledge about the metaphysical world, they nevertheless embrace Aristotelian ethics as a means toward understanding human desire – for the good, for knowledge, and for God. Deguileville and Langland explore a fully intellectual and fully affective pursuit of knowledge, yet emphasize the threat of excessive intellectual desire as both material and sexual, in modes similar to the courtly versions of the "mounted Aristotle" tales. In particular, I revise understandings of *Piers Plowman* as an essentially "ascetic" poem that advocates an "epistemology of suffering," arguing that the poem enacts a simultaneous epistemology of pleasure. Langland ultimately transforms Deguileville's images of insatiable desire – voiced by Aristotle – into an affective, imitative relationship to Christ's desire for men's souls – a philosophical and poetic union of the physical, intellectual, and volitional, of suffering, delight, and beauty. For Langland, God became man not, or not only, to save mankind, but to save God, his knowledge, and therefore our love for him.

Chapter 5 traces the possibilities for earthly happiness imagined in Chaucer's *Troilus and Criseyde*. Perhaps the largest controversy inspired by Aristotle's *Ethics* questioned whether happiness might be had on earth. The association of Aristotle with twofold earthly happiness, both political and contemplative, was widespread. Yet such a view challenged the position of a Christian afterlife as the sole site of true happiness. In this chapter I argue that fourteenth-century understandings of Boethius – especially those explored in the commentary tradition and in Dante's *Convivio* – complicate the prescription of otherworldly asceticism that medievalist literary scholarship typically identifies as "Boethian" in Chaucer's poem. The late medieval commentaries on Boethius' *Consolation of Philosophy* tend to emphasize Aristotelian doctrines such as the acquisition of knowledge through the senses, the educative power of empathy, and the impossibility of a stoicism that would require one to remain untouched by worldly sorrow. These commentaries allow space for earthly happiness at the same time that they acknowledge that "true" beatitude will only take place in the afterlife. I argue that Chaucer explores the clerkly dimensions of his lovers' "felicity" as a way to think through the ethical intersections of erotic and intellectual discourses, and thus to imagine a place for happiness in an unstable world. Happiness itself becomes unthinkable except through the language uneasily shared by clerks and lovers, a language that acknowledges human love as the experience that opens ethics toward the variety, mystery, and inexorability of the fortune-tossed world.

I close the book by exploring the fact that Chaucer's female characters are often his most "philosophical," the most given to exploring the vicissitudes of love in scholarly terms. I place this observation within the context of Lacanian psychoanalytic theories of "*jouissance féminine*," which

I argue are rooted ultimately in Lacan's evolving readings of medieval Aristotelianism. The figures of Criseyde, Dorigen, and Alcyone express their *jouissance* not through ecstatic or mystical discourse, but through an intellectual and erotic commitment to mutuality, courage, and contingency – a commitment now recognizable as an Aristotelian response to the full range of medieval ethical experience. As such, these figures offer a way to engage modern psychoanalytic critiques of the ethics of "courtly love" – so often deemed narcissistic, misogynist, and disabling. In the uncovering of a vigorous premodern conversation about the ethics of desire, pleasure, and happiness, I suggest, finally, that we might not only look to medieval poetry for the unethical origins of our desires, but for the ethical origins of our love; perhaps we need not break with the medieval, but instead look to uncover its less easily seductive and more bracing strands of affective life.

CHAPTER I

Enjoyment: a medieval history

FROM VIRTUE TO LOVE

Although this book's introduction emphasized the full translation of Aristotle's *Nicomachean Ethics* as a key moment in the transformation of medieval definitions of enjoyment, these definitions evolved constantly from antiquity forward. This chapter provides an intellectual history of enjoyment, examining understandings of pleasure and love as "goods" from the classical period up to the beginnings of the age of scholasticism and the translation and reception of Aristotle's works in Latin. This history is in some part the narrative of how Platonic virtue and Aristotelian happiness became Christian love, though Christian theology never left pagan philosophy behind. Enjoyment is in some ways a difficult idea to track, as the classical period did not have a single dominant way of thinking about the achievement of the good, as would the medieval in the wake of Augustine's definitions of *fruitio*. I thus orient the following discussion of happiness, pleasure, love, and the *summum bonum* around the idea of enjoyment not because this was consistently the term that classical or medieval philosophers use to signify the highest good, but because it was Augustine's use of the term that would allow medieval philosophers to define, over time, the experience that is the goal of both the human life and the eternal soul: loving God for his own sake.

Love, of course, was not something alien grafted onto the discourse of ethics by Christian theologians, and classical philosophy developed its own definitions of love. In Platonic, Aristotelian, and Stoic philosophy, love was not only considered as itself a topic worthy of ethical consideration, but was also inevitably part of many discussions of the virtuous good. Philosophers considered whether love was a component of the good and whether the good could be properly pursued through love. Plato's *Symposium* is famously devoted to a series of encomia to eros in which the speakers variously praise love as a route to civic virtue, a passionate desire rooted in lack, and finally, with Socrates' sharing of Diotima's wisdom, a hierarchical route toward virtuous love of the divine form of the beautiful itself. In the Latin translations of the *Nicomachean Ethics*, Aristotle speaks more often in terms of the pursuit of what is pleasing, rather than what is loved, though even in Aristotelian philosophy enjoyment of a pursued object shades into love. People find pleasure in the things that they love, as a horse-lover (*amanti equum*) is pleased by horses.[1] Love itself is taken up in the philosopher's discussions of friendship in the *Ethics*, where he defines *philia* as the love of someone else for his or her own sake – wishing good things to happen to him for no merely abstract or egoistic reason.[2] Gregory Vlastos argues that Aristotle's concept of *philia* would more aptly be translated as "love" rather than the more common "friendship," as the former word conveys more of the range of emotional bonds that Aristotle describes.[3] Despite the difference between the two philosophers – Plato attributes love to God, while for Aristotle the unmoved mover is immutable, not being prone to the motion that desire/love implies – both put an abstract idea of the "good" at the heart of love.[4] In Aristotle's highest form of *philia*, we love another individual because of the good that he embodies; for Plato, when we love other people, we in fact love the image of the good within them.[5] Ideal love in Plato's philosophy also contains the notion of loving an object for its own sake, but this object is abstract – "the Good" – or an individual imperfect instantiation of goodness. Each philosopher variously lays the foundation for the transformation of the highest good, and man's achieving of that good, into love and loving. Christianity will unite the self-sufficient good with the self-sufficient love for an object – with God as the good loved alone above all others, for his own sake.

Christian theologians acknowledge the classical lineage of Christian thought about ethics and love; Augustine has the distinction of not only writing this history, but making the most significant contribution to the Christian transformation of Greek and Roman ethical thought. The eighth book of Augustine's *City of God* elevates Plato and Platonic philosophy above all other pagan knowledge. The theologian accepts Plato's definition of philosophy as love of wisdom, redefining wisdom as God himself through scriptural authority, and asks, "If Plato says that the wise man is the man who imitates, knows, and loves this God, and that participation in this God brings man happiness, what need is there to examine the other philosophers?"[6] For Augustine, Aristotle is a worthy follower of Plato (though not such a great literary stylist), as is Plotinus, and several other Platonists and Stoics are worth harvesting for the odd anecdote.

While Augustine does not hesitate to criticize Plato where necessary (on the belief in multiple gods, for example), he uses the authority of Platonic doctrine to underwrite and found an understanding of Christian morality. As Marcia Colish observes, one can see in Augustine's writing the harmonizing of a Stoic psychology of self-sufficient happiness with neo-Platonic conceptions of the good as transcendent and eternal.[7] Plato – via the translations and summarizations of later philosophers – furnishes Augustine with his key understandings of the relationships between practical and speculative philosophy, the division of philosophy as a whole into moral, natural, and rational concerns, and his definition of moral discourse as that which addresses enjoyment: the pursuit of the *summum bonum*, sought for its own sake.[8]

Ethical enjoyment is an evolving concept for Augustine, and his writing demonstrates his wrestling with a variety of philosophical categories: love, virtue, contemplation, and the good. Virtue becomes for him an intermediary good, and the self-sufficiency of the soul is necessarily negated in the face of the necessity of God's grace. Most significantly, the virtues as *summum bonum* are transformed into the perfect love of God, and God becomes not merely an object of intellectual contemplation, but an object of love.[9] As to what specific word we should use to describe virtuous or divine love, Augustine ensures that all love's terms are equal participants in ethical discourse. In addressing the question of whether *dilectio* means something different from *amor*, he concludes that pagan philosophy, secular literature, and divine Scripture each tells us that "charity" (*caritas*), "fondness" (*dilectio*), and "love" (*amor*) all mean the same thing. All words for love can be used properly to describe the love of an individual for another person, for material objects, or for God; a rightly directed will is love in a good sense, and a "perverted" will is love in a bad sense.[10] In this way, love begins to subsume other closely related ethical terms. For example, happiness and pleasure are both subsumed by love; a love seeking possession is desire, and a love which possesses is joy. Enjoyment thus comes to encapsulate an ethical goal, the desire for that goal, and the activity that achieves or comprises that goal. Happiness and the true good for humanity, according to Augustine, are not in enjoyment of the body, or the mind, but in the enjoyment of God (*fruitio Dei*).[11] The highest good is the enjoyment of what one loves, and so happiness is defined "not in the loving, but in the enjoyment" – when making a distinction between desire and possession, enjoyment is disentangled from love.[12] Later, Augustine describes enjoyment, stating that "For our Good, that Final Good about which the philosophers dispute, is nothing else but to cleave to him whose spiritual embrace, if one may so express it, fills the intellectual soul and makes it fertile with true virtues."[13] In *De Doctrina Christiana*, we find his final formulation of *fruitio* as "inhering with love in something for its own sake."[14] The latter definition was cited throughout the Middle Ages as the highest goal of the human subject; happiness, enjoyment, and love thus coalesce in one perfected, eternal instance of love for the divine object. Yet as much as this definition sought to harmonize these ethical goals that had been the subject of philosophical debate for close to a millennium, medieval theologians did not hesitate to separate the strands of enjoyment for continuous analysis.

The sections below describe the lineage of Christian ethical thought about love, breaking down its reception of classical philosophy into a number of categories that mirror the concerns of this book as a whole: pleasure, intellectualism, labor, and human happiness. These categories were not necessarily considered distinct, or controversial, by each philosopher or theologian that I discuss, but these are the categories that were destabilized in a variety of ways by the reception of Aristotle's moral philosophy in the later medieval period. Thus I cannot claim to give anywhere near a full history of the Christian reception of classical ethics, but rather offer a series of necessarily partial stories of particular ideas about enjoyment.[15] In each case, I begin with Platonic and neo-Platonic ideas about the supreme good that influenced Augustine and his successors. I then trace these terms up through Augustine's discussions of use and enjoyment, Boethius' discussions of human happiness in the *Consolation of Philosophy*, and into the scattered discourse on enjoyment and the highest good that finds its place in early medieval collections of *sententiae* and elsewhere. There is no sustained or systematic treatment of ethics in what we would recognize as a "philosophical" sense until the twelfth century, though of course Christian moralists and theologians were consistently concerned with defining virtue, vice, and the highest good.[16]

This chapter leads us up through the poetry and philosophy of the twelfth century, including Peter Lombard's *Sentences*, a work which became a standard university text and which produced many surviving commentaries. The Lombard's text reaffirmed the centrality of enjoyment by treating the topic in the first "distinction" of the first book of his text; the foregrounding of questions of use and enjoyment in commentaries on the *Sentences* was thus ensured.[17] Yet the text that most explicitly illustrates a twelfth-century engagement with classical philosophies of enjoyment is Peter Abelard's *Dialogue between a Philosopher, a Jew, and a Christian*, dramatizing the points of agreement and dissent about love, pleasure, and the highest good in the debate between the philosopher and the Christian. Finally, I turn to a small corpus of troubadour poetry composed in the early to mid twelfth century. These songs demonstrate that vernacular love poetry was the location for a varied meditation on the relationships between earthly passion and ethical understandings of desire, pleasure, and goodness. From the compositions of the first known troubadour, Guilhem IX, this secular love poetry took joy – both physical and spiritual – as its matter, formal inspiration, and subject of inquiry.

THE PLEASURE OF ENJOYMENT

At first glance, speaking of pleasure as an aspect of enjoyment appears redundant. What is enjoyment if not pleasurable? And should we not experience the achievement of a final goal as the highest kind of pleasure? Yet as Jacques Lacan observes in *The Ethics of Psychoanalysis*, "thinkers in the field of ethics always return to the ethical problem of the relation of pleasure to the final good, whenever the guidance of human action from a moral point of view is concerned."[18] The basic ancient debates center on whether pleasure is itself the goal of the ethical life, or whether it instead "supervenes" upon the activity associated with the greatest good, occurring as a separate yet inextricably associated phenomenon. Ancient philosophers also consider whether pleasure should be understood in terms of conventional goods (health, friends, material wealth) or in terms of a transformed relationship to happiness whereby pleasure is experienced through the practice of virtue alone. In their late antique reception, Plato and Aristotle came to stand in for the two poles of the latter debate: Plato was thought to hold consistently that virtue was self-sufficient for happiness, while Aristotle stood for the notion that external goods are necessary for happiness, thus defined in a much more intuitive or common manner.[19] This polarity held despite Plato's concern for metaphysical and political topics in the *Republic* – topics which would suggest that the exercise of individual virtue is not wholly self-sufficient – and despite Aristotle's emphasis in the tenth book of his *Nicomachean Ethics* on the desirability and divinity of the contemplative life.

Pleasure is often unstable in Plato's dialogues, with perhaps the only stable pleasure being the pleasure of philosophical discourse. For the interlocutors themselves, this pleasure is constant, and only compromised by external misfortune, as when Phaedo describes his emotions visiting Socrates at the end of his life. He remarks that the pleasure (*oblectamentum*) that he was accustomed to feel in philosophical discourse was mixed with pain (*tristicia*), for he could not but reflect that Socrates was soon to die.[20] Socrates begins his conversation with his friends on the last day of his life by speaking about this mingling of pleasure and pain, two bodies "attached to a single head."[21] At the level of content, the *Phaedo* is a dialogue that rejects earthly pleasure (*voluptas*), arguing that a true philosopher joyfully relinquishes the false pleasures of life for the unification with his true love, wisdom, in death. These pleasures are rejected (along with pain) as tools that rivet the soul to the body like a nail, rendering the soul corporeal and subject to the body's knowledge.[22] Yet it would seem that this dialogue acknowledges a third kind of pleasure: the pleasure of a discourse that allows one to engage in an earthly pleasure so as to transcend it.

Plato discusses pleasure directly in the *Protagoras*, *Gorgias*, *Republic*, *Philebus*, and *Laws*. In some of the dialogues, pleasure is characterized as a spring from which one must learn to drink moderately and rationally in order to achieve happiness.[23] At other times, pleasure is never what the virtuous person directly chooses, but rather a phenomenon that supervenes when one acts virtuously. These two ways of thinking about pleasure are different ways of responding to the apparent necessity of rejecting the pleasure that people – and all animals – are understood to pursue irrationally. The goal of virtue cannot, for Plato, be physical pleasure. If we retain our intuitive understanding of the nature of pleasure, then pleasure must simply accompany virtuous activity as an epiphenomenon, thus appearing as though it might be our ethical goal, but in fact only emerging as a side effect. If, however, we are interested in maintaining the idea of pleasure itself as a natural pursuit, then it is pleasure itself that must be redefined. Pleasure is understood as a pleasure in being virtuous, and thus virtue and happiness become almost synonymous. The Stoics will push this definition of virtue further to claim that the noble man, happy despite being tortured, experiences pleasure in his virtuous resistance, and yet this version of pleasure and happiness is not assimilable to any common understanding of the terms.[24]

A Platonic view of pleasure was most readily available to medieval readers in Boethius' *Consolation of Philosophy*, the story of Philosophia's painstaking education of the prisoner as to what constitutes happiness. Modern scholars have read the text on a spectrum from didactic moral treatise to dialogic exploration of a variety of philosophical issues to a dramatization of the impossibility of resolving the conflict between one's earthly desires and divine aspirations. While no single medieval reading of the text emerges, it is clear that Boethius' text was a treasure trove for Platonic, neo-Platonic, Aristotelian, and Stoic philosophy on free will, the cosmos, and especially human happiness. As Philosophia explains to the prisoner, "nothing is miserable unless you think so, and on the other hand a man who bears all with contentment, finds every state a happy one."[25] The seeming pleasantness of happiness based on earthly fortunes is revealed to be "wretched" (*misera*) and therefore not pleasant at all. Philosophia acknowledges that happiness is not subject to pain, but the prisoner learns that he cannot seek "joy through pleasures" (*laetitiam voluptatibus*).[26] His education in the good culminates in the realization that happiness is divine, and that happiness ultimately *is* God, but to arrive at this point he must assent to counter-intuitive truths such as the non-existence of evil and the true lack of pleasure in the seeming pleasures of fortune. Self-sufficiency is the guiding determination of what constitutes happiness and the good, and Philosophia seeks to convince her pupil that "the true good is only produced when they [things that are sought as goods] are gathered as it were into one form which as efficient cause makes that which is self-sufficient thereby equivalent to power, respect, fame and pleasure."[27] Things that seem good and worthy of pursuit are only good inasmuch as they participate in God's sufficiency and unity; sufficiency itself is pleasure. Philosophia attempts to lead the prisoner on a path whereby he might understand that he should ultimately only desire virtuous sufficiency – the other goods are simply ephemeral and incidental. Pleasure is thus maintained as an ethical goal, but its nature has been transformed into the pleasure of the practice of virtue.

Aristotelian ethics, on the other hand, requires no such transformation of basic understandings of pleasure or happiness as that which is incompatible with misfortune and pain. Aristotle defines happiness as the sovereign good because it is pursued on its own account, and is accompanied by pleasure. On the question of hedonism, whether pleasure is an ethical goal in itself, Aristotle remains intriguingly agnostic. What seems a fundamental question of ethical motivation is irresolvable, according to the philosopher, and he states that "whether we choose life for the sake of pleasure or pleasure for the sake of life is a question we may dismiss for the present. Indeed they seem to be united and not to admit of separation, since there is no pleasure without activity."[28] While Aristotle did not think it necessary to resolve this motivational ambiguity, the pursuit of pleasure presents an important obstacle for Plotinus, outlined in the section of the *Enneads* on beauty. He cites the contemplation of sensual beauty as a starting point for the lifting of the soul toward higher things, toward contemplation of the divine. But the mingled pleasure and pain that beauty brings can also turn us away from the Good, toward a desire for material objects. The problem for Plotinus' narcissistic soul is thus not love for self or image, but that the pleasure of such a love does not goad one to higher things, trapping one in a cycle of earthly pleasures that cannot be escaped.[29] Choosing life for the sake of pleasure here is a dangerous mistake. In the late medieval reception of Aristotelian ethics, the problem of pleasure as a motivating factor will re-emerge in debates about whether pleasure is identical with love, a non-identical but necessary epiphenomenon, or wholly extricable from the experience of enjoyment.

In the texts that came down to the early Middle Ages, pleasure was either transformed or denied as a valid ethical goal. Access to philosophers who defend the pursuit of pleasure was either lost, as with Aristotle, or filtered through writers such as Cicero, who transmit their claims only to critique them. In his *Tusculan Disputations*, for example, Cicero does not allow for the possibility of an intellectual or spiritual pleasure, and thus dismisses the morality of Epicurus' pleasure. He understands (or at least claims to understand) Epicurus' "joy of mind" (*mentis laetitiam*) as simply the hope of bodily pleasures.[30] On such terms it is easy to dismiss the idea of an ethical pursuit of pleasure out of hand. The necessity of rejecting intuitive pleasures – relegating them to instrumental value, if any value at all – permeates Augustine's writings. Yet this rejection is no easy task, and the theologian is perhaps most wrenching and most acute about human nature when he discusses the necessity of exchanging physical for spiritual pleasures. In Book x of the *Confessions*, Augustine speaks of the tenacious hold that the pleasures of the ear have on him, confessing to being beguiled by the pleasures of the flesh, but also asserting his resistance to being "captivated" by them.[31] Even pleasure in holy words can be a sin if the enjoyment of the senses outruns reason in their stirring by voice and song; this sin Augustine confesses to. When music – secular or holy – is enjoyed for its own sake rather than for the sake of God (and thus properly *used*), this is the "peril of pleasure" (*periculum voluptatis*).[32] Augustine's sensitivity to music, to the beauty of forms and colors that might possess his soul, even to the beauty of beguiling daylight, threatens that he will be "miserably captured" (*capior miserabiliter*) by external beauties.[33] Even more perilous than physical pleasure, however, is the pleasure of satisfying intellectual curiosity. Such pleasure often seems antithetical to sensory pleasure, as it drives us to stare at mangled corpses and monstrous humans, and to watch tragic theater.[34] Desire to know the courses of the stars is here equivalent to the desire to become sad and pale in the face of real or performed death, and this critique of curiosity will shadow the late medieval Aristotelianism that raises intellectual contemplation to the level of the highest virtuous activity and source of the highest pleasure. For Augustine, desiring knowledge for its own sake offers only idle pleasures, and pleasure is allowed only insofar as it is subordinated to the goal of enjoying God.

The shifting ethical terrain created by Aristotle's valorization of earthly intellectual pleasure as an end in itself, a phenomenon inextricable from both contemplative activity and virtuous life, raised a number of questions about the definition and role of moral pleasure. In his commentary on Peter Lombard's *Sentences*, William Ockham discusses the relationship between enjoyment of intellectual pursuits and the intrusions of physical or other pain, and posits the existence of earthly things that deserve to be enjoyed for their own sake, if not as highest goods.[35] Most controversially, he offered an understanding of enjoyment of the highest good – beatific enjoyment – that did not necessarily include pleasure, thus severing pleasure from its inherent relationship to the love of God. Philosophers had to contend both with the Aristotelian location of enjoyment on an earthly plane and with the unsettling notion that pleasure and the highest form of love might not be so safely intertwined. Aristotle himself was disturbingly silent on the question of the motivation for pursuits of contemplative enjoyment, and medieval theologians would have to supply answers that articulated the relationships between earthly and divine pleasures, human love and God's will, and the pleasures of activity and contemplation.

THE LABOR OF ENJOYMENT

Labor or "practical activity" is a category that threatens to subsume the others. Is the experience of the highest good one of activity (*operacio*) or one of rest (*quies*)? Is virtue itself an activity? Defining pleasure or virtue in terms of activity does not necessarily entail a placement of "labor" at the center of these definitions, but a focus on activity nevertheless has implications for literary language and larger understandings of ethics that subsume such philosophical definitions under the categories of medieval ethical life. The relationship of activity to pleasure and virtue is a topic discussed by every philosopher who addresses the highest good, from Plato and Aristotle forward. The definition of this relationship has everything to do with whether one takes virtue to be primarily intellectual (and thus associated with contemplative activity), whether one locates happiness in the human sphere (and thus likely to be an activity or process) or in an afterlife (and thus associated with a state of rest), and how one describes the role of pleasure (an experience supervening on enjoyment or a goal in itself).

In Plato's *Meno*, the notion of virtue as action is revealed as a common and mistaken idea, locating virtue in its myriad effects rather than in its unifying cause; knowledge of virtue should rather be thought of as something like practical wisdom. In the *Meno*, Socrates' interlocutors are men who understand a virtue such as courage to be inherent in courageous acts, and he guides them toward a realization that these acts are unified instead by an intellectual conception of good and evil allowing for courage, thus redefining virtue itself as a skill or expertise inhering in recovered knowledge.[36] Plato's notion of virtue as knowledge – and therefore something that can be taught – is a precursor of Aristotle's conception of *habitus*, where virtue is inculcated through education and practice until it becomes an internal disposition of the soul. For Aristotle, like Plato, virtue itself is not an activity; however, in the tenth book of the *Nicomachean Ethics* he describes the way that the rational soul achieves the highest good in performing the activity of contemplation. In this context the contrast between the active and contemplative lives is displaced by the contrast between the active and resting intellect. For Aristotle, happiness is a life given as much as possible to "the most perfect activity [that] belongs to the best-conditioned faculty in relation to the most excellent object falling within its competence"; this activity is the rational mind's contemplation of truth and the divine.[37] Happiness is thus not a disposition, but a self-sufficient virtuous activity.[38]

Plotinus' conception of contemplative activity is not far from Aristotle's. Contemplation is not antithetical to activity, but is a form of action chosen by the stronger intellect.[39] His life of the mind is filled with endless activity that nevertheless is unwearying:

> Life, pure, is never a burden; how then could there be weariness There where the living is most noble? That very life is wisdom, not a wisdom built up by reasonings but complete from the beginning, suffering no lack which could set it inquiring, a wisdom primal, unborrowed, not something added to the Being, but its very essence.[40]

Here we find a tension between Plotinus' apophatic claim that the perfect experience of fruition in God is not tied to the intellect and a nevertheless persistent valuing of activity rooted in his Aristotelian affinities. The life of wisdom in some ways sounds much like Aristotle's contemplative ideal, but it is finally "not built up by reasonings," leaving the reasoning mind as we understand it behind.

The alternative to a conception of enjoyment as labor or activity, of course, is enjoyment as an experience of rest. For Philo of Alexandria, a Jewish theologian influenced by Plato and himself influential in early Christian theology, the beatific vision includes a mind at rest, experiencing joy in the contemplation of God's being in a prayer that is not in any earthly or active sense a prayer at all.[41] This experience is preceded by an immense commitment to a mortification of the senses and strict mental and moral discipline, a toiling upward that ends in rest. Yet this moment of joy is not the achievement of one's own labors, but a moment of grace, bestowed by God. The only thing "truly enjoyable" for Philo is rest in God, and the greatest good is equivalent to "undisturbed peace."[42] Likewise, for Augustine, we are understood to direct ourselves toward God with love (*dilectio*), "so that in reaching him we may find our rest, and attain our happiness because we have achieved our fulfillment in him."[43] Whereas in Aristotelian ethics, rest and pleasure are almost always understood as enabling further activity, in the Augustinian system we engage in activity so that we might one day achieve rest. Such a contrast has ramifications for understandings of ethical motivation, and also for a poetic tradition that will oscillate between a commitment to the endless activity of loving and writing and a celebration of the beloved as source of one's "hertes reste."[44] Nicole Oresme will later comment in his translation of Aristotle's *Ethics* that, in heaven, "rest" does not connote the complete cessation of activity, for the blessed continually understand and will in God ("les beneurés ont ilecques continuelment operacion de entendement et de volenté en Dieu"). When one speaks of repose in heaven, he avers, one speaks of the cessation of sorrowful, painful, or laborious activity, not of all activity.[45] Oresme's comment captures some of the tensions inherent in speaking about enjoyment as either rest or labor – labor is ethically valuable but also always connotes pain, while rest might be a means to an end or the end itself.

Later medieval theologians will discuss the virtuous activity and the laborious or restful nature of happiness with an orientation dependent upon whether they locate the intellect or the will as the primary seat of the experience of fruition. If enjoyment is located in the intellect, then it must be identical to intellectual activity: pleasure in the contemplation and love of God. But if enjoyment resides ultimately in the will, or in the will of God himself, then the heart's and desire's rest through the attainment of the beloved object must constitute the highest bliss. The question of whether enjoyment is an activity, and whether the pleasure that accompanies it is an activity or passion, is something that later medieval philosophers will debate, with implications for understandings of free will, grace, and charity. Love as labor becomes both a trope of lovers' sorrows and a parody of lovers' heroic sexual achievements. The Aristotelian notion of the highest good as pleasurable contemplation challenges both the Augustinian and the fourteenth-century emphasis on the will and a poetic commitment to the pain inherent in labor, and in love.

INTELLECTUAL ENJOYMENT

The role of knowledge and the intellectual faculty in ethical activity and pursuit of the good was controversial even within Plato's dialogues. In these texts and in the wider moral discourse that proceeded from them, there were a number of ways of thinking about the intellect: as a site of conflict between the contemplative and the political life, as an aspect of the practice of virtue, and as the mental site of experience of the highest good. The question of the primacy of the intellect in the pursuit of the highest good remained a controversy throughout the Middle Ages and into the fourteenth century. The very possibility of an intellectualist understanding of ethics must be placed in the context of varying understandings of the components of the soul.[46] In both classical and medieval philosophy, the activity of the intellect is traditionally opposed both to the activity of the body and to the activity of the "will." Plato's famous and influential division of the soul into three parts – rational, spirited, and appetitive – led to questions of whether humans are ruled by desire for pleasure or by reason, and further whether knowledge itself can be vulnerable to desire, pleasure, or love. The *Phaedrus*' enduring image of the soul as two horses driven by a charioteer is another way of conceptualizing the relationship between reason and other aspects of the soul. Such a self-alienated model of the soul is ultimately incompatible with Stoic notions of harmonious integration and the sufficiency of virtue for happiness.

Plato's *Protagoras* addresses the intellectual conception of virtue, asking the linked questions of whether pleasure is the same as "good," and whether virtue can be taught.[47] In this dialogue, Socrates moves toward a version of "hedonism" whereby pleasure is indeed to be sought as good, but knowledge is necessary in order that a person correctly calculate the pleasure that his actions will bring him over time. At the close, Socrates imagines the conclusion of the text itself personified, exclaiming, "You, Socrates, began by saying that excellence can't be taught, and now you are insisting on the opposite, trying to show that all things are knowledge – justice, soundness of mind, even courage – from which it would follow that excellence most certainly could be taught."[48] Here, as in other of Plato's early dialogues, the "virtues" threaten to collapse into a single virtue – that of knowledge. Such a collapse can be discerned in the Stoics, who embraced a monistic psychology in which the soul is entirely rational.[49] If virtue is identified with knowledge, as it is for many of the Stoics, then education should be sufficient to render a person virtuous.[50] "Socratic intellectualism" thus raises a matrix of concerns that encompass the division of the soul, questions of pedagogy (whether virtue can be taught), and the relationship between pleasure and the good.

While Aristotle insisted on reason as the most noble, divine human power, and therefore the part of our nature most singularly human, he resisted the reduction of virtue to knowledge. With Aristotle, we must also attend to the difference between his actual writings and his post-classical reception; this latter understanding of his position on knowledge and virtue was typically governed by the philosopher's basic stance that intellectual virtues are not sufficient for perfect happiness. Where late medieval theologians were more interested in Aristotle's claims about the felicity found in intellectual contemplation, late antique philosophers focused on the necessity of external goods. For these philosophers, Aristotle's originality inheres in his acknowledgment of the effects of fortune on the prospects for human happiness, as well as the necessity of conventional, external goods for the exercise of practical virtues such as liberality and justice. The Aristotelian version of the happy man needs health, moderate wealth, and friends, though these are not sufficient conditions for happiness. This practical model seems to be in tension with the contemplative version of happiness described in the last book of the *Nicomachean Ethics*, where perfect happiness is achieved through reflection on truth. Yet the practical, political life remains ethically valid, and Aristotelian contemplation – while central to the achievement of the highest good available to humans – provides in itself no guarantee of happiness.[51] While material goods are by no means identical with happiness, Aristotle affirms that even the virtuous man, engaged in the contemplative life, will not be happy if he suffers misfortune.

In contrast to both Plato and Aristotle, the neo-Platonist philosophers adapted a different model that placed the intellect at the center of ethical experience: the model of intellectual ascent. This version of intellectualism takes up Platonic topoi such as the world of Forms, the unreality of earthly life and matter, and mystical ascent to the divine. Plotinus sketches this ascent in explicitly intellectual terms; the only route to

God is through the mind.[52] The active life, if necessary as a pursuit for those without sufficient intellectual power, does not appear to be given much ethical value. Plotinus compares those who choose to pursue crafts or manual labor rather than study and speculation to "dull" children; they love material rather than spiritual beauty. The soul who has not yet rejected material beauty is likened to Narcissus, falling in love with its reflection in Matter.[53] Yet the ethically valuable experience of loving the beauty of "Moral-Wisdom" is not unlike that of Ovid's Narcissus or a courtly lover, "seized, with what pang of desire … flooded with awe and gladness, stricken by a salutary terror."[54] The object of such desire and wonder shifts, though experientially it is indistinct from love oriented toward the material world. If the good requires a first transformation from material beauty to moral beauty, it ultimately requires a final transformation whereby one's own intellect and love are subsumed by the divine, which itself enacts fruition and union. In Plotinus, as in later neo-Platonists such as pseudo-Dionysius, the intellect must finally be left behind in order to truly find the Good. Plotinus claims that all things strive after contemplation, "looking to Vision [*theoria*] as their one end"; this is true even of unreasoning animals.[55] Intellectual ascent is more than an ethical prescription, for it is also the origin of any creative or procreative act, and a description of the telos of all created beings. Neo-Platonism bequeathed medieval mystical discourse an intellectualism that emphasizes not education, but contemplation, and ultimately an intellectual contemplation whose goal is to leave the intellect behind.

Outside this mystical tradition, experience of union with God was not necessarily understood to transcend the intellect. Augustine – although he is typically associated with an emphasis on the primacy of the will, and occasionally describes joy as an act of the will – was clearly influenced by both Plato and the Platonists who describe the highest enjoyment in terms of cognition, knowledge, and self-reflection. For example, the theologian describes our resemblance to the Trinity as inhering in the fact that we exist, we know we exist, and we are glad of this existence and this knowledge.[56] Knowledge, self-reflection on that knowledge, and pleasure in that knowledge are the keys of divinity and thus of happiness. Yet any knowledge that partakes of an ultimate enjoyment will be granted by God, and will inhere in the desire for knowledge of him; this desire for knowledge is ultimately tantamount to love rather than a simple desire to understand. For Augustine, following Paul (1 Corinthians 12:8), knowledge (*scientia*) is ultimately different from the wisdom (*sapientia*) bestowed by God; we have knowledge about human things, and wisdom about the divine.[57] Yet this distinction between knowledge and divine sapience is often blurred, as Augustine cites descriptions of wisdom in a writer such as Cicero, who praises contemplative wisdom at the end of the *Hortensius*, and claims that the "use of reason and zeal of inquiry" will ease the ascent to heaven.[58]

The intellectualist approach to enjoyment created questions for the theologian about the role of virtuous action as well as the role of the will. In Christian doctrine, the question of the conflict between the virtue of the contemplative and active lives is always urgent. Just as desire for knowledge without love is ultimately empty, so is intellectual desire without action. For Augustine's teacher Ambrose (*c.*338–97), the desire for knowledge is a natural thing, and devotion to philosophical inquiry is honorable, but knowledge without actions is a hindrance in achieving the happy life.[59] Isidore of Seville's (d. 636) influential *Sententiae* describe the happy life as equivalent to the understanding of divinity – "Beata vita cognitio divinitatis est" – yet he does not espouse a strictly intellectualist ethical orientation.[60] Rather, he is instructive in the ways that, in the wake of Augustine, the distinctions between pursuits of virtue through the intellect, virtuous actions, or love of God all tend to collapse. At the beginning of the second book of his *Sententiae*, Isidore explains that the understanding of divinity, the virtue of good work, and enjoyment of eternity (*fructus aeternitatis*) are all equivalent.[61] In this way both practical virtue and the contemplative life are viewed as pursuing the same goal: the love and enjoyment of God. These later writers speak of happiness or blessedness in terms of cognition when the subject is wisdom, and in terms of love when the subject is love; there does not seem to be any controversy surrounding the matter. These are simply different ways of describing the same experience and goal. The Platonic and neo-Platonic union of love and the intellect is thus easily assimilated to Christian ideas of the role of cognition in the experience of beatitude. The later reception of the full *Nicomachean Ethics* will make this association controversial, for there the medieval philosophers found a description of felicity as an avowedly intellectual experience, born of study and contemplation of truth, the good, and the divine. As I will discuss in the following chapter, some thirteenth-century scholars were thus inspired to claim radically that only a life of philosophical speculation could lead one to the supreme good, but even unquestionably orthodox commentators such as Albert the Great noticed that Aristotle, in the last book of the *Ethics*, does not seem to leave any space for the love of God to participate in intellectual enjoyment – it appears to be irrelevant. In Chapter 4 we will find that this absence and the varied ways it was addressed by medieval philosophers and poets participated in the conflicts over intellectualism and voluntarism in the fourteenth century.

HUMAN HAPPINESS

Unlike pleasure, happiness is uncontested as an ethical goal for both the classical and the medieval periods, and as Augustine remarks in his *Confessions*,

> Happiness itself is neither Greek nor Latin, but it is that which Greeks, Latins, and men of all other languages long to attain. It is then known to all of them, and if they could all be asked: "Do you wish to be happy?" they would without doubt answer with one voice: "We do."[62]

This unanimity illustrates, for Augustine, that happiness must reside in human spiritual memory – a remembrance of the happy life (*beata vita*) in God. The question for classical discussions of happiness did not concern its desirability, or its appropriateness as a pursuit, but whether it was both desirable and possible on earth, or should instead be located in an afterlife or beyond of life. Plato is again not consistent on this topic across his dialogues. His emphasis in the *Theaetetus* and the *Phaedo* on imitation of the divine and on the irrelevance of worldly evil to the happiness of the virtuous man is in conflict with his insistence elsewhere that a life of virtue does not release one from concern for others, from responsibility in the world.[63] In the latter case, the relevance of earthly concerns to the virtuous man does not mean that happiness on earth is achievable. Accordingly, the ethical valorization of earthly activity does not in itself indicate that a philosopher endorses a concept of human happiness. This latter stance is perhaps taken to its extreme in Plotinus' writing, where the virtuous man will have civic virtues, but given his detachment from the world will be extremely unlikely to practice them.[64]

Just so, a validation of human happiness does not necessarily bring with it a rejection of the divine or the otherworldly. It is, perhaps surprisingly, at the end of the *Timaeus*, in a section not available to most medieval readers, that Plato's recipe for the "care of the soul" contains a recipe for happiness that is not unlike that which will be formulated by Aristotle. He admonishes that the man engrossed in earthly appetites will become fully mortal, while if a man's

> heart has been set on the love of learning and true wisdom and he has exercised that part of himself above all, he is surely bound to have thoughts immortal

> and divine, if he shall lay hold upon truth, nor can he fail to possess immortality in the fullest measure that human nature admits ... he must needs be happy above all.[65]

Both Plato and Aristotle outline a version of human happiness that demands a reaching toward the divine; both cite an element of the divine within us that we should nurture and allow to flourish. This version of the divinity of happiness is significantly different from the version that demands an escape from the world. In the *Theaetetus*, rather than pursuing justice, as evil can in any case never be conquered on earth, Socrates advocates escaping from earth to heaven. Evil will always haunt human life, and the only solution is to take flight, "becoming as like God as possible."[66] Socrates tells an anecdote, already well known to his contemporaries, about the philosopher Thales who, while gazing at the stars, fell into a well. Such tales of the star-gazing philosopher, oblivious to his earthly surroundings, were quite popular in the later Middle Ages, typically as evidence of the fallibility of the intellectual, a witness to the fact that every mortal person is subjected to the obstinacy of the material world and of human desire; no one is above or immune to the natural world. Yet in the version of this story in the *Theaetetus*, Thales is praised as being above the derision of the servant girl who teases him. The ideal philosopher "fails to see his next-door neighbour," and this is no fault.[67] As Julia Annas notes, this philosopher – oblivious to the world around him, uninterested in his neighbor, incapable of making a bed – seems an impossible figure of admiration. Yet it is precisely the distance between our common, intuitive identification with the servant girl and an admiration of the philosopher who has transcended earthly concerns that is the point of the tale. The *Phaedo* offers a perhaps more convincing topos for philosophers and theologians who wish to argue for the irrelevance of the mutable earthly world to happiness – the example of Socrates as the noble man who either pursues or humbly acquiesces to death in the name of virtue, or even in the name of happiness. As Philosophia will later remark in the *Consolation*, "if we know that many have sought the enjoyment of happiness not simply through death but even through pain and suffering, how can this present life make them happy, when its being past does not make them miserable?"[68]

Plato thus left a twinned legacy to later philosophers: a Stoic legacy focused on divinity as a life according to reason, in full engagement with the world, and a legacy in neo-Platonism, Judaism, and Christianity centered on the idea of "becoming divine" as a fleeing from the world toward the "perfect," divine good, necessarily outside of human experience. As Cicero summarizes the Stoic position, "the chances of mortal life are to be despised, death is to be disregarded, pains and toils are to be considered endurable."[69] He cites Plato's *Gorgias* in support of the dictum that "virtue is self-sufficient for a happy life."[70] In a Christian context, the "happy life" does not signify even supremely virtuous mortal life, but life in union with the divine after death. Aristotelian ethics was susceptible of both interpretations of the happy life. The philosopher emphasizes the achievability of perfect happiness in Book x of the *Nicomachean Ethics*, where happiness is defined as the activity of the highest aspect of human nature in accordance with its proper virtue: the exercise of the intellect in understanding the truth. Aristotle acknowledges that a life of such happiness is extraordinarily difficult to achieve, but he nevertheless contends that such is the goal of the ethical human life. This humanist optimism is overshadowed by his emphasis in the rest of the *Ethics* and in the other ethical treatises attributed to Aristotle in the Middle Ages (the *Eudemian Ethics* and the *Magna Moralia*) on the effects of fortune upon the chances for human happiness. While it is his theorization of the possibilities of happiness on earth that caused such difficulty for the late medieval theologians, his realism about the importance of external goods to happiness also made him a spokesperson for the near-impossibility of earthly happiness.

Augustine directly addresses the question of whether we can rightly or fruitfully pursue happiness on earth in Book ix of the *City of God*. Asking whether man can have genuine felicity, despite his mortality, he admits that this is a vexed question, and that various philosophers have given different answers; occasionally they argue that the wise person can achieve happiness. He concludes, finally, that "the more credible and probable position is that all men, as long as they are mortals, must needs be also wretched."[71] This answer affirms the Christian deferral of true blessedness until the afterlife while also giving an additional reason for the necessity of Christ's mediation between the mortal and the divine. If mortals could become truly happy, participating in the blessedness of the divine, they would logically serve as mediators, but as this is not the case, Christ must serve this purpose.[72] Plotinus, quoted rather freely, lends support to Augustine's judgment of the wretchedness of human life: "We must flee to our beloved country. There the Father is, and there is everything. Where shall we take ship? How can we flee? By becoming like God."[73] Augustine retains an intuitive understanding of happiness, but relocates it to the afterlife. Human happiness becomes instead "the life of happiness which follows death," and life itself is redefined in a variety of ways as a process of dying.[74] Ambrose had similarly equated the happy life (*vitam beatam*) with eternal life (*vitam aeternam*).[75] Augustine concludes that as the present life is still subject to death, deception, and distress, "life will only be truly happy when it is eternal," chiding the pagan philosophers, who "have wished, with amazing folly, to be happy here [on earth] and to achieve bliss by their own efforts."[76]

This rejection of human happiness informs the discourse of Philosophia in Boethius' *Consolation of Philosophy*, which might be read as a medieval update of the narrative of a philosopher going virtuously – if not wholly contentedly – toward his death. In the middle of Book II, Philosophia has already established that "happiness is the highest good of a rational nature" and thus that happiness cannot be equivalent to the "fortuitous happiness of the body."[77] By the end of book III, she has persuaded the prisoner to agree that "true happiness must reside in the most high God" and that happiness ultimately *is* God.[78] Therefore, "every happy man is a god," for he participates in divinity.[79] Philosophia unifies a Stoic moral philosophy, whereby nothing mutable contributes to happiness, with a Platonic and Aristotelian definition of happy life as a life that partakes of the divine.

Such a rejection of the physical world as a route to happiness does not mean, however, that one becomes unsusceptible to its beauties. Many of Philosophia's meters in the *Consolation* sing the praises of nature kept in harmony by a love that is both cosmic and human. And in one of the longest sections of the *City of God*, Augustine works toward a conclusion of the entire work by considering God's blessings, marveling over the beauties of the natural world and the artistic, architectural, and intellectual accomplishments of humankind. His deep appreciation for creation emerges as he describes the variety of plant and animal life, the wonders of ant colonies and of edible fruits, and offers a lyrical account of the spectacle of the colors of the sea: "putting on its changing colours like different garments, now green, with all the many varied shades, now purple, now blue."[80] Yet he finally judges that "these are the consolations of mankind under condemnation, not the rewards of the blessed."[81] Augustine and Boethius together bequeath a model of reconciliation between love for earthly beauty and rejection of earthly mutability – this literary model allows praise for the world once one's conversion away from the world has been effected, and consolation that springs from both mutable fortune, recognized as such, and a knowledge that a life beyond fortune exists after death.

Such melancholy comforts have perhaps never gone out of fashion. Yet in a philosophical context, morality that takes heavenly permanence as its starting point was often bracketed – if never entirely set aside – in the tradition of moral philosophy reinaugurated with full access to Aristotelian ethical thought. In its complete form, Aristotle's *Ethics* introduced a definition of the sovereign good that would prove difficult to assimilate to a Christian worldview. Human happiness is the starting point in this philosophy, a terrain of study in its own right. The tension between lyric desire for the permanence of beauty and a pragmatic analysis of the ethical goals achievable in this life animates both philosophy and poetry in the wake of the emergence of an earthly-oriented – not to say secular – ethics. While, in a Christian context, this happiness can never be allowed perfection, it can certainly be allowed investigation and pursuit, in terms of both the intellectual and the political lives. Defining the happiness achieved via self-reflection and contemplation as the highest happiness on earth demanded that ethical concepts of action, love, pleasure, felicity, and the good be re-examined and revised.

ETHICS AND ENJOYMENT IN THE TWELFTH CENTURY

Ethical understandings of enjoyment began to emerge as key issues in the twelfth century, as did philosophical and poetic discourses that treated human ethics as a terrain unto itself. A shift forward to this period finds the simultaneous beginnings of a systematic medieval treatment of ethics and the birth of vernacular love poetry. Early in the twelfth century, the second and third books of Aristotle's *Nicomachean Ethics* are translated into Latin (the *Ethica Vetus*) and they begin to generate commentaries.[82] Although it is not clear that Peter Abelard had access to these texts, his *Ethics* is unique and forward-looking in its treatment of ethical concerns – action, intention, religious culpability, and social justice – in a self-sufficient manner. His approach to human behavior as a subject worthy of its own discrete investigation harks back to the classical period and also looks forward to the reinvigoration of moral philosophy as a discipline in the scholastic period. Abelard's *Dialogus inter Philosophum, Judeum, et Christianum* – or *Collationes* – can be seen as a snapshot of mid-twelfth-century understandings of the relationship between pagan philosophy and Christian theology as they pertain to enjoyment. Likewise, Peter Lombard's *Sententiae*, a text written only a generation later, would contribute to a renewed focus on defining enjoyment in its full ethical and theological context.

Yet it is Abelard's *Dialogue* that articulates what might be thought of as a new version of the *City of God* for the late medieval period, in that it addresses the Christian inheritance of classical thought. In this text, a philosophical dream vision in which the narrator imagines himself as the judge of two dialogues – a Philosopher debating a Jew and Christian in turn – Abelard rethinks the relationship between pagan and Christian understandings of the highest good. The legacy of classical philosophy for Christian thought about aspects of enjoyment is rendered explicit in Abelard's dialogue – he is most fascinating when he explores the way a shared terminology masks crucial differences in how philosophers and Christians talk about ethics. Where Augustine sought to show that *amor*, *dilectio*, and *caritas* all describe the same phenomenon turned to various ends, Abelard is compelled to demonstrate that all understandings of *caritas* are hardly equivalent. Prodded by the questions of the Christian, the Philosopher parses the differences among the ancients regarding whether the highest good should be defined as virtue or as pleasure, and what these writers understood by pleasure. When the Christian turns to a discussion of differences in ethical vocabulary between the pagans and the Christians, the Philosopher at first maintains that they largely agree, but simply have different terms for the same things: "Epicurus I think calls this blessedness 'pleasure': your Christ calls it 'the kingdom of heaven.'"[83] The Philosopher tries to save philosophy by claiming that the pagan philosophers speak of the "ultimate *human* good" (*summum hominis bonum*) but the Christian will allow no earthly good to deserve the name of "ultimate," when the divine clearly surpasses it. A logical distinction – the Christian's criticism of the attribute "ultimate" being given to anything that is not in fact final – reveals that, as the Christian concludes, "our purpose and merits are quite different from yours, and we disagree quite a bit too about the ultimate good itself."[84]

Abelard's Philosopher is shown to stand in perfect agreement with Christianity, but only after he is educated in the true meanings of his terms. Early on in his portion of the dialogue, the Philosopher, invested in maintaining agreement between the two discourses, insists that the pleasure of the pagan philosophers is not carnal, but a tranquility of the soul, and that philosophers are great despisers of earthly happiness.[85] From Abelard's perspective, the demonstration that pagan philosophy finally agrees with Christianity is the only way that the content of such philosophy can be saved, and the Christian uses the philosophical method of logical disputation to critique the Philosopher. The Philosopher, for his part, minimizes the differences between those who would pursue pleasure and those who would pursue virtue, arguing that they are basically the same: the blessed are understood to be strong in virtues, and the virtuous are blessed with pleasure.[86] It is on this point that the Christian and Philosopher appear to part ways, for the Christian has not reoriented his definition of blessedness so that it becomes synonymous with virtuousness. He cannot disregard the pleasure of the beatitude offered in the afterlife, which will increase without an increase in virtuousness, while for the Philosopher the afterlife is irrelevant. The Christian uses logical treatises – Aristotle's *Categories* and Cicero's *Topics* – as evidence for his claim that even pagan philosophers agree that life on earth includes evils and suffering, and therefore cannot be the site of the ultimate good. He quotes Aristotle that "the contrary of a good is certainly evil," and Cicero that "if health is good, sickness is evil."[87] The use of a logical example as evidence in a moral argument is intriguing, and also perhaps telling of the desire to marshal any ethical writings possible in an environment in which not many texts are available.[88] The Philosopher ultimately capitulates to the Christian's line of reasoning, going so far as to recuperate Epicurus by reasoning that when he said that "the ultimate good is pleasure," he was referring to the pleasure of the afterlife. The desirability of the afterlife's blessedness as the ultimate good, now analogized to warmth after cold, clear skies after rain, has become "plain truth."

The other aspect of shared vocabulary dissected by the Christian is the common notion that the divine, or God, characterizes the ultimate good. The Philosopher sums up: "the ultimate good is God himself, or else his blessedness's ultimate tranquility that nevertheless we do not regard as anything other than him who is blessed from himself, not from something else."[89] The Christian's doctrine that God, the ultimate good, is also the ultimate human good, is "not unknown" to philosophy, as its spokesperson acknowledges. The ultimate *human* good for the Philosopher, however, is "the perpetual repose or joy everyone receives after this life in proportion to his merits, whether in the vision or cognition of God, as you say, or however else it happens."[90] This definition garners no response from the Christian, and it appears that he accepts it. While the Philosopher's belief in the divinity of the ultimate good has not shifted, his location of the human good as a participation in this ultimate good in the afterlife is a distinct transformation in his system.

While the Philosopher will allow for this relocation of the good, his agreement with the Christian cannot reach the same degree when it concerns the relationship between virtue and love – this relationship appears to be an insurmountable sticking point. The subsuming of both virtue and reward under the category of "love" by Christianity is demonstrated to cause difficulty for the Philosopher. In the first dialogue, the Jew and Philosopher both agree that "natural" law can be effectively summarized as the commandment to love both God and neighbor. The Philosopher's logical dissection of the Jew's beliefs turns on the Jew's claim that "love's perfection is enough to yield true blessedness" alongside his simultaneous insistence on the need for external works.[91] The Christian catches the Philosopher in a trap very similar to the logical snare that the Jew walks into: the Philosopher quite reasonably considers that if one's love for God is virtuous, and is increased on account of being given the gift of the divine vision in the afterlife, one should then merit further reward in heaven for increasing one's virtue of charity. But according to the Christian, human love is a necessary response to the "payment of a prize" of heavenly understanding, and so any increase of love in response does not "turn the reward itself into a merit again."[92] In other words, human souls upon entering heaven do not become more meritorious – what other reward could they expect? The dialogue ends, apparently incomplete, in the midst of a discussion about what things deserve to be called "good," and calling for any further points about the ultimate good to be brought forward. The dreamer is never called upon to judge the victor in these debates, but it hardly seems necessary, given the already determined outcome that Christianity will win (in fact has won, so far as Abelard is concerned), and given his mastery of both Christian and philosophical discourses. Yet the substance of the debate remains an illustrative example of the way that Christian ethics can harness philosophical logical method and content to its arguments, and the fact that philosophy can be won over to Christian doctrine, but only through dialectic and not through a simple claim that using the terms *summum bonum*, *caritas*, and *beatitudo* in common marks a shared understanding of the ethical orientation of a human life. Abelard's dialogue also shows that there are points of tension that are terribly difficult to resolve, if not irresolvable, between philosophical and Christian understandings of concepts such as virtue, love, and the good. Classical ethics is both the origin of Christian ethics and in some ways unassimilable to it.

Abelard's student, Peter Lombard, did not address the topic of classical ethics in such a systematic fashion in his enormously influential *Sententiae*. However, within this summation of Christian doctrine on a variety of topics, including vice, virtue, and the experience of the ultimate good in the afterlife, Peter does address questions about the relationship between intellectual contemplation and love of God, hierarchies of love for the supreme good and lesser goods, and the levels of enjoyment of the beatific vision.[93] He treats enjoyment most directly in the beginning of his book of *Sentences*; there we find again Augustine's definitions of use and enjoyment. Peter discusses these definitions, which things are to be used and which enjoyed, whether human beings and the virtues should be enjoyed, and whether God uses or enjoys us. He reiterates the definition of enjoyment in *De Doctrina Christiana* and emphasizes that the things of this world are only to be used:

> To enjoy is to inhere with love to some thing for its own sake; but to use is to apply whatever comes to one's hand in order to obtain that which is to be enjoyed … Among all things those alone are to be enjoyed which are eternal and unchangeable; as for the rest, they are to be used so that one may come to the full enjoyment of the former.[94]

He does not go on to elaborate at this point upon the vagaries of understandings of love, pleasure, fruition, or happiness. Yet later commentaries – several discussed in the chapters to follow – give quantities of space to discussing the controversies over enjoyment in their particular context. In the preface to her magisterial two-volume study of Peter Lombard, Marcia Colish remarks that a survey of the choices made by university students as to what aspects of the *Sentences* to focus on in their commentaries could give us a striking comprehension of geographical and chronological shifts in the history of speculative thought.[95] As Colish also notes, the theme of use and enjoyment, set out in the beginning, governs the *Sentences* as a whole: everything else points to God as the supreme being and supreme good to be enjoyed in and for himself.[96] Although the Lombard does not treat ethics systematically, he consistently addresses vice, virtues, free will, and moral law.

As the *Sentences* became a set text in the university curriculum and thus a consistent locus for debate about topics such as the psychology and ethics of enjoyment of the greatest good, it also became a site where Aristotelian philosophy was marshaled along with patristic doctrine to solve these debates.[97] As Abelard's renewed synthesis of classical and Christian ethics suggests, there was a continuing desire to repair the gaps between these two discourses, and an awareness that a reckoning of these differences was crucial to the ongoing project of formulating a medieval moral philosophy. The scholars of the late thirteenth and fourteenth centuries would take up the challenge of synthesizing the Lombard's Augustinian formulations of enjoyment with Aristotelian ideas about the relationships between love and pleasure, and love and intellectual activity, and about the place of enjoyment in human happiness. The focus on enjoyment in the first distinction of the *Sentences* ensured that it became a set topic in the commentaries of many theologians. These commentaries discussed the difference between the enjoyment to be had in this life (*fruitio viae*) and the enjoyment of the afterlife (*fruitio patriae*) and analyzed any number of other adjacent issues, including grace, charity, and the relationship between the intellect and the will. In this context the act of enjoyment (*fruitio*) is structurally distinct from the resulting pleasure (*delectatio*), and scholars debated whether or not the two terms could be effectively distinguished.[98] The thriving discourse of enjoyment in commentaries on the Lombard's text had its own influence on commentaries on Aristotle's *Ethics*. Debates about the identity or non-identity of pleasure, love, and happiness were recounted in comments on Book x as background to philosophical understandings of both human and divine happiness. In making pleasure and enjoyment common topics for discussion, late medieval theologians took up issues central to a theorizing of both the ultimate heavenly good and a terrestrial human good, wondering about the nobility of motivation through love or pleasure, and where in the soul the ultimate experience of enjoyment might take place. Such questions also animated another major ethical discourse of the late Middle Ages – poetry, and especially love poetry. The section below begins a description of the joint poetic and philosophical discourse of enjoyment that this book seeks to recover.

TROUBADOURS AND "LO GAI SABER"

The story about the relationship between poetry and philosophy that this book will tell is not a story about the unidirectional influence of the latter upon the former, but rather a picture of a period during which both poetry and philosophy together were addressing ethical questions about love. The poems of the troubadours reveal the way that, even prior to the full translation of Aristotle's ethical writings, this matrix of love poetry and philosophy created a space for thinking about secular ethical problems on their own terms. The Occitan poetry of the twelfth century has long been recognized as a site for meditation on the relationships among love, language, and joy.[99] The troubadours' penchant for repeated, common use of words such as *joi* (joy, enjoyment), *lo mielh* (the good), and *pretz* (worth, nobility) not only builds an ethical and erotic vocabulary, but also reveals a willingness to play with their own ethical systems.[100] The troubadours thus create, record, and constantly revise a courtly ethos that intersects with both secular and religious questions about valor, loyalty, service, goodness, desire, and happiness. Below, I will discuss lyrics by Guilhem IX (1071–1126), Jaufré Rudel (*c.*1125–*c.*1148), and Bernart de Ventadorn (*c.*1147–*c.*1170). These songs serve as material for exploring how the discourse of troubadour poetry intersects with the philosophical concerns I have narrated above, as well as an illustration of one of the main theses of this book, that vernacular love poetry takes the science of love and the good as one of its primary concerns, not simply as an independent genre, but as a participant in a larger late medieval ethical discourse.

The troubadours were celebrated by early scholars for what was understood as a chaste version of courtship with its accompanying elaborate codes and practices.[101] This commitment to chastity has more recently been exposed as a critical fiction, though the troubadours are still often noted for their creation of a mode of poetic desire that revels in desire itself and its accompanying sacrifices rather than its consummation. While this construction of desire is clearly a marked feature of much troubadour verse, and an important facet of the troubadour literary legacy, it is also clear that the question of the lyric subject's relationship to his desire was in constant flux from the very beginning of the troubadour *œuvre.* Troubadour poetry, considered as a whole, addresses many aspects of medieval philosophical debate about enjoyment: the relationships between virtue and love, and love and intellectual contemplation, definitions of pleasure and joy, and the possibilities of human happiness. Guilhem IX of Aquitaine sings that when spring returns, "Ben deu cascus lo joi jauzir / Don es jauzens" (each one should enjoy the joy / About which he is joyful, ll. 5–6).[102] This song, which begins "Pos vezem de novel florir," is dedicated to the sentiment that love without enjoyment is "nïens" (pointless, l. 18). The first stanza, with its play on the many grammatical forms of joy – enjoying joy (*joi jauzir*), receiving joyfulness (*jauzens*) – signals that the many ways to experience joy – as an object of desire, as something given or something actively enjoyed, or as an aspect of the activity of loving itself – are the subject of the poem. Guilhem expresses the possibility of separating enjoyment from love as a conflict over his duty to praise love despite its granting him no joy. The fact that the speaker, despite his advice to others, wants precisely what he cannot have means that he will have less pleasure from love, as well as less knowledge: "Per tal n'ai meins de bon saber / Quar vueill so que non puesc aver" (For this reason I have less good pleasure [knowledge] / Because I want what I cannot have, ll. 19–20). In Occitan as in Latin, the verb of knowledge (*saber*, *sapere*) is the same as the verb of tasting, and thus of "enjoying" in its range of senses. One often finds in troubadour poetry this deliberate play among intellectual knowledge, erotic knowledge, and intellectual and erotic enjoyment. The lyric subject might desire a person, the person's body, the person's desire, or knowledge itself. The beloved Lady is often described as wise as well as beautiful, and further as a source of wisdom; in this sense she is part of a long tradition stretching back to Augustine's praise of Sapientia and perhaps even the Platonic form of Beauty itself.

Jaufré Rudel similarly remarks that "Es amors bon' ab bon saber" (love is good when it has fine wisdom [pleasure] on its side, l. 14) in his poem "Quan lo rossinhols" ("When the nightingale").[103] He laments that he gains no wisdom ("bon saber," l. 21) from his lady's beauty despite the fact that when he dreams of her he has "joy meravelos / Per qu'ieu la ab joy jauzen" (marvelous joy / Because I rejoice there rejoicing with joy, ll. 17–18) and "Per qu'ieu la jau jauzitz jauzen" (rejoices joyfully on account of the joy from it, l. 18). Yet this love recedes the closer he comes to her; his poem creates the same goal of union with his beloved as the poem of Guilhem, and yet his goal appears in fact to be a goal of never arriving. The last two stanzas narrate the speaker's leave-taking of Love itself, parting joyfully, and apparently beginning a new pilgrimage to Bethlehem (l. 37). The lyric appears to exchange physical love for love of God, and the "bon saber" that the speaker could not gain from his beloved's beauty is finally achieved in the attendance of the "segura escola" (good school, l. 42) where Jesus teaches. In the context of this song, "saber" is moralized and the lamented distance of his lover is revealed as insurmountable; the singer gains more pleasure and wisdom by transferring his desire to God himself.

It would be mistaken, however, to dismiss this or others of Jaufré Rudel's songs as simplistically didactic, as the exchange of physical love for spiritual pilgrimage is collapsed in Jaufré's famous song "Lanquan li jorn son lonc en may" ("When the days are long in May"), perhaps the fullest exposition of his "love from afar."[104] The speaker in this song takes joy in distant birds and departs sadly and joyfully from a distant love. Yet rather than turning to God, we find that the poet will be granted the company of his distant love (who remains "distant" despite such conversation) through the Lord himself; God in fact "fermet cest' amor de loing" (fashioned this distant love, l. 37) and the poet's wish for pilgrimage would take him to his beloved's face, where "mos fustz e mos tapis / Fos pelz sieus bels huoills remiratz" (my staff and mat were gazed on by her lovely eyes, ll. 34–5). Such claims in the context of the matrix of troubadour song belie any simple notion that physical love might be sacrificed for spiritual love, as there is always the chance that one might simply hope that God would bring him or her to his earthly beloved. Both lover and pilgrim desire to gaze upon and contemplate the beloved's beauty and face. Guilhem's and Jaufré's poetry thematize the slippery relationships among desires for intellectual, erotic, and spiritual knowledge while attending to questions that were vital for medieval moral philosophy: the relationship between pleasure and love, the nature of the highest enjoyment, and the location of ethical desire.

Questions about love, knowledge, and religion remain vital for the later troubadours, though moral questions do not always address the gap between secular and spiritual desire. Bernart de Ventadorn's songs are often taken up with earthly questions that come with adopting one of two positions: the desiring subject or the object that is desired; this oscillation, it transpires, turns not on the alternation between the two poles of singing lover and far-off beloved, but rather his shifting relationship to other lovers and to himself. "Can vei la lauzeta mover" is one of the most archetypal (and popular) troubadour songs, written by the "archetype of the courtly troubadour."[105] Bernart begins his song with a moment of envy for the joys of others:

> Can vei la lauzeta mover
> de joi sas alas contral rai
> que s'oblid' e-s laissa chaser
> per la doussor c'al cor li vai,
> ai, tan grans enveya m'en ve
> de cui qu'eu veya jauzion
> meravilhas ai, car desse
> lo cor de dezirer no-m fon.[106] (ll. 1–8)

(When I see the lark beat his wings for joy against the sun's ray, until, for the sheer delight which goes to his heart, he forgets to fly and plummets down, then great envy of those whom I see filled with happiness comes to me. I marvel that my heart does not melt at once from desire.)

The poet watches a lark, Icarus-like, flying too high, forgetting itself in the joy of the sun's rays, and falling as a result of this intense emotion. Bernart follows this observation with a cry that a great desire or great envy takes hold of him when he sees any other joyful person, and he cannot believe that his heart does not simply melt from desire. Bernart tells us that he began to lose power over himself the moment he looked into his lady's eyes, into a mirror ("miralh," l. 20) that pleased him greatly. He claims to have lost himself just as Narcissus lost himself in the fountain. Here looking is privileged again, but instead of the voyeuristic looking upon another's pleasure that initiates the poem, the poet gazes into a mirror that could reflect his love object, the self, or an exemplary, ideal self. The myth of Narcissus complicates the earlier image of envious gazing, for the lark of the first line of the poem emerges more clearly as a figure for the poet himself – a songbird flying too close to the unattainable object of desire. The poet seems not to suffer out of envy or jealousy, but from the universal Ovidian dilemma of narcissistic desire: one is trapped by the too perfect possession of one's own self to properly experience desire.[107]

Bernart begins "Ab joi" with a meditation on the relationship between joy and the good, between beginnings and endings, and actions and reception:

> Ab joi mou lo vers e.l comens
> et ab joi reman e fenis,
> e sol que bona fos las fis,
> bos tenh qu'er lo comensamens.
> Per la bona comensansa
> mi ve jois et alegransa;
> e per so dei la bona fi grazir
> car totz bos faihz vei lauzar al fenir. (ll. 1–8)

(With Joy embarking I begin the verse, and with joy concluding it will end. Only when the ending is good, do I find the beginning good. In a good beginning, joy and happiness come to me, and so I shall welcome the good ending for I see all good deeds applauded at their end.)

Bernart seems here to be invoking a notion of the unity of intention and action, beginning and ending, in which joyful intentions will lead inevitably to good deeds. For Bernart, the end of the song confers meaning (here, joy) upon the beginning, for only if the end is good will he find the beginning good. In wishing "totz bos faihz" (all good deeds, l. 8) to be applauded at the end of his song, he is allowed to receive joy and happiness in its beginning. Here goodness and happiness seem to bracket his poem, sealing it off from the destructive forces of the outside world, guaranteeing an unbroken chain of promises, actions, beginnings and endings. Joy is demonstrated to be compatible with fear and anxiety ("paor e doptansa") about failing one's beloved; one's commitment to the courtly virtues necessary to be a "true lover" brings pleasure but also fear of failure. The fear of losing an ephemeral earthly good – the fear that compromises earthly happiness for Boethius and others – here is transformed into a fear that the self will not live up to the ethical demands of the beloved. Yet it is eminently compatible with the joy described by the poet; any pure lover ("fin' amansa") will experience this fear (ll. 13–14). As is often the case in troubadour lyrics, the poet demonstrates ambivalence about his desire to keep his love secret, as he wishes that his beloved be true to him "qu'enemics, c'ai fatz d'enveya morir" (so that I might make my enemies die of envy, l. 40). Thus the lady herself, Bel Vezers, does not come into visibility until the sixth stanza, when Bernart mentions her "bela bocha rizens" (beautiful smiling mouth, l. 41) and her kisses that slay him. Up to that point she has been either absent or an abstraction. It appears that when only the poet's desire and intention are present, happiness is possible. At the end of the poem, the promised happiness is more akin to Guilhem's claim that he "must" say good things about love; Bernart "dei aver alegransa" (ought to be happy, l. 61) because he loves such a worthy woman. She has his "esperansa" and is an expert about doing and saying pleasurable things. The broad claims about joy and happiness in the beginning of the poem give way to a less sure claim to happiness when an individual love object emerges. Bernart's poem dramatizes the conflict between the vagaries of earthly fortune and the human desire for stable happiness, as well as his ethical responsibility to praise love and to actually feel happiness when it seems that his happiness is compromised by anxiety about the desires of others and about his own virtue. Is enjoyment comprised by good deeds? By love? By assent to an ethical value system that praises love directed at a worthy object above all other practical matters? Bernart seems to suggest that such a system works well when considered in the abstract, but founders when it comes into contact with the community of the court, or even the community of two made up of the lover and his beloved.

The troubled relationship between self, desire, and other – often focused by an Ovidian lens – will remain the way in which the medieval poets work their way through the shared erotic and intellectual discourses of contemplation, love, and pleasure. The lyrics above reveal that questions about enjoyment were already animating vernacular poetry. The next century will witness a transformation in the textual environment of moral philosophy with the translation of the full *Nicomachean Ethics* along with many other texts in the Aristotelian corpus. In the *Roman de la Rose*, as we will see in the following chapter, Ovidian tales of Narcissus and Pygmalion function to allow the poets to explore the intersection of intellectual and erotic desires, along a range of experiences from a reveling in wonder and objectless delight to an idealized union of the creative and desiring impulses to a devastating and ironic critique of both courtly and scholarly ideas about ultimate possession and fruition.

CHAPTER 2

Narcissus after Aristotle: love and ethics in Le Roman de la Rose

Narcissus was always "after Aristotle," as my chapter title seems unnecessarily to remind us, but the succession was reversed for the Latin Middle Ages, in which Ovid preceded the Philosopher by centuries, at least in terms of textual reception.[1] There are any number of reasons why we might seek to find out what happens to Narcissus – Ovid's Narcissus along with his avatars, the self-reflexive, self-sacrificing protagonists of much love poetry – after Aristotle is fully returned to medieval discourse. Aristotle was, after all, no critic of self-love. In the thirteenth century, both philosophy and poetry grappled with shifting understandings of earthly and divine love, physical and intellectual pleasure, and human happiness. The Aristotelianism that came to dominate scholastic discourse in this period with the full translation and dissemination of most of the philosopher's works into Latin did not leave medieval understandings of love untouched. I concentrate below on the way that Aristotle's ethical writings transformed both poetic and philosophical understandings of love, taking as my focus the *Roman de la Rose* of Guillaume de Lorris and Jean de Meun. An examination of thirteenth-century Aristotelianism in this light will allow us to add another facet to our reading of Jean's transformation of Guillaume's *Rose*, to the poetic legacy of the conjoined text, and also to our understanding of the developing traditions of vernacular love poetry. The *Roman de la Rose* – as a poem at the center of the intellectual universe of the thirteenth century, and a poem that would immediately become and remain central to the traditions of love poetry, dream vision, encyclopedic narrative, personification allegory, and penitential and confessional narratives – is thus at the center of this story.

The modern recontextualization of the *Rose* within its full intellectual environment at the end of the thirteenth century is a project that began with Gérard Paré more than fifty years ago, and that remains uncompleted, though other critics besides Paré have located Jean de Meun at the heart of intellectual discourse and controversies.[2] Alastair Minnis argues for the similarity of Jean's "texts and intellectual pursuits" to those of the thirteenth-century Parisian arts faculty, noting that Jean was writing his *Rose* at the same time that Boethius of Dacia, the "radical Aristotelian," was active at the University of Paris.[3] Jean seems to be remarkably interested in the new learning of the schools, an interest that invites speculation that Jean chose to work with the commentary of William of Aragon – to him a very recent, very Aristotelian text – when writing his translation of Boethius' *Consolation of Philosophy*.[4] There is also evidence for an educated medieval audience for the poem: it was listed (as missing) in the 1338 inventory of the Sorbonne library and manuscript evidence points to readers who approached the poem with a wide range of perspectives and concerns.[5] A mid-fourteenth-century manuscript (MS Bibl. Nat. fr. 1560) demonstrates that at least one of its readers engaged with the poem as a part of philosophical discourse. This reader glosses the poem with references to Aristotle, among other learned writers, and specifically quotes the first book of the *Ethics* in reference to the personification of Reason: "Primo ethicorum. Semper ratio deprecatur ad optimam" (The first book of the *Ethics*. Reason always urges to the best, fol. 29^{r}, v. 4198).[6] Sylvia Huot reminds us that "for a fourteenth-century reader, there was nothing strange about seeking points of contact between poetry, philosophy, theology, law."[7]

I begin my examination of the Aristotelian aspects of the *Rose* with Guillaume de Lorris, in order to investigate why his poem (*c.*1230) might have provided such an attractive text for Jean's later experimentation (*c.*1270) with new ethical ideas. Below, I look at the way in which the "new Aristotle" affected courtly poetry by examining this famously bifurcated poem as a work divided not only by a temporal gap and a shift in authorship, but by the impact of the full translation of Aristotle's *Nicomachean Ethics* which takes place during that gap. Most importantly, this translation brought with it Aristotle's definition of contemplative activity as the highest human happiness, accessible in this life. This understanding of ethics as bound to the human sphere, and as oriented toward a good achievable in this life, would be particularly difficult for medieval philosophy to absorb. In this context of debate, Jean de Meun takes a poem already steeped in ethical categories of self-knowledge, desire, and free will and exploits its fissures in order to explore the erotic assumptions of both courtly poetry and scholastic philosophy. For Jean, this is still a poem about love, but it is additionally a poem about how the poetic expression of erotic desire must always also be about intellectual and spiritual desire. His renamed *Rose*, now the *Miroër aus Amoreus*, will ideally include all of the conflicting contemporary sciences of love in its polished surface.

GUILLAUME DE LORRIS: NARCISSUS AND THE *VITA ACTIVA*

Jean de Meun does not choose to work upon what he sees as a naive, earlier poem, but is interested in the "first *Rose*" precisely because Guillaume de Lorris seems to address Aristotelian ethical controversies *avant la lettre* – before the full translation of the *Nicomachean Ethics* into Latin (*c*.1246). Operating within a framework prior to the dissemination of Aristotle's contemplative definition of human happiness, Guillaume's poem explores the ethical implications of an erotic quest that remains firmly in a circular structure of desire and poetic activity, a structure that on its face does not seem to trouble the distinctions that medieval philosophy maintains between imperfect earthly goods and the perfect good reserved for divine illumination.[8] Instead the poem appears to adhere to conventional, ironic parallels between the unattainable love object and the *summum bonum* of the heavenly realm; in his dream vision Amant courts his inaccessible rose by maintaining the "commandments" given to him by Amor, the God of Love. It is Guillaume's exploration of erotic desire as expressed in a variety of activities associated with contemplation that makes his poem so relevant to later thirteenth-century ethics. Despite the poem's narrative form, Guillaume maintains the lyric stasis of Amant's quest through a collapsing of the distinction between productive and unproductive labor, especially with respect to the labors of self-reflection and writing love poetry. These terms will become key to medieval understandings of Aristotelian contemplation as a pleasurable activity, esteemed in itself; Guillaume's linking of the Narcissus myth, poetic activity, intellectual self-reflection, and physical labor will prove a fruitful nexus for his successor.

The protagonist-narrator Amant's entry into the garden of delight appears to be an entry into the perils not only of irrational desire, but irrational poetic activity. He is first welcomed by a figure named Oiseuse who unlocks the wicket garden gate. Earl Jeffrey Richards has argued convincingly that we should understand Guillaume's use of *oiseuse* as continuous with the twelfth-century use of the word to connote verbal folly or frivolity, a definition more encompassing than "Idleness," given in Charles Dahlberg's translation.[9] Richards argues that in the twelfth and early thirteenth centuries the term shifted away from its Latin etymology (though he notes that the word *otium* is itself polyvalent) and did not carry strong associations of either sinful idleness or the leisure necessary for study. Amant recounts his first impressions of Oiseuse's paradise, full of birds and their songs. In the midst of describing his past gratitude to the figure who offered him entry, the speaker shifts persona to become external narrator again, breaking into the present and future tenses to remark to his reader that he will describe the appearance of the garden:

> fui plains de grant joliveté
> et lores soi ge bien et vi
> qu'Oiseuse m'avoit bien servi,
> qui m'avoit en ce deduit mis.
> Bien deüsse estre ses amis,
> quant ele m'avoit desfermé
> le guichet dou vergier ramé.
> Des or mes, si con je savrai,
> tot l'afeire vos conterai. (ll. 682–90)

(I was filled with great joy and I saw that Oiseuse, who had placed me in the midst of this delight, had served me well. My love was due to her when she unlocked the wicket gate of the branching garden. From now on, I shall recount to you, as well as I know, how I went to work.)[10]

In Lecoy's edition of the poem (based on MS Bibl. Nat. fr. 1573), the narrator promises to tell us about the "afeire" or disposition of the garden, while Langlois' edition has the narrator promising to tell us "coment j'ovrai" (how I went to work, l. 690). In either case, the status of work, loving, and writing is immediately raised at this moment of entry and introduction; allegorically, Amant is allowed to enter the *locus amoenus* through his engagement with *oiseuse*, and this engagement is linked to the work of narrative, now associated with verbal frivolity.[11] Dreaming placed Amant in this position, we understand, but the narrator's poetic activity places him there again so that we may witness his experience. The personified Oiseuse suggests that Amant's primary activity will be a verbal activity, a learning about love "par parole" that will be the subject of critique by Amor himself.[12] The verb *ouvrer* as an intransitive verb means simply to work, but as a transitive verb *ouvrer* can mean to work materials, the material of language in this context. Amant's work and the affairs of the garden are the work of falling in love, of pursuing the rose, and ultimately continuing this pursuit in the very writing of the *Rose* itself. We will hear not only about Amant's dream-work, but about the art of the narrator. Just further on, the poem reveals the narrator's work to be narrative itself, for as he explains his task, he cannot convey the simultaneity of his experience upon entering the garden, but must "tot vos conteré par ordre" (tell you everything in order, l. 697), creating narrative out of a single moment of experience. Claire Nouvet has read the poem's conception of allegory as a split between an ideal vision that encompasses everything at once and the fallen, allegorical speculum that requires that we see things in a discrete, temporal succession.[13] Here the fate of fallen vision is coextensive with the experience of both reading and writing love poetry. Amant has a simultaneous, comprehensive experience, but transferring that experience into verse requires a fall into temporality and thus into *oiseuse* – the verbal frivolity associated with courtly delights and romance writing.

Given that the key emblem associated with this markedly active Oiseuse is the mirror in her hand, it is tempting to take her as an ironic figure for the contemplative life. In the appendix to his book *The Roman de la Rose* John Fleming suggestively places a manuscript illustration of Oiseuse with her comb and mirror next to an illustration from another *Rose* manuscript of Christ with his mirror of wisdom – both figures holding their reflected faces in the same manner.[14] Yet Fleming also states firmly that while mirrors in general in the late Middle Ages mean many things, including *luxuria*, self-knowledge, and the contemplative life, Oiseuse *is luxuria*, and her mirror has nothing whatsoever to do with the *vita contemplativa*.[15] While it seems unlikely that Guillaume is satirizing the contemplative life as idle or cupidinous, it is possible to imagine Oiseuse as a gently parodic figure of contemplation gone awry – turned to the vanity of her toilette and inviting Amant to engage in the irrational activity of writing romance narratives rather than rational pleasures.[16] Within the ethical landscape of the garden, she contrasts strikingly with Amor, whose commandments, and especially his proclamation that "covient vivre / les amanz, qu'il lor est mestiers" (lovers must live, for life is their occupation, ll. 2594–5), add up to a recommendation that Amant should choose the active life of loving rather than writing books about love – an irrational, unending project. For while up to this point the narrator's work has appeared to be the work of narrative, at other moments the work of romance writing is revealed to be definitively anti-narrative; it appears to condemn one to continual stasis. Just before his recommendation of "living" as an occupation, Amor tells Amant that

> Nes qu'em puet espuisier la mer,
> ne poroit nus les maus d'amer
> conter en romanz ne en livre. (ll. 2591–3)

(No more than one can empty the sea could any man recount in a romance or a book the woes of love.)

Considering that the *Rose* itself is largely constituted by the woes and joys of Amant, it appears that the poem is exactly the hopeless task that Amor warns against undertaking. The endless nature of romance writing is perhaps one more reason for the seemingly unfinished nature of the poem.[17] Rather than writing a romance for his beloved lady, the poet should be "living," according to Amor. At this moment the multiple subject positions of the narrator come to the fore again: as the character of Amant, he follows Amor's precepts, but as narrator and author figure he is engaged in pointless labor. Whereas the personified figure of Oiseuse had melded the notions of productive and unproductive activity by locating both loving and writing in the garden of delight, Amor disentangles the two kinds of activities.[18] Writing love poetry becomes an idle task in a negative sense, while loving itself is valorized, distinguished from merely participating in a scene of courtly flirtations and pleasures. Amor ethicizes this scene, makes distinctions and demands a particular kind of productive activity. With this contrast between Oiseuse and Amor, it appears that unfocused desire allows for the free play of both physical and intellectual pleasure, while focused desire brings with it a series of commandments and rules, prescribing activity oriented toward a particular end; in this way the recipe for the good, active (courtly) life comes into being. Guillaume's *Rose* seems interested in illustrating how the genre of love poetry depends upon a tension between deferred, specific desire that brings with it an elaborate code of conduct and a diffuse desire that remains objectless. He might agree with many modern readers of troubadour poetry who have understood the poets to be less in love with a particular person than interested in perpetuating desire itself.

The poem's unstable oppositions between productive and unproductive labor, writing and loving, are most poignantly expressed in the episode of Amant at the fountain of love. In recounting Amant's gaze into the perilous mirror of Narcissus, Guillaume sets up a parallel between the experience of encountering an exemplum as mirror, and the physical, immediate experience of self-reflection. Suzanne Akbari has explored the way that both Guillaume and Jean were deeply interested in the science of optics, both writing in the midst of new translations of philosophical and scientific texts from the Greek and Arabic.[19] She argues that Guillaume holds out the possibility that seeing might allow for self-knowledge, though this knowledge remains inaccessible to Amant.[20] Akbari usefully traces the optical theories that both poets of the *Rose* may have put to both poetic and ethical purposes; these optical metaphors are also inherent in ethical discourse, with its emphasis on reflection and self-knowledge. When

Amant comes upon the fountain, he does not immediately look in, but instead reads the inscription on the encompassing stone, an inscription written by Nature herself which reveals that the fountain was the site of Narcissus' death. The narrator then shifts to an extra-diegetic telling of the Narcissus myth. In Guillaume's version of the tale, Narcissus does not recognize himself (as he eventually does in Ovid's *Metamorphoses*), but rather mistakes his reflection for that of a beautiful child.[21] Overcome by the fruitlessness of his desire, Narcissus loses his sense and dies. The narrator then offers a gloss on this exemplum, stating that Narcissus received just punishment for having scorned Echo, and that all ladies should therefore take care not to neglect their lovers. The narrator refuses to find his own image (of himself as the young Lover) in the exemplum – the moral is instead thrust upon his beloved, in what is often read as a humorous and ironic attempt to reinforce his plea that she should return his love.[22]

Yet while the gloss may offer a moment of ironic humor, it is also a trenchant illustration of the way that Amant takes on the roles of both Echo and Narcissus. He is both Echo, the pursuer of the distant love object, the rose/lady, and the lover Narcissus gazing at his own reflection; he is Amant at the fountain and the narrator gazing upon his prior self. Not only does this version of Narcissus fail to recognize his own reflection, but with the ill-fitting gloss the narrator creates a textual precedent that implicitly endorses Amant's decision to gaze into the fountain and find his impossible object of desire. At the same time, he endorses his own position as the subject of desire for the lady "who deserves to be called Rose" outside the dream vision. His identification with both doomed lovers renders Amant's quest both super-determinedly unsuccessful and universalized. As other scholars have argued, the "narcissism" exhibited by Amant is not depicted as an avoidable pathology, but as a constitutive aspect of human desire.[23] Amant encounters the fountain of Narcissus, the narrator encounters the myth of Narcissus, but each fails to see the reflection of his desire. The Narcissus tale as recounted in the *Rose* is an illustration of the failure of a variety of modes of self-reflection – visual art, narrative, contemplation – to bring about self-recognition; the gloss recapitulates this failure.

At other points in the poem, the theme of failed self-reflection is clarified as unproductive labor. In her first words to Amant, the figure Raison assimilates the "perilousness" of Narcissus' mirror to the dangers of *oiseuse*, especially when *oiseuse* is understood as improper contemplation. Raison creates an equation between Oiseuse herself and the perilous mirror of Narcissus, telling Amant that,

Fox est qui s'acointe d'Oiseuse;
s'acointance est trop perilleuse. (ll. 2989–90)

(He who acquaints himself with Oiseuse is a fool; acquaintance with her is very dangerous.)

In this context, the entry of Amant into the garden of delight and into the hopeless task of recounting his narrative in romance is a peril that prefigures his gaze into the perilous fountain of Narcissus. Amant's acquaintance with Oiseuse has caused him to have "folement ovré" (worked foolishly, l. 2995) according to Raison, who would rather have him engaged in rational contemplation. Raison thus associates the "madness" of love with a loss of productivity:

Hons qui aime ne puet bien fere
ne a nul preu dou monde entendre:
s'il est clers, i piart son aprendre;
et se il fet autre mestier,
il n'em puet gaires esploitier. (ll. 3028–32)

(A man who loves can do nothing well nor attend to any worldly gain: if he is a clerk, he loses his learning, and if he follows some other trade, he can hardly accomplish it.)

Guillaume's Raison does not attempt to seduce Amant, as she does in Jean's *Rose*, nor does she advocate fruitful procreation, but her emphasis on work and productivity clearly points toward such later transformations. Amant responds to her critique, claiming that love itself is the only worthy activity, and that Raison herself "poriez bien gaster / en oiseuse vostre françois" (could waste her French in oiseuse, ll. 3072–3) arguing with him. Having rejected Raison, Amant continues in his pursuit of the rose, which, despite the narrator's assurances to the contrary, he will not achieve.

In fact, immediately after gaining an apparent triumph in kissing the rose, the narrator swears that he will pursue "tote l'estoire," implying both that there is a "whole" history that might be completed, and yet that it might be possible to write this history perpetually. He breaks into the narrative and swears:

Tote l'estoire veil parsuivre,
ja ne m'est parece d'escrivre,
por quoi je cuit qu'il abelise
a la bele, que Dex guerisse. (ll. 3487–90)

(I want to pursue the whole history, and I shall never be idle in writing it down as long as I believe that it may please the beautiful lady – may God be her cure.)

For while Amor urges Amant to "live" rather than write, the narrator seems to hold himself to an ethic of continuous writing. Here it seems that the "oiseuse" of literary production will in fact defend him from the more serious "parece." Though Guillaume's poem contains a promise to continue writing so long as it is pleasurable for the narrator's lady, the poem remains unfinished, breaking off about 500 lines later. Ending with a plea to Bel Acueil (Fair Welcome), expressing the woe and agitated desire of Amant, the poem is caught in just the position that Amor warned against – that of attempting to recount love's woes in a romance. Perhaps the narrator believes that his lady has ceased to be pleased by Amant's history, or perhaps his desire has been accomplished, thus rendering the writing of the poem both superfluous and obscene.[24] These possibilities remain unaddressed, and we are left with a poem about the relationship between unproductive and productive labor, overlaid upon physical and intellectual labor, explored through an erotic love that encompasses all forms of work. The ethical precepts of Amor are an alternative to the pleasurable but unproductive *oiseuse* of the garden and the non-amorous labor prescribed by Raison. Yet this version of the ethical, active life proves inextricable from Amant's narcissistic self-reflection on the one hand, and his inexhaustible writerly engagements on the other. The difficulty in disentangling productive from unproductive labor and the association of labor with both objectless desire and desire for a loved object are the key subjects of Guillaume's *Rose*. That ethicizing this desire and labor makes these distinctions no easier to maintain is one of its keener insights. The project of understanding intellectual and physical work via explorations of passionate and divine love – and thinking about love via explorations of work – will become a central mode of the reception of Aristotle's ethical writings. The nexus of love and intellectual activity is especially important for those writers concerned with the fact that the philosopher's investment in earthly happiness is constituted by a version of contemplation that seems to have nothing at all to do with love. Guillaume thus leaves Jean with a poem containing a set of meditations on productive and unproductive activity, lyric stasis and narrative work, writing and reflection that will prove ripe for development in a world seeking to come to terms with growing conflicts over the nature of human happiness and the sovereign good.

ARISTOTLE'S *ETHICS* IN THE THIRTEENTH CENTURY

Where Guillaume de Lorris writes within an ideological framework in which neither the *vita activa* nor the *vita contemplativa* offers any hope of earthly perfection, Jean de Meun writes within a new, controversial context of Aristotelian contemplation, where contemplation is the best life for man on earth and therefore confers human happiness. Suddenly, the earthly, bodily ethics offered within courtly poetry has a philosophical counterpart. With the full translation of the *Nicomachean Ethics* by Robert Grosseteste around 1246–7, it became impossible to sustain earlier medieval understandings of Aristotelian contemplation as oriented toward the love of God. In the final book, previously unavailable in Latin, the philosopher defines happiness as a life of contemplation – a life of perfect happiness that is theoretically attainable in the mundane world. Prior to the complete translation of the *Ethics*, medieval commentators on the incomplete versions largely agreed that Aristotle spoke only of political happiness, and not a final "true" happiness, and read his ethical writings as strictly practical guides for the virtuous life. This version of the "ethical life" as the active life harmonizes with the commentaries on the twelfth-century versions of Aristotle's *Ethics*, the so-called *Ethica Vetus* and *Ethica Nova*. These texts, comprising only the first three books of the *Nicomachean Ethics*, where Aristotle defines happiness and the good, *habitus*, the virtue of the mean, and voluntary action, were read as immediately practical guides for virtuous living.[25] On its face, contemplation as constituting happiness seems to be quite compatible with Christianity's emphasis on turning one's intellect toward God; other writers had explored the continuities between self-reflection, contemplation, and the beatific vision.[26] And where commentators did address Aristotle's theory of happiness, they almost invariably defined perfect happiness as a state of union with God, not the activity of contemplation.[27] Philosophical *felicitas* was equated with Christian *beatitudo*, and earthly happiness was always held to be flawed – a judgment sustained by Aristotle's own discussions of fortune.[28] A commentary thought to be by Robert Kilwardby is alone among the early commentaries in recognizing that Aristotle's philosophy restricts itself to earthly goods, and that his happiness is not to be equated with beatitude.[29] Subsequent commentators who had access to the explicit definition of contemplative happiness on earth as the sovereign good in Book x of the *Ethics* would shift from a definition of the good that takes God as its starting point to one that takes the perfection of human activity as its starting point.[30] The choice that the Kilwardby commentary presciently makes to focus on a separate, human happiness becomes necessary with the reception of the complete *Ethics*.

Beyond the difficulty of assimilating Aristotle's notion of happiness as an earthly activity lay the problem that this theory did not appear to include love. Aristotle's definition of happiness as virtuous activity accompanied by supervenient pleasure does not allocate space for joy in the beloved object.[31] Medieval readers were left to account for and justify this omission. Albert the Great wrote the first complete Latin commentary on the full *Nicomachean Ethics* in the years almost immediately after Grosseteste completed his translation (1248–52).[32] In his commentary on the tenth book of the *Ethics*, Albert must come to terms with Aristotle's definition of contemplation as the highest good for man, and the contemplative life as the happiest. In this section he addresses together the problems that Aristotelian contemplation appears to be an end in itself and that it does not appear to involve love for the object contemplated. He introduces the objection that contemplation of wisdom is not estimable in itself, explaining that contemplation should be considered vain if it were sought on account of nothing else. Further, Albert notes that enjoyment is completed in love ("fruitio completur in amore"), and that therefore contemplation must be ordered further toward love ("ergo contemplatio ipsa ordinatur ulterius ad amorem").[33] Albert resolves that "the contemplation of happiness is esteemed for its own sake, because it is principal, that is to say it is the contemplation of God, which according to the Theologian [Augustine] is the end of human life" ("contemplatio felicitatis diligitur propter se, quia ipsa praecipua est, scilicet contemplatio dei, quae est secundum THEOLOGUM finis humanae vitae").[34] Albert leaves the question of love unresolved, although God is reinstated as the object of contemplation.

Albert acknowledges, however, that Aristotelian contemplation is different from theological contemplation. Where many of the earlier commentators on the *Ethics* had conflated Aristotle's definition of happiness with Christian beatitude, Albert is careful to separate the two, making a strict distinction between happiness in this life and the beatitude of heaven.[35] The theologian contemplates through light infused by God ("per lumen infusum a deo") while the philosopher contemplates through acquired disposition of wisdom ("per habitum sapientiae acquisitum").[36] Where philosophy relies upon rational demonstration of certainty, theology rests upon truth without need of reason.[37] Thus, Albert explains, wonder is an indispensable aspect of theology, but not of contemplative philosophy. He ultimately avoids, however, confronting Aristotle's elevation of contemplative philosophy to the best life for man and the accompanying orientation of moral philosophy toward knowledge rather than practiced virtue. For Albert, Aristotelian ethics is still understood as having its scientific nature oriented practically toward "making us good."[38]

Albert's student Aquinas, however, is the first of the commentators on the *Ethics* neither to relegate Aristotle's philosophy to the purely practical nor subsume it to the theological. Other philosophers in the late thirteenth century have even fewer reservations in embracing Aristotle's definition of the good, and even go beyond Aristotle himself by disregarding practical, political considerations altogether, focusing on philosophical contemplation as the only way to happiness. Boethius of Dacia and Siger of Brabant both courted censure by arguing that the supreme good is only accessible to philosophers.[39] A rational, rather than divine, authority for Aristotle was espoused by certain members of the Paris arts faculty, and it was this type of authority that led the Bishop of Paris to cite several "Aristotelian" doctrines among the 219 theses condemned in 1277.[40] The source for these propositions is unclear, though they appear to correspond to the ideas of some contemporary Aristotelians: "No station in life is to be preferred to the study of philosophy," and "Happiness is to be had in this life and not in another."[41] Although Aquinas' writings are occasionally grouped with those of the "radical Aristotelians" by both medieval and modern critics, his commentary on the *Ethics* and the second section of his *Summa Theologiae* (on ethics) are both more interested in harmonizing Aristotle's philosophy with Christian doctrine, while being true to the Philosopher. Despite his assurance to his reader that Aristotle is speaking of happiness "such as can be ascribed to human and mortal life," and that perfect happiness is only possible in the afterlife, he clearly accepts, with Aristotle, that ethics should take earthly happiness as its subject.[42] Aquinas agrees with Aristotle unreservedly that contemplation of the truth is the highest good for man, the most virtuous of activities, and that contemplation of a truth already known is more perfect than investigation, because possession is more perfect (complete) than pursuit.[43] He states positively, "Thus it is clear that the person who gives himself to the contemplation of truth is the happiest a man can be in this life."[44] Because God himself exercises all his activity in the contemplation of wisdom, the philosopher is accordingly the happiest, and the dearest to God. Yet, as in Guillaume's *Rose*, there is no easy demarcation here between the active and contemplative lives, between the quietude of contemplation and earthly labor; with an Aristotelian understanding of happiness, both striving for the good and experiencing the good itself are spoken of in the language of action. In

Aristotle's discussion of the possibilities of earthly happiness, he states that we "must, so far as we can, make ourselves immortal, and strain every nerve to live in accordance with the best thing in us," for "the life of the intellect is best and most pleasant since the intellect more than anything else is man."[45] It is telling that rather than simply tending toward a life of reason as the life that is most in accordance with the basic definition of humanity, we must stretch and do everything possible ("omnia facere") to live according to our optimal potential. For humankind, teleology is not a simple gravitational pull or tendency, but a terribly challenging ethical imperative. The oscillation or tension between tendency and strain, teleology and desire, is a defining feature of the Latin reception of Aristotle. For where in the Greek, the *Ethics* begins by stating that "all things aim at [*ephiesthai*] the good," Grosseteste's Latin translation has it that "all things desire [*appetunt*] the good."[46] Aquinas comments that "this very tendency to good is the desiring of good," rendering desire both rational and teleological.[47] The very attainability of Aristotle's felicity is ironically what makes it compatible with Christianity, which has no virtuous place for the desire of unattainable objects. Aquinas and Aristotle share the same notion of ethical desire: it is finite, rational, and teleological. Infinite and shifting desire for Aristotle is irrational; for Aquinas it is also cupidinous.

This emphasis on telos, and the striving for an end, makes it necessary that desire for the unattainable, even spiritual desire, be rendered ethically problematic. Aquinas states that "a natural desire is nothing else but an inclination belonging to things by the disposition of the First Mover, and this cannot be frustrated … Therefore, it is impossible that we should proceed to an infinity of ends."[48] Aquinas' idea of "natural desire" is the "inclinatio" discussed in this case – desire is constantly being redefined as divinely implanted rational telos. Both joy (*gaudium*) and hope (*spes*) are differentiated from desire, which actually prevents one from attaining pleasure and doing the good. Desire is defined by the unattainability of its object, while hope implies that its object may be attained. In addressing Aristotle's discussion of the problems of fortune, and thus whether one can truly call a man "happy" in this life, Aquinas concludes "Since a natural desire is not in vain, we can correctly judge that perfect beatitude is reserved for man after this life."[49] A Christian understanding of rational desire may demand that perfect happiness be reserved for the afterlife, but it also simultaneously requires that imperfect human happiness be rendered a natural object of desire. Aristotle's discussion of rational contemplation and seeking after knowledge as the best life there is actually allows the field of moral philosophy to take a more optimistic view of life on earth. Virtuous pleasure is not reserved for either the afterlife or mystical experience, but is attainable, however imperfectly, in mundane existence.

Thus in order for Aristotle's emphasis on earthly ethics to be maintained in a Christian context, perfection must be exchanged for imperfection. Aquinas reconciles Aristotelian rational desire for attainable objects with Christian refusal to valorize desire for temporal goods. For Aquinas, Aristotle's happiness is "imperfect," but also continuous with the perfect happiness reserved for the afterlife. Aquinas' development of the concept of imperfect mundane happiness is crucial to the reception of the complete *Ethics*; in both his commentary proper and in the sections of the *Summa* that treat ethics, imperfect happiness is rendered a proper starting point for moral philosophy – replacing the ethical model which begins with the perfect happiness that one experiences after death in the contemplation of God. A teleological, earthly narrative begins to replace meditative lyricism as the way to approach the good, lending a new shape to morality itself.[50] In Aquinas' commentary on the *Ethics*, he states that "we are looking for the happiness that is the end of human acts,"[51] therefore cautioning that "In this work the Philosopher speaks of happiness as it is attainable in this life, for happiness in a future life is entirely beyond the investigation of reason."[52] Thus while true, infinite happiness is still reserved for the afterlife, it has been neatly removed from the purview of ethical knowledge. The pure, perfect good is bracketed so that Aquinas may continue his investigation of an earthly ethics without danger of heterodoxy.[53] The ethical good is now active, pleasurable, and achieved through a desire less assimilable to traditional ways of thinking about either spiritual or physical love.

Like courtly poetry, the new Aristotle offered many late medieval writers a challenge in thinking through the relationship between earthly desire and pursuits of the divine. As Lacan puts it, Aristotle's philosophy allowed Aquinas to invent a "physical theory of love … namely that the first being we have a sense of is our being, and everything that is for the good of our being must, by dint of this very fact, be the Supreme Being's jouissance, that is, God's."[54] For Aristotle, and for his commentators, contemplation is the best activity for man because it is closest to God, and therefore the most loved by God. God loves what is most like him, so the philosopher affirms the medieval notion of a contemplative, active God, taking pleasure in reflecting upon his own image. Narcissus is clearly not very far from Lacan's mind, nor, arguably, from the minds of medieval philosophers and poets. At the very end of his twentieth seminar, Lacan refers to the "mirage-like apprehension" ("appréhension de mirage") that emerges when one imagines that the relation of being to being is the harmony of either Aristotelian supreme *jouissance* or Christian beatitude.[55] This apprehension, in French as in English, is both a feeling of fear and a perception; when one approaches an "other," one perceives and fears a deluding "mirage." Both dread and understanding are generated as "true love" approaches being itself, giving way to hatred. Such apprehension might well be felt by Narcissus gazing at the mirage inside the perilous fountain, experiencing feelings of both love and destruction for his love object and for himself. For Lacan, Aristotle was instrumental in bequeathing medieval Christianity a God who enjoys the same way that we do, thus allowing us to sacrifice our *jouissance* for his. What Jean's *Rose* makes clear is that Aristotelian philosophy and the controversies it created were not so uniformly assimilated, even within the composition of one poem. The second *Rose* experiments with the ramifications of love and happiness defined through activity, with a love story that includes desire for an attainable object, with this-worldly and otherworldly locations of felicity, and with a poetic practice that investigates the potential of self-reflection through art to bring happiness, madness, love, and hate.

THE NEW NARCISSUS

Jean de Meun asks what Narcissus might look like in this new Aristotelian context, a context where self-reflection might inhabit a continuum including erotic love, intellectual contemplation, and the beatific vision. Jean asks how a lover might experience "well-ordered charity," and suggests that charity might range from the narcissistic to the social, from distance to possession, from mutuality to destruction. In Jean's *Rose*, questions of self-reflection, labor, and the good are taken up most extensively in the sections of the poem devoted to the discourses of Nature and Genius. These sections are overwhelmingly scholastic in content, and address issues such as the conception of pleasure as the ultimate ethical goal, the dangers of contemplation, and the relationship between labor, writing, and self-knowledge. Jean de Meun does not take up these issues in a strictly Aristotelian context, but addresses them in a way that is clearly influenced by and engages in contemporary controversies surrounding the definition of the good.[56] The second part of the *Rose* experiments with the assumption of Aristotle's narrative ethical system, where rational activity precedes love, self-knowledge determines love, and happiness consists in labor rather than rest.[57]

The exploration of the sovereign good in Jean's poem begins with the confession of Nature, where self-knowledge is rendered a condition of free will.[58] In this section of the poem, Amant absents himself as an interlocutor, as love itself is thus pushed aside, only to return in the content of the dialogue. In confessing to Genius, Nature recounts the story of Genesis and describes the earth and other planets, going on to complain of the sins of men, especially those who kill themselves or refuse to procreate.[59] Her "confession" is not a catalogue of sins, but the very narrative of the earth's creation and existence.[60] The only sins recounted are in fact the sins of mankind; Nature's interest is the harmonious perpetuation of the species, and man's refusal to cooperate in this goal is Nature's greatest sorrow. Human shortcomings lead to her long discussion of free will, where she acknowledges that some men believe that their premature deaths and failures to procreate are destined. However, Nature argues that through education and virtuous behavior, humans may exercise their free will and "obtain another result." Nature rehearses and rejects an argument in favor of free will that argues that God's foreknowledge does not confer necessity on human action, but rather that human actions and their results are the cause of God's foreknowledge.[61] She rebels against the claim that God's foreknowledge could be subordinated to the actions of humankind in such a manner. Instead, she argues that God's foreknowledge is free, complete, and self-sufficient, while also not constraining human action. Rather than using the traditional Boethian explanation for the coexistence of free will and divine omniscience, Nature focuses on the freedom conferred by self-knowledge. Just as God's foreknowledge is represented by an "eternal mirror" in which he sees all, so human beings seem to be granted the potential to reflect on their own conditions and to predict their own destinies. According to Nature, if a man knows himself well ("S'il est de soi bien connoissanz," l. 17544), and realizes that sin always struggles for mastery over his heart, then he will be able to maintain his free will ("frans voloirs," l. 17543) and control his destiny. It is knowledge of self that here trumps destiny and that allows for the expression of free will in action.

She somewhat unexpectedly goes on to discuss the benefits that could fall to mankind if he were granted foreknowledge of events such as storms or famine. According to Nature's logic, it appears that the maintenance of free will in the face of God's providence might actually replace destiny. Nature suggests, for instance, that if men could know that a harsh winter lay ahead, they could provide for themselves ahead of time. Yet she finally admits that only God could bestow such visions, and that free will, along with the exercise of good understanding, is the key to controlling one's destiny and living well. She states:

> mieux donc et plus legierement,
> par us de bon antandemant,
> pourroit eschever franc voloir
> quan que le peut fere douloir. (ll. 17681–4)

(Free will then, by the exercise of good understanding, could better and more easily avoid whatever can make it suffer.)

A man with knowledge of his birth and his current situation will not need to concern himself with destiny, but can make his own fortune.[62]

Yet immediately after this revelation, Nature makes a move that both sweeps aside the conflicts between free will and destiny and reveals their underlying significance. Following this discussion, Nature remarks:

> Des destinees plus parlasse,
> fortune e cas determinasse
> et bien vossisse tout espondre,
> plus opposer et plus respondre,
> et mainz examples an deïsse;
> mes trop longuement i meïsse
> ainz que j'eüsse tout finé.
> Bien est ailleurs determiné.
> Qui nou set a clerc le demande,
> qui leü l'ait et qui l'antande. (ll. 17697–706)

(I would speak more about destinies, I would settle the subject of Fortune and chance, and I would like very much to explain everything, to raise more objections, reply to them, and give many illustrations for them, but I would spend too much time before I finished everything. The good is decided elsewhere. He who does not know it may ask a clerk who had studied it and who may understand it.)

Nature's statement raises the question of whether "bien" resides outside a discussion of free will, or whether Nature herself simply does not want to pursue a clerical question best discussed "elsewhere," perhaps the university. Her refusal to bear out her discussion of fortune and chance may be an indication that twelfth-century concerns with *voluntas* in terms of ethical culpability have been superseded or at least joined by other, more pressing concerns. Her wager that human self-knowledge can trump destiny makes virtuous action contingent on "knowing thyself," pointing toward such knowledge as the way to freedom, the good, and bringing the soul out of suffering. In philosophical and moral terms, God's foreknowledge and human cupidity cease to be the prime obstacles to freedom, replaced by the problem of being able to reflect upon oneself. It becomes clear that the poem, through Nature's lengthy discussion of free will and predestination, addresses the problem of the good while it explicitly claims to ward it off.

Although in the context of the poem's "plot" the conversation between Nature and Genius seems to be removed from the concerns of the desiring Lover, love re-emerges as a core concern of Nature's confession. Free will and the capacity to resist evil is preserved for the person who knows himself entirely ("se connoit antierement," l. 17762) and this knowledge allows him to love wisely ("aime sagement," l. 17761). Love and knowledge are placed in a causal relationship: full knowledge enables love. In the *Summa Theologiae* Aquinas asks "whether knowledge is a cause of love," answering that

> some knowledge of a thing is necessary before it can be loved. That is why Aristotle says that sensory love is born of seeing a thing; and similarly, spiritual love is born of the spiritual contemplation of beauty or goodness. Knowledge is therefore said to be a cause of love for the same reason as is the good, which can be loved only when one has knowledge of it.[63]

Aquinas admits that perfect knowledge is not necessary for love, as one may love a thing better than it is known ("plus amatur quam cognoscatur"), for instance rhetoric or God.[64] But above all Aquinas gives us to understand that spiritual love is caused by knowledge in the same way that knowledge of physical beauty sparks love. Our understanding of physical love allows us to understand spiritual love; one is the mirror of the other and knowledge is a necessary condition of love for humans and God alike. In contrast, Nature comments that dumb beasts are undoubtedly without self-knowledge ("se mesconnoissent par nature," l. 17765). Yet she hazards that if they were given speech and reason, they would immediately challenge the mastery of men, refusing to submit to man's rule.[65] Most interestingly in the context of her discussion of self-knowledge in beasts and men, she appears to equate the acquisition of knowledge, especially self-knowledge, with the task of writing, or at least implies that the obvious next step upon recognizing one's self is to realize the ability to write. For if beasts were given reason, the monkeys and marmots among them could work with their own hands ("ouvreroient de mains," l. 17803) and rival humans in their craftsmanship; they could, Nature claims, be writers ("porroient estre escrivain," l. 17805), thus perhaps unexpectedly completing the notion of "working with one's hands" with the work of writing. The work that these newly rational animals would do is not only the work of making clothing and armor (so as to protect themselves against men), but the work of literary production. Writing is an imagined weapon in the arsenal of these newly rational, rebellious creatures. The result of self-knowledge for these animals is both a refusal of labor – the ox refuses the yoke – and a turning of that labor toward the necessary conditions of the exercise of free will: the destruction of humankind. The beasts undertake this action in whatever way they are able, from the buzzing fly to the writing marmot. Nature appears to subscribe to Aristotle's and others' dictum that reason, more than anything else, *is* man. But to reason she adds the important corollary of rational self-knowledge, the capacity for self-reflection, anticipating Genius by claiming writing as the activity that a rational creature should most fruitfully be engaged in.

However, this association of rationality, self-knowledge, and writing is complicated by Nature's excursus on mirrors further on in her "confession." This discussion of the fantastical characteristics of mirrors, showing both hidden truths and distorted realities, is the first of a series of episodes in which the poem appears to critique Aristotelian notions of contemplation as the greatest good. The stable connections that she has up to now created between rationality and self-reflection are troubled by her seeming "digression" on optical phenomena. For in her discussion of optics, in which she defers to Aristotle's book, mirrors become agents of deception – confusing distances, size, and the location of actual objects.[66] Even when mirrors reveal truths, they appear to do so only in aid of adulterous deception, as when Nature comments that if Mars and Venus had possessed the right kind of mirror, they could have magnified Vulcan's net and escaped his snare. Also particularly striking is Nature's discussion of the way that too much contemplation can create the appearance of false images outside the mind, in much the same way as mirrors can make images float in the air:

> voit l'an de ceus a grant planté …
> de trop panser sunt curieus,
> quant trop sunt melancolieus
> ou pooreus outre mesure,
> qui mainte diverse figure
> se font parair en eus meïsmes
> autrement que nous ne deïsmes

> quant des mirouers parlions,
> don si briefmant nous passions,
> et de tout ce leur samble lores
> qu'il sait ainsinc por voir defores.
> Ou qui, par grant devocion
> en trop grant contemplacion,
> font apparair en leur pansees
> les choses qu'il ont porpansees,
> et les cuident tout proprement
> voair defors apertement. (ll. 18314–32)

(One sees a great number of people who [are] … given to think too much in an unregulated way when they are very melancholy or irrationally fearful; they make many different images appear inside themselves, in ways other than those we told about just a short time ago when we were speaking about mirrors. And it seems to them then that all these images are in reality outside of them. Or there are those who, with great devotion, do too much contemplating and cause the appearance in their thought of things on which they have pondered, only they believe that they see them quite clearly and outside themselves.)

Here contemplation is a form of melancholia, a residing inside the self that results in the creation of false images. Thus rather than contemplation being defined as a rational thinking on the divine good, it becomes a sort of fantasmatic preoccupation with false images. The mistaken idea that an internal image is actually "outside" ("defores") oneself appears to be Narcissus' failure. Successful self-reflection demands a strict policing of the boundaries between inside and outside, self and other.[67] Love seems to function here as a limit case of the usefulness of mirrors. Although Nature opens up the possibility that self-knowledge may improve the life of man on earth, confer freedom, enable love and the ability to write, she also reveals the dangers inherent in such ideas. Artistic representations may be deceitful, excess of contemplation may lead to harmful fantasms, and a misguided sense of self will end in the acceptance of falsehoods rather than access to truth and good.[68]

Genius' response to Nature similarly contains foregrounded moments which appear to critique Aristotelian notions of the good, and further presses the question of what is essential about humanity. The figure of Genius would seem to be particularly apt to provide a definition of the good life for man, given that as "master of places, who sets all things at work according to their properties" ("des leus iestes dex et mestres, / et selonc leur proprietez / tretouz en euvre les metez," ll. 16256–8) he also acts as a personification of human nature itself, and an embodiment of the "genius" of humanness – in an Aristotelian sense, this characteristic is rational thought.[69] In the *Ethics* Aristotle claims in several places, in various formulations, that "contemplation is the highest operation, since the intellect is the best element in us and the objects of the intellect are the best of the things that can be known."[70] The *Rose*'s definition of genius as master of place and property seems a comfortable fit with Aristotle's teleological notion of human characteristics and the good. Yet Genius' speech points in multiple instances to the ways in which the notion of "the good" can be misread, misappropriated, and misused – by tyrants, by their subjects, and ultimately by all humankind.

Genius takes the link between labor and writing foreshadowed by Nature and makes it concrete, if slightly overdetermined. He preaches of the duty men have to procreate, and speaks, following Alain de Lille's *De Planctu Naturae*, in terms of the duty to write:

> quant il n'an veulent labourer
> por lui servir et honourer,
> ainz veulent Nature destruire
> quant ses anclumes veulent fuire,
> et ses tables e ses jaschieres …
> qu'el [tables] devandront toutes moussues
> s'el sunt en oiseuse tenues (ll. 19523–38)

(when they do not want to labor at serving and honoring Nature, but wish rather to destroy her by preferring to flee her anvils, her tablets and fallow fields … they [the tablets] will become all rusty if they are kept in oiseuse.)

Here we see a shift in the meaning of *oiseuse* toward its more familiar definition of idleness, as the idle tablets are not turned toward verbal frivolity, but rather not used at all. Writing, as metaphor for procreation, is the only way in which humankind might "live forever" – everyone must write so that all might continue to live. The *oiseuse* that Guillaume imagined as the state of tension between the labors of loving and writing has been transformed into a much starker alternative to writing and (re)production. But then, Genius is a decidedly non-courtly figure, unsympathetic to the lyric conventions of unfulfilled and non-procreative desire. For him, lyric stasis is not a satisfactory mode of desire – all should be for narrative and resolution. Lyric time is not for this world, but only for that "biaus parc" that one may hope to reach in the afterlife.

There has been much critical debate over whether Genius' sermon is to be taken ironically, and how to reconcile his priestly function with his apparently cupidinous advice.[71] I err on the side of taking Genius seriously, if not as a mouthpiece for an authorial viewpoint. His "naturalism" may be read as a screen for exploring ideas of poetic labor and competing ideas of the good. Accordingly, in Genius' sermon the audience witnesses a collision of two versions of "the good," the courtly and the Christian. He exhorts:

> Pansez de mener bone vie,
> aut chascuns anbracier s'amie,
> et son ami chascune anbrace …
> pansez de vos bien confessier,
> por bien fere et por mal lessier …
> Cil est saluz de cors et d'ame,
> c'est li biaus mirouers ma dame;
> ja ma dame riens ne seüst
> se ce biau mirouer n'eüst. (ll. 19855–72)

(Think of leading a good life; let each man embrace his sweetheart and each woman her lover … think of confessing yourselves well, in order to do good and avoid evil, and call upon the heavenly God whom Nature calls her master … He is the salvation of body and soul and the beautiful mirror of my lady, who would never know anything if she did not have this beautiful mirror.)

Genius' definition of the "bone vie" here is certainly not Christian, and even exceeds the courtly ethic with its emphasis on sexual procreation rather than passion and play. Still, he presents it as the central message of the "lovely Romance of the Rose" which, according to Genius, preaches the gospel of sexual procreation so that one may enter heaven. In urging his audience to confess he urges them to take Nature as a model, and states that Nature's own model is God himself, inverting the usual image of Nature as God's mirror. God here is at the service of Nature, imparting knowledge much as the *Miroër aus Amoreus* teaches its readers. Genius asks his audience (and by extension the reader) not only to take in his sermon, but to memorize it the better to spread his gospel, which "vient de bone escole" (comes from a good school, l. 19890). Playing the role of both priest and scholar, Genius outlines a method of reading that literalizes the notion that one should achieve self-knowledge through a self-reflexive relationship to literature. Genius' audience should absorb and actually become the text he has offered them, much as Nature creates an image in imitation of God's mirror.

While Genius preaches unreservedly the good of procreation, it becomes clear that his "naturalism" does not condone selfish hedonism in any way. Genius' later discussion of sensual pleasure as the sovereign good espoused by the tyrannical Jupiter seems to stage a critique of Aristotelian ethics based on a fundamental misunderstanding of Aristotle's terms. After Genius' description of the lyric space of the "biaus parc" that awaits those who pursue the good (as procreation), he remarks that not even the golden age knew a paradise so beautiful and pure. Yet the fall from the golden age, occasioned by the castration of Saturn by Jupiter, fits neatly with Genius' thesis that procreation is the greatest good, and that any strike against fertility is the greatest outrage. For in committing this sin against Nature, Jupiter inaugurated an age of vice and sorrow. In Genius' telling, Jupiter signifies an alternative definition of the pursuit of the good – the pursuit of individual pleasure:

> car deliz, si conme il disoit,
> c'est la meilleur chose qui soit
> et li souverains biens en vie
> don chascuns doit avoir anvie. (ll. 20075–8)

(As he [Jupiter] said, delight is the best thing that can exist and the sovereign good in life; everyone should desire it.)

Jupiter here espouses a vulgar understanding of "pleasure" as the good: pleasure as delight in food and other bodily pleasures, not in rational contemplation of the divine. Further, he has the relationship between pleasure and desire backwards – Aquinas, commenting on Aristotle's statement that "the good is what all desire," affirms the perhaps surprising conclusion that pleasure is good *because* all desire it; it is not desired because it is good. For Aquinas, the good is convertible with the movement of the appetite. He does not deny that some men desire evil, but explains that they only desire evil because they believe it to be good; the evilness of the object is therefore only incidental.[72] The force of teleology must come first in the causality of Aristotelian ethics: things naturally tend toward the good, people tend toward pleasure, and therefore we see that pleasure is the highest good.[73] Aquinas remarks that Aristotle "calls people in power tyrants because those who are occupied with amusements do not seem to strive for the common interest but for their own gratification … Thus then happiness is said to consist in pleasures of this nature because persons in power – whom men consider happy – spend their time in them."[74] Thus the corruption of the state corrupts the very definition of happiness, rendering it impossible for men to live good lives. The identification of the good with sensual pleasure is a misunderstanding rooted in perversions of civic society – when tyrants are in power, the good is necessarily obscured.

Furthermore, Jupiter's pursuit of his own pleasure is what leads to the fall from the golden age, to the necessity for labor, and thus to the creation of the arts.

> Ainsinc sunt arz avant venues,
> car toutes choses sunt vaincues
> par travaill, par povreté dure,
> par quoi les genz sunt en grant cure ... (ll. 20145–8)

(Thus have the arts sprung up, for all things are conquered by labor and hard poverty; through these things people exist in great care.)

In Genius' mythology, Jupiter defines pleasure as the highest good and a sensual good, and thus creates the necessity for labor. In a fallen world, the only way we have to overcome the excesses of tyrants and the obscuring of the good is through labor and "art." It is not an accidental irony that the very "plowing" that Genius was advocating earlier (on a literal level) is here the result of tyrannical corruption. Genius differentiates between Jupiter's unproductive pleasure on the one hand and the productive labor of the arts and reproduction. Such work unites productivity and pleasure, where pleasure both accompanies activity and serves as its reward. If Genius' followers procreate, they will deserve entry into a revised version of Guillaume's garden of delight, where the false, madness-inducing fountain of Narcissus is replaced by a health-giving, clear "fonteine de vie" (l. 20491). Genius' garden is both earthly paradise and Christian heaven, but for all his protestations, it is also not unlike Guillaume's courtly garden. Genius criticizes the "queroles qui faillirent" (carols that will pass away, l. 20325) contained in the mundane garden of love, but his heavenly park will contain people "chantant en pardurableté / motez, conduiz et chançonnetes" (forever singing motets, conducti, and chansonettes, ll. 20626–7). The reward for all of this labor is a return to the lyric stasis of the garden of Oiseuse, this time with guaranteed permanence. Genius' paradise illustrates how close fallen desire is to divine joy, and also captures some of the tensions between a traditional notion of rest as labor's reward and an Aristotelian ideal of continuous activity. Genius thus leaves his audience with an ideal of literary self-reflection, earthly labor, and the final reward of pleasurable activity disconnected from productivity or the pursuit of a desired object. Such is precisely the ideal one finds in Nicole Oresme's fourteenth-century translation and commentary on the *Ethics*, where he describes heaven as a place where the blessed experience continually the activity of understanding and willing in God – "beneurés ont ilecques continuelment operacion de entendement et de volenté en Dieu" – and where activity is released from its associations with painful labor.[75]

Nature's and Genius' explorations of art's relationship to pleasure, self-reflection, and the contemplation of the good are recapitulated and re-evaluated in the episode of Pygmalion.[76] Where the Narcissus episode and the discourse of Nature both emphasize the dangers of sight and reflection gone awry, Pygmalion perhaps embodies sight as it emerges in Aristotle's guiding metaphor for pleasure: an activity that is whole, complete, and grammatically perfect. Aristotle's image of the complete, pleasurable act of seeing is an image of a "Narcissus made good" – a figure that several critics have seen to reside at the center of Jean de Meun's *Rose*.[77] One of the promises upon which Pygmalion delivers is the potential for art to lead to self-recognition, and thus the potential for rational contemplation to lead to virtuous pleasure in this life. Initially, there is no evidence to support the idea that Pygmalion's love for his statue is a love that is being celebrated by the poem. Pygmalion himself cries that his love is horrible and unnatural ("mes ceste amour est si horrible / qu'el ne vient mie de Nature," ll. 20832–3). We are further told that Love had stolen his "sans et savoir" (l. 20894), leaving him completely bereft of comfort, and clearly bereft of sense and rationality. However, Pygmalion recognizes himself in the Narcissus myth, asking whether Narcissus did not love more foolishly than he, falling in love with his own face ("ama … sa propre figure," ll. 20846–8). Pygmalion thus displays the capacity to recognize himself in an exemplum – if somewhat self-servingly – and identify his desires with those of the subject of the tale, learning from this example.

The reward of such identification is not immediate – we witness the way in which he uses literary precedent to justify the continuation of his own clearly unnatural desires. He decides that he is better off than Ovid's lover, better off than other lovers who persist in loving though they are never given even a single kiss, and continues the work of creation – dressing the statue in fine clothing. It appears at first as though Pygmalion's myth might serve to expose the fictions underlying conventional courtly desire, illustrating that although courtly lovers may hold out hope for a kiss and love returned, their far-off loves may as well be cold ivory statues – in Narcissus' desire for his reflection, in Pygmalion's love for his statue, and in the courtly poet's love for his lady, the sexual relation does not exist. The gods are not happy with the sculptor, not because he is insane or perverse, but rather because the love is not mutual. Yet Pygmalion's renunciation of Chastity (chastity defined as an aspect of *oiseuse* by

Genius) convinces Venus to give life to the statue, transforming her into the damsel Galatea.[78] The narrator describes how Galatea gave Pygmalion every pleasure and that he was finally happy. This pleasure is importantly described as mutual, part of an ongoing exchange of happiness.[79] The closing of this tale offers both an erotic corruption of Aristotelian notions of pleasure and felicity and a narrative that describes how artistic labor might allow one to achieve self-knowledge and happiness.

For unlike Ovid's Pygmalion, Jean de Meun's sculptor is not motivated to escape corrupted women by taking refuge in his own pure creation; rather he simply desires "son grant angin esprouver" (to prove his skill, l. 20792). He thus works his greatest talent upon the most appropriate and valuable material, creating beauty for its own sake. From this activity and creation, love is born. Love or desire does not pre-exist, looking for a suitable object, but rather is engendered through one's own dedication to one's art. As Aristotle explains, since love resembles activity, it only makes sense that "love and the concomitants of love follow those who excel in activity."[80] The love of an artist for his creation is explored in Book IX of the *Ethics*, as an explanation for the observed phenomenon that benefactors seem to love those they have benefited more than these beneficiaries love their benefactors in return. Aristotle explains that the same inequality happens with craftsmen, "for each one loves his product more than he would be loved by it were the product alive. Likewise, it occurs especially with poets who love their own poems, doting on them as their children."[81] To this, Aquinas adds that "poems partake of reason – by which man is man – to a greater degree than other mechanical works."[82] Pygmalion's love for his sculpture thus partakes in a natural and ethical state of affairs, and it is only Galatea's equal love once she is vivified that exceeds this relationship. Rational activity, here aligned with artistic production, naturally leads to love; it is the love returned by the object itself that must be supplied by the artistic imagination, an imagination happily supplied by the poet. Jean de Meun, in his love for Guillaume's *Rose*, might thus be fantasizing a moment where his poem might come to life, and might love him equally in return.[83] Such a fantasy might be seen to give shape to feminine desire, to the subject of contemplation who is thus both loved by God and loving, and to poetry as the optimal vehicle for experiencing this love. This happy conclusion is shadowed by the possibility that this returned love will always be a fantasy, and Jean thus dutifully follows the lineage of Pygmalion and Galatea through to the incestuous romance of Myrrha and Cynaras and the birth of Adonis. Whether the violent ending to the Pygmalion digression, with Cynaras pursuing Myrrha in a murderous rage, should give us pause in thinking about the relationship Pygmalion pursues with his own artistic creation, we are not given time to consider, for we are returned quickly to the matter at hand. Yet it is clear that Pygmalion's love for his creation, considered from another perspective, might return us to the problem of melancholic narcissism, his love for Galatea another mistaking of "inside" for "outside," and thus aptly ending in murder and incest.

As he picks up his narrative directly after the Pygmalion digression, however, Jean reinforces its positive emphasis on love and labor by emphasizing his own labor and the labor of his reader. He refers to his "work" and compares his narration to plowing a field:

> Bien orroiz que ce senefie
> ainz que ceste euvre soit fenie.
> Ne vos vuell or plus ci tenir,
> a mon propos doi revenir,
> qu'autre champ me convient arer. (ll. 21183–7)

(By the time you have finished this work you will know what it means. But I won't keep you any longer on this subject; I should return to my story, since I must plow another field.)

Jean here takes Genius' metaphor of writing and makes it his primary meaning – plowing here metaphorically points us to writing, although the sexual connotation remains, and Jean's writing will include an involved (somewhat laborious) metaphorical description of a sex act between Amant and the rose. The reader must complete the work of reading the poem – "ceste euvre" – as Jean himself must complete his "plowing." One might read Jean's address to the reader – that he will understand what the myth of Pygmalion or his lineage "senefie" when he is done with the work – as a prescription for proper reading and self-recognition in a narrative exemplum. Just as Pygmalion's procreative, fruitful labor may be contrasted with Narcissus' folly, we might contrast the proper reading practices of both Pygmalion and the reader of the *Rose* with the first Lover's failed reading of the Narcissus myth.

Of course, the final procreative labor of the poem is the consummation of the affair between Amant and the Rose. The sex act is compared humorously with the labors of Hercules, and is in general represented as a strenuous bit of work.[84] And it concludes both productively, with the apparent impregnation of the rose, and destructively, as Amant "plucked" ("cuelli") the rose from the rosebush. This fruitful and then ultimately murderous union is both optimistic – an imagining of earthly fulfillment of desire – and fearful – filled with the uneasy humor that overlays the violence that such fulfillment might wreak.[85] And although the open-endedness of Guillaume's poem is finally closed, both by the capture of the rose and the waking of the dreamer, Jean does not offer a final resolution of the question of the desiring subject's ethical relationship to pleasure, the good, or the self. On a fairly overt metaphorical level, Jean's poem functions as a parody of Aristotelian theories of happiness, dissecting the all too easily imagined results of an ethics based on pleasurable activity as the achievable sovereign good. Yet if one reverses the metaphorical and literal levels, a reversal common in Jean's poem, this parody becomes a quite serious investigation of the ethical possibilities of the labor of reading and writing – both acts of creation in the poem. Whereas explicit acts of reading and writing in Guillaume's *Rose* typically express or perpetuate unattainable desire, creative labors bear fruit in Jean's continuation. We might read this contrast not only as a result of Jean's parody of the euphemisms of romance, but as an aspect of and further contribution to the reception of the new Aristotle. The fruition reached through labor at the poem's end is both grammatically perfect and ethically flawed – an apt representation of the good in a period trying to come to grips with Aristotle's moral philosophy. The irony of these flaws, however, should not obscure the very real possibilities for ethical reading that Jean's poem holds out. This version of ethical reading does not seek a moral or even a practical example of living well, but rather a reflection upon oneself and one's desires, bringing with it the pleasure that comes with the labor of rational contemplation. The activity itself disposes one to love, and is perhaps an act of love, though it is – as both Nature and Lacan remind us – prone to give way to fantasm, misapprehension, and even hate. This duality will become a distinctly late medieval way of thinking about ethics, dependent upon a deliberate yoking together of love, intellectual activity, and pleasure.

The questions raised in medieval Aristotelian commentaries and only partially resolved (how can contemplation be valued for its own sake? how can human happiness exist outside of love of God? what does it mean for pleasure to be the greatest good?) are taken to a variety of extremes in Jean de Meun's *Rose*. In the poem's various conversations and narratives, we witness self-sacrificing desire, teleological drive toward possession, love as action and love as rest, self-reflection as madness, and self-knowledge leading to love. Jean's *Rose* gets to the heart of late medieval questions about how to understand the relationship between bodily and intellectual pleasure, self-love, love of others, and love of God – without resolution, but resolutely on the side of working through the Aristotelian valorization of labor, this-worldly desires and goods, and poetry that de-sublimes some of love's most cherished metaphors. The new self-aware, active Narcissus limned by Jean's poem may experience desire as mutually delightful and productive or one-sided and destructive. Erotic desire shored up by the new philosophical language of human happiness may open avenues toward *jouissance* that need not be deferred, but these paths are fraught with potential for misapprehension. What remains clear, however, is that the *Rose* in its widespread and long-lasting influence bequeathed vernacular poetry a decidedly intellectual erotics, creating a tradition that would include Gower's confessing lover, framed by concerns for the common good; Chaucer's Troilus and Criseyde, wondering about freedom and "felicite" while they romance; and Guillaume de Deguileville's *Pèlerinage de Vie Humaine*, where we find an Aristotle intellectually unmanned by Sapience's broken mirror. Fourteenth-century poetry continued to speak in the shared vocabulary of lovers and clerks, and questions of how one should define and experience love, delight, pain, and desire continued to motivate all of the medieval discourses oriented toward human happiness.

CHAPTER 3

Metamorphoses of pleasure in the fourteenth-century dit amoureux

With the translation of classical texts into the vernacular, the fourteenth century marks not only an increased dissemination of scholarly and classical knowledge, but, as Claire Sherman has put it, "the development of modern languages as instruments of abstract and scientific thought."[1] Nicole Oresme's 1370 translation of the *Nicomachean Ethics*, commissioned by Charles V, alone coined dozens of words in French that are still in current use, including *abstraccion*, *contingentes*, *delectacion*, and *sujet*, and Oresme took care to include a "table des moz divers et estranges" at the end of his translation.[2] Even earlier, great portions of the *Nicomachean Ethics* and Aquinas' commentary were translated in a treatise titled *Li Ars d'Amour, de Vertu et de Boneurté*; the author included a glossary of technical terms such as *abis*, *fins*, *quidités*, and *philosophie* (defined as "amours de savoir, de viertut ou de verité").[3] The discursive matrix of philosophy and poetry developed in thirteenth-century Paris was thus perpetuated by a widening audience for "scholastic" texts and by increasingly philosophical vernacular languages, an environment that contributed to the intellectualization of erotic poetry alongside the impact of the *Roman de la Rose* – perhaps the most influential medieval vernacular poem after Dante's *Commedia*. As the vernacular and courtly turned toward the intellectual, the concerns of the university were already oriented toward love. An Aristotelian ethical focus on earthly life and the curricular prominence of Peter Lombard's *Sentences* generated concerns about the relationships between love and pleasure, and love and loss, and about the nature of beatific enjoyment. William Courtenay describes both English and Continental fourteenth-century philosophy as working out "a total analysis of human motivation and behavior that would theoretically cover daily experience and interpersonal relations as well as religious experience."[4] While the reception of Aristotle was by no means settled, monolithic, or uncontroversial by this period, Aristotelian ethics had entered the mainstream of medieval philosophical thought, and Aristotelian definitions of pleasure and enjoyment were applied to both earthly and heavenly experience. The dialectical investigation of Aristotelian teleologies of pleasure and an opposing contingent notion of happiness – itself ultimately Aristotelian – was one of the major projects of fourteenth-century philosophy and poetry. The philosophers ask what might happen if pleasure were disconnected from our experience of the final good, and how pleasure relates to our experience of intermediate, worldly goods; the poets ask how philosophical understandings of love and pleasure relate to an earthly realm ruled by the whims of fortune. As philosophy used secular ethics to understand both earth and heaven, poetry used the vocabulary of clerkly discourse to imagine the pleasure of love both immanent and transcendent. Both discourses were concerned with the nobility of the lover and the gap between natural and ethical responses to love realized and love lost.

The narrative poetry of Guillaume de Machaut and Jean Froissart offers perhaps the most conspicuous terrain for the intellectual and poetic legacies of Jean de Meun's *Rose.* Certainly if one restricts oneself to the genre of love narratives, it could equally be said of either poet that his work is largely "a commentary on *Le Roman de la Rose*."[5] Both poets wrote semi-allegorical dream visions about love and continued both Guillaume de Lorris' and Jean de Meun's experiments with narrative voice, clerkly and courtly personae, Ovidian mythography, and "realistic" representation. These *dits* are still rarely read as "philosophical" poems, unless that philosophy is descended from Boethius' *Consolation* and concerns traditional questions about the loss of will in love, the ways of Fortune, or the possible sources of comfort for a grieving lover.[6] In arguing for the relevance of philosophical discourse to Chaucer's dream visions, Kathryn Lynch admits that the visions' clearest debts are to French love poetry – an admission that appears to assume the incommensurability of this tradition with philosophical thought. Yet surely the lingering "earnestness … longing for moral clarity, [and] persistent ambiguity of meaning" that Lynch finds in Chaucer may also point to a tradition that reinvents itself both intellectually and erotically with the *Roman de la Rose*.[7] Jacqueline Cerquiglini-Toulet places Machaut's *Voir Dit* at a nexus of social, religious, moral, and philosophical crises of the fourteenth century – including debates over nominalism – arguing that the poet seeks a unified approach to these crises via the perspective of erotic love.[8] Sylvia Huot associates Machaut with an "intellectualization of love poetry," including the eroticization of Boethian discourse and the "creation of mythographic models of the love experience and the love poet."[9] More recently, Sarah

Kay has placed Machaut's *Jugement* poems in the context of fourteenth-century debates about knowledge of singular things and universals.[10]

I argue in this chapter that such an "intellectualization" includes the inheritance of the *Rose*'s association of erotic consummation with philosophical understandings of human happiness, and the conflation of artistic production and self-knowledge. In what follows I address a matrix of fourteenth-century love narratives – selected *dits amoureux* of Machaut and Froissart along with Chaucer's *Book of the Duchess* – as seemingly "light," elegant tales of courtly love that nevertheless place themselves at the center of fourteenth-century scholastic controversies about the relationship between pleasure and enjoyment. Machaut and Froissart do not simply adapt the motifs of dreams, pleasure gardens, fountains, and Ovidian lovers from the *Rose*, but also adapt and revise the questions the poem raises about the relationship between poetic creativity and desire for another person, about possibilities for earthly happiness, and about the beauty and violence inherent in love poetry. Long recognized as a brilliant compilation and revision of his French contemporaries, Chaucer's *Book of the Duchess* may also be read as a commentary on the French poets, an overtly ethical reading of the *dits amoureux* that contributes to a flourishing philosophical discourse of pleasure in the fourteenth century. Chaucer's inheritance of the French tradition, on full display in *The Book of the Duchess*, strikingly emphasizes how this tradition foregrounds the way love can elide important differences between joy and sorrow, and can thus obscure the motivations of desire, as well as judgments about good and evil.

As in the *Rose*, the fourteenth-century poets explored the ethics of desire through a tradition of reimaginings of the narratives in Ovid's *Metamorphoses*. As John Fyler remarks in the opening of *Chaucer and Ovid*, "Ovid becomes the Freud of the Middle Ages," allowing medieval poets to theorize the relationships among love, death, sublimation, and joy.[11] While Jean de Meun imagined Pygmalion as creator and lover of a work of art that might then return his love, Machaut, Froissart, and Chaucer all sustain an engagement with Ovidian love stories that resolutely follow their narratives beyond the moment of consummation and toward inevitable loss in betrayal or death. After Jean de Meun's engagement with the radical notion of human happiness and perfection, the poetry of intellectual eroticism begins to reckon more directly with conflicts between earthly happiness and the contingencies of earthly existence. Thus where Jean's idealization of the union of Pygmalion and Galatea was haunted by possibilities of narcissistic projection and violence, the later poets accept an ideal of mutuality while being troubled by its unsustainable nature. Such preoccupations lead to a series of transformations of the Pygmalion figure; he is at times arrested in his role as lover of an inanimate image, and at other times he is imagined not as a man whose artistry begets love, but a man whose love begets his artistry. Concern for the articulations of loss also animates the multiple retellings of the tale of Ceyx and Alcyone – a narrative found in Machaut, Froissart, Chaucer, Gower, Deschamps, and elsewhere.[12] The poets find a trove of possibilities in the tale, especially as it describes the dream as a space where one encounters both one's beloved and the knowledge of that beloved's loss. The mutuality of the love between Pygmalion and Galatea emphasized in the *Rose* is exchanged for the mutual love between Ceyx and Alcyone.[13] Yet this mutuality is importantly not the mutual delight of the artist and his animate creation, but rather a sharing of experience and emotion that encompasses both good and ill. As I discuss below, perhaps the most compelling feature of the tale of Ceyx for fourteenth-century poets is the figure of Morpheus – a figure whose shape-shifting allows for the fantasy that the dead king can tell his story, an impossible narrative of his own death.[14] Such an impossible perspective allows for this poetry to engage in ethical questions about the relationships among love, pleasure, and the shape of an entire human life. In the varied and focused attention given to the narrative arc of desire, fruition, and loss – and the attendant psychological responses to each state – one finds strikingly parallel discourses in fourteenth-century poetry and philosophy.

Even so, placing Chaucer and his French contemporaries in the midst of contemporary intellectual debates remains more challenging than the similar contextualization of Jean de Meun. The very notion of a project that attempts to put Chaucer's poetry into conversation with currents in scholastic philosophy is up against some long-held skepticism. The subject of Chaucer and philosophy continues to fascinate and to generate controversy, with some scholars arguing for the evident relevance of scholastic discourse to Chaucer's poetry and others (more often) noting interesting parallels, but prescribing skepticism and cautioning that we not "over-philosophize" Chaucer.[15] Yet even before William Courtenay invited scholars of Middle English literature to bring the world of Ockham together with the world of Chaucer, there was energetic and wide-ranging activity toward this goal.[16] In the last several decades, critics began researching the possible links between Chaucer and nominalist theories, thinking about the ways texts such as "The Clerk's Tale" might be influenced by William of Ockham's ideas about God's absolute power, the contingency of language and human experience, and epistemology.[17] There has as yet been no critical discussion of Chaucer and that area of medieval psychology that is closest in concern to medieval and modern ethics – specifically the fourteenth-century debates about enjoyment (*fruitio*) and pleasure (*delectatio*) as components of the sovereign good (*summum bonum*).[18] These debates centered on problems of ethical motivation – whether we love something for the pleasure it brings or for its own sake – and questions about the very intelligibility of love and pleasure – whether happiness or enjoyment can be understood or experienced without pleasure. Pleasure, in both philosophical and poetic contexts, becomes central to ethical, psychological, and epistemological concerns.

In a consideration of fourteenth-century ethical discourse about pleasure, we can speak about medieval literature and philosophy together without demanding direct lines of influence, reflecting instead upon a vigorous conversation about issues of particular urgency in the period. While the previous chapter illustrated the way that the medieval reception of Aristotelian enjoyment expanded the concept to include love, this chapter explores the way this expanded meaning radically destabilized understandings of love itself. The inclusion of love as a component of virtuous action and the enjoyment of virtuous objects made "happiness" more comprehensible to the medieval subject, but love's long association with suffering and sacrifice simultaneously made this happiness precarious and contradictory at its core. If love is the primary noble virtue, and love often brings suffering and loss, then happiness might comprehend sorrow – a medieval update of the classical image of the virtuous man, happy despite tortuous pain. The twinned medieval images of the virtuous subject included the lover of God, graced with the beatific vision, and the lover of a human paragon, continuing to love despite suffering; these two images had already begun to merge, from the very beginnings of vernacular love poetry. This poetry begins to find analogues for suffering love not only in discourses of theology and religious devotion, but in Aristotelian-influenced moral philosophy and psychology. In the fourteenth century, both poetry and philosophy explored what the new Aristotelian context of human happiness might mean for our experience of and our very understanding of love and pleasure.

PHILOSOPHICAL PLEASURES

The last book of the *Nicomachean Ethics* is clear on the inextricability of enjoyment and pleasure as a unified phenomenon, if not clear on the exact relationship between the two: pleasure "supervenes upon" and perfects activities in the way that beauty perfects youth ("velud iuvenibus pulcritudo").[19] For Aristotle, the activity equivalent with happiness entailed the pleasurable contemplation of truth, especially when this truth is knowledge possessed rather than sought. For medieval philosophers, the pleasure of enjoyment is the pleasure of the act of knowing and loving God. Without love, Ockham's objection that *fruitio* could persist without pleasure is all but unintelligible. Yet the ethical motivation that informs the psychology of the enjoying subject was less clear; the medieval reader of Aristotle was left to ponder: Do we live or love to experience pleasure, or does pleasure allow us to live and love?[20] Aristotelian aporiae about whether pleasure is an activity or a passion, and about whether love is a component of enjoyment, complicated ethical, psychological, and theological understandings of love.[21] The centrality of Aristotle in the universities meant that Aristotle's works became a touchstone for any discussion of ethics (along with a multitude of other topics) in theological as well as strictly philosophical writing. The *Sentences* commentaries of the fourteenth century are peppered with references to Aristotle, and yet the philosopher's writings are a source of tension as much as they are a source of knowledge for medieval theologians.

Because Aristotle left open the question of whether we live for the sake of pleasure, or pursue pleasure for the sake of life, questions of causality and motivation animated much ethical discourse in the wake of the institutionalization and dissemination of the *Ethics*. The relationship between desire and pleasure became a primary concern, especially inasmuch as it helped to illuminate the experience of the beatific vision, but also as it helped in understanding less lofty pursuits such as study, virtuous behavior, desire for objects, and love for people. Are we motivated to love by the pleasure that love promises and sometimes brings? Or do we love most purely when we have no regard for pleasure? What could it mean to imagine the highest love as lacking pleasure in its very fulfillment? How does loss affect our love for a person or a thing? Such questions – themes that had long been the subject of vernacular love poetry – became equally the terrain of fourteenth-century philosophy.

As one can see in the discourse of Abelard's Christian in his *Dialogue*, the blissfulness of heaven – a reward for earthly virtue and compensation for earthly sorrow – is a bedrock assumption of Christian doctrine. As Augustine puts it, "There is therefore nothing absurd in the assertion that the final complete happiness will be exempt from the spasms of fear and from any kind of grief"; he cites 1 John 4:18, "There is no fear in love," in support of his claim.[22] Where earthly pleasures are always compromised by their ephemeral nature, heavenly pleasures are complete and stable. Yet as influential a theologian as William Ockham claimed that love – even the highest love – is not equivalent to pleasure, and God's absolute power necessitates the possibility that the pleasure accompanying such love might be withheld. Ockham thus spends much time attempting to reconcile his theories of the will, intellect, and happiness with those of Augustine and other authorities. Both Ockham himself and the theologians who opposed the detachment of pleasure from love marshaled Aristotle to support their definitions of love, pleasure, and the identity or causality between the two.

The relationship between happiness and pleasure in Aristotle's *Ethics* was dissected in Albert the Great's first commentary, beginning with the question of whether pleasure is even an appropriate topic to discuss in relation to contemplative happiness. Albert acknowledges that pleasure is typically relevant to ethics in the context of moral decisions, and that morality requires one to flee pleasures, even according to Aristotle himself.[23] Yet, he concludes that pleasure is the measure of a human life, and those lives that have "good pleasures" ("bonas delectationes") are judged good, while those that have shameful ones are shameful.[24] Here he follows Book x of the *Ethics*, where Aristotle defines pleasure as the perfection of an enjoyable and rationally virtuous activity. Thus it follows that the highest pleasure would be the pleasure experienced upon the completion of the activity of contemplating the good. And indeed, Albert asserts that the "Commentator" Michael of Ephesus demonstrates that "happiness cannot be understood [or discerned] without pleasure."[25] In his commentary, Michael further asserts that the happy life appears pleasurable, and that "this perfect life is lacking nothing and self-sufficient, the highest and the utmost, wherefore it is also the most pleasant."[26] Pleasure well-chosen is thus both the indicator of a well-lived life and the very condition for the intelligibility of happiness. Happiness, as an experience or as an ethical end of human life, cannot be fathomed without pleasure.

Aquinas also picks up on this question of motivation in both his commentary on the *Ethics* and his discussion of pleasure in the *Summa Theologiae*. For Aquinas, the greatest good, perfect happiness (*beatitudo*), necessarily includes pleasure. On the question of whether pleasure (*delectatio*) differs from joy (*gaudium*), Aquinas argues that joy is one species of pleasure, as one experiences pleasure when one obtains an object of physical or rational desire, but one experiences joy from the actual exercise of reason.[27] Yet the question is also raised as to whether the ultimate end is

God himself (*ipse Deus*) or the enjoyment of God (*fruitio ipsius*). Aquinas acknowledges that one may equally say that the ultimate end of man is God himself, or that it is the enjoyment of God, but makes the distinction that the enjoyment of God is the greatest of human goods (*bona humana*).[28] Aquinas thus gives us two contexts from which to consider pleasure: from the perspective of the divine good, or from the perspective of the human good, where we encounter the problem of the priority of activity or pleasure. It is in a consideration of human happiness, thus, that ethical questions about pleasure come to the fore. In his *Ethics* commentary, the theologian addresses Aristotle's inquiry into whether we experience pleasure as a result of enjoyment, or whether perhaps we are given pleasure so that we might continue the labor of enjoyment. Aquinas restates the philosopher's view of indeterminacy, and yet goes on to give an answer: activity, not pleasure, is principal. He explains that "pleasure is a repose of the appetite in a pleasing object which a person enjoys by means of activity. But a person desires repose in a thing only inasmuch as he judges it agreeable to him. Consequently the activity itself that gives pleasure as a pleasing object seems to be desirable prior to pleasure."[29] Aquinas thus explains in his *Summa Theologiae* that pleasure functions in a similar way to sleep – it refreshes our souls so that we can continue our labors.[30] Having settled this, Aquinas seems to give no further thought to the problem of the priority of pleasure or activity. In discussing contemplation as the highest form of happiness, Aquinas accepts Aristotle's reasoning that "contemplation of wisdom is loved for itself and not for something else."[31] At this point, happiness has been defined as necessarily mingled with pleasure, and the love of contemplation for the sake of this mixture is not considered to be a conundrum of ethical motivation. Pleasure is not something external that would hinder the formula that such contemplation is loved "for its own sake," and yet its status as somehow "essential" to happiness is not secure.[32] The dissection of enjoyment in the commentaries on Peter Lombard's *Sentences* will zero in on this uncertainty and begin to break down the unity between enjoyment and pleasure.

The commentaries of both Albert and Aquinas remained influential, but the late thirteenth and early fourteenth centuries witnessed a transformation in the very terms of enjoyment. The focus on enjoyment in the first distinction of Peter Lombard's *Sentences* ensured that it became a set topic in the commentaries of many theologians. These commentaries discussed the difference between the enjoyment to be had in this life (*fruitio viae*) and the enjoyment of the afterlife (*fruitio patriae*) and analyzed any number of other adjacent issues, including grace, charity, and the relationship between the intellect and the will. In this context the act of enjoyment (*fruitio*) is structurally distinct from the resulting pleasure (*delectatio*), and scholars debated whether or not the two terms could be effectively distinguished.[33] In the late thirteenth and fourteenth centuries, questions about the identity or non-identity of pleasure and enjoyment became common topics for discussion. It is clear, in Aristotle, in commentaries on the *Ethics*, and on the *Sentences*, that defining pleasure brings into relief questions of ethical motivation, and makes urgent the task of determining (or saving) the nobility of love – for ourselves, for others, and for God.

Defining enjoyment in terms of the relationship between love and pleasure had long been a preoccupation of commentators on the *Sentences*. John Duns Scotus (*c.*1302) maintained that enjoyment was indistinct from pleasure, while Peter Aureoli (*c.*1316) determined that every love is pleasurable – two approaches to love and pleasure that maintain their alliance, and yet offer quite different understandings of the relationships between the two phenomena.[34] Either love and pleasure are somehow the same, or love is simply guaranteed to be accompanied by pleasure. The writings of William Ockham serve as a turning point in this conversation. In the wake of his commentary on the *Sentences* (1317–18), which controversially posited that enjoyment was distinct from pleasure, the question of the possible non-identity of these two experiences came to the forefront.[35]

Ockham's emphasis on voluntarism – in terms of both the primacy of God's free will and the human faculty of the will – had effects beyond his theorization of God's absolute freedom and the freedom and nobility of the human will. Voluntarism importantly shaped his understanding of both divine and human happiness, and particularly the relationship between love and pleasure. For Ockham, the understanding of enjoyment always returns to questions of cause, effect, and motivation; in life, the will causes love, while in heaven, love is caused by God.[36] He cites Aristotle's statement that "happiness consists in activity" and also that "pleasure is not activity but supervenes on activity," effectively separating pleasure from happiness.[37] This separation allowed Ockham to explore love both mundane and beatific that might involve sorrow rather than pleasure. He critiques the opinions of both Duns Scotus and Peter Aureoli, maintaining that love remains when pleasure is destroyed, and that this may be true for both earthly love and love directed toward God. He offers that an earthly, concupiscent desire such as revenge, for example, does not bring pleasure, and yet the desire remains. Similarly, he claims that "An intense act of love can exist with distress regarding the same object, namely, when someone is afraid of losing what he loves."[38] In refuting Peter Aureoli's opinion that pleasure and enjoyment are identical, Ockham marshals not only Augustine, but Aristotle, stating:

> according to the Philosopher in *Ethics* X, supreme distress excludes not only the pleasure opposite to it but also pleasure that is not opposed to it. For example, someone supremely distressed about the loss of a temporal thing does not take pleasure in investigating anything theoretical. But that distress does not exclude all love of that investigation.[39]

It is important to Ockham that love exists as an emotion and as a mental action even when the positive effects of love are not experienced; enjoyment, whether earthly or divine, must include not simply virtuous activity or the possession of an object, but persistent love.

Even proper enjoyment of God for his own sake – the highest vocation of the will – is not guaranteed to offer pleasure. For Ockham's belief in God's absolute power (*potentia absoluta*) demands that he acknowledge that God has the power to make even the experience of beatitude (*beatitudo*) a painful experience, replacing pleasure with distress.[40] Ultimately, these issues of definition become concerns about preserving the nobility of love. Ockham posits, provisionally, that "the act of love is without qualification nobler than pleasure."[41] He takes it as unarguable that "love in this life is more perfect than pleasure in this life; therefore, love in heaven is more perfect than pleasure in heaven, and consequently love as a whole is more perfect than pleasure."[42] Commentaries on Aristotle's *Ethics* become essential to this discussion, specifically as they resolve the question of whether we choose pleasure for the sake of activities or vice versa. Ockham cites Michael of Ephesus' comment on *Ethics* x that we pursue pleasure "for the sake of activities and in order to live … for however pleasant these [activities] are, it is not for the sake of pleasure that they are eagerly engaged in. For we choose many virtuous activities even though engaging in them is a cause of distress, labor, and grief."[43]

After Ockham, disagreement persisted in the terrains of *Sentences* commentaries and commentaries on the *Ethics*. In the commentaries of both Walter Chatton (*c.*1321–3) and Adam Wodeham (*c.*1329–32), enjoying love *is* a pleasure.[44] Wodeham's lectures on the *Sentences* are prime examples of the mobilization of Aristotle to argue both that enjoyment should be distinguished from pleasure, and that it should not. In his sixth question on the first distinction of the Lombard's text, Wodeham follows Ockham in addressing the question of "whether enjoyment is really distinguished from pleasure."[45] In the arguments for this distinction, Wodeham quotes Augustine on the definition of enjoyment as love of an object for its own sake and therefore an activity (*operatio*) and Aristotle on the definition of pleasure as a passion ("passio superveniens operationi").[46] In this case, Augustine gives us an understanding of enjoyment as an activity irreconcilable with Aristotle's definition of pleasure as a passion: an activity and a passion cannot be the same. Yet he later uses Aristotle's statement that the most pleasurable activity is the most perfect ("delectabilissima operatio est perfectissima") to support the notion that enjoyment and pleasure are the same and not distinguished from each other ("idem et non distinguuntur").[47] Aristotelian ideas about the nobility of spiritual pleasures and the particular pleasures of philosophical pursuits are given the same space and consideration as Augustinian discussions of the joy of the beatific vision. The Theologian and the Philosopher are demonstrated by Wodeham to be in harmony with each other and ultimately to show the harmony of enjoyment and delight.

The discussions of enjoyment in *Sentences* commentaries in turn had their effect upon commentaries on Aristotle's *Ethics*. Jean Buridan, in his *Quaestiones* on the *Ethics* (*c.*1340–50), directs his attention less to the relationship between love and pleasure than to the necessity of both for the constitution of happiness. Discussing the question of whether human happiness consists of one act or several, Buridan explicitly rejects the notion that happiness might involve sorrow or hate, or that God might detach love from the act of knowledge, and that this love could nevertheless constitute happiness. He offers a summary of the debate:

> if you say that the most noble act that can exist in a human being is the clear vision of God, then I prove that this would not be happiness essentially. For if it were happiness essentially, then with it alone remaining and all other acts being removed (as they could be by God's absolute power, as some theologians say), one would still be happy, as a stone would be white if whiteness remained in it and all other accidents were removed. Yet that conclusion is false, namely, that a human being who saw God clearly without any pleasure and without love of God would be called happy. For happiness must be most pleasant, as Aristotle says ... Those theologians say that God could form in Socrates' soul, together with a clear vision of God, an intense distress without pleasure and a hatred of God without love. Would he then be happy? I am sure that I would not wish for such happiness![48]

For Buridan, happiness requires both full understanding and full love of God; knowledge and love are both equally necessary. Aristotle's statement that happiness consists in perfect contemplation is glossed so that contemplation of God "is not knowledge of God without love or love without knowledge but is made up of both."[49] "Contemplation" itself is said to connote "just as the word 'happiness' does, the presence of love and pleasure naturally connected to that thought or vision [of God]."[50] In Buridan's final resolution, "happiness" signifies a single holistic act that connotes love of God, wisdom, perfect thought, prudence and moral virtues, and the virtues of the body and exterior goods.[51] In this way, human happiness encompasses Aristotelian practical virtue, Aristotelian contemplative happiness, and a Platonic/Boethian aggregation of all goods.

Buridan concludes that "Our best act, therefore, is the same as our most pleasant act" and, finally, that "by chief or primary purpose pleasure is for the sake of activity"[52] and thus cannot itself constitute the final good. Therefore, God is the most pleasant object, and the perception of God is the most pleasurable act, but it is the act that constitutes happiness – because pleasurable – and not the pleasure. He thus gives us finally an Aristotelian version of the Augustinian image of the beatific vision: "the blessed not only love and understand God, but they can understand reflexively, and they understand that they understand and love and take pleasure."[53] Buridan, as a member of the arts faculty, explicitly not writing as a theologian, neither approves nor rejects the statements that God could preserve a vision of himself in a subject while taking away "love and every act of will." Yet he makes a key distinction between the pleasure that necessarily accompanies the vision of God – inseparable from the apprehension "of an object under the concept of the good, present, and possessed" – and the pleasure that may very well be absent if one experiences love and volition without vision.[54] Thus the act of the intellect is nobler than the act of volition, because it is through understanding – not love – that one "immediately" attains God.

While it may seem to be on very fine points that these scholars disagree, they point to an interest in the psychology of the loving subject that is of great importance in fourteenth-century ethics.[55] As we will see below, Aristotelian-influenced medical understandings of lovesickness also focused on the psychological and ethical ramifications of being in love. Such questions animate the poets writing in the wake of the *Rose*: does love aim at possession? Does possession entail the reification of the loved person? What happens when the distinctions between joy and sorrow collapse? What motivations render the lover a noble lover? What if forces beyond human will render all of these questions moot? By tracing such questions and their multiple answers, we can recreate a picture of the way that both philosophers and poets approached very similar questions of motivation and causation as they searched for an ethical description of what happens when we love.

FOURTEENTH-CENTURY FRENCH ROSES

Guillaume de Machaut (*c.*1300–77) established the tone, themes, and generic spaces for the reception of the *Rose* in his century, and thus also created the space for the investigation of the questions outlined above. Machaut is one of the first poets to theorize his poetry in the vernacular, and, among the poets considered in this chapter, he is the most explicit regarding the relationship between joy, sorrow, and poetry. His love narratives are playful, ironic, detached, and profoundly interested in the interplay between poetry, song, authorship, material textual production, and lived experience. This interplay might be understood within the categories of "Musique, Rhetorique, et Sens"; these "gifts" are the children of Nature, given to the poet in his *Prologue*, a poem composed toward the end of his career, and which served as an introduction to his poetic *œuvre* in manuscript compilations.[56] Perhaps the signal ethical effect of his focus on the uneasy split between narrator and author and the material modes of writing resides in the way his poetry insists upon a recognition of the several players involved in the production of meaning and the sharing of emotion.[57] In his *Prologue*, the poet sustains a dialogue with Love and Nature, explaining that poetry is, by definition, joyous. For even if the poet has "triste matiere" (sad matter, v.43), "est joieuse la maniere / Dou fait" (the style of their treatment / Is joyful, v.44–5). Music itself creates joy and is created from the pleasant memories of one's beloved. The possibility of composing in sadness is acknowledged, but dismissed as inferior to composition born of happiness; even Orpheus is brought in as an example of the happiness music can bring, releasing Eurydice from the underworld.

In such moments, Machaut redefines our understandings of poetic joy itself. Much in the way that certain of Plato's dialogues ask that we understand the practice of virtue as tantamount to happiness, Machaut asks us to understand poetry born of love and received in joy as equivalent to joy itself, never mind the sorrow of the composer. Machaut's insistence on the superior quality of joyful music is shadowed by the barely submerged acknowledgment that much poetry is (at least imagined to be) born of sorrow and loss. In poetry, however, love is tantamount to joy, even allowing for such loss. Several of Machaut's poems address the ethics of poetry created from grief and the consolations and knowledge gained through dreaming. His masterpiece, *Le Voir Dit* (*c.*1363–5), is an encyclopedia of poetic genres – prose letter, verse narrative, lyric, dream vision, mirror for princes, commentary – as well as an ongoing representation of a psychomachia taking place within the narrator's mind, a battle between Hope and Desire.[58] In a lay contained in the center of the poem, the Lover describes how the Lady's sweet look "D'ardant Desir fist un dart / Et un d'Esperence" (Made one dart of burning Desire / And one of Hope, ll. 4360–1). Desire is consistently a source of pain for the Lover, while Hope brings comfort, here in the form of "Plaisence / En ma iolie souffrance" (pleasure / In my sweet suffering, ll. 4371–2).[59] While pleasure in suffering is a time-honored affect of the troubadours and other poets of lovesickness, Machaut shifts the association of such pleasure with desire to the much more ethically appealing emotion of hope. Hope allows the sorrow of love unconsummated to be transformed into the pleasure of suffering so that poetry may take place. Even the joy of love's consummation seems to take the form of poetry, as the Lover, having achieved some kind of union with his beloved ("mes desirs fu acomplis," l. 4001) while hidden in a cloud created by Venus, takes the opportunity to compose a song (ll. 4032ff).[60] The productive desire of the earlier love poets has given way to an equally productive hope – equivalent in suffering and pleasure, but oriented more fully toward a poetry that comprehends consummation and its aftermaths as well as perpetual longing.

In theorizing love, hope, and pleasure in this manner, Machaut opens up the possibility of an engagement between philosophical and poetic ideas about pleasure; for Machaut poetic pleasure is already philosophical. One sees that he does not take suffering love for granted, but rather – like Ockham and his contemporaries – dissects the relationships among activity, pleasure, and the end goals of love. Love is preserved as a purer place of nobility and pleasure, while suffering is associated with imagining the future. One might attribute to Machaut an affinity with Ockham in that love and pleasure are separate entities that may or may not coincide, and yet also with an Aristotelian philosopher such as Buridan in the insistence that the noblest activity – in this case, poetry – is *always* pleasurable. Machaut also locates the ethical questions raised by love and pleasure squarely in the relationships between people – not only between lover and beloved, but among lovers, poets, and readers of poetry.

Machaut's *Fonteinne Amoureuse* (*c.*1360–2) thus begins by foregrounding the disjunction between the sorrow of a lover's seemingly spontaneous lyric outpouring, and the delight that this performance gives to the narrator. We are told that the lover "commença piteusement, / Et je l'escri joieusement" (began piteously / While I wrote with pleasure, ll. 233–4).[61] The *Fonteinne* in particular appears to be captivated by the transformation of emotions as they travel between people and into poetry. For Machaut, and for Froissart and Chaucer after him, the understanding of the relationship between love, pleasure, and pain is demonstrated to be the product of a triangle of representation and reflection constituted by the person in sorrow or joy, an empathetic figure (the narrator/poet), and a spectator (the audience/reader).[62] It is this multi-layered circuit of representation and response that allows for the intelligibility of emotions in love – in fact creates their necessary conditions. As a poem that explores the possibilities of transforming sorrow into aesthetically pleasing art, or physically and spiritually comforting dreams, it is no wonder that Chaucer harvested some of the *Fonteinne*'s central motifs, and especially its retelling of the Ovidian tale of Ceyx and Alcyone, for his poem of consolation *The Book of the Duchess* (*c.*1368–70). Both poems center their narrative and emotional energy on the scene of a grieving lover telling his sorrows to another man.

Machaut's version of the Ovidian narrative comes into view in a complaint inserted early in the *Fonteinne Amoureuse*; Machaut's Lover reveals his sorrow and the absence of his beloved; he laments that writing a letter may not be efficacious, and sending a messenger might risk public revelation. He presents the tale of Ceyx and Alcyone as an alternative – a tale in which a queen's hyper-vigilance over the absence of her king is rewarded first with dreaming news of his death at sea, then ultimately with a transformation of both lovers into seabirds. The Lover imagines that he might entreat the Morpheus of the tale – Ovid's shape-shifting son of the god of sleep – to take on his form and present his cause to his beloved. The Lover is sure that although Pygmalion created an ivory statue that he loved and prayed to, "il n'ot pas si tres noble victoire / Ne tel eür / Comme j'aray, se Morpheüs avoire / Ce que je tieng qui sera chose voire" (his achievement was not as noble, / His luck was not the same / As I will have should Morpheus persevere with / What I think should prove true, ll. 965–8). Pygmalion, in this poem and in the others I discuss below, is almost always a sculptor, a man in love with an image, and almost never the lover of a woman come to life.[63] The transformative power of art so important in the *Rose* is denied to these later Pygmalions. Morpheus appears instead to be the privileged figure – an agent of metamorphosis and a figure for the poet – perhaps the reason that the *Fonteinne Amoureuse* is alternatively known as "The Book of Morpheus."[64] In the Lover's first proposing that Morpheus take his form, followed by his request that the narrator compose a complaint, the narrator takes on the role of Morpheus; when the narrator presents his already made copy of the Lover's plaint, he fulfills the role of Morpheus metamorphosed into the shape of the Lover himself. In this context, Morpheus and metamorphosis in general become figures for identification as a mode of narrative and poetic production – an appropriate role for Morpheus especially, as the "craftsman and simulator of human forms" ("artificem simulatoremque figurae").[65] The twinning of Machaut's two characters is reinforced when both men fall sweetly asleep together and dream the same dream: the narrator with the Lover's head in his lap, the narrator's head soon falling into slumber upon his companion's head. They sleep by the "fonteinne amoureuse," of which both the marble bowl and the ivory pillar on which it sits are attributed to Pygmalion and are carved with the histories of Narcissus and the Trojan War. In their shared dream they are visited by Venus, who tells the tale of the golden apple she is holding, and the Lady from whom the Lover desires his comfort.[66] After the dream, in which the Lover and the Lady exchange "ymages" and rings, the Lover expresses gratitude to Morpheus, who he is sure has visited the Lady in his shape. Any happiness here achieved is attributed to the capacity of Morpheus/the poet to inhabit another's subjectivity and shape.

The final image of the poem portrays the Lover, setting off on the sea, singing a rondel expressing desire to return to the country of his Lady. The Lover appears to promise reparation for the tragedy of King Ceyx's death at sea that would not demand otherworldly metamorphosis; he will go on the sea in order to return to his beloved, not to find his death in her absence. Yet the reader is left wondering whether the Lover has perhaps unwittingly placed himself in the role of Ceyx, setting off to sea with his other half, our narrator, remaining ashore as Alcyone.[67] As is often the case in Machaut, consolation in poetry is shadowed by the persistence of the possibilities of loss and sorrow, and this ending in particular raises questions about whether the privileged couple should be the Lover and his lady, or the Lover-patron and the narrator-poet, and about whether the sea of worldly fortune can ever prove a medium for uniting two lovers. In other words, it is unclear whether poetic metamorphosis ends up replacing the love relationship with a textual and social relationship, and whether either poetry or love are able to provide happiness in a contingent world.

These are among the questions that Machaut's poetry will encourage his successors to address. Machaut leaves his successors a body of work that articulates the relationships between love and poetic production, dreams and consolation, sorrow and poetic joy, and love, loss, and transformation. The intrusions of fortune create sorrow, but also opportunities to transform that sorrow into hope – what Machaut terms "iolie souffrance." Poetry thus offers a meta-perspective on fortune, a perspective most fully embodied by the figure of Morpheus/Ceyx, narrating his own demise. Such poetry is self-reflective about the way that hope is often channeled into the transformation of beloveds and love experiences into textual artifacts, and both Froissart and Chaucer will ask if this is the only mode of possession allowed to the loving subject. These poets share the project of rendering Machaut's ethical poetics more explicit. The problem – for both philosophy and poetry – is that preserving the nobility of love may compromise the success of that love: one may arrive at a painful beatific vision, or pleasurably love only an idealized or reified object. Pleasure for a reader or interlocutor may mean sorrow for the speaker-poet, and the activity of poetry may replace the supposed sought-for pleasure of union with the beloved. Aristotle's contention that choosing life for pleasure or pleasure for life cannot be determined could not be left untested and untried. Froissart will dissect his Machauldian inheritance through an Ovidian invention that allies clerkliness with love and ethics, while Chaucer will pursue the problem of the indeterminacy of joy and sorrow as a route to the height of human love and happiness.

FROM LAUREL TO LADY: THE NARRATIVE POETRY OF JEAN FROISSART

The Machauldian transformations of the *Rose* into a treasure trove for thinking about poetic production are transformed again by Froissart and Chaucer into spaces for thinking through the ethical difficulties of composing poetry about consolation and metamorphosis. Active at the same time and in the same court circles, both poets were heir to Machaut, and especially to his use of the *Rose* to engage questions of consolation, change, and shared emotion.[68] In *L'Espinette Amoureuse* (*The Hawthorn Bush of Love*, *c.*1369), Froissart places himself squarely in the tradition of the *Roman de la Rose*, writing a poem about love, roses, mirrors, and dreams.[69] He alludes to the *Rose* in claiming that "Dreams are but vain things" ("Songes nest fors que vainne cose," l. 677) and plays upon the earlier poem's favorite rhyming association of "mençonge" (lie, l. 685) and "songe" (dream, l. 686) in arguing that his experience is one of truth (*verite*) and therefore not a dream at all. It is in this poem that Froissart begins a poetic project of coming to terms with amorous and poetic desire for possession that will culminate in an ethical transformation of the very terms of creative metamorphosis.

Celebrated for its opening depiction of childhood play, the poem is largely about the transformation of that elemental play (quite literally elemental – the narrator admits to having preferred mud to more sophisticated toys) into games of love. These games consist of reading romances and exchanging lyrics, gifts, and gestures. The speaker is also the Lover, in this poem, and the many lyric insertions represent the lover/speaker's own voice and, once, the voice of the lady. After realizing that a ballade the narrator has hidden in a romance, lent to his beloved, has been returned apparently unread, the narrator composes a complaint. In this song (ll. 1556–2355), the narrator expresses his desire for the Lady, already a flesh-and-blood woman, to be turned into an object. After telling the tale of Apollo and Daphne, the Lover cries,

Pleuïst or au Roi de lassus
Que ma dame, qui de refus
S'esbat a moi et fait ses jus,
Fust devenue
Uns biaus loriers vers et foillus! (ll. 1780–4)

(Now if it had only pleased the King above
That my lady, who entertains herself at my expense
With her refusals and plays her games,
Had become
A beautiful green and leafy laurel!)

He justifies this desire by citing Pygmalion's love of his sculpted image and Candace's love of the portrait of Alexander in *Le Roman d'Alexander*, not mentioning that in these cases the image was a necessary or precursory substitute for a person. The narrator rationalizes that "n'i voi damage" (I see no harm, l. 1807) if his harsh beloved were turned into "vredure" (greenery, l. 1806). Upon reflection, however, the lover realizes his transgression, claiming, "J'ai dit, au regarder droiture, / Un grant outrage" (I realize that I have said, in truth, / An outrageous thing, ll. 1810–11).[70]

The narrator begins to berate himself for having wished to turn his lady into a "fourme villainne" (base form, l. 1816). He blames Fortune for having made him express such a wish, but appears to rue the verbal expression rather than the sentiment behind it. His wish to reify her continues to haunt what seem like conventional formulations: for example, that his lady "blance et vermelle / Est com la rose" (is white and red / Like a rose, ll. 1946–7). Comparing his beloved's coloring to a rose could not be more traditional and courtly, and yet given the context of both the *Roman de la Rose* and his stated desire to turn her into another plant, the laurel, the comparison becomes slightly sinister, and even "villainne." The same image concludes the complaint, as the lover wishes his beloved lady to advise him on his failed rhymes and embrace his pretty rhymes to her red and white cheeks (ll. 2345–7).

The lover appears more satisfied by his lady's form when she is absent, when he goes abroad and she gives him the gift of her mirror. Frustrated that he can see only his own reflection, rather than the image of the lady that the mirror must have held many times, the lover takes consolation in his own imagination. Through the powers of his own mind, the lover sees a perfect impression of

> ma dame et de sa figure
> Qui se miroit ou mireoir
> Et tenoit d'ivore un trechoir
> Dont ses cevelés demi lons
> Partissoit, qu'elle eut biaus et blons … (ll. 2630–4)

> (my lady and of her face
> Which was reflected in the mirror,
> And she held an ivory comb,
> With which she parted her long
> Hair, which was beautiful and blonde …)

His lady, viewed in the mirror through the power of his imagination, looks like no one so much as the Oiseuse of the *Rose*. Yet while Oiseuse held a mirror and comb, symbols of her vanity and her parodic contemplation, the lady appears to have fully entered the mirror and holds only her ivory comb. She has lost her contemplative agency, now given over to the lover who can determine the contents of the mirror with his "imagination."[71] And yet the narrator leaves open the possibility that the lady still gazes upon herself (*se miroit*) in the mirror – the verb is ambiguous as to whether she is passively reflected, or whether she may still somehow gaze upon herself, retaining some agency and contemplative power. She is simultaneously rendered a more passive object of desire and yet exceeds the lover's attempts to make her wholly an object of his imagination. Given the possibility of the lady's gazing upon herself in a mirror while the lover looks at her in another version of that very mirror, the lover begins to appear rather concretely as a double of the lady; her posture and gaze determine his, and yet her gaze is directed beyond his reach.

It is thus finally the lady herself who accepts her role as laurel, attributing the role to her own imagination. The lover begs to hear his beloved's voice, and she responds with a poem wherein she transforms the image of the laurel tree into a symbol of constancy and faithfulness, claiming that she is "au lorier me figure / A tous bons grés" (quite happy to / Imagine myself as the laurel, ll. 2867–8). Upon the completion of her poem, the lover sees her face disappear from the mirror, and wakes disconsolate, blaming Morpheus for bringing false mercy ("grasce vainne," l. 3027) in his sleep. This version of metamorphosis – of the beloved into an object to be possessed – is clearly dissatisfactory. The lover's frustration stands in marked contrast to the sentiment of Froissart's earlier *Le Paradis d'Amour* (*c.*1361–2), which takes place almost entirely inside the dream of a suffering lover, ending with the dreamer's praise of Morpheus for having comforted him in sleep.[72] Froissart seems to have traveled a path in which the notion of consolation through dreams or the imagination becomes increasingly hard to sustain; he appears in the end to demand that dreaming consolation have an effect in reality, or at least to acknowledge that dreaming pleasure does not compensate for waking sorrow. Rather than a representation of an uncomplicated source of consoling pleasures, the dream becomes a vehicle for exploring the possibilities and limitations of poetic metamorphosis and empathy for addressing loss.

This exploration reaches its climax in Froissart's *Prison Amoureuse* (*c.*1372–3).[73] In addition to a Machauldian exercise in dramatizing the material modes of poetic production, this poem might be seen as a meditation on the Ovidian poetics of desire present in Froissart's previous poems, bringing to bear an Aristotelian psychology in his descriptions of lovesickness. In the *Prison Amoureuse*, one finds an encounter with Ovidian mythology that presents an exploration of the problems inherent in love and creativity, carried out in the clerkly language of ethics. Froissart is concerned here not only with love as an ethical activity, but with love as an emotion that allows or impedes ethical thought and action. In this narrative of poetic exchange between a poet "Flos" and his patron "Rose," Froissart rewrites the Pygmalion myth along with the myth of Pyramus and Thisbe as the tale of Pynoteüs and Neptisphelé.[74] The narrator describes this pseudo-Ovidian tale as more "amoureuse" and "belle" (l. 1310) than any other material. His hero Pynoteüs is notably more clerkly than chivalrous, having been "de lettre fu moult bien duis" (well instructed in letters, l. 1319), having studied the seven liberal arts, and being expert in "l'escripture" (writing, l. 1321). He falls in love with Neptisphelé and with her enters a golden age garden in which they have no use for such things as bowls and cups. After they have carried on this innocent, Edenic love affair for "moult lontainne saison" (quite a long time, l. 1380), Neptisphelé is devoured by a fierce lion. Pynoteüs' loss renders him melancholy and lovesick, as one might expect, but it also specifically leaves him unable to make ethical decisions. He dwells on the contrast between his former self, a counselor and diplomat, and his present inability to counsel even himself; he fears the mockery of those who would see that the wise poet "qui savoit, sans lui marir, / Autrui consellier et garir, / Ne s'est sceüs garir lui mismes" (who infallibly knew what / To advise or how to cure everyone else / Didn't know how to solve his own problems, ll. 1662–4). He is lost, unable to counsel himself or others, or to protect or save ("garir," l. 1664) himself. Although once without suffering ("grever," l. 1670) he could tell right from wrong ("le bien et le mal dessevrer," l. 1671), now he has no way of discerning between the two. Pynoteüs' suffering and his loss in love are repeatedly redescribed as suffering that proceeds from a loss of ethical knowledge.

In the redescribing of grief in love as an injured ethical sense, we can see the intersection of Aristotelian psychology and ethics with medicine emerging in the context of vernacular love poetry. Mary Wack has illustrated that the medical discourse of lovesickness, disseminated largely via commentaries on the *Viaticum* of Constantine the African, was self-consciously philosophical and influenced depictions of love in a wide range of literary texts.[75] Wack notes that glosses such as those written by Gerard of Berry in the late twelfth century already reveal intersections between clerical university culture and vernacular literature.[76] Medicine was as influenced by Aristotle as other disciplines, and thirteenth-century commentaries on the *Viaticum* used the terms of Aristotelian and Avicennan faculty psychology to discuss the malady of *amor hereos*, which was located by both Gerard and Peter of Spain (d. 1277) in the *virtus estimativa*. The imagination's fixation on a single object leads the estimative faculty to overvalue it, judging it to be better, nobler, and more desirable than any other object.[77] Peter elaborates that while non-pathological love is seated in the heart, *amor hereos* affects the brain, as it is a melancholic fixation that consists in a disordered imagination that disturbs self-control and governance.[78] Thus lovesickness in both medical literature and poetry could signify the ramifications of passion in ethical as well as physical terms. For Pynoteüs, love itself is not pathologized, but rather the state of grief he inhabits after the loss of his love object. Being in love is associated with right judgment and ethical counsel of oneself and others, being able to tell "le bien" from "le mal." The cure for lovesickness, in the case of Pynoteüs, turns out to be a desire for knowledge and creative activity.

The bereaved lover finally decides that he will create what is essentially a new Galatea, though he will pray to Phoebus rather than Venus, emphasizing the connections between love and knowledge over love and desire. Furthermore, his recreation of Neptisphelé with earth is art inspired by love rather than Pygmalion's art that inspires love.[79] This Pygmalion figure is not out to prove his great skill, as in the *Rose*, but in the tradition of Orpheus is seeking to remedy his lost love. Pynoteüs is in some ways a manifestation of the refusal to sublimate desire through art; he consciously recognizes that art is the imperfect solution to temporal loss. Imperfect, because he does not expect his new Neptisphelé to actually *be* the same as the person he lost. And yet in this refusal he finds his solution: if art is to repair loss it must be conceived in ethical terms. Thus in praying for her to be granted the spark of life, Pynoteüs strikingly addresses Phoebus rather than Venus. His prayer, before which he "Une foelle de lorier prit / Et ou rai dou solel le serre" (took a leaf from the laurel tree / And holds it up to the sun's rays, ll. 1739–40), emphasizes through a reference to the laurel crown of poets that his prayer is directed through poetry to Phoebus Apollo, god of poetry and knowledge as well as the sun. His use of the laurel leaf as a totem in prayer sheds some light on this choice. The lover of the *Espinette* who desired outrageously that his beloved be turned, like Daphne, into a laurel so that he might keep her in sight, is in some way atoned for by this lover who wishes that Phoebus would kindle that same leaf so that his inanimate creation might breathe. The "real" loss through death that Pynoteüs suffers appears to clarify the fact that love is not satisfied through possession alone. Pynoteüs first doubts that this maiden can be the same Neptisphelé, for he has just shaped her with his own hands ("mes mains"); he even wonders if the entire interlude of death and loss was a dream. The poem forces Pynoteüs to realize that he will never be sure that his experience of his beloved is not mediated by – or even fully created by – his own shaping, but he nevertheless commits himself to seeing this love through.[80] The maiden "wakes" from her slumber, desiring to see her friends and family, and Pynoteüs himself.[81] The narrator experiences the initial loss of his Lady as an ethical crisis, solved only by creation in the service of a love that recognizes the other as a subject in a web of social relations. Here it is the dream that is the space of loss and sorrow, and "reality" that is a space of consolation and happiness. Yet what the "dream" of loss seems to illustrate is that love allows for ethical decisions and actions, and loss brings on an ethical malaise; art can repair this loss, but it should be in the service of love, knowledge, and ethics. The true *amor hereos*, for Froissart, is the disturbance of the ethical faculties that idealization/reification and loss both engender. As a lover and a poet/artist, Pynoteüs asks for knowledge to be able to love properly; love is both Edenic – natural and simple – and the product of study and intellect.

The subsequent playful double-glossing of this narrative by the narrator, Flos, and its generation of allegorical dreams for his interlocutor, Rose, points to the way that this invented myth guides much of the rest of the poem and also exceeds any single attempt to interpret its meaning. Rose dreams an allegorical social landscape in which Justice, Pity, and Reason are left weeping – a seemingly pointed commentary on current events.[82] Those same virtues, along with Prudence, Moderation, and Knowledge, crop up at the end of the poem in Flos' final gloss on the Phaeton tale (part of Pynoteüs' prayer): Phaeton, incarnation of wild Desire, fails to live up to the model of rational Love represented by his father Apollo. One might be tempted to think about the whole of the *Prison Amoureuse*, with its context in consolation of the poet's imprisoned patron, as an exploration and a gesture of rational love – the possibility of a love that would not disturb the mind's judgment, but enhance it. Such a love is not subordinate to creativity, but rather inspires and guides it, allowing objects of love to be reanimated. The loving couple turns outward, as does the revivified Neptisphelé, to friends and family, and society in general. In Froissart's examination of his debts to Machaut and the trajectory of his own corpus of love narratives, the ethical stakes of love and love poetry are finally shown not to be concerned with the impossible pleasure of absolute possession, but with mutual consideration of desire in the face of contingency. For Froissart – and for Chaucer, as we will see below – the problem of identity or distinction between love and pleasure is manifested as a revision of philosophical ideas about lovesickness. Absent or selfish love creates psychological disturbances that inhibit proper judgment and counsel, while a full understanding of love and pleasure allows for a sound mind and body – the proper functioning of the *virtus estimativa*, and a seemingly paradoxical experience of rational passionate love.

THE ETHICS OF "ALIKENESS" IN CHAUCER'S *THE BOOK OF THE DUCHESS*

Reading Froissart's 1372 poem alongside Chaucer's *Book of the Duchess*, composed sometime between 1368 and 1370, reinforces one's sense that these poems are both engaged in a self-consciously ethical response to the tradition of the *Rose* and the fourteenth-century amorous dream vision. In many respects, the poem orients its narrative as a direct descendant of the poetry of Machaut and Froissart.[83] The poem opens with a portrayal of melancholy and sleeplessness, a first-person account of sorrowful unrest that is also a loose translation of the opening lines of Froissart's *Paradis d'Amour*. In allying his narrator's sleeplessness with the insomnia of Froissart's poem, Chaucer raises the specter that insomnia is not simply a physical malady, but an obstacle toward entering a state of consolation and ethical exploration. As we have seen, sleep is not simply a physical necessity in the French dream vision, but a state conducive or necessary to exploring possible reparations for waking discontents. Insomnia – the refusal to embody others and represent their sorrows and joys – is fully realized in Chaucer's poem as a disease akin to lovesickness with devastating ethical consequences. In *The Book of the Duchess* we see the full flowering of Froissart's later version of *amor hereos* in the *Prison Amoureuse* – what one might call "ethical lovesickness": the deadening of the ethical senses brought on by loss. In Chaucer's transformation of Froissart's earlier poem, lovesickness becomes an intentionally indeterminate malaise. His narrator begins:

I have gret wonder, be this lyght,
How that I lyve, for day ne nyght
I may not slepe wel nygh noght;
I have so many an ydel thoght
Purely for defaute of slep
That, by my trouthe, I take no kep
Of nothing, how hyt cometh or gooth,
Ne me nys nothyng leef nor looth.
Al is ylyche good to me –
Joye or sorowe, wherso hyt be ...[84] (ll. 1–10)

While Froissart's narrator quickly offers his reader a reason for his suffering in the tenth line of his poem – his memory of the beautiful woman whom he loves – Chaucer's narrator never satisfies us with the cause of his sickness, instead offering himself as the victim of a generalized ethical apathy.[85] And where Froissart's speaker is a markedly active lovesick subject – he and his thoughts are constantly in a process of laboring/suffering (*travellier*), and his general state is one of painful effort (*travel*) – in Chaucer's poem, thoughts are idle. Although his narrator claims to "be in sorowe" (l. 21), his overriding problem is the incapacity to distinguish between joy and sorrow – all emotions are "alike" to the narrator (ll. 9–10). His sickness is thus manifested as an inability to participate in ethical reasoning, to discriminate between bad and good, joy and sorrow, and to know thereby "what is best to doo" (l. 29). *The Book of the Duchess* diagnoses the ethical anesthesia of the melancholic, a malady that will be addressed through an exploration of various kinds of indistinction between joy and sorrow. Throughout the poem, pain and pleasure coincide, first in a kind of lovesickness, then in an immature subjectivity that has yet to experience love, and finally in the heights of mutual romantic love.

The identity of pain and pleasure as a pathology speaks both to moral philosophical questions about the motivations of desire (Chaucer's narrator is neither "leef nor looth") and medical questions about the way love can become a physical and spiritual malady. Constantine's *Viaticum* defined eros as an extreme form of pleasure ("eros delectationis quedam est extremitas"), in opposition to loyalty, which is an extreme form of love ("dilectionis ultimitas").[86] Aristotle's *Ethics* speaks to the potential incompatibility of the experience of passionate pleasure and prudence, for "while it [sexual pleasure] is being experienced no one is capable of turning his mind to anything."[87] Aquinas glosses further that "no one is capable of exercising the act of understanding at the time of the act of pleasure."[88] The heights of erotic pleasure are understood to interfere with cognitive reasoning, and yet Aristotle's *Politics* claims that the response to pleasure is part of what fundamentally makes human beings rational and political animals. Aristotle explains the nature of man as a "political animal" by rooting the difference between human and animal in the interpretation and communication of pain and pleasure. While all animals make sounds that signify experiences of pain and pleasure to each other, human speech alone communicates the transformation of that experience into moral judgment. Aristotle explains that human beings are more suited to "political" associations than bees and other animals because although all animals use signs to express sadness and pleasure, human speech

> serves to make clear what is beneficial and what is harmful, and so also what is just and what is unjust. For by contrast with the other animals man has this peculiarity: he alone has sense of good and evil, just and unjust, etc. An association in these matters makes a household and a state.[89]

Having lost his fundamental discernment between joy and sorrow, the narrator of *The Book of the Duchess* cannot communicate properly with others at a basic, animal level, let alone at the human level that transforms sensory experience into a moral understanding of good and evil, and that allows for the formation of relationships and communities.

In response to this state of affairs, the poem charts a movement from aesthetic and thus ethical apathy to an understanding of the sovereign good, moving from an "alikeness" marked by undifferentiated emotions and actions to an "alikeness" born of love and the good itself. Chaucer's narrator, driven almost mad by grief and lack of sleep, experiences an insomnia that, in the context of medical, philosophical, and amorous discourse, is not simply a physical malady but a bar to the ethical exploration of love. The political implications of the narrator's numbness come to the fore in a dream sequence in which he is unable or unwilling to connect a mourning knight's song with the knight's affect. The re-establishment of human community and communication via the interpretation of painful and pleasurable love experiences guides the trajectory of the dream vision.

Chaucer's poem – likely written to commemorate the death of John of Gaunt's wife Blanche[90] – has inspired ongoing critical debate about the consolation that the poem affords diegetically to the Black Knight, and extra-diegetically to John of Gaunt,[91] yet the narrator is the only character within the fiction of the poem who could truly be consoled.[92] A possible cure for the narrator's malady is explored through his empathetic stance to the Black Knight's tale in his dream – an "alikeness" born of a full relationship to "the good" and to another person.[93] Several different forms of "alikeness" emerge in relation to the poem's notion of "the good." The Black Knight suffered his own idle "alikeness" in his youth, a malady that could be cured through composing lyrics:

> For that tyme Yowthe, my maistresse,
> Governed me in ydelnesse;
> For hyt was in my firste youthe,
> And thoo ful lytel good y couthe,
> For al my werkes were flyttynge
> That tyme, and al my thoght varyinge.
> Al were to me ylyche good
> That I knew thoo; but thus it stood. (ll. 797–804)

In his youth, the knight "couthe" little good – he did not know the good and had no mastery of the good as a skill.[94] Like the narrator at the start of the poem, the idle, restless thoughts of the knight thwart his capacity for fruitful work, and render all objects "ylyche good." According to the knight's narrative, his ethical apathy is immediately broken when he chances to see the object of his love – he is inspired with the thought that it "were beter serve hir for noght / Than with another to be wel" (ll. 844–5). Like Pynoteüs, the Black Knight's service is more than a conventional instantiation of the chivalric ethos, but carries the weight of a variety of ethical discourses – chivalric, courtly, medical, and philosophical. The nobility of his love resides in its desirability for its own sake, for no pleasure or reward. In telling the narrator about his efforts to properly worship his lady, he reveals that "for to kepe me fro ydelnesse, / Trewly I dide my besynesse / To make songes, as I best koude" (ll. 1155–7). The knight thus writes lyrics as best he knows how, his skill in composing and singing remedying his earlier lack of skill in "the good." In serving his lady, he strives to act without pretence, without "slouthe" (l. 1100), and in proper labor. It is this lady, White, whom the knight has described in his first lyric as not only fair, fresh, and "fre," but "So good that men may wel se / Of al goodnesse she had no mete" (ll. 485–6). He describes her superlative qualities in a lengthy blazon – the "alderfayreste" (l. 1050) and "chef myrour of al the feste" (l. 974). If the knight chiastically embodies and encompasses sorrow – "y am sorwe, and sorwe ys y" (l. 597) – then White seems to embody the sum of all goods. Thus while the knight has the good in his sights he is able to labor fruitfully, but since its loss, the very distinction between idleness and labor has collapsed: "In travayle is myn ydelnesse / And eke my reste" (ll. 602–3).[95] The knight's equation of idleness, labor, and rest is part of a complete transformation of all goods into their opposites. He laments, "my wele is woo, / My good ys harm" (ll. 603–4).[96] The transformation of his fortunes seems to have endowed him with the narrator's lovesickness: unable to distinguish between good and bad, all is "ylyche" to him.

An ethically positive version of alikeness is introduced through the now familiar figure of Morpheus and the tale of Ceyx and Alcyone, the tale of mourning love that the narrator reads before falling asleep. The narrative of Alcyone's realization of the death of her lost husband – a message brought to her in Chaucer's version by Morpheus inhabiting Ceyx's corpse – sends the narrator himself off to sleep, and to dream of a similarly bereft figure. The mournful cry, "To lytel while oure blysse lasteth!" (l. 211), spoken by this dead but supernaturally animated King Ceyx to his grief-stricken wife, functions as the poem's first linking of joy and romantic love, of bliss with earthly happiness. The tale of the mournful Alcyone both consoles the narrator and leaves him more sorrowful than before – he claims both that it saved his life and that it gave him "such pittee and such rowthe / To rede hir sorwe that, by my trowthe, / I ferde the worse al the morwe / Aftir to thenken on hir sorwe" (ll. 97–100). The tale itself prepares him for his own dreaming invention which will help resolve his ethical dilemma, as his "pittee" and "rowthe" foreshadow the "routhe" (l. 1310) he will feel for the loss of the Black Knight.[97] As in Machaut, there is comedy in the narrator's mobile empathy and his lighting upon the "use factor" of a tale that inspires him to pray to the newfound god of sleep, Morpheus, for a cure for his insomnia. The narrator's emphasis on the Morpheus figure is both comically utilitarian and seriously invested in the fantasy of Morpheus' power both to give voice to the dead and to offer poetic models of metamorphic compassion. The Black Knight's tale of the loss of his great love parallels and expands upon the brief tale of Alcyone's woe, and the "routhe" to which it moves the narrator is even more profoundly healing. The doubling of the narrator as the dreamer of the tale and a sympathetic dream-listener reinforces the link between reading/listening and creating, as well as the link between compassion and poetic productivity. As the narrator moves from "reading" to "thinking" in the lines quoted above, he models a mode of literary reception for Chaucer's own narrative of sorrow.

This particular version of Ovid's tale does the important work of linking dreams with narrative as well as with a reality obscured by daylight and revealed through the animation of dead, mourned objects. Chaucer significantly alters several features of Ovid's tale, but one of the most striking is his description of Morpheus appearing not in the image of Ceyx, but in his actual corpse. Rather than having Alcyone reunite with Ceyx's body at the seaside, as in Ovid, Chaucer locates this physical reunion in her dream, emphasizing the dreamscape and imagination as a place of reality, embodiment and physical communication. It is Ceyx's animated body that allows Alcyone, and thus the dreaming narrator, to hear a particular truth that might console or kill – the king's lament that life's bliss is too short. There is no question in Ceyx's speech that bliss is located on earth, though one's response to this bliss is left open. In Ovid's tale, the brevity of this bliss is repaired in the metamorphosis of the two lovers into seabirds, but, as many commentators have remarked, Chaucer leaves out the metamorphosis in his tale of Ceyx and Alcyone – a typically Chaucerian move that leaves us with a tragic narrative devoid of comforting transformation or the metamorphosis that allows moralization in the *Ovide Moralisé*. Without the seemingly deathless seabirds, we are left only with a choice of how to respond to imperfect, brief, contingent earthly bliss. And without this final metamorphosis, we are left only with Morpheus as a model for the poetic ability to speak as another and to offer a perspective on love and life that would otherwise be unavailable.

Yet it seems that Chaucer may not have entirely ignored the moralized version of Ovid's story.[98] The French text tells us that the tragic nature of the love story is inevitable, given the protagonists' attachments to earthly loves and pleasures. We should learn from the tale that all earthly love, no matter how true or passionate, is doomed to loss at the hands of fortune. For the author of the *Moralisé*, the Ovidian tale is another version of the familiar tale of the vulnerable human as a ship in the sea of mortal life ("la troubleuse mer dou monde").[99] Earthly, secular life ("li siecle") is full of pain and sadness, and to covet the little joy available is to commit the sin of "veine gloire." We must learn to cast off earthly delight for the blessedness of heavenly "clarté." While these admonitions do not inspire Chaucer to moralize Ovid's tale, nor to make a similar moral clear in his own tale of tragic romantic love to follow, I would argue that they do inform Ceyx's cry that "To lytel while oure blysse lasteth."[100] This statement is an end in itself, a realization that is not followed by a recommendation of pursuit of a more lasting bliss. Instead, Chaucer's poem focuses on the best way to pursue and experience this earthly happiness, given that it is so fleeting, so rare, and so often ends in pain.

This refusal of transcendence may further account for the changes Chaucer makes to Ovid's narrative. As with Froissart's *L'Espinette Amoureuse* and *La Prison Amoureuse*, dreams are a place where loss is experienced and recognized rather than a place of escape and consolation. Chaucer's Alcyone simply dies of grief three days after her dream. In order to dramatize the narrator's movement from numb despair at the vagaries of fortune to a productive empathy and narrativity, Alcyone serves as a useful foil.[101] Chaucer telescopes all of the meaningful action of Ovid's tale so that it occurs within Alcyone's dream vision. She grieves, realizes Ceyx's death, reunites with Ceyx's body, and recognizes the brevity of earthly bliss all in a single unified state. Her choice to respond to Ceyx's command to "let be her sorrowful life" by dying rather than giving up her sorrow is the interpretive choice – an ethical and existential choice – that she makes after having this dream. Chaucer's narrator will dream again and interpret otherwise.

Perhaps the most important aspect of the tale told in the *Ovide Moralisé*, also conspicuous for its absence, is the desire on Alcyone's part for shared experience and emotion with Ceyx. In both Machaut's and Chaucer's version of the tale of Ceyx and Alcyone, Alcyone's long speech asking Ceyx not to go alone over the sea is excised. The version of the speech in the *Ovide Moralisé* is thrice the length of the speech in Ovid's poem – a result not solely of translation from Latin to vernacular, but of dilation and repetition in Alcyone's pleas and questions. Alcyone cautions Ceyx about the power of the ocean and its winds, but ends her speech with an appeal that he take her with him, for above all she wishes that they share whatever good or bad fortune might bring:

> Faite un poi de mes aviaux
> Si m'en menez o vous, seviaux,
> Si verrai lors que vous ferez
> Et savrai de ce que arez
> Bien ou mal, que que vous avaigne
> Comme parçonniere et compaigne
> De tout ce que vous avendra:
> Ensi si ne me convendra
> Douter, fors tant que je verrai
> Que je meïsmes soufferai,
> Si serons compaignon et per
> Ou de noier ou d'eschaper.
> Ensamble irons par mer nagant. (XI.3084–96)

(Undertake a portion of my desires; if you lead me with you, at least I will see how you are and will know in what way you come to good or ill; I will see whatever happens to you as a partner and companion of all that befalls you: Thus it will not be fitting for me to fear, as long as I will see that I will suffer in the same way. Then we will be companions and equal whether we are killed or we escape. Together we will navigate the sea.)

Alcyone repeats her desire that they be together and, if they must suffer, at least suffer the same events. Ceyx, of course, rejects both her requests: he cannot give up his voyage, and he cannot put his wife at risk. Her wish to accompany her husband on his travels is not simply the desperation of a pessimistic wife, but an ethical stance about what it means to be in love. Her version of love and happiness is not one of unmitigated possession and pleasure, but rather a shared joy and sorrow with one's beloved, experiencing the good and ill of fortune together. This love that admits the contingency of pleasure, encompassing the possibilities of both joy and sorrow, would not, in the end, be alien to the noble beatific love theorized by Ockham.

Although neither Machaut nor Chaucer represent Alcyone's plea, her desire for togetherness and shared suffering re-emerges in *The Book of the Duchess* first in the terrible, numbing "alikeness" that the narrator suffers as a result of his insomnia, and later, transformed into the "alikeness" shared by the Black Knight and his beloved White. The Black Knight's idle youth, as well as his idle grief-filled solitude, biographically bookend an experience of joy and love that is placed at the very end of his narrative. In his description of his requited love for White, the "alikeness" that is the keynote of his ethical apathy is transformed into the condition of highest joy. The poem reaches its climax when the knight describes his lady's gift of her mercy and her ring as rendering him "Of al happes the alderbeste, / The gladdest, and the moste at reste" (ll. 1279–80). In this, the conclusion of the knight's tale, he claims that in being taken into his lady's governance

> Our joye was ever ylyche newe
> Oure hertes wern so evene a payre
> That never nas that oon contrayre
> To that other for no woo.
> For sothe, ylyche they suffred thoo
> Oo blysse and eke oo sorwe bothe;
> Ylyche they were bothe glad and wrothe;
> Al was us oon, withoute were.
> And thus we lyved ful many a yere
> So wel I kan nat telle how. (ll. 1288–97)

This joy is notably a joy that encompasses pleasure and sorrow, happiness and anger – it is the shared status of these emotions that makes them equally joyous. The language of suffering one bliss and one sorrow calls to mind Alcyone's desire that she suffer the same "bien ou mal" as her husband. The compatibility between joy and sorrow recalls not only the long tradition of love's paradoxes, but also ethical concerns about what constitutes earthly happiness, and what the relationship might be between love, pleasure, and pain.[102] The coexistence of enjoyment and pain that Chaucer explores is not the pain inflicted by a capricious God, acting willfully outside the bounds of his *potentia ordinata*, but rather the love of an object that is not love in exchange for pleasure.

Thus the knight's maturation from callow youth to fulfilled lover is a passage toward a particular understanding and experience of the good, one that is rooted in an "alikeness" of will, whether that will encounters joy or sorrow. It is a passage that the narrator must travel as well, one that he halts at this specific point, for the lines quoted above are the last words the knight speaks before the narrator's question "where is she now?" (l. 1298) breaks him out of his reverie. At this point the knight reveals that White is dead, to which the narrator can only reply, "Is that youre los? Be God, hyt ys routhe!" (l. 1310). "And with that word" the hart-hunting is finished, all return home, and the narrator wakens with Ovid's book in his hand. Upon waking he marvels at his strange dream and commits to writing it down "be processe of tyme" (l. 1331). Peter Travis persuasively contends that the abruptness of this ending deliberately creates a sense of discomfort and incompleteness, a way for the narrator to conclude his "talking cure" by assimilating his own lack.[103] I would argue further that the rapid conclusion serves to focus the succession of narration, sympathy, waking, and writing, thus encouraging the reader to consider the efficacy of consolation and its relationship to poetry.

In waking with the book "of Alcione and Seys the kyng" (l. 1327) in his hand, the narrator asks his audience to consider how the book they have just heard or read will change their dreams and thoughts. And he returns to the question of what Alcyone and Ceyx have to do with the poem's Black Knight, White, and dreaming narrator himself. Morpheus sends the narrator to sleep to remedy an unspecified illness, and he encounters a figure mourning for a love relationship that embodies the empathetic, ethical opposite of the numbing "alikeness" between joy and sorrow from which he and the narrator now both suffer. The tale of Ceyx and Alcyone reveals that fortune both demands an enjoyment that encompasses joy and sorrow and guarantees that this enjoyment will have an end. We might understand the mourning knight as an incarnation of an Alcyone who was granted her wish for a fully companionate existence, but who nevertheless does not escape the fact that one cannot "navigate the seas" of death with another person, no matter one's commitment to courage in shared destinies. Morpheus, god of sleep and human metamorphosis, allows the narrator to experience the slow comprehension of another person's "alikeness" through that person's narrative; the ending of the poem reinforces Machaut's insight that another name for shape-shifting sleep is poetry.[104]

Ceyx's impossible narration of his own death begets a meditation on his insight that our bliss on earth is but too brief. By exchanging the metamorphosis of the two lovers for the metamorphosis of Morpheus as he animates Ceyx's body, the poem chooses the corporeal and contingent, yet nevertheless seeks a comprehensive perspective. Where in Jean's *Rose* we cannot help but love and enjoy because we are creative beings, for Machaut, Froissart, and Chaucer we cannot help but create because we are loving beings. Art is at the service of love, and this love is sought not for pleasure, nor for the promise of pleasure, but for the "pure expenditure" of enjoyment alone, preserving the nobility of *fruitio* in much the same terms as Ockham – love is still love without pleasure. In *The Book of the Duchess,* pleasure and pain are the basis of shared experience that can be interpreted by a political community that makes judgments regarding whether such pleasure should be "leef [or] looth." Lovesickness is not evidence that passion inhibits rational thinking, but a spur to imagining possibilities for rational love. Love comes first for the fourteenth century, a period grappling with ways to preserve the intelligibility and integrity of love while dissecting its very components. What philosophers from Ockham to Buridan demonstrate is that any attempt to define love in simultaneously Aristotelian and Christian terms will inevitably bring about a crisis of motivation and a disjunction within the very experience of enjoyment – up to now assumed to be a seamless experience of love and pleasure. In the space between the integrity and coherence of the loving subject and the integrity and coherence of the love experience – two poles now seemingly at odds – the poets imagine subjects who acknowledge that the impossibility of possession and the contingency of happiness change our very understanding of love and pleasure. The experiences of alikeness – of two lovers, of narrator and interlocutor, of poet and reader, of bliss and sorrow – offered by this poetry provide moments where pleasure is inextricably bound up with shared experience and a shared moral sense of the world. In these cases, choosing pleasure for the sake of life or life for the sake of pleasure would indeed appear to be one and the same.

CHAPTER 4

Love's knowledge: fabliau, allegory, and fourteenth-century anti-intellectualism

Historians have traditionally credited the 1277 condemnations of "radically Aristotelian" theses with marking a shift in focus in scholastic philosophy at the close of the thirteenth century.[1] Aristotle's emphasis on contemplation as the highest kind of happiness allowed for occasionally dangerous-seeming claims about the role of the intellect as a privileged faculty of the soul, or the superiority of the life of the philosopher. In the wake of controversies surrounding the "intellectualist" understanding of happiness, theologians debated the emphasis on reason, teleology, and rational pleasure along with the relative roles of the will and the intellect as seats of enjoyment. John Duns Scotus, William Ockham, and other late thirteenth- and early fourteenth-century philosophers made reason the handmaiden of the will, questioned Aristotelian teleology, and continued debates about the nature of enjoyment as the highest good. While there is thus a true "anti-intellectualist" strain in the narrow sense of the intellect as a mental faculty, however, the period is not at all anti-philosophical or anti-Aristotelian. And "independent thinkers" such as Godfrey of Fontaines maintained an opposition to the condemnations of 1277, arguing for the superiority of the intellect over the will.[2] Any resistance to overemphasis on the intellectual faculty may be described more justly as a critique of radical medieval Aristotelians rather than a critique of Aristotle himself.[3]

A theologian directly affected by the condemnations – denied his *licentia docendi* because of controversial claims in his commentary on the *Sentences* – Giles of Rome went on directly to produce one of the most influential works of political Aristotelianism, his *De Regimine Principum* (*c.*1277–80). Matthew Kempshall observes that while Giles is careful to restrict himself to a discussion of political happiness in his commentary on Aristotle's *Rhetoric*, he directly addresses contemplative happiness in the *De Regimine*, recommending that a king should have both an active and a contemplative life, so that he might rule his subjects by means of the active life, and rule himself by contemplation, devotion, and love of God.[4] Giles nevertheless offers a modest critique of those who would locate true happiness solely in contemplation. Book I, Part I begins by defining felicity, citing it as the "end" of all action. Yet he judiciously criticizes those who have said that speculation is enough for true perfect felicity, for "they placed contemplative life in pure speculation, which is false, for one is never perfected in such a life, unless he has in him love of God and charity."[5]

Thus the basic equation between philosophical contemplation and happiness continued to be controversial – and in vernacular "literary" texts as well as in politics and theology. Questions about the unique claims of the intellect may be found not only in scholastic discourse, but in secular literature, with its often comical distrust of stargazing clerks. This intellectual comedy may be read not simply as lay resistance to the claims to special knowledge made by university types – though such resistance is certainly present – but as an investigation of the claims of the intellectual faculty itself – intellectualism in this narrow sense. Vernacular poetry has its own questions to ask about the relationship between the intellect, the will, and the individual or common good. Thus just as poetry and philosophy shared a discourse of loving pursuit of ethical and erotic ideals, so too did they share a vocabulary for investigating the dangers of overreaching intellectualism and the multiplying mirrors of truth, love, and narcissism.

The perils of an intellectual pursuit that might become a "passion" became a common topos in a variety of medieval genres, and one telling way of mapping shifting attitudes toward contemplation is available through the medieval variants of the oft-told tale of Thales. In most versions, the tale relates the fate of a philosopher who kept his mind so focused on the pursuit of truth that he walked unnoticing into a well. In Plato's *Theaetetus*, Thales serves as an example of a man who successfully disregards his body and the material world so that he may pursue the task of contemplation without distraction. Socrates presents Thales as an admirable figure – comical to the servant girl who laughs at his misfortune, but, to the intellectually inclined audience, the philosophical ideal.[6] In its medieval context – a context where such an ideal comes under critique from Christian, courtly, and popular perspectives – the tale becomes exceedingly flexible, available in myriad versions. Thales and his philosophical brethren may indeed signify the contemplative ideal, or may demonstrate the unreliability of all sensory experience, the vulnerability of the male will to female seduction, the dangers of excessive intellectual curiosity, or the vulnerability of the intellect to the intrusions of the material world. The tale appears to have offered its medieval audience a context for investigating the nature of the intellect itself and the limits – both earthly and divine – that human reason encounters.

Later versions of the tale do not always include the laughing servant girl; in Aesop's earlier, but quite similar, fable of an unnamed astronomer, the hapless man is scolded by an anonymous passer-by.[7] Yet the girl – occasionally transformed into an old woman, as in Christine de Pizan's *L'Avision Christine* – often functions as a feminine, physical intrusion into the rarified world of the philosopher.[8] The laughing, admonishing woman stands for physicality, the material world, and the body in all its comedy and demands. In an early modern version of the tale, in Michel de Montaigne's *Apology for Raymond Sebond*, there are additional details that reinforce the connection between femininity, the material world, and sexuality. In Montaigne's version, Thales stumbles over a stone deliberately placed near the well by the girl. No longer an innocent, if gossipy, witness, the girl is now the agent of Thales' fall, having attempted to teach him a lesson about the importance of observing the world around him before looking at the stars. Montaigne claims to

> gladly acknowledge the Milesian girl, who, seeing the philosopher Thales constantly amusing himself in the contemplation of the celestial vault and always keeping his eyes upward, put in his way something to make him stumble to show him that it would be time to amuse himself with things in the clouds when he had provided for those at his feet.[9]

Distancing himself from the perspective of the girl, Montaigne uses this anecdote to make a point about such seemingly transparent observation: we have no easier access to the observed world close at hand than we do to the stars or more remote truths.[10]

The tale of the stargazing Thales is told in a variety of manners in medieval literature, and by no means do they indicate an increasingly homogeneous attitude of skepticism. In Chaucer's "Miller's Tale," the tale is alluded to by the carpenter, John, who laments that the scholar Nicholas – feigning catatonia – has lost his wits by paying too much attention to the stars. He cries that

> Men sholde nat knowe of Goddes pryvetee.
> Ye, blessed be alwey a lewed man
> That noght but oonly his bileve kan!
> So ferde another clerk with astromye;
> He walked in the feeldes for to prye

> Upon the sterres, what ther sholde bifalle,
> Til he was in a marle-pit yfalle;
> He saugh nat that. (ll. 3454–61)

John's brief parable points to the virtues of the simple man of faith over the prying attempts of the clerks to understand divine mysteries. Yet the Miller, in his Prologue, has already set up the parallel between "Goddes pryvetee," the secrets of God's mysteries, and the "pryvetee" of a man's wife – signifying both her genitalia and the mystery of the way she parcels out the gifts of her body and love.[11] The tale's irony here lies in the fact that while John believes that Nicholas has been injured through his attempted violation of God's secrets, it is John himself who will be injured – indeed will fall – because of his participation in Nicholas' scheme to outwit the supposedly impending flood. Nicholas will also be wounded – not for prying into God's secrets, but in the process of carrying out his needlessly elaborate plans for adultery and the humiliation of Absolon. In "The Miller's Tale," "pryvetee" comes to signify the object of an excess of desire – both intellectual and erotic; yet this very excess is what appears to define desire as experienced naturally by humankind. It is Alison alone who seems to escape the trap in which one desires what one cannot have and devalues what has been given.[12]

In "The Miller's Tale," the single-minded philosophical pursuit of truth takes on characteristics of the sexual drive. I would argue that this implication is not so much Chaucer's invention as his revelation of an aspect of the tale of Thales that was always lingering under the surface, the implicit underside of the servant girl's critique: inquiry into the stars is – if not necessarily misdirected sexual energy – energy that should be directed toward concerns in the material world, and the body will inevitably have its desublimating revenge. In considering the discourse of anti-intellectualism as it circulated in sermons and fabliaux, it becomes clear that the stargazing philosopher is understood to tend inevitably toward either a pit in the earth or the pit of desire.[13] These critiques of intellectual pursuit are bound up with a humor rooted in the intractability of the material world and sensuality. Whether that intractability is lamented, as it often is in sermon or advice literature, or comically celebrated, as it is in courtly contexts, it becomes clear that the intellect is not only vulnerable to the passions, but is itself a kind of passion, and that the philosopher hardly merits his position as limit case of man's invulnerability to material concerns or sexual desire – a position we will see that he holds in the imagination of the sermon exemplum. Rather, the philosopher becomes a figure for the inherent susceptibility of the intellect and the intellectual, and for the location of the virtuous person within the world, a dethroning of Aristotle that Aristotle himself might well have predicted.

While the previous chapter explored the way that Aristotelian ethics contributed to a poetic and philosophical engagement with enjoyment that encompasses both joy and sorrow, the current chapter explores the way that Aristotelian definitions of cognitive pleasure contributed to a similar engagement with an enjoyment that encompasses both intellect and will. Below I explore a tradition that seems to diverge from the strand of courtly "play" with clerkly terminology and ideas that this book has focused on thus far; the two texts that are my greatest concern here – Guillaume de Deguileville's *Pèlerinage de Vie Humaine* and William Langland's *Piers Plowman* – are notable for their resistance to intellectualism, and in some instances their outright critique of Aristotelian philosophy. Deguileville identifies himself as a monk and writes a poem interested in the ethical adventures of the human life, while Langland similarly invests his poem with concerns for contemporary politics and transcendent truth. Yet Deguileville, in his first version of the *Vie Humaine*, locates his inspiration in the *Roman de la Rose*, and both poets engage with and transform the *Rose*'s erotic discourse into a larger meditation on human desires. The erotic–intellectual tradition that grew out of the *Rose* thus exceeded its courtly context, influencing poetry that was neither of the court nor of the university, and the nexus of eros and intellect became a site for ethical speculation and exploration in poetry outside the contours of the genres of romance and *dit*.

I argue here that fourteenth-century poetry engaged with the *Rose* as a way of exploring Aristotelian transformations of enjoyment as an ethical and volitional goal. Both Deguileville and Langland write about love as a means to the ethical life while occupying two poles of late medieval critiques of intellectualism: one pole stresses the limits of the intellect in the face of God's wisdom, while the other stresses the vulnerability of intellectual pursuit to the intrusions of sexuality and materiality. In the imagination of vernacular poetry, these two modes of critique persistently serve to place both God's grace and human sexuality outside the purview of Aristotelian philosophy. Aristotelian rationality alienates the Philosopher from both miraculous illumination and earthly eroticism and makes him vulnerable to seduction and critique from both divine and physical perspectives. Yet despite the overt attempts that both Deguileville and Langland make to distance themselves from clerkly pursuits of ontological and ethical knowledge, they nevertheless work in the terms of both Aristotle and the *Rose*. Thus Deguileville critiques Aristotle as not having access to the whole of wisdom, which includes the miraculous and paradoxical truths enabled by the grace of God, yet remains indebted to Aristotle's knowledge about the natural world and human ethics. Langland, on the other hand, is more interested in the way that the intellect is limited by its susceptibility to eros and the material world, and the possibility that intellect, will, and grace might be unified. Both poets explore the ways in which the intellect alone will not tell the abstract human will or embodied pilgrim about God's truths or how to "do well." As we will see below, both scholastic philosophy and poetic allegories were concerned that morality not be made a simply speculative problem; the ability to do well must inhere in subjective desire as well as in accurate judgment of proper action in a particular or general case. And yet, of course, it is this same desire that provides the most intractable ethical challenges to living a good "vie humaine." By making speculative reasoning an act of love – and thus rendering love a rational act – medieval Aristotelian philosophy threatened the centrality of desire as the dramatic site of sin, virtue, and alienation from or enjoyment of God. The erotic mirror of love thus became a site for exploring the renewed battle between the will and the intellect for the heart of human ethical experience.

ARISTOTLE GOES TO COURT

The synthesis of Aristotelian philosophy with Christian love was reflected in the courtly literature of the thirteenth century, though in a much more playful manner. The apparent disconnection between Aristotelian philosophy and understandings of the human will begin to account for Aristotle's association with intellectualism, and thus for the fact that he was transformed into a fabliau character at just about the same time that he was entering the canon of medieval philosophy.[14] While scholastic philosophers were translating and commenting on newly available Aristotelian texts, Aristotle became a figure of fun and a symbol for the power of erotic love, such that he could later be witnessed in a parade of conquered men by the narrator of Gower's *Confessio Amantis*: "Aristotle … Whom that the queene of Grece so / Hath bridled … That he foryat al his logique."[15] This topos of the "mounted Aristotle," bridled by the queen of Greece, was deployed in all manner of contexts, but at least one strand focused on the philosopher as a figure for the dominance of the intellect at the expense of both bodily and spiritual desire, with the seduction and humiliation of Aristotle functioning as revenge for intellectual hubris. At possibly the same time that Guillaume de Lorris was writing his *Roman de la Rose* (*c*.1230), Henri d'Andeli was writing his popular *Lai d'Aristote* (*c*.1200–40), a humorous tale of Aristotle's seduction by the paramour of his student, Alexander.[16] An engagement with philosophical concerns is not surprising in the poetry of Henri, author of four *dits* including the *Bataille des Sept Arts*, and one of the earliest of vernacular Parisian poets. Writing in the milieu of the University of Paris, Henri has been understood to respond to the new dominance of Aristotelianism in a variety of ways.[17] There is clear appeal to both an educated Parisian audience and a non-intellectual audience in a light-hearted story in which the Philosopher himself is shown to disregard his own teachings and to fall victim to the seductions of a beautiful woman; Henri's tale appears to be the first textual version of the widely popular "mounted Aristotle" story.[18] In its various versions, Alexander's lover – scorned because of the advice given by Aristotle – revenges herself by convincing the philosopher to let her ride upon his back. Henri's courtly tale was followed by versions told in Latin sermons, where men tricked by women are made into exempla, and in iconographic depictions of the bridled philosopher in sculpture, tapestry, and manuscript decoration.[19]

In these contexts, images and tales of the seduction of Aristotle were often used to demonstrate the extreme sexual vulnerability of all mankind, made manifest by the fall of the archetype of the wise philosopher, and also used to explore the vulnerability of the intellect itself as it ignores the force of the physical world and human desire. While medieval moralists were drawn to a tale easily interpreted in terms of the dangers of wily women and sexuality in general – so dangerous that even Aristotle is compelled to fall – the poets were equally drawn to dissect the assumptions that allow us to accept that an intellectual should be considered least vulnerable to such compulsion, or that human reason always functions as a check to desire. The pursuits of the intellect are themselves already rendered erotic through the tradition of vernacular love poetry, associated with the world of learning in the wake of Jean de Meun's *Rose*. The "mounted Aristotle" thus offered the medieval reader and viewer a rich topos for an investigation of the inherent connections between philosophy and eros, rather than a simple proof of the universality of masculine weakness and feminine sexual treachery.

A focus on philosophy and eros is manifest in Henri d'Andeli's version of the tale, which emphasizes the seductress' manipulation of the philosopher's narcissism. Aristotle, having advised Alexander to cast off his lover and focus on more pressing matters, arrives at abashed self-knowledge and knowledge about the ways of desire through the clever revenge of the maiden. In the *Lai d'Aristote*, the philosopher falls in love with the beauty of his pupil's paramour, but he is particularly charmed by her evocation of masculine desire as she sings. The first moment of lyric seduction narrated by the poem, as Aristotle gazes at the girl in "li vergers plains de verdure" (the garden full of greenery, l. 285), offers him the spectacle of a beautiful woman voicing the desire of a man gazing upon a beautiful woman:

> C'est la jus desoz l'olive
> Or la voi venir, m'amie!
> La fontaine i sort serie,
> El glaioloi, desoz l'aunoi
> Or la voi, la voi, la voi,
> La bele blonde! a li m'otroi![20] (ll. 303–8)

(There beneath the olive tree, now I see her arrive, my sweetheart. There the fountain flows gently, and the gladioli beneath the alder. Now I see her, I see her, I see her, the beautiful blonde. To her I surrender myself.)

Placed in the traditional *locus amoenus*, this parodic lover gazes not into the fountain beneath the olive tree, but at the lovely "bele blonde." Yet even without the conventional mirror-gazing evoked by the presence of the fountain, the narcissistic structure of the desire awakened in the philosopher is inescapable: he falls in love by being presented with the lyric image of his own desire. Anne Ladd observes that the first two songs, both from a man's point of view, are meant not to express emotion on the part of the speaker, but to create an attitude in the listener, and the trick is spectacularly successful.[21] Aristotle exclaims, "Ha! Diex … quar venist ore / Cist mirëors plus pres de ci! / Si me metroie en sa merci" (Ah, God, [if] this mirror might come closer! I would place myself in her mercy, ll. 326–8). Aristotle has here, much like the troubadour poets or the Lover in the *Rose* of Guillaume de Lorris, fallen prey to an idealized image of his own desire – one might say he has fallen for poetry itself. The mirror of truth now holds an image of the sage in love, and Aristotle is inevitably entranced.

Beyond the courtly pleasure in the performance of the "pucele" and her lyrics, or the comic pleasure of the philosopher saddled by the girl and paraded to the satisfaction of Alexander, the poem offers a variety of ways to interpret the tale; its "moral" is offered and revised several times by the poet.[22] Aristotle himself offers the poem's audience the first lesson, and one that will prove appealing for future moralists: he claims that if his fall surely illustrates the difficulty that the emperor of wisdom has in escaping seduction and shame, so much more then should the youthful and lusty Alexander be wary of such a fate. Such a face-saving moral offered by the shamed Aristotle, just having been "dismounted" by the girl, is all too tempting to dismiss. The narrator voices the possibility of cynicism at Aristotle's moralizing, and gives us a second lesson in Cato's adage that "Turpe est doctori cum culpa redarguit ipsum" (The teacher is a fool when his guilt contradicts his teaching, l. 521). Aristotle's foolishness is compounded here, as we are reminded that he was not simply seduced into acting the fool, but seduced after giving advice against love that he himself could not follow. Finally, at the very conclusion of the *lai*, the narrator, now identified in the third person as "Henri," interprets his tale as an illustration of the power of love: "amors vaint tout et tout vaincra / Tant com cis siecles durera" (love conquers all and all will conquer, as long as time itself endures, ll. 578–9). As love is a universal, natural, inescapable phenomenon, lovers and their beloveds should thus be free from blame. This final conclusion leads Susan Smith to observe that the *Lai d'Aristote* – in contrast to other versions of the legend – works as an "argument in favor of the courtly principle that love is all-powerful and the source of happiness."[23]

The poem thus offers a variety of readings, and several explicit interpretations of what the audience witnesses in the moment that Aristotle "falls" for the "pucele." He may be the universal male subject, his wisdom cast aside in the moment that a beautiful woman appears. He may be the foolish teacher, inevitably fated to engage in behavior opposed to his advice. Or he may be a courtly lover, compelled by Nature and Love to surrender to the love object who appears in the proper place – the garden with a fountain of love. Surely he may be all of these at once – conquered man, fool, and idealized lover – for all of these figures inform the reception of the "fallen Aristotle" myth into the late medieval and early modern period. The strand I will follow here is the strand that associates the compulsions of Nature and Love with Aristotle as an intellectual figure – a combination of the figures of the foolish teacher and the lover. This Aristotle is not simply tricked despite his wisdom, but tricked *because* of his wisdom; he is a figure for the notions that intellectual pursuit cannot work as a prophylaxis against desire, and that intellectual contemplation can in fact leave one vulnerable to the very physical world that one attempts to transcend. Intellectual pursuit is all too easily transformed into erotic pursuit – or revealed to have been originally transformed from erotic desire as these comic narratives reveal the sublimation at work in the discourse and the material circumstances of homosocial philosophical study. The initial partnership of Aristotle and Alexander is eroticized by its association with the tale of seduction that ensues; such a reading is often encouraged by the depiction of the narrative in the visual arts, as the knight–clerk "couple" is shown to be disrupted by the maiden, who creates another visual pairing.[24] Alexander might furthermore be understood to "top" Aristotle via his proxy, the maiden, thus securing his continued access to his own erotic pleasures. This critique combines courtly verities (the power of love) with fabliau sensibilities and medieval Christian discomfort with the idea that one can reach any kind of truth through philosophy alone. As "the Philosopher," Aristotle is an easy target for such critique, though we might acknowledge that the inescapability of fortune and the physical world are truths taught by the sage himself.[25]

It is this wise Aristotle whom we find rehabilitated in Jacques de Vitry's sermon, which along with Henri's lay was the earliest and best known of the versions of the Aristotle legend.[26] In Jacques de Vitry's narrative, Aristotle's face-saving moral – if "the most prudent of all mortals" ("prudentissimum inter omnes mortales") could be held captive, then so much more should his pupil fear for his own seduction – is judged acceptable by Alexander and thus stands as the moral of the sermon itself.[27] With his wise words, the philosopher soothes the king's anger and closes the sermon's narrative. While in Henri's tale the courtly appreciation of the power of love wins out, Jacques' sermon asserts the power of sexual desire as a debilitating, feminizing, humiliating force.[28] Yet this moral does not critique the philosopher's disdain for earthly concerns, but rather uses Aristotle as an example of the wise man who should be *least* vulnerable to physical seduction. In another Latin – and later vernacularized – version of the tale, Aristotle's status as philosopher is much more important. The *Lamentationes* of Matheolus, translated by Jehan le Fèvre (*c.*1371–2), tells this tale of "woman over wisdom" and emphasizes the inversion of grammar, logic, gender, and nature when a woman "rode" Aristotle.[29] The speaker, Matheolus, scornfully asks why "nature, reason, and justice" did not gallop to the philosopher's aid, and finally wonders "What will philosophy say when the great master was tricked by the figure of amphibology?"[30] In this instance, Aristotle does not stand for the weakness of men or humankind in the face of sexual seduction, but for the weakness of philosophy itself in the face of feminine ambiguity, doubleness, and sexuality. Matheolus avers that "practitioners of the liberal arts are in constant and perpetual confusion" because of Aristotle's actions.[31] An Aristotelian commitment to reason, justice, and the virtuous operations of the intellect in no way insulates a man from the madness of passion. Aristotle's fall does not here demonstrate the fallibility of all men, but rather the confusion wrought upon philosophers when sexual desire turns their particular world upside-down, giving the lie to the idea that the cultivated life of reason insulates one from the vagaries of the will. Aristotelian philosophers, who privilege intellectual contemplation as the best ethical life and the route toward truth about things both human and divine, are particularly susceptible to such confusion.

With this very brief survey I do not pretend to have singled out a particularly dominant strand of interpretation of the "mounted Aristotle" topos, but simply wish to point out a possibility that has not garnered much attention in recent criticism. As Smith points out, the topos of the "mounted Aristotle" has no single textual referent, no dominant univocal interpretation, and no stable context across religious, courtly, or philosophical discourse.[32] The Aristotle legend spoke to a variety of interests and anxieties that have been widely acknowledged – the power of women, the power of eros, the fallibility of wise men, and the conflict between secular and clerical values – but it also spoke to a simultaneous fascination with and skepticism about the power of the intellect. As we saw in the *Roman de la Rose*, the erotic mirror and the speculative mirror are linked by a spectrum of loving, narcissistic, and contemplative behavior, and the philosopher's mirror is perhaps less immune to the dangers of desire than one might expect. The intellect as vulnerable to the concupiscent will and, even more markedly, the intellect as itself an aspect of overcharged sexual desire, are pointed concerns of fourteenth-century poetic discourse.

WILL'S PLEASURE

Before turning to the critiques of intellectualism in the allegories of Deguileville and Langland, it will be useful to turn to scholastic concerns about the integrity of intellectual enjoyment. A conflict between intellectualism and voluntarism, as the introduction to this chapter discussed, was a marked feature of fourteenth-century philosophy, meaning that many philosophers wrote about the affective or volitional versus rational aspects of human nature, the active or free character of the will with respect to reason, or the freedom of God's will. Another hallmark of voluntarism, and the one with which I am most concerned here, is the notion that beatitude or happiness inheres more in the will than in the intellect.[33] This will – the faculty that seeks the good and chooses to act rightly or wrongly – is distinctly not the sensual or concupiscent appetite, but the rational or intellectual appetite.[34] Much scholastic resistance to intellectualism was rooted in the observation that people simply do not always act with the good as a goal; we do not, as Aristotle would have it, consistently orient ourselves toward "some good," whether that good is mistaken or not. Voluntarist philosophers were concerned with the seeming problem that if the only impediment toward moral action is a proper intellectual understanding of the good, then all ethics becomes speculative.[35] As Bonnie Kent summarizes, "The desire for happiness is natural, and reason enables us to pursue happiness in a suitably enlightened way, but reason is not what makes us free, and even the rational pursuit of happiness is not what makes us morally admirable."[36] As with the concern for the motivations of love of God, discussed in the previous chapter, scholastic concern about the seat of enjoyment derives at least in part from a concern for love's nobility. For a human being to love ethically, to have a well-directed will, he or she must do more than act rationally; one must choose among many competing desires, and choose God despite the attractions of other competing objects. Choosing God out of clear-sightedness is simply not as morally admirable as choosing God and all attendant actions in a victory of the will that is pulled in many different directions, not all of them "good."

In influential texts, such as Bonaventure's *Itinerarium Mentis in Deum*, concerns about the dominance of the intellect can seem like wholesale anti-intellectualism. Bonaventure (*c.*1217–74) describes the seventh stage of the mind's journey as one in which "all intellectual operations should be abandoned, and the whole height of our affection should be transferred and transformed with God."[37] The Franciscan quotes pseudo-Dionysius' *Mystical Theology* advising that the seeker of God should "abandon [his] senses and intellectual operations."[38] In a series of binary opposites that sum up a mystical voluntarism, Bonaventure addresses his reader, advising "If you should ask how these things come about, question grace, not instruction; desire, not intellect; the cry of prayer, not pursuit of study; the spouse, not the teacher; God, not man; darkness, not clarity …"[39] Bonaventure does not deny the importance of intellectual pursuit more generally, but we are clearly a world away from Aristotle's elevation of philosophical reason as the key to the highest human happiness. John Duns Scotus (*c.*1265–1308) similarly held that happiness is an act of the will, arguing that the will is the seat of virtues such as temperance, fortitude, and justice, as well as the location of the desire for happiness; the will desires happiness in particular ("in particulari") and not as a universal, and so happiness is an object of the will rather than the intellect.[40] Yet while Scotus revises Aristotle, who locates temperance and fortitude in the concupiscent appetite and justice alone in the will, he nevertheless argues his case with support from the *Nicomachean Ethics*, *Metaphysics*, and *Physics* quite easily alongside St. Paul's letters to the Corinthians and Philippians. He takes pains to preserve the freedom of the will, arguing that while "the will of a pilgrim in this life" ("voluntas viatoris") mostly wishes for happiness, he does not *necessarily* will it either in general or in particular.[41] As with the definitions of pleasure discussed in the previous chapter, most theologians sought to harmonize the Aristotelian and Augustinian perspectives, and marshaled Aristotle in arguments for the primacy of the will as well as the primacy of the intellect. As we will see below, each philosopher works to recruit Aristotelian philosophy for his way of understanding enjoyment, often in ways that render attempts to summarize "Aristotelianism" nearly impossible.

Ockham's commentary on the *Sentences* explicitly attempts to reconcile arguments for the primacy of the intellect versus the will. For Ockham, enjoyment is a product of both awareness of God and love of God; he emphasizes, however, that there is no pleasure without the operation of the will – i.e., love.[42] Ockham presents Aristotle's definition of enjoyment, lending support to the argument that enjoyment is an intellectual act: "Enjoyment [*fruitio*] is formally [the same as] blessedness, because it is so called from 'fruit,' which is something ultimate, and blessedness is like this. But according to the Philosopher in *Ethics* x [7] and i [7, 1098a15–17], blessedness is an activity of intellect. Therefore enjoying will be an activity of intellect."[43] Against this idea, Ockham introduces Augustine's definition of enjoyment as love, affirming that love is solely an act of will. Ockham sides with the voluntarist perspective, stating that enjoyment is thus "solely an act of will," and yet he saves the Aristotelian argument by assuring us that

> it is important to understand that when I say that enjoying is solely an act of will, I do not mean to deny that properly speaking and in virtue of [the strict meaning] of the terms [*de virtute sermonis*] enjoying is an act of the intellect, for as I will show elsewhere intellect and will are entirely the same [thing]. Hence whatever is in the intellect is in the will and conversely.[44]

Still, enjoyment is not *cognitive* for Ockham, not an act of understanding or knowing, but rather the "showing" of an enjoyable object to the will by the intellect. In this life, the will actively responds to this beloved object, while as regards the beatific act, the will is only passive.[45] The freedom of the will must be preserved, but so too the freedom of God, for ultimately God alone is the "effective cause" of enjoyment, and "this [is] because of the nobility of blessedness itself."[46] Medieval writers did not understand this vision as standing in contrast to Aristotelian philosophy, but rather as the necessary fruit of Christian love, Aristotelian felicity, and *theoria*.

Jean Buridan's questions on the *Ethics* similarly situate enjoyment as an act of both the intellect and the will. For Buridan, simply, these are the two powers by which we understand and love God, respectively.[47] Buridan's understanding of the Aristotelian sufficiency of happiness demands that happiness consist in an act of the will and an act of the intellect: happiness is "not knowledge of God without love or love without knowledge but is made up of both."[48] Speaking as an Aristotelian in his commentary on the *Ethics*, Buridan is fully comfortable with happiness defined as an aggregate with many different connotations and components. He works successfully to synthesize Boethius' Platonic definition of happiness as a perfect condition consisting in the union of all goods with Aristotle's definition of felicity as the most excellent faculty of the human mind engaged in the most virtuous activity, with the best object. He affirms that "what is best is an act of thought regarding the divine essence," but adds that this act should not be cut off from its "connotations" ("connotationibus") of all good things that are prerequisite to this act, nor the good things that follow from it.[49] Buridan's happiness is thus defined primarily as a contemplative act of the intellect, though it includes a contemplative act of the will. Buridan allies happiness with self-reflection, noting that "the blessed not only love and understand God, but they can understand reflexively, and they understand that they understand and love and take pleasure."[50] While enjoyment may be separated into its component parts – the clear vision of God (intellect) and loving God (will) – the happiness of the soul as a whole consists in this love and vision combined. For Buridan, furthermore, this definition of happiness as an act of knowledge and of love applies equally to the afterlife and to this life on earth, and is as true for laypeople as it is for clergy dedicated to the contemplative life.[51]

Yet even in texts that are unqualifiedly in concert with thirteenth-century Aristotelianism – as in Nicole Oresme's translation and commentary on the *Ethics*, which takes much of its content from the commentary of Aquinas – there is a marked concern that intellectualism not lead to an assumption that perfect knowledge is available to people during their mortal lives. Oresme, who affirms that "parfaicte felicité est en speculacion," nevertheless warns his reader that this does not mean that mortals should seek after divine truths.[52] He echoes Aquinas' gloss on Aristotle's statement that we should not follow those who advise us that "homme doit seulement sentir et savoir choses humaines, ne homme mortel ne doit savoir fors seulement choses mortels" (human beings should only understand and learn human things, and mortals should study only mortal things), noting that such restriction was wrongly advised by Simonides the poet. Aquinas only affirms and explains Aristotle's meaning. Yet Oresme notes that it seems as though Simonides had a point, for Cato says, "Cum sumus mortales, quaesitum mortalia," and Ecclesiasticus 3:22 advises "Altiora te ne quaesieris" (Do not seek after things that are too high for you). He concludes that

> il est a entendre que l'en ne doit pas enquerir des secréz de Dieu ne de choses curieuses et lesquelles l'en ne pourroit savoir. Mais il est tres bon d'enquerir de Dieu et des choses divines ce qui est possible a savoir en ceste vie.[53]

> (One must understand that one should not inquire about the secrets of God nor about curious things and those things about which one cannot know. But it is very good to inquire about God and divine things about which it is possible to know in this life.)

Whether Oresme is warding off criticism or making his own intervention, it is clear that he saw the need to defend Aristotelian intellectualism from overstepping its bounds into the realm of curiosity.[54] Assent to reason as the highest human faculty, even the most divine of human faculties, and to speculation as the happiest of enterprises, does not mean that one assents to the idea that such contemplation can grant access to "God's secrets."

Thus, much like the scholastic discussions of pleasure, discussions of the relative participation of the will and the intellect in enjoyment sought to preserve the integrity, freedom, and nobility of both the pursuit and experience of human and beatific happiness. While Aristotelian ethics was committed to the primacy of the intellectual faculty, it was demonstrated to be not incompatible with voluntaristic understandings of ethics and enjoyment. In their various attempts to understand the mental and spiritual location of bliss, philosophers clearly chose their sides in the conflict between wit and will – offering greater nobility or controlling status to one faculty or the other – but Aristotle's philosophy was saved by both sides. Such harmonizing was not necessarily the goal of the vernacular literature that addressed the dangers and limits of intellectualism, though this literature is similarly invested in Aristotelian ethics. The comic appeal of the wayward Thales and the conquered Aristotle intersected with earnest inquiries into the nature of the human mind and soul, the desire for earthly and divine happiness, and the mind and will of God himself.

THE PILGRIMAGE OF HUMAN LIFE

Explorations of the composition of human desire and experience made their way into vernacular literature in various guises, from allegorical narratives of the conflict between "wit" and "will" to the narrative of the soul's ascent to the beatific vision in Dante's *Paradiso*. These vernacular poetic representations of the faculty of the will range from a stark contrast between "Witte þe wise kyng" and "Wille þe wick" in the fourteenth-century allegory *The Conflict of Wit and Will* to an imagining of the will as the site of the highest enjoyment, aided by the intellect.[55] It is within such a range of responses that we find Guillaume de Deguileville's *Le Pèlerinage de Vie Humaine*, a poem that seems at first glance to be fairly uncompromising in its dismissal of Aristotelian philosophy as a route to understanding of the world or of the divine. Yet its dialogic structure in fact illustrates the necessity of philosophical pursuit of the good. In its form – a combination of allegorical narrative and allegorical dialogue – the poem exposes its inheritance from the *Roman de la Rose*, an inheritance also explicitly alluded to by the poet.[56] The narrator tells us that while awake, he had read, studied, and looked closely at "the beautiful *Romance of the Rose*," and that this poem was what "moved" him to have the dream he will relate.[57] The influence of the *Rose* colors a poem that does not at all seem to be a part of either the scholastic or the courtly world, nor is it interested in the vagaries of erotic desire, but rather in the narrative of the human soul as it struggles against temptation and seeks after virtuous living. The audience is quickly introduced to a recasting of the *Rose*'s garden of delight as the high-walled and beautiful city of Jerusalem, seen from afar in a mirror, "large beyond measure."[58] It is clear that this dream inspired by the *Rose* will have a different path of desire in mind – poverty is here a necessity for entering the *locus amoenus* where in the *Rose* it was a certain barrier, captured in a portrait on the outside of the garden wall – yet Deguileville's poem is no less committed to the pursuit of a love object. *Le Pèlerinage de Vie Humaine* does not invert the imagery of Guillaume and Jean's poem simply to undermine its courtly, secular themes, but rather turns its compelling narrative of desire to heavenly ends.

As in the *Rose*, this narrative is a process of ethical self-knowledge, a knowledge that occupies the space between the two poles of narcissism and contemplation of divine truth. The centrality of self-knowledge to Deguileville's poem inheres not only in the image of the mirror but, as Sarah Kay notes, in "the consistently human dimension of the space of the poem," as its spaces of action are identified most often with human usage (house, hedge, ship, etc.).[59] Deguileville thus redirects the energy of the *Rose*'s engagement with Aristotelian philosophy so that it might serve to expose the dangers and the limits of human desire. The Lover's dream that proved so productive for both Guillaume de Lorris and Jean de Meun, allowing for an exploration of desire as it encounters other people, received wisdom, courtly mores, linguistic boundaries, and creative possibilities, is here universalized, freed from courtly constraints and erotic context. In this dream of everyman, desire is for metaphysical and ethical knowledge, yet it is a desire no less threatened by the irrational, the passionate, and the philosophical.

An obvious episode in which one might investigate the poem's attitude toward Aristotelian philosophy occurs in the character Grace Dieu's recounting of a debate about the Eucharist staged between Aristotle – acting as Nature's clerk – and Sapience. At first glance, Deguileville's depiction of Aristotle seems to function as a dismissal of the philosopher, a clearing away of all rational impediments to faith in the miracles of Christianity. Aristotle overtly serves as a figure of stubborn rationality in the face of the miracle of the Eucharist, yet his role as Nature's clerk opens up a dialogue about human desire in all its dimensions. Sapience herself corrects the philosopher's resistance to the notion that bread could be composed of the body of Christ, or that the part of any substance could be equal to or greater than the whole. She reminds him that she did not in fact impart to him the whole of her art, but rather withheld some of her knowledge, rendering Aristotle's philosophy a discourse in which wisdom may only be sought with the knowledge that some unidentifiable portion of art and science will always remain unreachable. It is not that Aristotelian philosophy – or, by extension, philosophy in general – differs in kind from Christian wisdom, but that it differs only in its claims to completeness. By introducing this lack into Aristotelian philosophy, Sapience renders it irrational in Aristotle's own terms, under which rational, ethical desire must be for something that we can actually obtain. In the poem, Aristotle accepts this description of his learning and proceeds to engage in debate about the relationship between the part and the whole, and between the appearance and the substance of objects.

It is the dialectical space between intellectual pursuit – identified with Aristotle – and wisdom – identified with God's grace – that offers an experience and understanding of both earthly creation and beatific enjoyment. In correcting Aristotle's views on the relationship between the inner and outer appearances of things, Sapience asks if he had "ever seen either outside or inside how big the human heart is?" ("Veis tu onques ne hors ne ens / De cuer d'omme la quantite?" ll. 3128–9), and what it would take to fill or satisfy an organ so small that, as the philosopher admits, a hungry bird would not find it satisfying. Aristotle answers that "if [the heart] had the whole world at its command, that would not be enough to fill it up and satisfy it" ("li sauoler, / Li remplir et assasier / Tout li mondes pas ne pourroit, / Se tout a son vouloir l'avoit," ll. 3143–6). Here Aristotle redefines lack: it is not constitutive of the world, but rather constitutive of human desire; one might possess everything it is possible to possess, and yet remain wanting. His emphasis is not on the fact that the world is missing something, but that the heart by its very nature can never be filled. Nevertheless, he claims a few lines later that one sovereign good will fill it completely (l. 3158).[60] Aristotle's articulation of this paradox is used to demonstrate the emptiness of his initial criticism of Sapience's eucharistic doctrine. Sapience may now argue that an object which exceeds the world – the sovereign good – can nevertheless be contained in the small space of a person's heart. This "biau conte" inspires the pilgrim with great hunger, and he asks Grace Dieu if he might eat some of this bread "Pour mon vuit cuer assasier" (To fill my empty heart, l. 3314).

What interests me about this exchange is that although Aristotle must be schooled in the miracle of the Eucharist, his knowledge about human desire and its relationship to the sovereign good goes unchallenged. It is through the dialogue between the goddess, Sapience, and the Philosopher, Aristotle, that the reader comes to an understanding of the insatiability of human desire and the miraculous capacity for God, as sovereign good, to satisfy this desire. In an example that takes us back to the opening of the poem and the mirror that displays the object of human desire (Jerusalem, a rose), Sapience further refutes Aristotle's physical theories by pointing out that the shards of a broken mirror each contain the complete reflection of the whole. While the mirror itself has multiplied, its multiplicity produces unity and singularity; rather than a singular mirror – a fountain of love – creating desire for a contingent object, these multiple mirrors contain one unchanging image. Yet while the shattered mirror may metaphorically refute Aristotelian physics (as a smaller substance contains the same amount as a larger substance), it harmonizes with Aristotelian ethics – every act and person seeks the good, and the sovereign good may thus be seen in every mirror. Even after the debate ends, or rather founders – Aristotle admits that he can win nothing against Wisdom herself – Aristotelian philosophy, and particularly the *Ethics*, remains a resource of wisdom about desire, pleasure, and the good. Grace later points the dreamer to this book for an understanding of the ways that not all things bring pleasure or use-value in the same way to everyone (4705–8).[61] In the famous "ABC" prayer of the third book, later translated by Chaucer, the poet closes with an "et cetera" that claims

> Ethiques s'avoie lëu
> Tout recorde et tout scëu
> Et aprez rien n'en ouvrass. (ll. 11169–71)

(I have read the Ethics, and understood and remembered it all, but afterwards did nothing about it.)[62]

While the content of the *Ethics* may be irreproachable, book learning is clearly not sufficient for moral behavior; the narrator has done no work (*ouvrass*) with the materials of the *Ethics*. Far from a rejection of Aristotle, Deguileville's poem demonstrates the ways that Aristotelian philosophy, in dialogue with beliefs in Augustinian grace, can guide the human pilgrim in the good life.

Deguileville's versions of Aristotle offer a way to keep the central insights of Aristotelian ethics – that self-knowledge is tied to pursuit of the sovereign good, that desire for the changeable good is endless and irrational, that virtuous action requires more than mere speculative understanding – while maintaining space for grace and unknowable miracles. Deguileville's version of the "mounted Aristotle" – in this case dialectically mastered and topped by Sapience herself – gives us a mirror of intellectual desire, its revelations and its limits. Such is the desire we encounter in Langland's *Piers Plowman*, a poem that also narrates a human pilgrimage in search of the "good life," and yet this desire is not simply rebuked and silenced but rather transformed – the yearning for full intellectual and volitional experience placed in a simultaneously human and divine context through a meditation on the desires of God.[63]

PIERS PLOWMAN AND LOVE'S SOVEREIGN SCIENCE

Langland's allegorical protagonist, Will, has been taken by generations of readers to be a representation of the author, an everyman figure, any number of different "types" of individuals, and the mental and/or spiritual faculty of the will; the poem gives encouragement at different moments for all of these interpretations.[64] While I am interested in the moments when a psychological understanding of Will comes to the fore, I am also interested in the poem's depictions of desire generally, and especially the desire for knowledge.[65] Like the *Pèlerinage*, Langland's poem critiques the intellect as an enactment of concupiscent desire for total knowledge, but also pursues a notion of knowledge as love, an intellectual love tied to pleasure that would look familiar to any medieval Aristotelian. James Simpson has influentially read *Piers Plowman* as demonstrating a movement from rational to affective knowledge, and from scholastic to devotional modes of inquiry and reading.[66] In Simpson's narrative, Will is represented as "passing through" the intellective faculties on his way to a more "direct" experiential knowledge of God, an experience seated in the will.[67] It is clear that Langland is interested in the conflict between rationalist approaches to understanding the world and God and an insistence on love as either a mode of knowledge or an experience that supplants knowledge from outside. Piers himself, according to the figure Clergie, has "sette alle sciences at a soppe save love one" (B.XIII.125).[68] In recent scholarship, however, accounts of this conflict have been nuanced to take into account the poem's evident and continuous interest in philosophical discourse and in the full range of mental activity engaged through learning, meditation, and prayer.[69]

In *Piers Plowman*, critical binaries such as will and intellect, *sensualitas* and *voluntas*, love and study, monasticism and scholasticism, reason and affect are often subtly destabilized. For as much as love is a science in the poem, in some ways supplanting conventional or scholastic modes of knowledge, it also transforms our understanding of science – what it means to know. Thus while Will may move cumulatively away from reading practices of disputation and toward reading practices of devotional meditation, the role of the intellect and will in one's pursuit of the good and God are not thereby resolved – such questions exceed reading practices as much as they remain circumscribed by them. One might claim that Will's rational powers are not "exhausted" (*pace* Simpson) but are rather transformed. The poem constructs a model of a rational will, or combination of will and reason, that looks not unlike the models constructed by the scholastic philosophers, who were equally concerned to preserve the centrality of love in ethical and spiritual experience. Masha Raskolnikov privileges the figure Liberum Arbitrium as the most fully developed alter ego of Will, emphasizing that he is "a will with a resoun" (C.176). She notes Britton Harwood's suggestion that Liberum Arbitrium represents a "faculty which serves 'to account for choice by coming between the reason's judgment of the good and the will's desire for the good – yet one composed of reason and will.'"[70] In *Piers Plowman* we find an intricate investigation of what it might mean to pursue "knowledge through love," engaging both the will and the intellect.

The poem not only articulates the ideal of a fully intellectual and fully affective pursuit of knowledge, but emphasizes the problem of excessive intellectual desire as a material and sexual excess, thus figuring the threat to intellectual pursuit in much the same manner as the "mounted Aristotle" tales. As Andrew Galloway has noted, Will is swayed far more by intellectual transgression than sensual indulgence, and I would add that the poem accordingly imagines the intellect as itself a form of concupiscence.[71] The threat to Will, understood as a personification of the mental faculty, is less a slippery slope between the rational and sensual wills than a slide into passionate rationality – an intellect in knowledge-hungry overdrive. The poem presents a search for a mode of intellectual desire in harmony with charity, a loving knowledge marked by union with God rather than separation and suffering. A focus on exactly how Langland characterizes the operations of the intellect allows us to see that what is at stake is also an understanding of desire for the sovereign good not as an endlessly deferred experience earned through suffering, but rather an experience possible through an exemplary imitation of God's unification of will and pleasure. Rather than "the most ascetic of the great didactic, Middle English allegories,"[72] *Piers Plowman* might be understood as an investigation of salutary pleasure, of a unification of desire and pleasure modeled on Christ himself. Langland ultimately transforms Deguileville's images of insatiable desire – voiced by Aristotle – into an affective, imitative relationship to Christ's desire for men's souls – a union of the physical, intellectual, and spiritual, of suffering, delight, and beauty.

This ideal, rather than being threatened by Nature – as in Deguileville's poem – is presented as itself natural, inasmuch as nature is a product of the divine will. Where the French poet focuses on Nature's overreaching impetus to complete knowledge, in conflict with Sapience, Langland allies the forces of nature and wisdom. Nature does not signify a desire for total knowledge, or the domination of the world by rational, "natural" science, for it is Will who acts unnaturally – "unkindly" in the poem's vocabulary – in desiring to know "Alle the sciences under sonne and alle the sotile craftes" (B.XV.48).[73] Where Deguileville's Grace Dieu relates the story of Aristotle's debate with Sapience in the context of the pilgrim's desire for knowledge about the Eucharist, thus warding off any attempt at full wisdom without grace, Will is given no such pre-emptive narrative. Anima chides that perfect knowledge belongs only to Christ, and a desire for such complete knowing is "ayeins kynde" (B.XV.52). "Kynde" – a term that has a broad range of signification but typically refers in some way to "nature" and innate experience, knowledge, and emotions – here has become a guarantor that humankind cannot overreach and make any claims to full wisdom.[74] Nature becomes a guardian of proper knowledge-seeking.

Nature is thus the boundary by which love is enabled to pursue knowledge in a proper, ethical manner. By allying Nature and Love, however, Langland courts the possibility that "kindness" will not only guarantee that Will renounces any claims to full knowledge, but might create a situation where knowledge is "devoured" by natural passions.[75] Nature as limiter of human knowledge and keeper of the keys to knowledge of sexuality emerges in the twelfth Passus of the poem. Here, the same barrier that prevents one from knowing why one of the thieves crucified with Christ "yielded" rather than the other thief also prevents one from knowing where the "floures in the fryth" (B.XII.220) get their clear, bright colors. The "why" of natural beauty is as dark to Clergy and Kind Wit as the "why" of biblical history. Only "Kynde" knows the answers to these questions because he himself is the cause of such characteristics and occurrences. As we are told, "Kynde kenned Adam to knowe hise pryvé membres, / And taughte hym and Eve to helien hem with leves" (B.XII.229–30). The secrets of secrecy itself – what should be hidden and why – belong to Kynde. Unlearned men may seek out clerks to ask why Adam did not instead cover his mouth – that shameful organ that ate the apple – rather than his thighs, but "Kynde knoweth whi he dide so, ac no clerk ellis!" (B.XII.234). The limits of learning and knowledge are thus figured as the limits created by divine nature, and sexual desire – the shame attached to Adam and Eve's "privy members," the mating practices of birds – is emphasized as a realm where "seeking after whys" will come to nothing.[76] Dame Studie had predicted Ymaginatyf's response to Will's questioning, stating that he will answer Will's "purpose," and advise him as Augustine did, "Non plus sapere quam oportet ..." (B.X.118*a*), reanimating the overlapping senses of "sapere": to know, taste, and delight. Studie appears to demand a similar tamping down of curiosity, recommending that those who wish to "wite the whyes of God almyghty" should place "his eighe ... in his ers and his fynger after" (B.X.124–5).[77] Excessive intellectual desire is itself figured as concupiscent, and its desired object is – among other things – the mystery of concupiscent desires and practices. Ymaginatyf might say, along with Chaucer's Miller, that "An housbande shal nat been inquisityf / Of Goddes pryvetee, nor of his wyf" (ll. 3163–4). For both

Ymaginatyf and the Miller, inquisitiveness is itself excessive and therefore concupiscent, and the objects of its questioning are primarily figured as sexual.

Yet in figuring the very limits of knowledge, the mysteries of the divine will, Ymaginatyf offers a key to the ethical functioning of the desiring intellect. In warning the dreamer that he should not ask why one thief who was crucified with Christ yielded to faith, but not the other, he contends that the answer to the question "Quare placuit?" is simply "Quia voluit" (B.XII.215*a*). Why did it please him? Because he willed it. Here the pleasure and will of the thief are shadowed by the pleasure and will of God – the line in the poem transforms the statement of Psalm 134:6, "Whatsoever the Lord hath willed, he hath done" ("*omnia quae voluit Dominus fecit*"), into a question and answer: Why did it please him? Because he willed it so. The poem emphasizes that God was pleased ("*placuit*") in addition to carrying out his will ("*voluit*"). God's will, his pleasure, and his actions are unified by definition – he does what is pleasing to him and he is pleased by what he does – and this unification yields what should be intellectual satisfaction for the questioner. There is no "why" beyond the unity of God's will and pleasure – this pleasure is tantamount to knowledge. The poem invites us to think about how one might close the gap between what one sees as good and takes delight in ("*placeo*") and what one wills and does, and even how one's intellect, delight, and volition might imitate that of God. While concupiscent intellectual desire is rebuked by the poem, an experience of desire and action in which the will, intellect, and pleasure are unified is said to belong to God himself.

The mysteries of beauty and desire thus allow us to rethink the poem's relationship to pleasure, and especially its interest in the possibility of moving "from delights to delights" ("*de deliciis ad delicias*"). The transition from sensual or even literary pleasures to higher pleasures is a path that the poem continually marks out as a desired route, but one that never seems to be traveled. We are reminded in the midst of Haukyn's confession in Passus XIV that a pleasurable life on earth makes it all the more difficult to ensure a pleasurable afterlife. Though the faint possibility of "double hire" and "double rest" for the rich if not the wicked is held out by Patience (B.XIV.144*a*–148), the poem consistently affirms that "*de deliciis ad delicias*" is a difficult transition to make indeed. Yet the poem encourages us to wonder – even more than how to get into heaven if one is cursed with earthly wealth – how we might move from delights to delights while still on earth, how to reject the pleasures of the gut and the eye for the pleasure of the loving will. The satisfaction held out is not perfect beatitude, but rather an earthly experience of well-directed love and its associated pleasures.

Pleasure and love, however, hardly have an obvious and untroubled relationship in *Piers Plowman*. At many moments in the poem, the science of love appears to be a practice of suffering love associated with Patience, a suffering of worldly poverty, of the sins of others, of all manner of injustice and pain. As Wit explains, "Dowel is to drede God, and DoBet to suffre" (B.IX.204). Where doing well is to fear the law, and healing is provided by doing best, the love associated with Do-Better is equated with suffering. It is no accident, I think, that this equation is made by Wit, for the pursuit of rational knowledge is a necessarily suffering pursuit – often associated in the poem with frustrated desire, a disconnect between emotion and intellect, and the discipline of the schools.[78] This desire's constant frustration is what allies it with erotic, concupiscent desire. Reason also instructs Will in the desirability of suffering, asking "Who suffreth moore than God? … he suffreth for som mannes good, and so is oure bettre" (B.XI.379–81). He concludes that Holy Writ thus teaches men to suffer. Suffering is both what we take on after having been instructed by Scripture and a punishment for seeking too much knowledge. According to Anima, God suffered for us in example that we should suffer also (B.XV.266). Yet the poem is careful to emphasize that a suffering ideal is not simply the taking on of pain, and does not demand a passive attitude toward the world. The poem makes a distinction, though a slippery one, between suffering – the patient bearing of worldly fortune – and suffering *for* – either the sacrificial taking on of pain for the good of another or the pain experienced in the pursuit of knowledge and pleasure.[79] Simple "suffering" in the poem more resembles a stoic acceptance of external happenstance, although Langland certainly does maintain desire that earthly poverty and injustice could be righted. The poem navigates the margin between a subordination of earthly justice to heavenly reward and a deep concern that the poor be taken care of, both physically and spiritually. The prescription of suffering applies to the steady suffering of fortune or misfortune, and being, like Griselda, as "glad of a gowne of a gray russet / As of a tunycle of Tarse or of trie scarlet" (B.XV.167–8). One should not covet earthly things, but should bear both good and bad fortune "mildly." Yet pleasure is as much a part of knowledge as pain may be, and the poem's epistemology of suffering might be understood also to encompass – not paradoxically – an epistemology of pleasure.[80] Learning is not associated solely with suffering, but with the pleasure of understanding and of experience. The poem affirms that pleasure and learning are allied in that knowledge is gained through the experience of opposing states, an experience which is also the key to pleasure.

In the most joyous and dramatic Passus of the B-version, Passus XVIII, suffering as a path toward pleasurable, active knowledge is emphasized. Readers have noted that Langland does not linger here over the details of his narrative of Christ's Passion, declining to engender an extended affective, compassionate response in his audience.[81] Rather than the compassion we should feel for Christ's suffering, it is God's own compassion that is emphasized. According to the figure Peace, it is because we cannot understand happiness without experience of woe that God allowed Adam to introduce suffering into the world; suffering allows Adam "To wite what wele was, kyndeliche to knowe it" (B.XVIII.220). And so it follows that God became man:

> And after, God auntrede hymself and took Adames kynde
> To wite what he hath suffred in thre sondry places,
> Bothe in hevene and in erthe – and now til helle he thenketh,
> To wite what alle wo is, that woot of alle joye. (B.XVIII.221–4)

God becomes man to understand human experience, to undergo it bodily. Man's "suffering" is identical to all of his experience, not only his pain. God became man to understand what Adam suffered in heaven, on earth, and in hell.[82] As Lacan contends in his twentieth seminar, the Incarnation and Passion do not function to save man, but rather to save God, and particularly to save his knowledge of hatred and love. A God ignorant of hatred and pain is a terrifically ignorant God. God imitates us in all our human woe and lack – we need not pursue additional pain.[83] And as Amy Hollywood has argued in another context, this way of understanding the Incarnation renders the suffering human condition itself a state of union with God; passivity in the face of outside forces becomes an active pursuit of knowledge, and there is no need to demand still more suffering in the service of an ideal of *imitatio Christi*.[84] The oft-repeated maxim of the poem's fourth vision, "*pacientes vincunt*," thus loses some of its force as a prescription – that one should become like those suffering ones – and gains more force as description. God as suffering man conquered sin and the devil; as humans, we suffer by definition, and will also triumph. Such a reading of the Incarnation and Crucifixion demands a philosophy of knowledge through bodily experience and empathy, and a pursuit of knowledge through not only painful, but also pleasurable love.

Christ himself finally exemplifies how one can transform "bely joye" into a higher joy, the joy of love, to move from delights to delights. Christ proclaims to the devil that he must drink the bitterness he has brewed, while Christ imbibes love:

> I that am lord of lif, love is my drynke,
> And for that drynke today, I deide upon erthe.
> I faught so, me thursteth yet, for mannes soule sake;
> May no drynke me moiste, ne my thurst slake,
> Til the vendage falle in the vale of Josaphat,
> That I drynke right ripe must, *resureccio mortuorum*.
>
> (B.XVIII.366–71)

He thirsts endlessly for men's souls, but enjoys their sweet taste all the while. This image of insatiable earthly desire, but one in which sensual goods are replaced by spiritual goods, with even deeper satisfactions, would seem to be the ideal way to pass from delights to delights. The miraculous nature of the sovereign good, represented in the debate between Aristotle and Sapience in the *Pèlerinage de Vie Humaine*, is here rendered in Christ's own voice. He endlessly thirsts for love, and can never be sated, except that one drink of "new wine" ("right ripe must"), the resurrection of the dead, will slake his desire.

Such a spectacular image of satisfaction, unity, and delight is revealed to the dreamer at the end of this Passus. Peace reprises her theme of knowledge through contraries, this time in song: the sun is brighter after much cloud, love is brighter after hate, weather warmer after rain, friends dearer after war:

> Thanne pipede Pees of poesie a note:
> *'Clarior est solito post maxima nebula Phebus;*
> *Post inimicicias clarior est et amor.*
> After sharpest shoures,' quod Pees, 'moost shene is the sonne;
> Is no weder warmer than after watry cloudes;
> Ne no love levere, ne lever frendes
> Than after werre and wo, whan love and pees ben maistres.
> Was nevere werre in this world, ne wikkednesse so kene,
> That Love, and hym liste, to laughynge ne broughte,
> And Pees, thorugh pacience, alle perils stoppede.'
>
> (B.XVIII.410–17)

Deprivation or hardship here does not bequeath understanding, but rather intensifies pleasure – or, rather, knowledge is here tied to pleasure. The experience of "suffering for," of undergoing pain so that one can gain knowledge, is here transformed into a scene where pain gives way to pleasure and understanding. We are not told that rain is colder after a time of basking in the sun. Contrary experiences intensify sensory experience, but also the affective experience of love and friendship. Here love's "mastery" is manifested in the activity of simultaneous understanding and pleasure. Following Peace's piping of poesy, the elusive unification of peace and justice, mercy and truth, is achieved; Truth sings in praise of God, Love sings in praise of the goodness and delight of people united, and amidst this festival of caroling and celebration, the dreamer wakes up. At the end of this vision, faith in the miraculous and a commitment to truth and knowledge are joyously reconciled, an image of a union that Deguileville could not or did not want to dream of. Peace asks the group that they let no one "parceyve that we chidde" (B.XVIII.420), though it is the chiding, of course, that makes the reunion that much more poignant and sustaining.

While the poem admonishes that it is very difficult to move from delights to delights, it is possible, perhaps, to move from suffering love to joyous love, and to have that movement not be temporal – suffering on earth rewarded with joy in heaven – but epistemological: human knowledge through suffering replaced by knowledge through joy. The sovereign good for *Piers Plowman* would appear to be the seemingly unreachable ethical knowledge of how to reconcile mercy and truth. We leave the poem with Will still searching for this knowledge, amidst a church and society in crisis. Toward the end of the poem, he asks Kynde, "what crafte be best to lerne?" "Lerne to love," Kynde answers, "and leef all othere" (B.XX.207–8). The language of science has been replaced with the language of craft, a term that better captures the fact that Will is not searching for a unit of truth, but rather seeking a process, a skill, a way of life that is both intellectual and physical, both an art and a practice. We might then reread Dame Studie's advice to Will: "loke thow lovye as longe as thow durest / For is no science under sonne so sovereyne for the soule" (B.X.207–8). Love is not a replacement for the intellect, but a way of understanding ethical intellectual pursuit. Suffering, pleasure, and knowledge all at once – this love is without desire for complete possession, and without the singleness of intellectual purpose that sent Thales into the ditch. The recognition of the paradox of bottomless desire – it cannot be satisfied by the entire world, and yet one waits for one single miraculous substance to fulfill it – allows Langland to give this desire to God, thus offering humankind hope of relief from a monstrous burden.

Piers Plowman thus imagines what it might mean to possess an intellect and will that, in Ockham's terms, are "entirely the same." Such a model of the soul's faculties brings the threat of concupiscent desire for knowledge, a focus on nature's mysteries that bespeaks a delight in lingering amidst the pursuit of unknowable truths – a pursuit of those truths precisely because of their unknowability. But it also brings the possibility of a loving pursuit of knowledge, the loving contemplation that the classical Aristotle does not quite arrive at. The medieval vernacular poetry of love that distances itself from both the erotic and the intellectual still investigates its subject through the language of clerkly erotics and erotic clerkliness. And it is both scholastic discourse and vernacular romance that offer models – the loving will, Christ the Lover-Knight, the debating Aristotle and Sapience – for an ethical experience of loving God. Yet love's knowledge – as both a science of love and a passionate experience – remains both dangerously and delightfully close to the desire for a maiden, a poem, or one's own mirror image.

CHAPTER 5

On human happiness: Dante, Chaucer, and the felicity of friendship

Chaucer's *Troilus and Criseyde* famously begins with a statement of purpose, "The double sorwe of Troilus to tellen." Telling of sorrow, not happiness, informs the activity of the poet, and Troilus' double sorrow structures the consolatory context of the poem as it is most broadly read: Pandarus first consoles his friend by conveying his loved object to him, and the loss of Criseyde inaugurates another period of sorrow that is consoled only in death. Yet despite the narrator's initial foreboding announcement, and the fact that almost every medieval reader knew precisely the trajectory of Troilus and Criseyde's love affair, Chaucer still allows for an experience of love's bliss at the center of his poem.[1] In Book III, when the lovers are finally joined together, the narrator asks his audience to consider erotic happiness in the terms of clerkly discourse. Deliberately placing his words in the context of moral philosophy, he speaks of the joy experienced by the two lovers:

> This is no litel thyng of for to seye;
> This passeth every wit for to devyse;
> For ech of hem gan otheres lust obeye.
> Felicite, which that thise clerkes wise
> Comenden so, ne may nought here suffise;
> This joie may nought writen be with inke;
> This passeth al that herte may bythynke (III.1688–94).

The joy experienced by Troilus and Criseyde is beyond the conceptual capacities of writing, clerks, or the heart. Suddenly, clerkly happiness appears not to be happiness at all, for it is not "sufficient." Still, although the narrator finds the clerkly concept of "Felicite" somehow wanting as a descriptor for the enjoyment shared between Troilus and Criseyde, he does not attempt to find any other discourse that would serve this function. On the contrary, it is the nexus of courtly and clerkly felicity that animates the ethics of *Troilus and Criseyde*, revealing that what is at stake for Chaucer is not the inadequacy of clerkly language to describe erotic felicity, but the knowledge that clerks and lovers share a language, and share a notion that pleasure and happiness constitute the end of human desire, for good or ill.

According to the narrator, what places the lovers' felicity in the context of – and yet beyond – the felicity of clerks is their unified desires. The facet of Troilus and Criseyde's joy that renders it beyond the grasp of language to "devyse" is the way each person obeys the desires and pleasures of the other, such that their "lust" is indistinguishable – "ech of hem gan otheres lust obeye."[2] The elevation of this erotic unity would seem to bring the poem into conflict with the foundation of medieval Christian ethics, which roots itself in the conviction that the things of this world are unstable and ephemeral, and thus unworthy of desire. Happiness is to be found not in goods governed by fortune, but in the stable, self-sufficient goods of heaven and divine union. While this orientation is scriptural in origin, its late medieval expression is often mediated by Boethius' *Consolation of Philosophy*, a dialogue in which Philosophia teaches the speaker that true happiness is found in God and nowhere else: "God and verray blisfulnesse is al o thing," in Chaucer's translation (Book III, prose 10, ll. 245–6). The rejection of worldly desires as a route to happiness is thus "Boethian" in medieval literature, as much as it is Christian, and it is assumed that this ethic is itself immutable. It is perhaps inevitable, then, that it is in *Troilus and Criseyde*, Chaucer's most Boethian poem, that we find the poet's most ambitious meditation on the felicity of erotic love. Such a felicity is threatened simultaneously by earthly misfortune, which impedes it, and heavenly stability, which renders it small and fleeting by comparison.[3]

This chapter considers the ways that new approaches to Boethius' dialogue – new in both the fourteenth and the twenty-first centuries – can help us to see that Chaucer's *Troilus* explores fortune as the very ground of earthly felicity, and *philia* as a route to human happiness. I ask below what it might mean to take Chaucer's narrator's claims about the lovers' felicity seriously, investigating his suggestion that Troilus and Criseyde's felicity is relevant to a consideration of clerical discourse, and that this felicity might exceed the happiness of moral philosophy on its own terms.[4] It is important, in this context, that the narrator states that the felicity commended by clerks may not "suffise" to speak about the bliss of the lovers. In the language of Boethius and indeed all medieval discourse on moral philosophy, it is not sufficient, as any good must be. If clerkly language does not "suffise" to speak about all felicity, then it must not be an end in itself, must either be ordered to some other end or require accompanying goods to be desirable. It is erotic love, that missing element of the happiness described by "clerkes wise," that renders this language insufficient. An ethics of felicity needs the two lovers as much as it needs Boethius and Aristotle.

This emphasis on mutuality and compassion runs throughout the *Troilus* and allows us to place the lovers' erotic and ethical felicity in a fourteenth-century philosophical as well as a contemporary critical context. Both contexts complicate what is typically taken to be the Boethian trajectory of *Troilus and Criseyde*: the gradual rejection of earthly happiness as unstable, anxiety-ridden, and therefore self-contradictory at its core. Co-feeling, between narrator, audience, and characters, between lovers and friends, is at the heart of the poem, and this "doubling" of feeling includes joy as well as sorrow. As Martin Camargo has observed, Boethius' *Consolation* offered not only thematic, but also dramatic substance to Chaucer's poem, and through the figure of Pandarus, Chaucer animates Philosophia as a friend.[5] My reading of *Troilus and Criseyde* continues a long line of criticism that has been interested in Chaucer's depiction of friendship in his poem – between lovers, male and female friends, niece and uncle – and that reads this friendship in the light of Chaucer's relationship to Boethius' book. I would like to add to this matrix the ways that fourteenth-century readers of Boethius – Latin commentators and Dante – see Boethius in the light of the new Aristotelian learning, and give us a version of the *Consolation* that imagines the pursuit of philosophy as a pursuit of mutual love that is best enacted through educative identification with friends pursuing happiness in the face of fortune. For Dante, Philosophia herself is a friend in the highest sense. This version of the happiness prescribed by Boethius' book allows us to see that Chaucer's lovers are in harmony with a simultaneously Boethian and Aristotelian ethic of friendship in their moment of mutuality, and it is the dissolution of this ethic in the face of war and contingency that constitutes the dissolution – the "double sorwe" – of their love.

THE NEW BOETHIUS

The clerkly context of Troilus and Criseyde's felicity is generally taken most immediately to be Boethius' *Consolation of Philosophy*. Bernard Jefferson argued over ninety years ago that "Chaucer's whole conception of this fundamental question of the end of life or of 'felicitee,' as he commonly terms it, is unmistakably and to a large degree influenced by Boethius … he discusses the problem in Boethian language, and … he reaches the same conclusions which Boethius reached."[6] Much the same perspective informs Ralph Hanna and Traugott Lawler's remarks in their introduction to Chaucer's English translation of the *Consolation*, the *Boece*: "Chaucer's understanding, not only of love but of human life itself, seems to have been fundamentally Boethian."[7] Yet if the term "Boethian" once appeared transparent, this transparency and critical agreement no longer hold. Recent scholarship, Mark Miller's *Philosophical Chaucer* in particular, has begun to question precisely what we mean by the term "Boethian," for Boethius' *Consolation* also gives voice to the impossibility and undesirability of renouncing earthly attachments.[8] The medieval Stoic tradition was beset not simply by the difficulty of dealing with earthly loss and its possibly inadequate consolations, but by the difficulty of experiencing and representing pleasure and plenitude in an environment where earthly pleasures are devalued on the level of normative discourse. One may understand that true, full happiness lies elsewhere, but that knowledge does not in itself confer happiness, and it certainly does not insulate a person from the desire for earthly delight, nor from the unexpected, fortunate encounter with joy. Miller argues that rather than containing an extractable "set of philosophical doctrines," the *Consolation of Philosophy* offers instead a dialogic exploration of human psychology which reveals both the attractions of a normative rejection of worldly happiness and the resistance to the self-dissolution that such a rejection would demand.[9] In the end, Miller claims, what is "Boethian" about Chaucer is his understanding of "the production of narrative as a paradigmatic site for fetishistic reification," of poetry as a medium in which we attempt to historicize the sense of loss that accompanies subjectivity.[10] In other words, Chaucer is being Boethian when he refuses to validate poetry as a place for the recuperation of a lost time when people were not alienated from their desires, and when everyone naturally tended toward the sovereign good. Narrative poetry may encourage us to create such a nostalgic "Former Age," an era prior to lack, but this creation, for Chaucer, is always revealed as false, and even sometimes acknowledged to be distinctly undesirable. The "Boethianism" of the *Troilus* may finally involve a rejection of nostalgia and an ethical space for earthly pleasure. This re-evaluation of the *Consolation* allows us a richer understanding of Boethius' dialogue, as well as of Chaucer's engagement with it. We have grown used to a Chaucer who is "subversive of priestly absolutes,"[11] but in the process may have grown too complacent in our certainty about the absolutes he was subverting, and about who was voicing them. In moving from an exegetical perspective on Chaucer as a vehicle for pious Christian doctrine toward a Chaucer who resists that doctrine, or engages in a dialectic that shows its gaps, we may have missed an opportunity to think about the spaces for subversive or at least unconventional thinking in the writings of the men of "gret auctorite" who provide Chaucer with so much fodder for thought.

This unexpected version of Boethianism is not just the province of recent scholarship, but also a facet of the reception of the *Consolation* in the thirteenth and fourteenth centuries. Beginning in the late thirteenth century, the *Consolation* became the subject of "Aristotelianizing" commentators who sought to bring the new learning of the schools to bear on Boethius' work. The extent to which late medieval commentators on Boethius, particularly Nicholas Trevet, departed from the widely influential commentary of the neo-Platonist William of Conches has been exaggerated in past scholarship, but there is no question that access to full translations of Aristotle's *Ethics*, *Politics*, *De Anima*, and *Metaphysics* had a transformative effect on the reception of Boethius.[12] Aristotelian earthly happiness was complemented by the reception of *De Anima*, which similarly demanded that greater emphasis be placed on the sensible world. We come to knowledge, even knowledge of concepts and greater truths, through our sensory contact with earthly things. For medieval Aristotelians, we even learn to turn our desires away from the earth and toward the divine through sensible experience.[13] The world of sense and the body thus gains a much more central place in the pursuit of knowledge and the good. Felicity starts to become a more earthly affair.

The effect of the "new Aristotle" on Boethian commentaries is seen most readily in the way that Aristotle's works were used to recalibrate the reception of controversial Platonic ideas such as the doctrine of reminiscence, the world-soul, and the pre-existence of souls and primal matter.[14] In addition to "correcting" heterodox-seeming Platonic ideas, Aristotle was also used to address less obviously controversial topics such as the turning of human desires toward false or proper goods, the proper way to consider fortune as it applies to happiness, and the way poetry and all arts tend toward the good. It is these topics to which I will turn, for they are the places where an assumed rejection of the sensible world and unstable happiness are most deeply called into question, and are troubled in such a way as to highlight the mutuality and compassion at the heart of *Troilus and Criseyde*. The commentaries' recourse to an Aristotelian ethical pedagogy of shared experience demonstrates the way that the changing context for definitions of human happiness had profound consequences for an ethical understanding of the friendship and shared emotion at the heart of consolation.

The happiness of Troilus and Criseyde appears contrary to the happiness defined by Philosophia, not only because it is of this world, but because their mutual delight highlights the fact that her austere felicity is not an emotion that another can participate in or empathize with. Both Aristotelian philosophy and the *Troilus* itself characterize shared happiness as sensory, earthbound, and mutable, and empathetic friendship as similarly sensible, mundane, and subject to fortune. For although Aristotle, like Lady Philosophy, affirms that happiness cannot be judged on the basis of fortune, Aristotle's ethics of friendship demands that instability and shared happiness go hand in hand. Aristotle's discussion of friendship in the *Ethics* assumes conditions of shifting prosperity and adversity, and the virtue of friendship depends on each friend's response to these conditions: friendship is "more necessary in adversity," but "more honorable in prosperity."[15] He goes on to claim more broadly that "Every man wishes to share with his friends whatever constitutes his existence or whatever makes his life worth living."[16] As Jacques Derrida observes, there is a "perhaps" at the heart of friendship, for "to love friendship, it is not enough to know how to bear the other in mourning; one must love the future. And there is no more just category for the future than that of the 'perhaps.'"[17] He remarks that in both Platonic and Aristotelian philosophy, friendship depends just as much on instability as on the stable or constant (*bébaios*). Aristotle insists that perfect friendship is "unchanging and enduring," but the lastingness of any friendship is tested by the fact that men themselves change.[18] Lack and instability do not destroy friendship but form its foundation. Lest we imagine that this instability is essential solely to allow for the sharing of misery and subsequent consolation, Derrida reminds us that what "makes the friend" is "*Mitfreude* and not *Mitleiden*, joy among friends, shared enjoyment (*jouissance*) and not shared suffering."[19] It is in this spirit that Chaucer's narrator tells his audience at the beginning of Book III that it is a part of the poet's ethical responsibility to narrate pleasure as well as sorrow. He vows that he must, though he may labor a full year, speak about the "gladnesse" of the lovers as well as he has spoken about their "heavinesse" (III.1196–7). This vow to hard labor, and his later failure of speech at the high point of Troilus and Criseyde's joy, point to the difficulties inherent in such a project, but also to its importance. The narrator's responsibility and challenge is to speak of a pleasure that is present, full, and shared. Such pleasure is always threatened by the "perhaps" of fortune, and yet constituted by it; a Boethian relationship to "future tyme" (v.748) demands both an embrace of fortune as the condition of friendship and an acknowledgment that fortune "imedles" happiness with care and sorrow.[20]

Thinking Boethius through Aristotle puts questions of earthly pain and pleasure, shared emotion, and sensible experience into high relief. While there is only one of these late medieval commentaries on Boethius that we know Chaucer to have read – that of Nicholas Trevet – it is instructive to glance at the commentary of the "arch-Aristotelian" William of Aragon. His commentary on the *Consolation* rehabilitates the sensory world, departing in striking ways from the pre-Aristotelian tradition of commentary on the text, offering original readings that often foreground his critique of William of Conches' Platonism.[21] The later William uses a variety of Aristotelian texts to reconcile both Boethius and Plato to a late medieval Aristotelianism, so as to "bring down the Platonic atmosphere of Boethius' text to the Aristotelian world of sense."[22] He accomplishes this descent in a number of ways, most importantly by linking man's knowledge of intelligible goods to the sensual world. While William's commentary does not seem to have been spectacularly popular (only five manuscripts survive), it was certainly read by Jean de Meun, who translated the prologue for his own French version, *Le Livre de Confort de Philosophie*.[23] This prologue was subsequently used in two other popular French vernacular translations of the *Consolation*, giving William's prologue, if not the body of his commentary, much greater exposure than the number of surviving Latin copies would suggest.[24]

His prologue, in which he explains why he – a scholar of medicine – will be lecturing on the *Consolation*, underscores humanity's unavoidable immersion in sensible things, and emphasizes that so long as our souls remain embodied, the only path toward intellectual knowledge is through the senses. He begins with a citation of Aristotle's *Politics*, that "all things seek the good,"[25] and proceeds to naturalize this dictum, offering examples of plants turning toward sunlight and animals drawn to kind owners. Human beings, however, pursue the good in a confused and haphazard way. What makes human beings unique, in William's reading, is not their rational capabilities (though as a good Aristotelian he would admit this as well), but that "man alone, out of all other creatures, needs practice in acting and needs to be taught in the matter of exercising his choice so that he may be brought closer to what is good for him by a direct route and without deviation."[26] The natural world in this view is marked by a harmony with the good, rather than by a bestial pursuit of sensory pleasure. As in Will's vision of middle-earth in

Piers Plowman, William observes that while humans are the only creatures capable of cultivating *habitus*, they are also the only creatures that *require* it. Humans need these habitual practices that inculcate virtue and allow for the judicious choice of an appropriate good in a sensory world where many felonious things appear good. However, William does not advocate a turning away from the sensory world, but simply an education of the senses that will allow for an understanding of intelligible as well as sensual goods. He thus acknowledges that the world of sense is disordered and confusing, but he also maintains that it is the only route by which people can come to an understanding of intelligible goods. Philosophy is essential to one's education, but he insists that we gain knowledge of the good "first of all through sensation."[27] Man is confused by the sensible world, but also nurtured ("nutritur") by it for a very long time.

William's prologue also highlights the impossibility of simply denying the attractions of earthly goods. Boethius' dialogue, along with Aristotle's *Ethics*, can teach us that the truly good person withstands the blows of fortune with strength and wisdom, but will never tell us that we should be "impervious" ("insensibilitatem") to worldly sorrow.[28] We should not ignore the delights and pains of the world, but learn how to sustain them bravely. This version of Stoicism might not seem like such a dramatic shift, but it runs counter to the usual notion that Boethius' dialogue teaches us to mortify our attachments to worldly objects. What William would like us to avoid is the "mental turmoil" ("turbatio animi") that the weak mind suffers when subjected to misfortune. The properly "Boethian" subject, according to William, keeps his teleological compass intact, pointing ultimately toward the sovereign good, even when he or she suffers a finite loss. That he will suffer, however, is never in question. It is "part of the human condition to feel intensely, and grieve over, misfortunes which occur in relation to those [sensible] goods."[29] Aristotle remarks in Book VII of the *Ethics* that although fortune is not identical with happiness, it is nonsensical to imagine that even the virtuous man remains happy when overcome by misfortune.[30] In William's version of Stoicism, then, we can learn to sustain grief wisely, but we cannot learn not to grieve at all. His Aristotelianism appears to allow for a certain compatibility between the pursuit of the good and attachment to worldly objects, and between consolation and lingering sorrow. Consolation in William's terms emphatically does not mean an absence of pain, though such relief is clearly a deeply held desire for many other medieval and modern readers of Boethius' book.

William of Aragon's rejection of imperviousness allows him to develop an empathic theory of human happiness in the context of his commentary on the Orpheus myth in Book III, meter 12. William's interpretation of the first two words, "felix qui," plays on the double meaning of happiness as the sovereign good and as a stroke of luck or chance. William notes various philosophers who have offered different paths toward perfect happiness: discovering the causes of things, never experiencing prosperity, caring not who rules the world – all of these paths are contingent stances or experiences that enable a person to better orient himself to the final good.[31] William himself prefers the proverb, "Happy is the man made cautious by other people's dangers"[32] or, as Pandarus might put it, "wyse ben by foles harm chastised" (III.329). He explains that there are two ways that men learn to be disposed toward the good: the first through one's own experience and the second through witnessing the experiences of others. The latter, William tells us, is much more efficient. In this he echoes Aristotle who explains that happy men have need of friends not only because solitary life is unpleasant, but because "we can study our neighbors better than ourselves and their actions better than our own."[33] The recommended path toward happiness is thus followed in its most generous sense not only by observing fools, but through friendship and empathy. William's emphasis on learning through the experiences of others points to an Orpheus who might not only tell us about the danger of looking back at earthly objects of desire, but also about the empathetic pleasure of poetry, the virtuous aspects of earthly love, and the way that all of our neighbor's experiences – of happiness and of its loss – are worthy of sharing and essential to one's ethical education.

Nicholas Trevet, on the other hand, was a more conservative commentator, maintaining a respectful treatment of William of Conches' work while using Aristotelian philosophy to reconcile the earlier commentator's Platonism to Christian doctrine.[34] Trevet's commentary was more popular, and was a key source for Chaucer during his composition of the *Boece*.[35] But Trevet also highlights the workings of empathy in the *Consolation* and in ethical life generally. His prologue makes compassion the central goal of the *Consolation*, giving particular power to poetic form to rouse this emotion. His prologue suggests that Boethius begins his book in meter because a *planctus* moves us to compassion more readily, for music is inherent in metrical language rather than prose, and it is music that has the capacity to move us.[36] For Trevet, one of the main goals of Boethius' book is to move us to compassion via poetic form itself. The Aristotelian context of his commentary most often takes him into concerns about precisely how Boethius' book theorizes the way that people learn or are moved. He cites the second book of the *Metaphysics* as explaining that not everyone learns the truth in the same way ("non omnes recipiunt veritatem eodem modo") and that diverse natures and education mean that some will learn through logical demonstration, some through authoritative proof, and some through the veils of fabulous narratives ("per integumentum fabularum"). While the notion of truth veiled by fable is hardly new, Trevet places this standard justification of fiction within a context of education that is keyed to an individual's circumstances and character. He occasionally adds details to Boethius' narrative that further highlight the variety of responses to a story or a song; where Boethius' Orpheus laments the cruelty of the gods after the death of Eurydice, Trevet explains that Orpheus had attempted to soothe the celestial gods with melodies ("modulationibus deos superos placare sategit"). When this did not work – the cruel gods could not be moved – he took his songs to the underworld.

Trevet's commentary emphasizes the workings of poetry both within the Orpheus fable – song has the capacity to move those susceptible to such movement – and in the workings of the *Consolation* itself. The banishing of the muses in the opening of the book tells us that Philosophia desires only one kind of song – that which will elevate our thoughts to the divine. Yet through the earthbound concerns of the doomed Boethius and the lovelorn Orpheus who must direct his music toward whoever will receive it, our affections are often drawn in opposing directions. The simultaneous attractions of both celestial contemplation and human ethics and love become central to even the most Platonic moments of the book. Mark Gleason argues that Trevet develops an Aristotelian framework for explorations of love in the *Consolation*, so that a Platonic expression of cosmic love and creation such as Book III, meter 9 ("O qui perpetua") may also be read in terms of Aristotelian causes and understandings of the sovereign good.[37] For both Boethius and Trevet, human reason, will, and moral intelligence are understood not as subjected to the greater force of the divine will, but rather as operating within an ethical framework founded on the premise of God's love for the universe.[38] Gleason concludes that the *Consolation* and Trevet's commentary offered Chaucer resources to explore "how far the love that harmonizes the universe can unite and harmonize human hearts when nature only is the guide."[39]

Both William's and Trevet's commentaries thus make an ethical space for poetry that imagines the compassion inspired by metrical language and the educative possibilities of witnessing another's experience – either in life or in fable. Bruce Holsinger has suggested that Chaucer made up for his prosing of the *Boece* in his short "Boethian" poems, restoring "lyric integrity to one of the great vernacularizing enterprises of his career."[40] One might imagine the poet engaged in a similar formal enterprise in the *Troilus*, an investigation of the way meter moves us to compassion and identification, and a probing of the ethical and aesthetic limits of human encounters with others. Both Boethius' dialogue and Chaucer's poem explore the possibilities of learning by example of happiness as well as sorrow. The Aristotelian commentaries on Boethius allow us to speculate about the ways in which the shifting environment for the reception of Boethius' book – made possible or even necessary by the new Aristotle – may have shaped certain possibilities for Chaucer as a "Boethian" poet and his readers as "Boethian" subjects. Boethius glosses Aristotle as much as Aristotle glosses Boethius. An Aristotelian notion of the relevance of the sensual world to pursuits of both erotic pleasure and the sovereign good allows for a revised approach to earthly goods. The new Aristotle offered readers of Boethius an innovative context for thinking through not only obviously controversial topics such as the pre-existence of souls or prime matter, but also topics that were not so clearly orthodox or heterodox, yet were clearly essential to Christian ethics: how to pursue the good in the context of both lived and read experience. While neither William of Aragon nor Nicholas Trevet was interested in exploring romantic passion as an ethical good, each insists on an approach to the good as sensible and as perceptible through the experience of others. Bringing the world of the intellect down to the realm of the senses (or the senses up to the world of the intellect) allows the compassionate education recommended by the Boethian commentators to take place. This context sharpens Troilus' lesson learned in the first book of the poem, when he laments – with an unmistakable air of self-satisfaction – that foolish lovers cannot learn from each other's suffering: "Ther nys nat oon kan war by other be" (1.203). It is, of course, Troilus who has not learned from others that he is just as susceptible to love as they are. Having climbed the stairway of pride, Troilus must descend to the realm of those made subject unto love. As both he and Orpheus know, "may no man fordon the lawe of kynde" (1.238).

DANTE AND THE CONSOLATIONS OF FRIENDSHIP

In Dante's writings we find not only the exploration of Aristotelian theories of happiness, but also vernacular sites for the rereading of Boethian felicity in the light of Aristotelian philosophy. Dante offers a fairly radical estimation of Aristotelian theories of earthly happiness in his Italian *Convivio*, as well as in the Latin *Monarchia*. For Dante, Aristotle is the supreme philosopher, and in his world the Peripatetic school of philosophy "tiene questa gente oggi lo reggimento del mondo in dottrina per tutte parti, e puotesi appellare quasi cattolica oppinione" (at present holds universal sway in teaching everywhere, and their doctrine may almost be called universal opinion).[41] In his treatise on government, *Monarchia*, Dante gives Aristotle full authority on happiness, claiming that it is fruitless for anyone to write again on the topic, with the Philosopher having already done so.[42] Robert Lerner refers to Dante as having an "integrally Aristotelian position" in the *Monarchia*, distinguishing between the final goal for each human life and for all of humankind.[43] Dante writes that divine Providence "set before us two goals to aim at: i.e. happiness in this life, which consists in the exercise of our own powers and is figured in the earthly Paradise; and happiness in the eternal life, which consists in the enjoyment of the vision of God (to which our own powers cannot raise us except with the help of God's light) and which is signified by the heavenly paradise."[44] The first end has been "entirely revealed to us by the philosophers" while the other has been revealed by the Holy Spirit, prophets, and sacred writings. While at the end of the *Monarchia* Dante concedes that mortal happiness is in "some sense" ordered toward immortal felicity, it seems clear that he defines human happiness as Aristotle defines it – an end in itself, constituted by philosophical contemplation.[45] Lerner argues that Dante's commitment to dual happiness may be found in the *Commedia* as well, and observes that Dante reaches earthly Paradise in the *Purgatorio* through a pilgrimage "accomplished by means of philosophy, not theology."[46] While this earlier journey prefigures the later journey through Paradise, this parallel need not obviate the fact that there are two paths. Olivia Holmes reads Dante's relationship to these two felicities through the lens of erotic choice, but illustrates that they are unified in a female love object; she notes, "First in the *Convivio*'s Donna Gentile, and later in the *Commedia*'s Beatrice, Dante embraces both meanings of Philosophy, the secular/classical and the scriptural."[47] For Dante, although the fullness of both felicities cannot be experienced in this life, desire for earthly happiness need no longer be defined by its frustrating and unfulfillable nature.[48]

Chaucer knew at least parts of Dante's *Convivio* – the Wife of Bath attributes the loathly lady's speech about "gentilesse" to Dante, and parts of her meditation on nobility come from this text. Chaucer also seems to quote the treatise in *The Legend of Good Women* ("vertu is the mene, / as Etik seith," F.165–6), though the echo is decidedly brief. Although it is possible that Chaucer was working with a fragmentary knowledge of the *Convivio*, it is just as likely that he had knowledge of the full treatise.[49] In this unfinished text, Dante theorizes the pursuit of philosophical knowledge as an erotic pursuit, placing it within a Boethian framework. In the first book, Dante allies himself almost incidentally with the author of the *Consolation*, justifying his choice to speak about himself by observing that Boethius used the pretext of consolation to clear his name from infamy. Such a motivation guides his commentary on the first canzone, revealing that virtue, not passion, moved its author. In the second book, Dante identifies himself far more closely with Boethius, revealing that when he had lost "lo primo diletto de la mia anima" (the first delight of [his] soul), he read the *Consolation* alongside Cicero's *On Friendship*, and through this reading discovered that Philosophy was a "somma cosa" (great thing), and he began to imagine her fashioned "come una donna gentile" (as a gentle lady, II.12.6). The Donna Gentile of the *Convivio* is a noble lady, a beloved, and Philosophia all at once. In taking the position of the prisoner consoled by Philosophy, and yet placing that consolation in the delight of human happiness – experienced by friend, lover, philosopher – Dante gives us a radically changed Boethianism. In the *Convivio*, the pursuit of philosophy does not demand a turn from the world, but rather an embrace of *philia* that gives consolation.[50]

The *Convivio* defines philosophy by exploring the relationship between the philosopher and his love object; happiness itself – in its earthly form – is constituted by this relationship. Citing Book IX of the *Ethics*, Dante defines the end of true friendship as delight in what is good, and the end of philosophy as "quella eccellentissima dilezione che non pate alcuna intermissione o vero difetto, cioè vera felicitade che per contemplazione de la veritade s'acquista" (that most excellent delight which suffers no cessation or imperfection, namely true happiness, which is acquired through the contemplation of truth, III.11.14). The *Convivio* is thus an allegory of and commentary on love, friendship, and philosophy – three categories which collapse entirely by the end of the work. For Dante, a philosopher is most importantly a friend of wisdom, a participant in a love affair that is mutual, engendering good will on both sides (III.11). Following Aristotle, the delight that accompanies "true" friendship and true philosophy is rooted in stable truths rather than contingent, accidental desires, though located in a world of contingency. Philosophy itself comes to be defined through friendship, for "Filosofia è quando l'anima e la sapienza sono fatte amiche, sì che l'una sia tutta amata da l'altra" (philosophy exists when the soul and wisdom have become such friends that each is wholly loved by the other, III.12.4). While Aristotle's ideas of friendship proceed from his definition of happiness, Dante turns this relationship inside out, showing his readers that philosophy *is* friendship, modeled on human relationships. While Dante is clearly imposing simultaneously courtly and Aristotelian ideas onto Boethius' incarnation of Philosophia, he may also be drawing out an idea of philosophy as love/friendship that is latent in Boethius' own writings. Peter Dronke finds a parallel notion in Boethius' commentary on Porphyry, where he states that "Philosophy is the love and pursuit and in a sense friendship of Wisdom."[51] Dante draws out the implications of Boethius' Philosophia, who was so easily transformed into a courtly lady by late medieval readers.[52]

Dante leaves no doubt that he speaks about happiness in this life, emphasizing that when his canzone says "quella gente che qui s'innamora" (those down here who fall in love, III.13.3) such words signify that he speaks of "filosofia umana" (human philosophy) and those who fall in love "'qui,' cioè in questa vita" (here, that is, in this life, III.13.3). While Dante acknowledges in the fourth Book that the speculative intellect cannot reach perfection in this life (IV.22.13), it is nevertheless clear that he allows for the pursuit of human happiness in its own right. For Dante, we first come to blessedness imperfectly, through the active life, but later find it "almost perfectly" in the exercise of the intellectual virtues (IV.22.18). The necessary qualification of "almost" and warnings about the impossibility of intellectual perfection in this life do little to modify Dante's praise of intellectual contemplation as the highest calling of human reason, offering its own delights, and a happiness that is proper to this world – not happy in that it partakes of some quality of the happiness of the afterlife, but happy in that it fulfills human earthly potentiality. Dante speaks not only of friendship with wisdom, but of human need for companionship in the social world. "A life of happiness [*vita felice*]," he observes, is not attainable "without the aid of someone else" (IV.4.1). While Aristotle's theory of happiness allowed for the pursuit of perfect enjoyment in this life, the transformation of contemplative happiness into *imperfect* earthly happiness was foundational for a medieval ethics of human felicity. Perfect happiness might always be deferred until the afterlife, but human happiness could nevertheless be a true, real, and realizable activity.

Chaucer left Dante's Aristotelian material behind in building his discourse on nobility in "The Wife of Bath's Tale," seemingly uninterested in the scholastic context of the *Convivio*'s discussions of virtue.[53] Yet in

Troilus and Criseyde we find an embodied, narrative version of Dante's alliance of the pursuit of philosophy with the pursuit of a mutual love and an engagement with philosophical questions made possible by falling in love and being in love. In the *Convivio*, Chaucer would have found the collocation of delight, eros, happiness, and clerkliness that marks the height of love in *Troilus*, Book III.[54] Dante's *philia* goes beyond the common or natural, does not hide itself from the loved one, manifests itself in devotion or dedication, loves every part of the beloved, and exists both between two people and between an individual and wisdom. Chaucer does not go so far as Dante in locating perfect happiness on earth, and yet he goes further. While Dante emphasizes love as a stable source of happiness amidst a world of turbulent change, Chaucer gives his lovers a contingent happiness that nevertheless transcends the felicity of the clerks. And while Dante uses courtly models of human behavior and relationships to explain the felicities of philosophy, Chaucer uses a unified vision of philosophical and courtly happiness to explore courtly love and friendship. All of the concerted power of philosophical and courtly discourses is necessary to understand human relationships in Chaucer's *Troilus*.

THE DOUBLED JOYS OF TROILUS AND CRISEYDE

By placing Chaucer's *Troilus and Criseyde* in the context of the Boethian commentaries and Dante's *Convivio*, we may avoid the binary crux that has so often guided interpretations of the lines with which I opened this chapter, lines that describe the lovers' joy against which clerkly felicity appears insufficient. With these lines, Chaucer leaves his audience wondering whether Troilus and Criseyde's joy surpasses clerkly happiness, or perhaps simply stands outside of it. Readers have typically wondered about the narrator's sincerity – is he serious when he tells us that the lovers' erotic encounter exceeds the sovereign happiness commended by clerks, and that it is in fact ineffable? Such a question leads inevitably to one of two options: either the narrator is sincere, and is an example of someone who misidentifies sensual pleasure as true happiness (or is reluctant to identify it as false), or the narrator is ironic, pointing out the vain, misguided ways of the two lovers who mistake their brief delights for the highest bliss.[55] It is clear, however, that romantic happiness is one field of worldly felicity that Chaucer did not find so easy to dismiss, and that he consistently returned to the difficult relationship between erotic pleasure and clerkly felicity. As in Dante, erotic, intellectual, and spiritual pursuits of happiness manifest themselves in the same experience of *philia*, and are thus not so easy to disentangle. The infamous clerks of the passage quoted above make their appearance elsewhere in Chaucer's poetry, as in "The Merchant's Tale" where the narrator explains that

> Somme clerkes holden that felicitee
> Stant in delit, and therfore certeyn he,
> This noble Januarie, with al his myght,
> In honest wyse, as longeth to a knyght,
> Shoop hym to lyve ful deliciously. (ll. 2021–5)

In this instance, it is clear that January has either ignorantly or quite cleverly misunderstood the clerkly belief that felicity is equivalent to pleasure. The qualifying "Somme" at the beginning of the statement might signal that Chaucer was aware of contemporary philosophical debates as to whether enjoyment (*fruitio*) was the same as pleasure (*delectatio*), and thus whether happiness as a human *summum bonum* was necessarily constituted by pleasure. Contemporary philosophical allusion or no, January transforms the delights of philosophical contemplation into the delicious pursuit of voluptuous pleasure with a much younger wife. But even January worries that he will have "so parfit felicitee" (l. 1642) in marriage that he will pre-emptively have his heaven on earth. Chaucer was obviously delighted by the comic potential inherent in a clerkly discourse that centered on the high moral pursuit of happiness and pleasure, but he also took a genuine interest in the ethical and poetic implications of a moral discourse that acknowledged the desirability of happiness and pleasure, indeed judged "the good" by the very fact of its desirability, and yet sought to discipline or even construct those same desires. Those who identify either an unreliable or an ironic narrator in the *Troilus* have created a largely false choice, for both options deny the poet and the reader an engagement with the complicated problems evoked in this stanza. In drawing his comparison, Chaucer plays on the fact that lovers and moral philosophers share a common understanding of happiness as the sovereign good. A knowing disregard for the lovers' bliss would evade the basic confluences and conflicts between clerkly ideals of spiritual and intellectual happiness and the natural attractions of erotic love, which has its own spiritual and intellectual involvements. Such disregard also denies the poem a serious engagement with these philosophical definitions of human happiness – if we take it as obvious that the "felicite" so commended by clerks is the one we should desire, how exactly is it defined? Who are these clerks who commend it so, and what is their relationship to human happiness?

For a poet like Chaucer, interested in the relationship between human love and loss and final ends, the reconsideration of paths toward happiness opened up myriad possibilities for the poetry of epic romance. Rather than a hymn to stability and self-sufficiency, the *Troilus* is better understood as an exploration of happiness in a world of instability and contingency – not in defiance of "clerkes" and their prescriptions, but as a poetic contribution to a larger inquiry into the nature of human happiness and sensible pleasures. The poem asks its audience to share in its lovers' sorrows and joys, and to imagine an ethical response to their shared delight. The narrator opens the poem by calling upon lovers that bathe in "gladnesse" (1.22) to identify with the adversity that faces other, less fortunate lovers, and claims that he himself will have compassion on them as though he were their own brother (1.50–1). This plea for compassion in sorrow is nothing unusual, but it becomes more complicated in the context of the shared joy at the center of the poem. The sharing of emotion is an ethical necessity, given Paul's command that we should "gaudere cum gaudentibus flere cum flentibus" (rejoice with those who rejoice, weep with those who weep, Romans 12:15). The author of the pentitential treatise *Fasciculus Morum*, speaking about the diabolical nature of envy, extends Paul's statement beyond law and claims that Paul says it is human nature ("humanum est") to share joy and sadness.[56] Sharing joy may thus be read as anything from perfectly ethical to dangerously (because sexually) voyeuristic. *Troilus and Criseyde* raises many questions about the propriety of the witnessing – both by Pandarus and by the audience – of the erotic bliss of its eponymous couple. Yet the narrator replaces questions of propriety with larger ethical questions when he balks at describing their consummation not because he is too polite, but because their joy exceeds the *summum bonum*.

Placing the lovers' consummation in the context of its potential relation to the highest good usefully shifts our relationship to the questions of complicity and voyeurism that have long haunted readers' perceptions of the lovers' happiness. Pandarus' role in the poem often calls up questions of consent and propriety, and raises the possibility that our witnessing of the two lovers' bliss is an act of voyeurism. His and Troilus' desires are at times virtually indistinguishable in the poem, and he shares in the knight's losses and triumphs, pains and joys. Pandarus' vicariousness invites readers to see themselves in the same terms, and thereby encourages us to consider the ethics of our participation in the felicity and the sorrows of the two lovers. A. C. Spearing remarks on both the distance created by Chaucer's narrator, ignorant in the ways of love, and the distance bridged by Pandarus, who experiences vicarious sexual pleasure through his machinations.[57] The poem appears to slide very deliberately between vicariousness and empathy, voyeurism and consolation. Lee Patterson has argued for an ethical mode of identification with the lovers, recommending that "the experience [of reading *Troilus and Criseyde*] should be one not of moral superiority but rather complicity."[58] Yet describing the audience's response as "complicit" implies that we guiltily participate in a crime or other transgression; instead the poem works to bridge the gap between complicity and compassion by making mutuality a central aspect of happiness. The question raised by the reader's participation in the lovers' happiness is how such a partaking can be consonant with the "felicite" learned through experience. If we are not soothed by Orpheus' song of grief, but rather witnesses to a song of joy, what response should this provoke?

This question of how friendship should be understood as a mutual pursuit of happiness is refracted through each of Chaucer's three protagonists. The most explicit advocate for the sharing of joy is Pandarus, whose version of happiness and friendship is sensual, contingent, and shared. It is perhaps for this reason that it is Pandarus who introduces the Orpheus myth into the world of the poem. The question of compassion in relation to love poetry is essential to the tale of Orpheus in every version, as Orpheus' song of grief for Eurydice invariably soothes not only earthly creatures but the denizens of hell. The tragic irony of Orpheus' song in Boethius' *Consolation* is that though it subdues nature and relieves hell's tortures, it cannot soothe its master.[59] We constantly take pleasure in the well-rendered sorrows of others; such is perhaps a description of the better portion of poetry. Yet Pandarus, from whose mouth the allusions to those conquered by Orpheus fly fast in Book I of the *Troilus*, would much rather take pleasure in others' happiness and do whatever he can to make that happiness come about. And Pandarus will not, above all, allow his friend to wallow in the lyric enjoyment of his suffering. In this moment, Pandarus appears to diagnose Troilus' transgression of psychoanalytic ethics – Troilus has given up on his desire and prefers rather to enjoy his pain; this pleasure in sacrifice is precisely what Pandarus asks Troilus to give up, exhorting him to "Delyte nat in wo" (I.704). The ever-optimistic Pandarus is the poem's problematic spokesperson for an earthly happiness that might evade the Law of the Father, trick Fortune at her own game, and might disturb our convictions that earthly happiness, because necessarily fleeting, is a foolish or even impossible pursuit. That such questions about the relationships among poetry, empathy, and happiness are raised by the Orpheus myth would not surprise Albert the Great, who tells us that in the opening lines of Book III, meter 12 ("Felix qui potuit boni") of the *Consolation*, we find "drawn together and grasped" ("trahitur et tangitur") all of Book X of the *Nicomachean Ethics*.[60]

In a scene in Book II that seems to deliberately parody Chaucer's earlier foray into Boethian consolation, *The Book of the Duchess*, Pandarus reports to Criseyde that he has encouraged his friend to tell him the cause of his sorrow. Pandarus claims to have overheard Troilus in the palace garden groaning and praying to God to "have routhe upon [his] peyne" (II.523). Like the Black Knight, Troilus reportedly repents of his youthful dismissal of love and beseeches God to demand his penance. And like the *Book*'s dreaming narrator, Pandarus pretends not to have heard Troilus' cries and allows him to feign a "fresshe" countenance, until he later finds him weeping in his chamber and finally convinces him to reveal the source of his grief. The ambiguity of *The Book of the Duchess* as to whether Chaucer's narrator understands the source of the Knight's grief or not is clarified to comic effect in this episode of the *Troilus*; we might understand Pandarus as the answer to the Black Knight's adamant assertion that neither "al the remedyes of Ovyde, / Ne Orpheus, god of melodye" (ll. 568–9) could heal him. Troilus' physician intentionally feigns ignorance as a ploy to gain his patient's confidence, encouraging him to reveal his grief so that a cure might be found. In his conversation with Criseyde, Pandarus rewrites Chaucer's dream vision and creates a narrative path toward a happy ending – to be authored, naturally, by him. Consolation arrives in the form of a confident procurer of happiness – a possibility that could not have been entertained by the earlier poem. Pandarus walks a fine line between vicarious, intrusive pleasure and literal incarnation of the Aristotelian ideal of the friend – he shares with Troilus those things that constitute his existence and make his life worth living. The poem both raises the possibility that Pandarus is no more than a bawd, and emphasizes that he acts selflessly, for no hope of reward (III.415). He and Troilus are mutually satisfied by the actions of the other, holding each other "wel apayed," or rewarded (III.421).

Troilus is not only a recipient of the benefits of such friendship, for he shares his joys with his friend, and his emotional response to love in the aftermath of the affair's consummation exceeds the private space of the loving couple. His renewed compassion appears at first to render Troilus the typical courtly lover, ennobled by love, but the poem emphasizes not only his valor in war and his generosity, but his increased capacity for friendship, and his sharing of his joy most of all with Pandarus. While delighting in his love affair with Criseyde, Troilus lives "In suffisaunce, in blisse, and in singynges" (III.1716). He gathers about him "a world of folk," the best men and women that Troy has to offer. This Troilus in love consoles those who are in sorrow, and lacks all envy, feeling only gladness when others fare well (III.1790–1). He takes Pandarus often into the garden to share his joy in Criseyde's "wommanhede" and beauty, and sings him a Boethian hymn to cosmic love. His song that begins "Love, that of erthe and se hath governaunce" (III.1744) praises Love in its capacity to join people together while assuring harmonious change – a world ruled by love varies, but in such a way that it remains stable. Troilus may not here be wrenching Boethius' meter out of its proper context, but rather celebrating its new context of Dantean courtly Aristotelianism. His song is the embodiment of stable love in the face of instability – necessary in adversity and even more honorable in prosperity – that Aristotle praises.

Like Troilus, Criseyde experiences love in relation to friends outside the private couple, in the context of a homosocial community and in an even more overt context of philosophical debate. Earlier in the poem, we witness a Criseyde who is first opened up to the possibility of love through her relationships with her women. She is the figure most concerned about the brittleness of false happiness, and of the main figures in the poem she emerges most explicitly as an ethical subject – one who expresses concerns about Fortune and freedom, right action and reputation, and is ever asking what "fyn" she is living for.[61] As a widow, she stands in the beginning as someone whose involvement in life's tumult is past, someone for whom "the mooste stormy lyf" (II.778) is something to be avoided. The traditional moralizing voice (of the *Ovide Moralisé*, for instance) would recommend holding oneself aloof from the storms of earthly life, safe in the boat of the church and of faith.[62] Yet Criseyde, for better or worse, plunges in. We first witness Criseyde being brought to love in Book II when she witnesses her niece Antigone's song. Criseyde is naturally skeptical about the possibility of happiness through earthly love, and she wonders aloud if there is actually such bliss among lovers as they describe in their songs (II.885–6). Antigone's song expresses the notion that being in love will allow for a life consistently "In alle joie and seurte out of drede" (II.833) while simultaneously acknowledging that the most heartfelt possible wish for one's beloved is the wish for good fortune: "Now good thrift have he, wherso that he be!" (II.847). Criseyde is silent in response, but we are told that she printed every word that she had heard upon her heart, thus beginning to lose her fear of love, and to grow "somwhat able to converte" (II.903). Rather than being swayed by testimony or proof, Criseyde learns from the example of her friend, and is moved by music. She resembles the reading subject of the *Consolation*, as theorized by Nicholas Trevet: moved to compassion by musical language and finally brought to knowledge via various modes – example, logical discourse, and fabulous narrative.

Of course, the possibility that Criseyde does not participate in the felicitous mutual love ("I love hym best, so doth he me") described by the poem is repeatedly raised.[63] For it is directly after Criseyde hears Antigone's song and becomes less fearful of love that she dreams of a white eagle who rends her heart from her breast, an image that is echoed later in the description of Criseyde as an innocent lark caught in the grasp of the sparrow hawk (III.1191–2). The felicity of the lovers is threatened not solely by its avowed earthliness, but by the possibility that Criseyde is an unwilling participant, that she is only an object to be enjoyed. This anxiety both "imedles" their felicity and sharpens the reader's belief in the importance of mutuality, our desire to believe what the poem overtly insists upon – that Criseyde loves and experiences joy with Troilus. The mutuality of the lovers' delight is integral to the narrative, and is finally the reason for the narrator's loss of words. The union of the two lovers – a central lyric moment in the midst of a narrative punctuated by songs, letters, and interior philosophical debate – is a moment in which concerns for the mutuality of the affair are meant both to dissipate and yet also to heighten. The poem's oscillation here in regard to the possibility of true mutual consent appears tied to the consolations provided not only by sensory pleasures but by language itself. The audience is presented with a moment of pre-symbolic bliss, where language need not, cannot enter. In the face of the seamless union of Troilus' and Criseyde's wills and enjoyment, words fail. Still, at other moments the poem attempts to reverse the Lacanian and Platonic understanding of language whereby words themselves signify lack. Chaucer fantasizes a space where language is for joy fulfilled, not joy desired, where his lovers rehearse the history of their courting in lines that sound quite a bit like the poem itself: "how, and whan, and where / Thei knewe hem first, and every wo and feere / That passed was" (III.1397–9). In this joyous retelling, both happiness and sorrow are recalled, but all "hevynesse" is turned to "gladnesse" and tales of woe are broken by kissing. The two lovers "recover bliss" without a loss of self or speech, implying that if we could only inhabit their bliss for this instant, we might have our reading or listening experience transformed into an experience of full, joyous language without lack, and compassion without pain.

The couple's process of falling in love and loving is a foray into the *filosofia umana* that Dante describes; they are "la gente che qui s'innamora" exploring the possibilities and limits of human happiness and friendship, and the philosophical questions animated specifically by an eroticization of that happiness and friendship. To what extent can one recognize the will of another, and how much freedom can one discover in one's own will? How can learning from others not only lead to happiness, but in fact constitute happiness itself? For Aristotle, friendship is not simply a tool leading to greater virtue and happiness, but is an end in itself. Community has its benefits, but is pursued for its own sake, and people "desire to live together even when they have no need of help from one another."[64]

Thus when the sun rises and the world impinges on the lovers' moment of bliss, just as it will on their later moment of quiet, ineffable mutuality, this turning of Fortune's wheel need not demonstrate that we should never have enjoyed the poetic depiction of worldly happiness in the first place. Worldliness, in "questa vita," is the substance of their philosophy. And thus Criseyde's betrayal is born not out of her fickle femininity, nor necessarily out of political pragmatism, but out of a desire to keep her worldly felicity stable, a refusal to accept the "perhaps" at the heart of her and Troilus' friendship and love affair. Criseyde ventriloquizes Boethius when she asks how one can ever be truly happy, for "if to lese his joie he sette a myte, / Than semeth it that joie is worth ful lite" (III.832–3). Chaucer's interest in Boethian discourses of consolation accords not only with representations of sorrow in need of amelioration, but with representations of mundane joy that are unavoidably riddled with anxiety. The *Consolation* gives voice to the fragility of such joy and to its uncertain ethical value. Philosophia consoles Boethius by encouraging him to see that his earthly misfortune does not actually dilute his happiness, if this happiness is only appropriately defined. As Aristotle explains in the first Book of the *Nicomachean Ethics*, we cannot determine the happiness of a man by the vagaries of fortune, as though he were a chameleon – happy one moment and then unhappy the next. Such unstable, insufficient happiness is not happiness at all. This definition is the cornerstone upon which Lady Philosophy builds her pupil's understanding of the *summum bonum* as "verray blisfulnesse." Secular happiness, "worldly selynesse," is simply not to be trusted – either it is compromised by anxiety or it is only a phantom emotion. Yet Aristotle's rejection of fortune-based understandings of *eudaimonia* are taken to a radical extreme by Philosophia, who argues that fortunate circumstances do not contribute to a full life of happiness in *any* meaningful way. For William of Aragon, as for Aristotle, it is the human condition to feel misfortune deeply – a far remove from Philosophia's insistence that bad fortune is to be embraced as revealing a truth about the world. In her betrayal of Troilus, Criseyde appears to oscillate between an Aristotelian acceptance of fortune – "bityde what bityde" (v.750) – and an acceptance of Philosophia's definition of happiness.

After their fortunes have turned, Criseyde comforts herself by looking forward to a time when in "the feld of pite, out of peyne, / That highte Elisos, shal we ben yfeere, / As Orpheus and Erudice, his feere" (iv.789–91). The rhyme of "yfeere" and "feere" calls up an absent third homonym, "fear," suggesting the anxiety that underlies Criseyde's Elysian fantasy. She appears later to assent to earthly felicity, stating boldly that she calls felicity her "suffissaunce" (v.763), yet her earlier Orphic desires betray her. Criseyde seems to have in mind the Orpheus and Eurydice not of Boethius but of Ovid's *Metamorphoses*, where Orpheus' death at the hands of a horde of Thracian women allows him to reunite permanently with his Eurydice in the Elysian fields. In their shared afterlife the couple stroll together, each occasionally leading the other, with Orpheus able finally to look back safely at his love, without fear, loss, or pain.[65] It is the Criseyde who has removed her desire from the unstable, contingent world who finally loses her resolve to pursue felicity through love. She is not punished with loss for looking back at worldly goods, but rather inflicts loss by looking beyond the world to a static Elysium. Of course, there is no Elysium for Troilus and Criseyde – only war-wracked Troy. Once Criseyde turns her gaze toward the Elysian fields, in an inversion of the Orpheus myth, the serpent that bit the fleeing Eurydice becomes a simple thread that can find no purchase in Criseyde's breast – both Troilus and Troy slide "knotteles" through her heart (v.768–9).

The lovers who in fear and trepidation gave themselves up to mutual bliss experience a felicity beyond words, beyond clerks, though not beyond time. That they quickly lose this bliss points not only to the inexorable turning of Fortune's wheel, but to the difficulty of maintaining one's appreciation for the felicity wrested from this "brotel worlde." Once experienced, one cannot help but wish for eternal, Elysian bliss, though not the way Lady Philosophy intended. Criseyde's desire for stability and constancy over anxiety-ridden worldly happiness is hardly a turn toward the divine. Her knotless string will metamorphose once again to become Diomede's "hook and lyne" (v.777). The poem's palinode raises the possibility that Troilus has managed to make this happy turn, though his laughter has traditionally demanded that Chaucer's audience make a choice that is the mirror image of the choice that the "clerks" of Book III seem to ask for – an anti-Boethian irony or a Boethian sincerity. One might persuasively dismiss the last stanzas of the *Troilus* as "not a language for serious, moral, religious, or psychological inquiry,"[66] yet it is precisely as commonplaces that they necessitate investigation.

Martin Camargo allies Troilus' final laugh with his earlier (and equally conventional) laughing disdain for love and lovers, thus enacting a "parody" of the man that Lady Philosophy would like Boethius to become.[67] As the narrator tells us, "thus bigan his lovyng of Criseyde, / As I have told, and in this wise he deyde" (v.1833–4). Troilus' laugh need not be ironic or insincere, but he has been converted to the enjoyment of divine, not human, happiness; such should well be his end in the afterlife, akin to the turn in Dante's *Paradiso*, when the poet leaves Virgil behind for Beatrice. We do not need the intervening story of Troilus and Criseyde, or their songs, to arrive at the narrator's exhortation to "yonge, fresshe folkes" to give up worldly vanity, and that is what is so jarring, and thus so important, about these "commonplaces" – they do not accommodate lived or shared experience. They are correct in a strict sense, though they do not tell half the story, or any story. The Lord whom Chaucer addresses in the final stanza as "uncircumscript," but which "al maist circumscrive" does in fact encompass, circumscribe all of the experiences contained in the poem, though that does not mean that he constrains them. From the perspective of Philosophy, or from the perspective of God that she attempts to show the prisoner of the *Consolation*, the world is entirely harmonious and provident, no matter the experiences of any particular individual. And yet, as Joel Relihan has argued, the *Consolation* nevertheless leaves the prisoner and the reader with a view of the world in all its complexity, rather than a view of the heavens.[68]

At the end of *Troilus and Criseyde*, we are given both perspectives: Troilus' view of "This litel spot of erthe" (v.1815) and the narrator's Dantean prayer to "Thow oon, and two, and thre, eterne on lyve" (v.1863). Troilus experiences "pleyn" – full and perfect – felicity, but it does not compromise the "felicite humaine" of the earlier narrative. Whereas the *Consolation* traces an oscillation between attachment to worldly goods and individual desires and their transcendence, *Troilus and Criseyde* traces a double trajectory toward imperfect human happiness and the full felicity of the afterlife. Troilus' laughter, while an evolution from his earlier scoffing, is not an evolution available to "la gente che qui s'innamora." The lovers' felicity remains both twinned with and distanced from the felicity of the clerks. The Aristotelian reception of Boethius brought the happiness commended by clerks closer to worldly happiness in all its mutuality and sensuality, but it cannot, of course, entirely collapse the two. Chaucer's Boethian characters, like the poet himself, cannot think about happiness without thinking through the language uneasily shared by clerks and lovers. This doubleness opens Chaucerian ethics beyond the dicta of "clerkes wise," both grounding and heightening his lovers' doubled joy.

In giving us these Boethian lovers, and placing an Aristotelian and Dantean *philia* between them, Chaucer locates happiness not in a single individual's pursuit of the good, or of an object of love, but in the couple – variously formulated as heterosexual and homosocial. *Troilus and Criseyde* is filled with conversations regarding the ethics of love – between friends, lovers, in letters, in response to song. In the poem, philosophy is love and love is philosophy. In Dante's *Convivio*, contemplation is understood through the categories of human friendship, while for Chaucer, actual engagement with human friendship and love are the grounds of the pursuit of philosophy – not as a vehicle or allegory for philosophical truths, but as a route toward a philosophy that is nurtured by sensory experience, animated by poetic compassion, and constituted by shared conversation about the pursuit of the good. Such an understanding of love as philosophy does not guarantee the integrity or perfection of human happiness – Troilus and Criseyde pursue felicity by loving the future together, and then abandon themselves and their love by hoping for an Elysian or impossible bliss. Human felicity "suffices" precisely because it strives for delightful mutuality in the face of earthly instability, for a goal that is itself inchoate. As Aquinas, Dante, and Chaucer's lovers remind us, the tense of human happiness is always the imperfect.

Coda: Chaucer's philosophical women

Female characters such as Alcyone and Criseyde often make the strongest cases in Chaucer's poetry for an ethical relationship to love, embodying what I have called "erotic Aristotelianism." The course this book has traced from Pygmalion to Criseyde begins to map a complicated terrain that features the gendering of the subjects of ethical love, one in which feminine characters are often the ones who take up the role of the amorous philosophical subject. We might not be surprised by this, given Jane Burns' observation that women in Old French literature create possibilities for a larger range of desiring experiences – beyond the paradigm of unrequited male desire – and disrupt the binary structure of the conventional Western romantic love story.[1] Both Burns and Simon Gaunt have argued that feminine and queer subjects in medieval romance trouble dominant modes of desire, sublimation, and sacrifice, and thus offer ways of critiquing the ethics of courtly love from within; as Burns puts it, we can productively look back to those medieval heroines "who broke the rules but still stayed in the game."[2] These women break the "rules" by neither remaining silent objects of desire nor inhabiting the subject position of masculine desire for such a silent object. I would argue that in the wake of the reception of Aristotelian ethics, such possibilities expand, and, as we have seen in the figures of Pygmalion, Pynoteüs, Alcyone, the Black Knight, and Criseyde, the subject of courtly Aristotelianism expresses desire for shared fortune, for a lover who speaks, for an "alikeness" that does not reduce the beloved to a mirror image. These desires are not often fulfilled, or not for long, but their expression opens up a space for thinking about love that embodies an ethical relationship to the other, and a new relationship to human happiness.

The privileged position of women in relation to the "thought" of love is something that has been emphasized within post-Freudian psychoanalytic discourse. Alain Badiou argues that feminine truth is distinctive because love is its condition; the feminine subject may approach truth through science, art, or politics, but it is love that allows any of these "truth procedures" to confer value on humanity.[3] For the masculine subject, by contrast, each type of discourse confers value without reference to the existence of the others.[4] Badiou stresses that the loving subject does not "think itself" – love for him is not self-reflexive – but he suggests that the woman in love "inquires," she (or he) wanders and tells stories, and her statements aim at ontological truth. Jacques Lacan also associates feminine subjectivity with ontological truth, and his subject of feminine *jouissance* is not only a philosophical subject, but an explicitly Aristotelian subject. As I illustrate below, Lacan's ideas about love grew out of his study of medieval Aristotelianism, and his psychoanalytic ethics do not so much critique "courtly love" as they make explicit the ethics of late medieval poetry – an earthly ethics of love between subjects at the mercy of fortune, an ethics "after Aristotle" in all senses of the phrase.

LACAN AVEC ARISTOTLE

An insistence upon the alliance of Lacanian *jouissance féminine* with Aristotle may appear strange or even perverse, given that if Lacan tells us anything about the ethics of psychoanalysis in his seminar on the topic, it is that it constitutes a definitive break with Aristotelian ethics. For Lacan, it is the continuing relevance of Aristotle's morality that provides the foundation for the subversiveness of Freud; after Freud, he argues, Aristotle is rendered incomprehensible.[5] Lacan's Freudian critique of Aristotle is founded centrally on the notion that Aristotle situates sexual desire outside the moral register. Aristotle's theory of virtuous love, with the highest form of love consisting of a shared pursuit of the good, does not at first seem to square with Lacan's insistence on the irrationality, the contingency, and the narcissism of desire. According to Lacan, Freud offers something "completely new" to ethical discussions of pleasure: a contingent notion of the good that roots "happiness" in a chance "happening" rather than in an irrefutable teleology that guides rational man on the path toward enjoyment.[6] Yet Aristotle is never simply discarded by Lacan; the ancient philosopher is a constant touchstone in his writings on ethics, and, if anything, is not overturned but reinvented.[7] As Lacan seeks to create an ethics of psychoanalysis that will supersede Aristotelian ethics, he leaves behind his exhortations not to give way on one's desire ("ne pas céder sur son désir"), and it appears that he leaves this fidelity to desire behind in favor of an "ethics of the real" that is closer to an ethics of love – an ethics that has manifest connections with Aristotelian *philia*.[8]

Lacan's recasting of his seventh seminar, *The Ethics of Psychoanalysis*, as a new *Nicomachean Ethics* for our time is not made explicit until his twentieth seminar on feminine sexuality. Lacan reminds his audience that "In dealing, a long time ago, a very long time ago indeed, with the ethics of psychoanalysis, I began with nothing less than Aristotle's *Nicomachean Ethics*."[9] He talks about the impossibility of reading Aristotle in French translation, stating that the incomprehensibility of available editions should not be attributed to the fact that "we have but badly taken notes."[10] Lacan allies himself with the Greek philosopher by discussing his own earlier seminar on ethics and the unauthorized version published by an enthusiastic note-taker. Stating that he will rewrite and republish this seminar, seemingly in hope of avoiding the fate of Aristotle's *Ethics*, Lacan nevertheless optimistically claims that "reading the *Nicomachean Ethics* in the French translation, you understand nothing in it, of course, but no less than in what I tell you ("vous n'y comprendrez rien, bien sûr, mais pas moins qu'à ce que je dis"), and thus it suffices all the same."[11] Aristotle is distant and difficult, but no more or less comprehensible than Lacan's own discourse ("ce que je vous raconte"). In the end, Lacan allies himself quite closely to Aristotle, at the same time as he insists upon the philosopher's strangeness, his blindness to sexuality, his misguided metaphysics of telos. It is thus both surprising and predictable when Lacan unequivocally states, "whatever else may be said, I prefer Aristotle to Jaufré Rudel."[12]

What does it mean for Lacan to prefer Aristotle to the twelfth-century troubadour Jaufré Rudel, famous for his depictions of love from afar? One might not want to take this rejection of Jaufré Rudel too seriously; after all, his medieval Provençal biographer gives him credit for "bons sons, ab paubres motz" (fine melodies, but poor words).[13] But Lacan is surely not making a purely aesthetic judgment here. Directly after he tells us that courtly love is "the only way to elegantly pull off the absence of the sexual relationship" – elegant and fraudulent because we imagine that we ourselves have erected barriers to impossible *jouissance* – he tells us that Aristotle's work has more of a key to the obstacle than the courtly poet Jaufré Rudel. Where, for Lacan, courtly poetry offers a way to exchange self-shattering *jouissance* for the more easily domesticated delights of words and meanings that endlessly circle the sublimed object (*jouis-sense*), Aristotelian philosophy offers wider possibilities for enjoyment.[14] In this seminar, Lacan speaks about a love that is "horsexe" (beyondsex), setting this love apart from the sacrificial, narcissistic desire that he associates with courtly love. Narcissism is contrasted with a *jouissance féminine* that is aware of the paradoxes inherent when one addresses oneself to an Other who can never live up to one's demands and admiration; this *jouissance* is allied with a version of Aristotelian *philia* that reaches out to another person in his or her fragility and terror as she attempts to stand in relation to precisely this same Other. This kind of love verges upon an "ethics of the real" in Lacan's terms, approaching the real behind the knowledge not only that the "Other does not exist," but also that we nevertheless each construct our identities by desiring this non-existent Other. He thus chooses Aristotle's theory of the *ĕnstasis* – the "instance" or "obstacle" – over Jaufré's. Lacan describes the project of his twentieth seminar, at least in part, as trying "to integrate [his] four formulas ... into Aristotle's work."[15] Ultimately, Aristotle's philosophy can tell us more about the "*jouissance* of being," and about the possibilities of subjectivity within language, than the poetry of the troubadours, or at least the most conventional of troubadours – the tenso of Arnaut Daniel quoted in the seventh seminar, a poem that reveals the obscene emptiness of the "Lady" of courtly love, would be an exception.[16]

It becomes increasingly clear in his twentieth seminar that it was Lacan's reading of medieval Aristotelian philosophy – mostly Aquinas – that allowed him to rediscover Aristotle as a philosopher of contingency and love, as a philosopher of the real. Medieval scholasticism becomes a place where supposed Aristotelian blindness to sexuality is transformed into a learned discourse on eros, narcissism, and the imagination – a discourse not unlike Lacanian psychoanalysis. At the end of the seminar, Lacan describes love in the following terms:

> Regarding one's partner, love can only actualize what, in a sort of poetic flight, in order to make myself understood, I called courage – courage with respect to this fatal destiny. But is it courage that is at stake or pathways of recognition? This recognition is nothing other than the way in which the relationship said to be sexual – that has now become a subject-to-subject relationship, the subject being but the effect of unconscious knowledge – stops not being written.[17]

Lacan's discussion of love makes it clear that the distinction between desire and love is one of inevitability versus contingency, ceaselessness versus the event, repetition versus transformation. His phrase of contingency, "stops not being written," stands in contrast to the impossible sexual relationship which "doesn't stop not being written" and the necessary, which "doesn't stop being written."[18] To "stop not being written" offers the promise of a present-tense moment of love and recognition without the numbing repetition of the "necessary." Love is a moment of beginning over, of contingent meeting and happening, with an impossible promise that the sexual relationship could exist.[19]

The contrast between contingency and necessity is precisely what underwrites the distance between Freud and Aristotle, according to Lacan's seventh seminar, where Aristotle's telos, the irrefutable attractions of the pleasurable good, is superseded by Freud's notion of a happiness that is an encounter, a happening, a bit of good fortune. And yet, as Lacan must know, while Aristotle's good is undoubtedly teleological, Aristotle is also the philosopher of contingency and fortune. He disagrees with the Stoics who would advise us to be impervious to the workings of fortune and the material world, happy in our virtuousness; happiness, for Aristotle, is a complicated pursuit that involves birth into a good family, self-fashioning, physical well-being, good friends, and material sustenance – in other words, a great deal of good luck. The best kind of happiness, contemplative happiness, requires leisure, but is hard work, and even then it might be thwarted by any exterior event. Thus Lacan's "poetic" definition of love as courage, given above, has some close affinities to his restatement of Aristotle's definition of *philia* in Seminar 20:

> What Aristotle evokes with the term *philia*, namely, what represents the possibility of a bond of love between two of these beings, can also, manifesting the tension toward the Supreme Being, be reversed in the way in which I expressed it – it is in their courage in bearing the intolerable relationship to the Supreme Being that friends, *philoi*, recognize and choose each other. This ethics is manifestly "beyondsex."[20]

Aristotelian *philia* is here rewritten not as the love of the good manifested in the other, but the recognition that both subjects are striving toward a manifestation of that good, both desiring the love of an Other whom they know does not exist. For Lacan, the relationship to the Supreme Being, the Aristotelian unmoved mover, is not manifested in a participation in its goodness, but in a participation of "radically Other" feminine *jouissance*.[21] Such a recognition is a love that is "beyondsex" – not the sexual relationship that "doesn't stop not being written," but a relationship of love that has the potential to "stop not being written" – to cross the line of impossibility. As Slavoj Žižek observes in *The Metastases of Enjoyment*, "true love can emerge only within a relationship of 'partnership' that is animated by a different, non-sexual goal … Love is an unforeseeable answer of the real: it (can) emerge(s) 'out of nowhere' only when we renounce any attempt to direct and control its course."[22] For

Badiou, love is an encounter in which both masculine and feminine subjects escape the trap of narcissistic desire – passing through desire to love "like a camel through the eye of a needle."[23] His man and woman do not "recognize" each other, but rather speak from a perspective in which the impossible-to-conceive "two" has already come into being. In love, two are not merged into one, but rather allowed to "inquire into the world" from a perspective that Badiou calls "post-evental": it is only from this impossible position that one can inhabit the truth of sexual difference, which is not the same as "knowledge" of the other sex.[24] It is ironically the pursuit of this non-sexual goal that creates the possibility for the existence of the sexual relationship – a mutual pursuit of enjoyment that does not reduce the other person to an object or mirror.

In reintroducing Aristotelian philosophy here not in its purely classical version, but in the version given to us by thirteenth-century Christian theologians, especially Thomas Aquinas, Lacan gives us an Aristotle who is a Freudian philosopher of love.[25] Aquinas and others created an Aristotle who repaired the ignorance Lacan diagnoses in the antique tradition, which covered *jouissance* over with knowledge, and did not recognize that speech concerns enjoyment.[26] Lacan's Aristotle is after the "*jouissance* of being" itself, recognizing the way that the enjoyment of God is modeled on our own enjoyment, that philosophical "wondering" is not only pleasurable, but a form of loving God. This Aristotle emerges from the Latin authors who tried to reconcile an ethics oriented toward human happiness in this life with a Christian ethics, largely Augustinian, that tells us that the only object rightfully to be enjoyed is God.

It is in the beyond of *jouissance* where the love poetry of the late Middle Ages reaches toward the contingency that Lacan describes in his twentieth seminar. One wonders what Lacan would have made of the ethical discourse of the fourteenth century, where he would have found a congenial skepticism about the narcissistic reflexivity of beatific enjoyment and ongoing struggles to understand the relationship between love and pleasure in this life and the life beyond. I can only imagine that Lacan would have the same "delirious admiration" for the poets and philosophers of the new Aristotle as he did for Aquinas, that perhaps their reinjection of contingency, fortune, knowing and ignorant narcissism, and *philia* into the book of courtly love might have him "rolling on the floor laughing" at their audacity.[27] And yet even without this explicit encounter, Lacan appeared to move toward a synthesis of Aristotelian logic, *philia*, and medieval poetry, claiming in his twenty-first seminar that contingent love, love "beyondsex," love that becomes possible as one ceases not to write it – "que l'amour c'est l'amour courtois" (that love is courtly love).[28]

The subjects of love in medieval poetry express a *jouissance féminine* not through ecstatic or mystical discourse – the locations Lacan highlights in his twentieth seminar – but through an intellectual and erotic commitment to mutual experience and emotion, courage, and contingency, a commitment now recognizable as an Aristotelian response to the full range of medieval ethical experience. This is not to say that courtly poetry has at this point renounced the idealization of the thoroughly conventional Lady as cipher – beautiful, wise, grey-eyed, and slender – nor the attractions of suffering love from afar. But these ideals and pleasures are increasingly ironized and placed in the context of a newly world-oriented ethics. The love born of impossibility and contingency can never cross into necessity, but the poetry of Chaucer and his contemporaries gives witness to this desire and its discontents. Aristotelian ethics allows medieval poets to explore the possibilities of a love that would evade both the numbing necessity of the possible as well as the impossibility of the sexual relationship; for Lacan, Aristotle opens up possibilities of love rooted in contingency and happening – happiness. In their intolerable relationship to the stormy sea of life, Alcyone and Ceyx might choose each other. Alcyone's ideal of love as a facing of fortune together has clear affinities with Lacan's idea of love, of "courage – courage with respect to this fatal destiny." This courage is tantamount to Badiou's encounter in which the couple faces the world from the perspective of two that do not collapse into one; it is from this perspective that the sexual relationship may be said to "stop not being written" – to flare into existence, even if only for a moment. Alcyone thus embodies not the archetypal courtly desire to encircle the impossibility of object-possession with sublime poetry, but the formulation that we can recognize as both Aristotelian and Lacanian: "every man wishes to share with his friends whatever constitutes his existence or whatever makes his life worth living."[29] As Lacan remarks, in a particularly Aristotelian moment, "In love what is aimed at is the subject, the subject as such, insofar as he is presumed in an articulated sentence, in something that is organized or can be organized on the basis of a whole life."[30] One loves a person not as an image, and not in a discrete moment, but as a being who can be imagined as having a past, present, and future. Such love is difficult to sustain, and Badiou describes the labor of love as an oscillation between a collapsing of the "two" back into one, and an expansion of the two conducted via "innumerable common practices, or shared inquiries about the world, without which love has no scene of its own except as a sexual adventure."[31] Love is both an event that fleetingly introduces into reality an impossible perspective and a more mundane labor of sharing common practices and "whatever constitutes one's existence."

PHILOSOPHICAL DORIGEN

This collocation of Aristotelian *philia*, psychoanalytic ethics, and the feminine subject of love emerges vividly in Chaucer's "Franklin's Tale" – a narrative that might be understood to epitomize the themes of this book in miniature. The tale ostentatiously offers amorous conflict as a location for considering ethics, famously ending with the question of who is most "fre." Although it appears that the Franklin's heroine Dorigen is excluded from the category of the "fre," it is her actions and desires that drive the narrative, and her internal meditations on love and fortune that occupy the bulk of the tale's attention. It is in fact Dorigen who creates the conditions under which men can be "fre," and who speaks as a philosophical subject of courtly *philia*. As Burns notes, "Agency in these revised contexts is not something wielded by an empowered and dominant protagonist of either gender."[32] As women open up the range of possibilities of amorous configurations and subject positions, they shift the possibilities for men as well.[33] While Dorigen is not explicitly offered by the Franklin as a "fre" subject, her resistance to and embracing of fortune, and her registering of the conflicts created by her desire to protect herself and her husband from the vagaries of God and nature, are what set the tale and its ethical quandaries in motion.

The Franklin introduces his Breton matter by describing what he understands to be an ideal marriage, one without "maistrye" and lived in "quiete and in reste" (l. 760). He makes it clear that Dorigen and Arveragus – yet to be named at this point – constitute the ideal couple, loving each other without constraint, exhibiting patience and preemptive forgiveness in the face of the inevitability that the other will "dooth or seith somtyme amys" (l. 780). Dorigen's happiness is troubled only by her husband's absence, and she is something of a comic foil for the Alcyone of Ovid's tale. While Arveragus seeks honor overseas in England, Dorigen mourns, weeps, and fasts, so desirous is she of her husband's presence that she can care for nothing else in the world. Yet, unlike Alcyone, she receives regular letters from her husband regarding his welfare, and is eventually "emprented" (l. 831) with the consolation of her friends.

Dorigen is not so thoroughly consoled, however, that she does not fear for Arveragus' safe return, a fear compounded by the presence of "grisly feendly rokkes blake" along the coast of Brittany. She laments their presence, manifesting a desire to control and domesticate Fortune. While acknowledging that clerks may argue that "al is for the beste" (l. 886) – and she herself quotes the Aristotelian commonplace that "In ydel, as men seyn, ye [God] no thyng make" (l. 867) – she nevertheless prays that God would sink these rocks into hell.[34] Dorigen acknowledges the possibility of clerkly discourse (specifically Aristotelian discourse) as a source of consolation and an ethical guide to how to encounter the world, and the world of fortune, but she rejects it.

Her desire to remove any natural obstacles to Arveragus' return informs Dorigen's "pley" with Aurelius in the episode that follows. After informing her ardent admirer that she will never be untrue to her husband, she offers to grant him her love if he should remove every rock from the coast of Brittany. She clearly imagines that she is secure in this play, for she has set Aurelius an impossible task ("this were an inpossible!" he cries, l. 1009), and yet there is something serious in her request. In her fear for Arveragus' life, the remover of the rocks would surely earn her love and gratitude. Dorigen asks us, and Aurelius, to imagine a scenario in which her husband is allowed to live only through the actions of her adulterous lover; Dorigen would then be both true wife and betrayer, Aurelius the savior of Arveragus and the agent of his cuckoldry.

The tale avoids this situation by rendering Aurelius' task otiose; Arveragus returns home safely, and only then does Aurelius succeed in removing the rocks (or at least creating the illusion that they were removed). The submerged rocks come to signify not the conquering of Fortune, but the "magical" knowledge of the stars, moon, and tides – the manipulation of natural knowledge to create the fiction that nature has been tamed. With Arveragus home safely (though conveniently "out of town"), Dorigen suddenly desires to defend the "process of nature," and laments that it has been thwarted by her persistent suitor. She blames Fortune for her woes, and laments her untenable situation. Again, we are witness to her internal struggle, articulated in the terms of clerkly discourse – this time a hundred-line summary of Jerome's *Adversus Jovinianum* that offers a catalogue of noble wives who have sacrificed themselves either to maintain their honor and fidelity to their husbands, because they did not want to live without their husbands, or for the sake of their husbands' lives. Dorigen's lengthy interior debate, said by the narrator to last "a day or tweye" (l. 1457), underscores the repetitive solution to any threat to wifely honor – death – and conveys that these endless exempla do not offer a solution to Dorigen's plight. Dorigen intends to die, but her complaint cannot bring itself to resolution; it is only Arveragus' return that halts her lamenting and cataloguing.

In her complaint, Dorigen appears to blame Fortune, but she in fact belatedly accepts the Aristotelian wisdom that had earlier seemed so empty: fortune and the natural world are hard facts, like fiendish rocks, and are not to be manipulated by human beings. Dorigen, by continuing to complain, survives and continues to live her story, accepting the world as it is. Jill Mann accordingly reads Dorigen's "failure" to kill herself as indicative of "human resistance to stasis, to finality." Dorigen's "commitment to story is, like patience, a commitment to *movement*, a commitment to follow events rather than force them into a pre-determined shape."[35] As Susan Crane observes, "other characters do not find themselves so swept along in the flow of events as are Dorigen and the narrator."[36] She is Badiou's "woman," the "she (or he) who makes love travel and who desires that her speech constantly reiterate and renovate itself" – not the "mute and violent" man, but the woman who "gossips and complains."[37] Dorigen's commitment to story, to wandering, gossiping, and complaining as a way of suffrance, is recognizable as the Franklin's science of love, expressed in his most Langlandian moment: "Lerneth to suffre, or elles, so moot I goon, / Ye shul it lerne, wher so ye wole or noon" (ll. 777–8). Dorigen's desire for shared experience, and her constant confrontation with a fortune that will not cooperate with her own desires, with her designs on her future, lead her to despair and intellectual impasse, but she persists in her story. It is in Dorigen that we most clearly see love as courageous, as an "aventure."

In his seventh seminar, Lacan explains that God's power inheres in his capacity to "advance into emptiness," to move into the pure realm of the "perhaps" and create where nothing had existed before; it is in our understanding of the nature of this power that we realize that "the recognition of another reveals itself as an adventure (*aventure*)," and this recognition retains all of the "accents of militancy and of nostalgia we can invest in it."[38] The recognition of another is, Lacan might well have said, a medieval romance. It is in the adventure and contingency of love that medieval courtly poetry finds its positive ethical legacy in the modern period. J. Allan Mitchell has recently noted that Levinas finds medieval poetry a fertile ground for investigating the ethics of erotic fortune. Levinas' readings of medieval poetry lead to his conclusions that ethics originates in contingency, that fortune is the condition of human flourishing, and that the insistent thwarting of the love relationship, in its insistence that possession and union are never quite possible, is "an assurance that the ethical relation is about to happen."[39] A modern ethics of fortune and friendship may thus not only be grounded in Aristotle, but in the medieval romance, which is, as Mitchell points out, a genre of "adventure" and fortune above all.

Lacan's definition of love as contingent, coinciding with the logic of the impossible, always "about to be written," and never "written," is finally just as much Chaucerian, Froissartian, and Langlandian as Thomist or Aristotelian. And thus we might look for an ethical legacy of medieval love poetry that gives us not – or not only – Lacan's "elegant fraud," but an elegant and searching examination of this very fraud. Love after the medieval Aristotle is no less narcissistic, self-sacrificing, and deferred, but reaches toward shared experience, imperfection, and present bliss – a sacrifice of the sacrifice, as Žižek has termed it. Late medieval *philia* is not an innocent practice – it may be selfish, coercive, and rejected altogether when inconvenient. But it survives on its own terms, no longer simply a pale imitation of the heavenly "face to face." No poet denies that Alcyone's pleas may go unanswered, or that Dorigen as a "new Alcyone" might manage to jeopardize a love that seemed threatened only by the unforgiving material world, yet these are nevertheless not women raised "to the dignity of the Thing," but women facing their "fatal destiny," making sure that their stories continue to be written.

Notes

INTRODUCTION: LOVE AFTER ARISTOTLE

1 See Fernand van Steenberghen, *Aristotle in the West: the Origins of Latin Aristotelianism*, trans. Leonard Johnston (Louvain: E. Nauwelaerts, 1955); D. A. Callus, "Introduction of Aristotelian Learning at Oxford," *Proceedings of the British Academy* 29 (Nov. 1943): 229–81; Martin Grabmann, *Methoden und Hilfsmittel des Aristotelesstudiums in Mittelalter* (Munich: Verlag der Bayerischen Akademie der Wissenschaften, 1939); Maurice de Wulf, *History of Mediaeval Philosophy*, trans. Ernest C. Messenger (New York: Dover, 1952; trans. of 6th edition, 1934–7); and Bernard G. Dod, "Aristoteles Latinus," in *The Cambridge History of Later Medieval Philosophy: from the Rediscovery of Aristotle to the Disintegration of Scholasticism, 1100–1600*, ed. Norman Kretzmann, Anthony Kenny, and Jan Pinborg, assoc. ed. Eleonore Stump (Cambridge University Press, 1982), pp. 45–79. On the reception of the *Ethics* in particular, see Georg Wieland, "The Reception and Interpretation of Aristotle's *Ethics*," and "Happiness: the Perfection of Man," in *The Cambridge History of Later Medieval Philosophy*, pp. 657–72 and 673–86.

2 Wieland notes that the *Nicomachean Ethics* was not adopted as a regular textbook in the arts faculties until the second half of the fourteenth century (Wieland, "Reception and Interpretation," p. 657), though several books of the *Ethics* were granted six to twelve weeks of study at Paris in 1255. See P. Osmund Lewry, "Robert Kilwardby's Commentary on the *Ethica Noua* and *Vetus*," in *L'homme et son univers au Moyen Âge: actes du septième congrès international de philosophie médiévale*, ed. C. Wenin, Philosophes médiévaux 27 (Louvain-la-Neuve: Institut supérieur de philosophie, 1986), pp. 799–807 (p. 799); and *Chartularium Universitatis Parisiensis*, ed. Émile Chatelain and Heinrich Denifle (Paris: Fratrum Delalain, 1889–97), I, n. 246, p. 278. The *Ethics* was a subject of disputation examinations as early as the 1230s in Paris, and commentaries and lectures are documented at Oxford in the 1240s (Dod, "Aristoteles Latinus," pp. 72–3).

3 Cary J. Nederman, "Aristotelian Ethics before the *Nicomachean Ethics*: Alternate Sources of Aristotle's Concept of Virtue in the Twelfth Century," *Parergon* 7 (1989): 55–75, and "Nature, Ethics, and the Doctrine of 'Habitus':

Aristotelian Moral Psychology in the Twelfth Century," *Traditio* 45 (1989–90): 87–110.

4 Dod, "Aristoteles Latinus," includes a table of medieval Latin translations of Aristotle's works (including pseudo-Aristotelian and related works). Robert Grosseteste's translation survives in 33 manuscript copies; the revision, now accepted as the work of William of Moerbeke, in 246. For a history of the debate about the authorship of the revision, and an argument for attribution to Moerbeke, see Jozef Brams, "The Revised Version of Grosseteste's Translation of the *Nicomachean Ethics*," *Bulletin de Philosophie Médiévale* 36 (1994): 45–55.

5 Alastair Minnis argues for the influence of the reception of the earlier books of the *Nicomachean Ethics* and a positive, secular re-evaluation of the active life. See Minnis, "The Biennial Chaucer Lecture: 'I speke of folk in seculer estaat': Vernacularity and Secularity in the Age of Chaucer," *Studies in the Age of Chaucer* 27 (2005): 25–58.

6 Aristotle, *Ethica Nicomachea*, x.5.27–8 (1174b31–3): "Perficit autem operacionem delectacio non sicut habitus que inest, set ut superveniens quidam finis velud iuvenibus pulcritudo." References to the *Nicomachean Ethics* will include book, chapter, and line numbers from the *Aristoteles Latinus*, vol. xxvi, parts 1–3, fasc. 4, ed. R. A. Gauthier (Leiden and Brussels: Brill and Desclée De Brouwer, 1972–4), unless otherwise stated, along with the page and line numbers from Immanuel Bekker's edition of the Greek text (Berlin, 1831), the standard form of reference in most modern editions and translations. Translations, with some emendations, are from C. I. Litzinger's translation of Thomas Aquinas' *Commentary on Aristotle's Nicomachean Ethics* (Notre Dame, IN: Dumb Ox Books, 1993), which includes the Aristotelian text (based on William of Moerbeke's revision of Grosseteste's translation); I have also consulted Terence Irwin's translation of the *Ethics* (Indianapolis, IN: Hackett Publishing Co., 1985) and found the text and notes very helpful. Throughout the book, I quote from published translations where they are available; unreferenced translations are my own.

7 The *De Anima* had been translated by James of Venice in the mid twelfth century, but was revised by William of Moerbeke by 1268 (most surviving manuscripts – 268 of 474 – are in this version); the *Politics* was not available in Latin before William of Moerbeke's translation *c.*1260 (107 mss), and the *Rhetoric* had limited circulation (8 mss survive from the mid thirteenth century) until William's translation (100 mss). The *Economics* were available in an anonymous translation (15 mss) and its revision (79 mss) in the late thirteenth century. See Dod, "Aristoteles Latinus," pp. 74–8.

8 Matthew Kempshall explores the way that thirteenth- and fourteenth-century theologians negotiated the introduction of the idea of a common good that did not only mean moral goodness, but also a practical political goodness that ensured the material security and peace that enable human virtue. See *The Common Good in Late Medieval Political Thought* (Oxford: Clarendon Press, 1999).

9 Aristotle, *Politics*, Book III, chapter 4, section 3 (1278b30); for the translation by William of Moerbeke, see *Aristotelis Polticorum Libri Octo cum Vetusta Translatione Gulielmi de Moerbeka*, ed. Franz Susemihl (Leipzig: Teubner, 1872). For both the *Politics* and *Economics*, I have followed the chapter and section numbers of the Loeb editions: Aristotle, *Politics*, trans. H. Rackham (Cambridge, MA: Harvard University Press, 1932); Aristotle, *Metaphysics, Oeconomica, and Magna Moralia*, trans. G. Cyril Armstrong (Cambridge, MA: Harvard University Press, 1936).

10 Aristotle, *Politics*, Book III, chapter 4, section 2 (1278b19–22).

11 Pseudo-Aristotle, *Economics*, Book III, chapter 4, ll. 26–7. Albert Menut's edition of Nicole Oresme's translation of the *Economics* also contains appended the medieval Latin text; see "Maistre Nicole Oresme: *Le Livre de Yconomique D'Aristote*, Critical Edition of the French Text from the Avranches Manuscript with the Original Latin Version, Introduction, and Translation," ed. Albert Douglas Menut, *Transactions of the American Philosophical Society*, n.s. 47.5 (1957): 783–853 (p. 849). No Greek exemplar of the third book of the *Economics* is known, so it is not included in Bekker's edition.

12 Pseudo-Aristotle, *Economics*, Book I, chapter 3, l. 3 (1343b20); 852 in Menut's edition.

13 Kempshall, *The Common Good*, p. 133; see also J. J. Murphy, "Aristotle's Rhetoric in the Middle Ages," *Quarterly Journal of Speech* 52 (1966): 109–15.

14 Judson Allen, *The Ethical Poetic of the Later Middle Ages: a Decorum of Convenient Distinction* (University of Toronto Press, 1982), pp. 6–12; see discussion of *divisio scientiae* in Rita Copeland, *Rhetoric, Hermeneutics, and Translation in the Middle Ages: Academic Traditions and Vernacular Texts* (Cambridge University Press, 1991), pp. 5, 207–12.

15 Allen, *Ethical Poetic*, p. 12.

16 *Ibid.*, p. 32.

17 John Dagenais, *The Ethics of Reading in Manuscript Culture: Glossing the "Libro de Buen Amor"* (Princeton University Press, 1994), p. xvii.

18 Adam Phillips, *Going Sane: Maps of Happiness* (New York: Fourth Estate, 2005), p. xx.

19 Jean Buridan, *Quaestiones super Decem Libros Ethicorum* (Frankfurt: Minerva, 1968; facs. Paris 1513 edition), Prologue, p. 2^r, col. b: "Cum igitur non nisi secundum moralia sit innatus appetitus alienare judicium rationis, hinc est, quod in aliis artibus et scientiis sufficit nobis logica simpliciter, sed in moralibus indigemus logica speciali. Huius autem moralis logice due sunt partes, scilicet rhetorica, et poetria, que sic differunt: quia rhetorica claram scientiam desiderat, et verbis utitur in sua propria significatione retentis. Poetria vero scientiam delectabiliter obscurare nititur per verborum transumptionem vel alio modo."

20 Buridan, *Quaestiones super Decem Libros Ethicorum*, Book x, q. 4, sect. 4e, p. 211^v, col. b, and "Questions on Book X of the Ethics," in *Ethics and Political Philosophy*, ed. Arthur Stephen McGrade, John Kilcullen, and

Matthew Kempshall, Cambridge Translations of Medieval Philosophical Texts 2 (Cambridge University Press, 2001), p. 557. For a discussion of these lines in the context of whether Buridan espouses a "nominalist ethics," see James J. Walsh, "Nominalism and Ethics: Some Remarks about Buridan's Commentary," *Journal of the History of Philosophy* 4.1 (Jan. 1966): 1–13 (p. 10).

21 On enjoyment and love as subjects of medieval scholasticism, see L. O. Aranye Fradenburg, "Amorous Scholasticism," in *Speaking Images: Essays in Honor of V. A. Kolve*, ed. R. F. Yeager and Charlotte C. Morse (Asheville, NC: Pegasus Press, 2001), pp. 27–53.

22 Recent work that explicitly treats medieval literature as an ethical discourse includes J. Allan Mitchell, *Ethics and Exemplary Narrative in Chaucer and Gower* (Cambridge: Boydell and Brewer, 2004), and *Ethics and Eventfulness in Middle English Literature* (New York: Palgrave Macmillan, 2009); Hugh White, *Nature, Sex, and Goodness in a Medieval Literary Tradition* (Oxford University Press, 2000); L. O. Aranye Fradenburg, *Sacrifice Your Love: Psychoanalysis, Historicism, Chaucer* (Minneapolis: University of Minnesota Press, 2002); Glending Olson, *Literature as Recreation in the Later Middle Ages* (Ithaca, NY: Cornell University Press, 1982); and Alcuin Blamires, *Chaucer, Ethics, and Gender* (Oxford University Press, 2006). Fradenburg treats Chaucer's poetry from the perspective of psychoanalytic ethics; Olson examines medieval commentaries on Aristotle's *Nicomachean Ethics* in order to discover medieval ideas about the pleasure of reading (pp. 93–104). For an examination of the "moral imagination" shared by philosophical and literary works in the early modern period, see Christopher Tilmouth, *Passion's Triumph over Reason: a History of the Moral Imagination from Spenser to Rochester* (Oxford University Press, 2007), pp. 8–11.

23 William Courtenay, "Between Despair and Love: Some Late Medieval Modifications of Augustine's Teaching on Fruition and Psychic States," in *Augustine, the Harvest, and Theology (1300–1650): Essays Dedicated to Heiko Augustinus Oberman in Honor of his Sixtieth Birthday*, ed. Kenneth Hagen (Leiden: E. J. Brill, 1990), pp. 5–20 (p. 14).

24 Arthur S. McGrade, "Enjoyment at Oxford after Ockham: Philosophy, Psychology, and the Love of God," in *From Ockham to Wyclif*, ed. Anne Hudson and Michael Wilks, Studies in Church History, Subsidia, 5 (London: Blackwell, 1987), pp. 63–88 (p. 86).

25 Recent work that addresses this intersection includes Nicolette Zeeman, *"Piers Plowman" and the Medieval Discourse of Desire* (Cambridge University Press, 2006); Sarah Kay, *The Place of Thought: the Complexity of One in Late Medieval French Didactic Poetry* (Philadelphia: University of Pennsylvania Press, 2007); and Steven Rigby, *Wisdom and Chivalry: Chaucer's Knight's Tale and Medieval Political Theory* (Leiden: Brill, 2009).

26 Alastair Minnis observes a moment where moral philosophy takes note of the relationship between Aristotelian love and the love described in secular poetry: Nicole Oresme, fourteenth-century translator of Aristotle, acknowledges the mutual concerns with love in Aristotle's *Economics* and Ovid's *Ars Amatoria*, though Oresme "disingenuously" describes Ovid's book

as concerning the same "rational" love that the philosopher describes. See Minnis, "'I speke of folk in seculer estaat,'" p. 51, n. 78.

27 In Chapter 3, I explore scholastic considerations that enjoyment might include pain, a possibility that brings it closer to Lacanian *jouissance*, as well as to vernacular poetry.

28 Henry George Liddell and Robert Scott, *A Greek–English Lexicon*, revised and augmented throughout by Sir Henry Stuart Jones with the assistance of Roderick McKenzie (Oxford: Clarendon Press, 1996). The entry for δαίμων contains several definitions, including "god, goddess," "the Divine power," "chance," and "the power controlling the destiny of individuals." Definitions of εὐδαιμονία include "prosperity, good fortune, opulence," and "true, full happiness."

29 See J. L. Ackrill, "Aristotle on *Eudaimonia*," in *Aristotle's Ethics: Critical Essays*, ed. Nancy Sherman (Lanham, MD: Rowman and Littlefield, 1999), pp. 57–78 (pp. 66–7).

30 See Matti Rissanen, "In Search of *Happiness*: *Felicitas* and *Beatitudo* in Early English Boethius Translations," *Studia Anglica Posnaniensia* 31 (1997): 237–48 (240–1). *Felicitas* and *felix* are also used to speak about true happiness when Boethius is not concerned about making a distinction between the two kinds of happiness. See also James McEvoy, "Ultimate Goods: Happiness, Friendship, and Bliss," in *The Cambridge Companion to Medieval Philosophy*, ed. A. S. McGrade (Cambridge University Press, 2003), pp. 254–75.

31 Indeed, in Aristotle's *Nicomachean Ethics*, the words *eudaimōn* (happy) and *makarios* (blessed, or blessedly happy) are used interchangeably. See *Nicomachean Ethics*, trans. Irwin, p. 388.

32 Adam Potkay follows the concept of joy from the Bible through the twentieth century and explores the opposition between happiness and joy as an inheritance from classical philosophy – an opposition between active human flourishing and passive joy; see *The Story of Joy* (Cambridge University Press, 2007), pp. 20–4. As Potkay observes in his brief discussion of Aquinas, however, late medieval theology sought to reconcile Christian joy with Aristotelian happiness in pursuit of a concept of the "joy of the ethical life" (p. 31).

33 Augustine, *De Doctrina Christiana*, ed. Joseph Martin, Corpus Christianorum Series Latina (hereafter CCSL) 32 (Turnhout: Brepols, 1962), 1.4, ll. 1–2: "Frui est enim amore inhaerere alicui rei propter se ipsam."

34 Jacques Lacan, *Encore*, ed. Jacques-Alain Miller (Paris: Seuil, 1999), pp. 66–7, and *On Feminine Sexuality: the Limits of Love and Knowledge (Encore), 1972–3*, trans. Bruce Fink (New York: Norton, 1998), pp. 70–1.

35 Geoffrey Chaucer, *The Riverside Chaucer*, gen. ed. Larry D. Benson, 3rd edn. (Boston, MA: Houghton Mifflin, 1987). All subsequent citations of Chaucer will refer to this edition, cited parenthetically by line number when the reference is clear.

36 Mitchell, *Ethics and Eventfulness*, examines fortune and contingency as the grounds of ethics in medieval English poetry. He addresses the influence of Aristotle on late medieval ideas about fortune at pp. 19–20, 57–61.

37 Fradenburg, *Sacrifice Your Love*, p. 2.

1 ENJOYMENT: A MEDIEVAL HISTORY

1 Aristotle, *Ethica Nicomachea*, I.4.11–12 (1099a9). For a discussion of the relationship between the pursuit of an end and pleasure in that end, with reference to the prefix "philo" in the Greek, see also J. C. B. Gosling and C. C. W. Taylor, *The Greeks on Pleasure* (Oxford: Clarendon Press, 1982), pp. 281–3. As Aristotle was available to medieval western European writers in Latin, I give quotations based on the thirteenth-century Latin translations of his texts. Where possible in this chapter, I give the medieval Latin versions of texts originally written in Greek.

2 Aristotle, *Ethica Nicomachea*, VIII.3.1–5 (1156b6–10).

3 Gregory Vlastos, "The Individual as Object of Love in Plato," in *Platonic Studies* (Princeton University Press, 1973), p. 4. On translating *philia*, see also David Konstan's introduction to his translation of the Greek commentaries on Books VIII and IX of the *Ethics*: *On Aristotle's Nicomachean Ethics 8 and 9: Aspasius, Anonymous, Michael of Ephesus* (Ithaca, NY: Cornell University Press, 2001), pp. 1–7.

4 Plato, *Timaeus: a Calcidio Translatus Commentarioque Instructis*, ed. J. H. Waszink (London and Leiden: Warburg Institute and Brill, 1975), pp. 22–3 (29d–30c). Plato's God in the *Timaeus* is motivated by a supreme goodness and absence of envy, desiring to create a world in the likeness of himself.

5 Vlastos, "Love in Plato," p. 31.

6 Augustine, *De Civitate Dei*, ed. Bernard Dombart and Alphonse Kalb, CCSL 47–8 (Turnhout: Brepols, 1955), VIII.5, ll. 1–3: "Si ergo Plato Dei huius imitatorem cognitorem amatorem dixit esse sapientem, cuius participatione sit beatus, quid opus est excutere ceteros?" Translations are from Augustine, *Concerning the City of God against the Pagans*, trans. Henry Bettenson (New York: Penguin, 1972).

7 Marcia Colish, *The Stoic Tradition from Antiquity to the Early Middle Ages*, 2 vols. (Leiden: Brill, 1985), vol. II, pp. 212–16.

8 Augustine, *De Civitate Dei*, VIII.4–8.

9 Colish, *The Stoic Tradition*, vol. II, p. 216.

10 Augustine, *De Civitate Dei*, XIV.7, ll. 40–1: "Recta itaque voluntas est bonus amor et voluntas perversa malus amor." Though cf. *De Trinitate*, ed. W. J. Mountain, CCSL 50–50a (Turnhout: Brepols, 1968), VIII.7, ll. 5–6: "atque ita cupidi abusive dicuntur diligere quemadmodum cupere abusive dicuntur qui diligunt" (we misuse language when we say of those who covet that they love and of those who love that they covet).

11 Augustine, *De Civitate Dei*, VIII.8, ll. 26–9.

12 *Ibid.*, VIII.8, ll. 43–4: "non se beatus putant amando, sed fruendo."

13 *Ibid.*, X.3, ll. 31–4: "Bonum enim nostrum, de cuius fine inter philosophos magna contentio est, nullum est aliud quam illi cohaerere, cuius unius anima intellectualis incorporeo, si dici potest, amplexu veris impletur fecundaturque virtutibus."

14 Augustine, *De Doctrina Christiana*, I.4, ll. 1–2: "Frui est enim amore inhaerere alicui rei propter se ipsam."

15 Some larger studies of this reception include Colish, *The Stoic Tradition*; Terence Irwin, *The Development of Ethics: From Socrates to the Reformation*, 3 vols. (Oxford University Press, 2007), vol. 1; Richard Sorabji (ed.), *Aristotle Transformed: the Ancient Commentaries and their Influence* (Ithaca, NY: Cornell University Press, 1990); and Stephen Gersh, *Middle Platonism and Neoplatonism: the Latin Tradition* (University of Notre Dame Press, 1986).
16 John Marenbon, *Early Medieval Philosophy (480–1150): an Introduction*, 2nd edn. (London and New York: Routledge, 1988), p. 157.
17 Courtenay, "Between Despair and Love," p. 15.
18 Jacques Lacan, *L'éthique de la psychanalyse*, ed. Jacques-Alain Miller (Paris: Seuil, 1986), p. 46; *The Ethics of Psychoanalysis, 1959–1960*, trans. Dennis Porter (New York: Norton, 1997), p. 36.
19 Julia Annas, *Platonic Ethics, Old and New* (Ithaca, NY: Cornell University Press, 1999), pp. 50–1.
20 Plato, *Phaedo*, ed. Laurence Minio-Paluello, Plato Latinus 2 (London: Warburg Institute, 1950), p. 7 (59a). Translations are from *Phaedo*, trans. David Gallop (Oxford: Clarendon Press, 1975).
21 *Ibid.*, p. 8 (60b–c): "velut ex una vertice counita duo existencia."
22 *Ibid.*, p. 42 (83d): "omnis voluptas et tristicia tamquam clavum habens acclavat ipsam ad corpus atque affigit."
23 Plato, *Laws*, trans. A. E. Taylor (London: Dent, 1960), 636d–e; see also Annas, *Platonic Ethics*, p. 141.
24 On the Stoic example of the man tortured within Phalaris' bull, see Marcus Tullius Cicero, *Tusculan Disputations*, trans. J. E. King (Cambridge, MA and London: Harvard University Press and W. Heinemann, 1945), p. 164.
25 Boethius, *The Theological Tractates and "The Consolation of Philosophy"*, ed. and trans. Stephen Tester (Cambridge, MA: Harvard University Press, 1973), Book II, prose 4, ll. 62–4: "nihil est miserum nisi cum putes contraque beata sors omnis est aequanimitate tolerantis."
26 *Ibid.*, Book III, prose 9, l.6.
27 *Ibid.*, Book III, prose 11, ll. 12–15: "Tum autem verum bonum fieri cum in unam veluti formam atque efficientiam colliguntur, ut quae sufficientia est, eadem sit potentia, reverentia, claritas atque jucunditas."
28 Aristotle, *Ethica Nicomachea*, x.5.20–3 (1175a18–21): "Utrum autem propter delectationem vivere eligimus vel propter vivere delectationem; dimittatur in presenti; coniungi quidem enim hec videntur et separacionem non recipere. Sine operacione enim non fit delectatio."
29 Plotinus, *Enneads*, trans. Stephen MacKenna (Burdett, NY: Larson Publications, 1992), I.6.8, "Beauty," p. 71.
30 Cicero, *Tusculan Disputations*, p. 274.
31 Augustine, *Confessionem Libri XIII*, ed. Lucas Verheijen, CCSL 27 (Turnhout: Brepols, 1981), x.33. Translations are from *Confessions*, trans. Edward Pusey (New York: Collier Books, 1961).
32 *Ibid.*, x.33, l. 30.
33 *Ibid.*, x.34, ll. 51–2.
34 *Ibid.*, x.35.

35 For Ockham's discussion of external distress disturbing the pleasure of intellectual investigation (but not hindering love of that investigation), see *Quaestiones in Librum Quartum Sententiarum*, in *Opera Philosophica et Theologica*, ed. Rega Wood and Gedeon Gal (Bonaventure, NY: St. Bonaventure University, 1984), Liber 1, Dist. 1, q. 3, p. 409; Ockham refers here to *Nicomachean Ethics*, Book x (1175b16–24). On the question of whether anything other than God should be the object of enjoyment, see *Quaestiones*, Liber 1, Dist. 1, q. 4, pp. 429–47. See Arthur S. McGrade, "Ockham on Enjoyment –Towards an Understanding of Fourteenth-Century Philosophy and Psychology," *Review of Metaphysics* 34.4, issue 136 (June 1981): 706–28; McGrade discusses desires that persist without pleasure at pp. 712–13 and "weak enjoyings" of earthly objects at pp. 709–10, 720.

36 Plato, *Meno*, ed. Victor Kordeuter, Plato Latinus 1 (London: Warburg Institute, 1940; repr. Nendeln, Liechtenstein: Kraus, 1973); see Annas, *Platonic Ethics*, p. 68.

37 Aristotle, *Ethica Nicomachea*, x.5.17–19 (1174b21–3): "Delectabilissima autem perfectissima, perfectissima que bene habentis ad studiosissimum eorum que sub ipsam"; see also x.8.14–15 (1177a16–17): "huius operacio secundum propriam virtutem erit utique perfecta felicitas" (Perfect happiness is the activity [of the most divine part of the soul – whether intellect or something else] in accordance with its proper virtue); and again x.8.8 (1178b7–8): "Perfecta autem felicitas quoniam speculativa quedam est operacio" (Perfect happiness is a form of contemplative activity).

38 *Ibid.*, x.8.1–2 (1176b5–6): "Nullo enim indigens felicitas, set per se sufficiens" (Happiness lacks nothing and is self-sufficient).

39 Plotinus, *Enneads*, III.8.4, "Nature, Contemplation, and the One," p. 276.

40 *Ibid.*, v.8.4, "On the Intellectual Beauty," p. 489.

41 Philo of Alexandria, *De Fuga et Inventione*, in *The Works of Philo: Complete and Unabridged*, trans. C. D. Yonge (Peabody, MA: Hendrickson Publishing, 1993), pp. 91–2; cited in Henry Chadwick, "Philo," in *The Cambridge History of Later Greek and Early Medieval Philosophy*, ed. A. H. Armstrong (Cambridge University Press, 1970), pp. 137–57 (p. 148).

42 Philo, *De Fuga et Inventione*, p. 337.

43 Augustine, *De Civitate Dei*, x.3, ll. 30–1: "ut perveniendo quiescamus, ideo beati, quia illo fine perfecti."

44 Chaucer, *Troilus and Criseyde*, III.1281.

45 Nicole Oresme, *Le Livre de Éthiques d'Aristote published from the text of MS 2902, Bibliothèque Royale de Belgique*, ed. Albert Menut (New York: G. E. Stechert & Co., 1940), p. 517, n. 20: "Et en ce ont repos a parler de repos pour cessacion d'operacion triste, penible et laborieuse et non pas de reposeront de leurs labeurs."

46 See Annas, *Platonic Ethics*, chapter 6.

47 Plato, *Protagoras*, trans. C. C. W. Taylor (Oxford: Clarendon Press, 1991), pp. 45–57 (352a–62a).

48 *Ibid.*, p. 56 (361b).

49 Annas, *Platonic Ethics*, p. 120.

50 See Colish, *The Stoic Tradition*, vol. 1, p. 45; the Stoics also allowed that becoming virtuous might be accomplished in a moment of understanding and choosing to become good; in any case, virtue is not the result of anything like Aristotelian *habitus*.

51 The question of whether Aristotle has a unified position on happiness is still a subject of controversy. See J. M. Cooper's chapter "Contemplation and Happiness: a Reconsideration," in *Reason and Emotion: Essays on Ancient Moral Psychology and Ethical Theory* (Princeton University Press, 1998) for a relatively recent treatment of the problem, arguing for a coherent theory of happiness in the *Nicomachean Ethics*. My own understanding accords with that of Georg Wieland ("Happiness"), who states that Aristotle believes contemplation to be the best kind of happiness, and thus the best life for man; political, active happiness is "second best," but it is also in its own way a highest good – self-sufficient and desirable for its own sake.

52 See A. H. Armstrong, "The One and Intellect" in *The Cambridge History of Later Greek and Early Medieval Philosophy*, pp. 236–49 (p. 239).

53 Plotinus, *Enneads*, 1.6.8, "Beauty," p. 71: "is there not a myth telling in symbol of such a dupe, how he sank into the depths of the current and was swept away to nothingness? So too, one that is held by material beauty and will not break free shall be precipitated, not in body, but in Soul, down to the dark depths loathed of the Intellective-Being, where, blind even in the Lower-World, he shall have commerce only with shadows, there as here."

54 *Ibid.*, 1.6.7, p. 70.

55 *Ibid.*, III.8.1, "Nature, Contemplation, and the One," p. 273.

56 Augustine, *De Civitate Dei*, XI.26, ll. 7–8.

57 Augustine, *De Trinitate*, XIV.1, ll. 54–6: "rerum divinarum scientia sapientia proprie nuncupetur, humanarum autem proprie scientiae nomen obtineat."

58 *Ibid.*, XIV.19, ll. 40–1: "in ratione et investigandi cupiditate."

59 Ambrose, *De Officiis*, ed. and trans. Ivor J. Davidson (Oxford University Press, 2001), 1.125.

60 Isidore of Seville, *Sententiae*, ed. Pierre Cazier, CCSL 111 (Turnhout: Brepols, 1998), II.1.1.

61 *Ibid.*

62 Augustine, *Confessionem Libri XIII*, X.20, ll. 27–31: "… res ipsa [beata vita] nec graeca nec Latina est, cui adipiscendae Graeci Latinique inhiant ceterarumque linguarum homines. Nota est igitur omnibus, qui una voce si interrogari possent, utrum beati esse vellent, sine ulla dubitatione velle responderent."

63 Annas, *Platonic Ethics*, p. 62.

64 Plotinus, *Enneads*, 1.2; see Annas, *Platonic Ethics*, p. 69.

65 Plato, *Timaeus*, 90c.

66 Plato, *Theaetetus*, trans. M. J. Levett (Indianapolis, IN: Hackett Publishing Co., 1992), 176b.

67 *Ibid.*, 174b.

68 Boethius, *Consolation*, Book II, prose 4, ll. 97–101: "Quod si multos scimus beatitudinis fructum non morte solum verum etiam doloribus suppliciisque quaesisse, quonam modo praesens facere beatos potest quae miseros transacta non efficit?"

69 Cicero, *Tusculan Disputations*, IV.24: "contemnendae res humanae sunt, negligenda mors est, patibiles et dolores putandi."

70 *Ibid.*, V.12: "virtutem ad beate vivendum se ipsa esse contentum."

71 Augustine, *De Civitate Dei*, IX.15, ll. 1–3: "Si autem, quod multo credibilius et probabilius disputatur, omnes homines, quamdiu mortales sunt, etiam miseri sint necesse est …"

72 *Ibid.*, IX.14.

73 *Ibid.*, IX.17, ll. 5–7: "Fugiendum est igitur ad carissimam patriam, et ibi pater, et ibi omnia. Quae igitur, inquit, classis aut fuga? Similem Deo fieri." See Plotinus, *Enneads*, I.6.8.

74 Augustine, *De Civitate Dei*, X.1, ll. 8–9: "beata vita, quae post mortem futura est"; XIII.

75 Ambrose, *De Officiis*, II.1.

76 Augustine, *De Civitate Dei*, XIV.25, l. 25: "Tunc igitur beata erit, quando aeterna erit"; XIX.4, ll. 17–18: "hic beati esse et a se ipsis beatificari mira vanitate voluerunt."

77 Boethius, *Consolation*, Book II, prose 4, ll. 79–80, 94–5: "beatitudo est summum naturae bonum ratione … fortuitam felicitatem corporis."

78 *Ibid.*, Book III, prose 10, ll. 37–8: "beatitudinem in summo deo sitam esse necesse est."

79 *Ibid.*, ll. 88–9: "omnis igitur beatus deus."

80 Augustine, *De Civitate Dei*, XXII.24, ll. 183–5: "cum sese diversis coloribus velut vestibus induit et aliquando viride atque hoc multis modis, aliquando purpureum, aliquando caeruleum est."

81 *Ibid.*, XXII.24, ll. 198–9: "haec omnia miserorum sunt damnatorumque solacia, non praemia beatorum."

82 Forty-eight manuscript copies of the *Ethica Vetus* survive, and forty of the *Ethica Nova* (Book I of the *Ethics*, translated in the early thirteenth century). See Dod, "Aristoteles Latinus," p. 77. Six fragmentary commentaries on the partial texts of the *Ethics* survive, all produced by arts masters at Paris before 1250. On the reception of the *Ethics*, see Aristotle, *L'Éthique à Nicomaque*, ed. R. A. Gauthier and J. Y. Jolif, 3 vols., 2nd edn. (Louvain: Publications Universitaires, 1958–9), I.74–85, and *Ethica Nicomachea: Praefatio*, in *Aristoteles Latinus*, vol. XXVI, fasc. 1, pp. 15–16. On the commentaries on the *Ethica Vetus* and *Nova*, see Anthony J. Celano, "The Understanding of the Concept of *Felicitas* in the pre-1250 Commentaries on the *Ethica Nicomachea*," *Medioevo* 12 (1986): 29–53 (pp. 31–3); and Irene Zavattero, "Moral and Intellectual Virtues in the Earliest Latin Commentaries on the *Nicomachean Ethics*," in *Virtue Ethics in the Middle Ages: Commentaries on Aristotle's Nicomachean Ethics, 1200–1500*, ed. István P. Bejczy (Leiden: Brill, 2008), pp. 31–54.

83 Abelard, *Dialogus inter Philosophum, Judaeum et Christianum*, ed. Rudolf Thomas (Stuttgart-Bad Cannstatt: Friedrich Frommann Verlag, 1970), p. 104,

ll. 1713–14: "Quam, ut arbitror, beatitudinem Epicurus voluptatem, Xpistus vester regnum celorum nominat." Translations are from *Ethical Writings: "Ethics" and "Dialogue Between a Philosopher, a Jew, and a Christian"*, ed. and trans. Paul Vincent Spade and Marilyn McCord Adams (Indianapolis, IN: Hackett Publishing Co., 1995).

84 *Ibid.*, p. 104, ll. 1721–3: "nostra in hoc et vestra intentio quam merita sunt diversa, et de ipso quoque summo bono non modice dissentimus."

85 *Ibid.*, p. 100, ll. 1532–7.

86 *Ibid.*, p. 100, ll. 1545–7.

87 *Ibid.*, p. 102, ll. 1609–10, 1618–19: "Contrarium ... bono quidem ex necessitate est malum ... Si bona est ... sanitas, mala est egritudo."

88 Sarah Kay, *Courtly Contradictions: the Emergence of the Literary Object in the Twelfth Century* (Stanford University Press, 2001), discusses the fact that for many medieval writers (e.g., Boethius) logical argument is oriented toward ethical truths, while others pursued logical controversy and contradiction for its own sake (pp. 16–17).

89 Abelard, *Dialogus*, p. 120, ll. 2309–12: "summum bonum Deus ipse est vel eius beatitudinis summa tranquillitas, quam tamen non aliud quam ipsum estimamus, / qui ex se ipso, non aliunde, beatus est."

90 *Ibid.*, p. 120, ll. 2312–15: "Summum autem hominis bonum illa est perpetua quies sive letitia, quam quisque pro meritis post hanc vitam recipit, sive in ipsa visione vel cognitione Dei, ut dicitis, sive quoquo modo aliter contingat."

91 *Ibid.*, p. 81, ll. 846–7: "dilectionis perfectio ad beatitudinem veram promerandam sufficiat."

92 *Ibid.*, p. 124, ll. 2490, 2497: "premii retributio ... rursum ipsum premium convertamus in meritum?"

93 See Marcia Colish, *Peter Lombard* (Leiden and New York: Brill, 1994), pp. 510, 750–1, on contemplation of God and the "ladder of love," respectively. See Philipp Rosemann, *Peter Lombard* (Oxford University Press, 2004), pp. 189–91 on the relationship between Peter's understanding of the beatific vision and the "many mansions" of the Father's house described in John 14:2.

94 Peter Lombard, *Sententiae in IV Libris Distinctae*, tome 1, part 2, Books I and II (Grottaferrata: Editiones Collegii S. Bonaventurae ad Claras Aquas, 1971), Book I, Dist. I, chapter 2: "Frui autem est amore inhaerere alicui rei propter se ipsam; uti vero, id quod in usum venerit referre ad obtinendum illud quo fruendum est ... In omnibus rebus illae tantum sunt quibus fruendum est, quae aeternae et incommutabiles sunt; ceteris autem utendum est, ut ad illarum perfruitionem perveniatur." Translations are from Peter Lombard, *The Sentences, Book I: The Mystery of the Trinity*, trans. Giulio Solano (Toronto: Pontifical Institute of Mediaeval Studies, 2007).

95 Colish, *Peter Lombard*, p. 1. She also notes that the practical obstacles to such a project are staggering.

96 *Ibid.*, pp. 718–19.

97 Monika Asztalos describes the theological curriculum at Paris in the thirteenth century, noting that the only required texts for theological study were the Bible and Lombard's *Sentences*. See "The Faculty of Theology," in

A History of the University in Europe, vol. 1: *Universities in the Middle Ages*, ed. Hilde de Ridder-Symoens (Cambridge University Press, 1992), pp. 409–41 (p. 418). Partial commentaries and glosses on the *Sentences* survive from as early as the 1160s, and it became the subject of formal commentary in the 1170s.

98 The enjoyment of the proper goal of human nature (love of God) was a prominent topic in the *Sentences* commentaries of Scotus, Ockham, Durandus of St. Pourçain, and Peter Aureoli. On the influence of these scholars throughout the fourteenth century, especially in England, see William Courtenay, *Schools and Scholars in Fourteenth-Century England* (Princeton University Press, 1987), pp. 282, 361. On the discourse surrounding enjoyment at fourteenth-century Oxford, see McGrade, "Enjoyment at Oxford."

99 See, for example, Leslie Topsfield, *Troubadours and Love* (New York: Cambridge University Press, 1975). Topsfield reads the *lo mielhs* of Jaufré Rudel as "probably analogous to the *omnium summum bonorum* of Boethius" (p. 44) and defines *jois* as supreme individual happiness; for him the early generation of troubadours (Guilhem IX, Jaufré Rudel) places the search for *jois* over the search for *amors*. Potkay reads troubadour *joi* as these poets' term for an "exquisitely unsatisfied desire" (*The Story of Joy*, p. 50), a kind of joy in a complex relationship – both parody and enactment – with Christian joy (p. 51). Moshe Lazar suggests that Occitan *joy* derives from both *gaudium* (joy) and *jocus* (play); he reviews the opinions of other scholars who have argued, for example, that troubadour *joy* is identical with Augustinian *delectatio*; a sensual term derived from Greek paganism; or a wholly new sentiment. See Lazar, "Fin'Amor," in *Handbook of the Troubadours*, ed. F. Akehurst and Judith Davis (Berkeley: University of California Press, 1995), pp. 61–100 (p. 77).

100 Laura Kendrick uncovers wordplay that points to an erotic, obscene, playful interpretation in many troubadour lyrics – restoring a level of "gaiety" to the "gaya sciensa" – in *The Game of Love: Troubadour Wordplay* (Berkeley: University of California Press, 1988), pp. 95–120 and *passim*.

101 This understanding was perhaps most influentially formulated by C. S. Lewis in *The Allegory of Love* (London: Oxford University Press, 1938).

102 All citations and translations of William IX are from *The Poetry of William VII, Count of Poitiers, IX Duke of Aquitaine*, ed. and trans. Gerald A. Bond (New York and London: Garland Publishing Co., 1982).

103 All citations and translations of Jaufré Rudel are from *The Songs of Jaufré Rudel*, ed. Rupert T. Pickens (Toronto: Pontifical Institute of Mediaeval Studies, 1978).

104 In *Love and Death in Medieval French and Occitan Courtly Literature: Martyrs to Love* (Oxford University Press, 2006), Simon Gaunt opens with a discussion of Jaufré's pilgrimage poem, observing that the poem is ambiguous as to whether we should read it as an erotic charging of spiritual desire, or a religious ennobling of an erotic or other earthly desire (pp. 1–2).

105 Topsfield, *Troubadours and Love*, p. 111.

106 All citations and translations of Bernart are from *The Songs of Bernart de Ventadorn*, ed. and trans. Stephen Nichols, John Galm, and A. Bartlett Giamatti, with Roger Porter, Seth Wolitz, and Claudette Charbonneau (Chapel Hill: University of North Carolina Press, 1962; rev. 1965).

107 D. Vance Smith reads the Narcissus myth as an exemplum for all experiences of possession in *Arts of Possession: the Middle English Household Imaginary* (Minneapolis: University of Minnesota Press, 2003), p. xviii. Gaunt reads "Can vei" as an exemplary sacrifice of *jouissance* for the pleasures of displeasure (*Love and Death*, p. 38).

2 NARCISSUS AFTER ARISTOTLE: LOVE AND ETHICS IN *LE ROMAN DE LA ROSE*

1 Boethius performed the earliest surviving Latin translations of Aristotle's philosophy, but completed only the *Categories*, *De Interpretatione*, *Prior Analytics*, *Topics*, and *Sophistici Elenchi*. For a narrative of translations of the Aristotelian corpus into Latin, see Dod, "Aristoteles Latinus," pp. 45–79.

2 Daniel Heller-Roazen makes this observation in *Fortune's Faces: The "Roman de la Rose" and the Poetics of Contingency* (Baltimore, MD: The Johns Hopkins University Press, 2003), p. 78, as a prelude to his own consideration of the poem's depiction of Fortune in the context of Aristotelian philosophy (pp. 79–99). See Gérard Paré, *Les idées et les lettres au XIIIe Siècle: "Le Roman de la Rose"* (Montréal: Centre de Psychologie et de Pédagogie, 1947), and *Le "Roman de la Rose" et la scholastique courtoise* (Paris and Ottawa: Publications de l'Institut d'Études Médiévales d'Ottawa, 1941). Giorgio Agamben situates the *Rose* in the context of thirteenth-century theories of imagination, lovesickness, and language in *Stanzas: Word and Phantasm in Western Culture*, trans. Ronald L. Martinez (Minneapolis: University of Minnesota Press, 1993). Suzanne Akbari places both Guillaume and Jean, along with Dante and Chaucer, in the context of scholastic interest in optics in *Seeing through the Veil: Optical Theory and Medieval Allegory* (University of Toronto Press, 2004). The *Rose* has more often been read in the context of twelfth-century neo-Platonism, as in Winthrop Wetherbee, *Platonism and Poetry in the Twelfth Century* (Princeton University Press, 1972).

3 Alastair Minnis, *Magister Amoris: The Roman de la Rose and Vernacular Hermeneutics* (Oxford University Press, 2001), pp. 4–6.

4 Minnis, "Aspects of the Medieval French and English Traditions of the *De Consolatione Philosophiae*," in *Boethius: His Life, Thought, and Influence*, ed. Margaret Gibson (Oxford: Blackwell, 1981), pp. 312–61 (pp. 323–4).

5 Sylvia Huot, *The Romance of the Rose and its Medieval Readers* (Cambridge University Press, 1993), p. 84.

6 Described *ibid.*, p. 50.

7 *Ibid.*, p. 74.

8 On the circularity of Amant's quest in Guillaume's *Rose*, see David Hult, *Self-fulfilling Prophecies: Readership and Authority in the first Roman de la Rose* (Cambridge University Press, 1986), p. 183.

9 Earl Jeffrey Richards, "Reflections on Oiseuse's Mirror: Iconographic Tradition, Luxuria, and the *Roman de la Rose*," *Zeitschrift für romanische Philologie* 98.3–4 (1982): 296–311 (p. 309). Richards distinguishes his approach to Oiseuse from D. W. Robertson's and John Fleming's who both caution against reading this figure as anything but idleness and the gateway to cupidity; see Fleming, *The Roman de la Rose: a Study in Allegory and Iconography* (Princeton University Press, 1969), pp. 73–81; and D. W. Robertson, *A Preface to Chaucer* (Princeton University Press, 1962), pp. 92–3. Agamben resolves the binary question as to whether Oiseuse means lechery or leisure by interpreting her mirror – and thus Oiseuse – as imagination itself, encompassing spiritual contemplation and false fantasy (*Stanzas*, p. 88, n. 16). Frédéric Godefroy gives a variety of definitions for *oiseuse*: oisiveté, lâcheté, paresse, chose oiseuse, inutile, parole vaine, futilité; see *Dictionnaire de l'ancienne langue française* (Paris: F. Vieweg, 1881–1902).

10 All internal references are to Guillaume de Lorris and Jean de Meun, *Le Roman de la Rose*, ed. Félix Lecoy (Paris: Honoré Champion, 1965–70). I will occasionally refer to *Le Roman de la Rose*, ed. Ernest Langlois (Paris: Firmin-Didot, 1914–24). The translations are from *The Romance of the Rose*, trans. Charles Dahlberg (Princeton University Press, 1971), though I have silently amended this translation in limited places, and have left the word *oiseuse* untranslated.

11 Hult suggests that the birdsong (the songs of the "oisiaus") directly before this narrative intrusion calls up associations with poetic activity and thus in effect calls the narrator/poet into being at this moment (*Self-fulfilling Prophecies*, p. 162).

12 Richards, "Reflections on Oiseuse's Mirror," p. 311.

13 Claire Nouvet, "An Allegorical Mirror: the Pool of Narcissus in Guillaume de Lorris' *Romance of the Rose*," *The Romanic Review* 91.4 (Nov. 2000): 353–74 (p. 367). Nouvet cites Augustine's *Confessions* on "intellectual heaven" (*caelum intellectuale*) as the place where the intellect is privileged to "know all at once" (*nosse simul*, XII.13).

14 Fleming, *The Roman de la Rose*, appendix images 17 and 18: Pierpont Morgan MSS M. 0324, fol. 5v and M. 0132, fol. 130v.

15 Fleming, *The Roman de la Rose*, pp. 76–8; Richards notes in opposition that the vice of *luxuria* was not typically depicted with mirror iconography in the thirteenth century, but more often with an image of a woman whose abdomen has been set upon by toads or snakes ("Reflections," pp. 296–304).

16 For a reading of Guillaume's *Rose* as addressing the difficulty of attaining self-knowledge through figures of deceptive vision and mirrors, see Akbari, *Seeing through the Veil*, pp. 19–20 and chapter 3.

17 On the "finishedness" of Guillaume's poem, see Hult, *Self-fulfilling Prophecies*, p. 174; and Kevin Brownlee, "Pygmalion, Mimesis, and the

Multiple Endings of the *Roman de la Rose*," *Yale French Studies* 95 (1999): 193–211 (p. 195).

18 Here my reading of Oiseuse has some affinities with Gregory Sadlek's interpretation; he argues that even more than leisure, "nonproductivity is the hallmark of [Oiseuse's] character"; see *Idleness Working: the Discourse of Love's Labor from Ovid through Chaucer and Gower* (Washington, DC: The Catholic University of America Press, 2004), p. 123.

19 Akbari, *Seeing through the Veil*, p. 19.

20 *Ibid.*, p. 76.

21 Narcissus also recognizes himself in the twelfth-century French poem *Narcisus.* Frederick Goldin discusses the importance of this recognition scene in *The Mirror of Narcissus in the Courtly Love Lyric* (Ithaca, NY: Cornell University Press, 1967), pp. 75–6.

22 Goldin argues that the dreamer escapes Narcissus' fate because he knows the Narcissus story, and has learned to see things besides his own image in the fountain; for Goldin, Guillaume's poem narrates the progress of the dreamer toward his ideal self (*The Mirror of Narcissus*, pp. 54–5).

23 See, most recently, Mark Miller, *Philosophical Chaucer: Love, Sex, and Agency in the Canterbury Tales* (Cambridge University Press, 2004), p. 168; also Sarah Kay, *The Romance of the Rose* (London: Grant & Cutler, Ltd., 1995), p. 79; and Hult, *Self-fulfilling Prophecies*, pp. 285–7.

24 In Hult's reading, the "translation" of the allegory of Amant taking the castle would not be physical consummation, but the winning of the lady's good graces (*Self-fulfilling Prophecies*, p. 172).

25 Wieland, "Reception and Interpretation," p. 661. See Wieland, *Ethica, scientia practica: die Anfänge der philosophischen Ethik im 13. Jahrhundert* (Münster Westfalen: Aschendorff, 1981), pp. 105–18.

26 See, for example, Aelred of Rievaulx, *De Speculo Caritatis*, in *Opera Omnia*, ed. A. Hoste and Charles H. Talbot, CCCM 1 (Turnhout: Brepols, 1971).

27 Celano, "The Understanding of the Concept of *Felicitas*."

28 *Ibid.*, p. 38. See also Robert Lerner, "Petrarch's Coolness Toward Dante: a Conflict of 'Humanisms,'" in *Intellectuals and Writers in Fourteenth-Century Europe*, ed. Piero Boitani and Anna Torti (Tübingen and Cambridge: Gunter Narr Verlag and D. S. Brewer, 1986), pp. 204–25 (p. 210, n. 19).

29 Celano, "The Understanding of the Concept of *Felicitas*," p. 43. The attribution of the commentary on the *Ethics* to Kilwardby is uncertain. Lewry argues for Kilwardby's authorship in "Robert Kilwardby's commentary." See discussion in Wieland, *Ethica, scientia practica*, pp. 172–7.

30 See Wieland, "Reception and Interpretation," pp. 657–8 and *passim*, and "Happiness"; also, Don Adams, "Aquinas on Aristotle on Happiness," *Medieval Philosophy and Theology*, 1 (1991): 98–118 on the difference between Aristotle's definition of contemplative happiness in Book x and the definitions of happiness in the preceding books.

31 Aristotle, *Ethica Nicomachea*, x.5.27–8 (1174b31–3).

32 Albert later wrote a second commentary, *c.*1263–7; see Wieland, "Reception and Interpretation," p. 660.

33 Albertus Magnus, *Super Ethica*, 2 vols., in *Opera Omnia*, ed. Wilhelm Kübel, tome XIV (Monasterii Westfalorum: Aschendorff, 1968–87), Book X, lectio 11, section 899, p. 754.
34 *Ibid.*
35 On earlier commentators, see Wieland, "Reception and Interpretation," pp. 658–9, as well as Steenberghen, *Aristotle in the West*, pp. 95–105.
36 Albertus, *Super Ethica*, section 927, p. 774.
37 *Ibid.*, Book X, lectio 16, section 928, p. 775.
38 *Ibid.*, Prologus, section 5, p. 4; Wieland, "Reception and Interpretation," p. 661.
39 Boethius of Dacia, *De Summo Bono*, in *Topica – Opuscula*, pars. 2, ed. Niels Jørgen Green-Pederson, in *Boethii Daci Opera*, Corpus philosophorum Danicorum Medii Aevi 6 (Hauniae: G. E. C. Gad, 1976); Siger of Brabant, *Quaestiones Morales*, in *Écrits de logique, de morale et de physique*, ed. Bernardo Bazán (Louvain: Publications Universitaires, 1974). Boethius is careful to define a "philosopher" as any man who lives according to the right order of nature and who has acquired the best and ultimate end of human life, a slightly tautological saving definition.
40 The introduction to this condemnation explicitly names the *De Amore* of Andreas Capellanus, a work condemned along with books on witchcraft, necromancy, etc. The full text of the condemnation is found in the *Chartularium Universitatis Parisiensis*, vol. I, pp. 543–61, and translated as "Condemnation of 219 Propositions" by Ernest L. Fortin and Peter D. O'Neill in *Medieval Political Philosophy: a Sourcebook*, ed. Ralph Lerner and Muhsin Mahdi (New York: Free Press of Glencoe, 1963), pp. 335–54. See also Roland Hissette, *Enquête sur les 219 articles condamnés à Paris le 7 Mars 1277* (Louvain: Publications Universitaires, 1977), especially pp. 263–73 on the ethical articles.
41 Quoted in Wieland, "Reception and Interpretation," p. 663: *Chartularium Universitatis Parisiensis*, vol. I, n. 473, Sent. 40: "quod non est excellentior status quam vacare philosophiae"; Sent. 176: "quod felicitas habetur in ista vita et non in alia."
42 Thomas Aquinas, *In Decem Libros Ethicorum Aristotelis ad Nicomachum Expositio*, ed. Raymund Spiazzi (Taurini: Marietti, 1964), Book X, lectio 13, 2136: "qualis potest competere humanae et mortali vitae." Translations are from *Commentary on Aristotle's Nicomachean Ethics.*
43 *Ibid.*, Book X, lectio 10, 2092.
44 *Ibid.*, Book X, lectio 11, 2110: "Sic ergo patet, quod ille qui vacat speculationi veritatis, est maxime felix, quantum homo in hac vita felix esse potest."
45 Aristotle, *Ethica Nicomachea*, X.9.14–24 (1177b31–1178a8): "Oportet … in quantum contingit immortalem facere, et omnia facere ad vivere secundum optimum eorum que in ipso … homini utique, quae secundum intellectum vita, si quid maxime hoc homo, iste ergo felicissimus."
46 This aspect of the translation is noted in *Summa Theologiae*, vol. XIX (*The Emotions*, Ia IIae 22–30), ed. E. D'Arcy (Blackfriars and New York:

McGraw-Hill, 1972), pp. 76–7, fn. c, in reference to Aquinas' understanding of the term "appetitus."

47 Aquinas, *Ethicorum Aristotelis Expositio*, Book 1, lectio 1, 11: "Ipsum autem tendere in bonum, est appetere bonum."

48 *Ibid.*, Book 1, lectio 2, 21: "naturale desiderium nihil est aliud quam inclinatio inhaerens rebus ex ordinatione primi moventis, quae non potest frustrari. Ergo impossible est, quod in finibus procedatur in infinitum."

49 *Ibid.*, Book 1, lectio 16, 202: "Et quia non est inane naturae desiderium, recte existimari potest, quod reservatur homini perfecta beatitudo post hanc vitam."

50 Vivian Boland reconciles Aristotle's notion of the "good as attractive" with the neo-Platonist (pseudo-Dionysian) notion of the "good as ecstatic" by suggesting that Aristotle's ethical vision is of a human being searching for what he has already received from the First Mover; see "Thinking about Good: Thomas Aquinas on *Nicomachean Ethics* I, *Divine Names* IV–V and *De Ebdomadibus*," *New Blackfriars*, 83.979 (2002): 384–400 (p. 391).

51 Aquinas, *Ethicorum Aristotelis Expositio*, Book 1, lectio 8, 98: "Quaerimus enim felicitatem, quae est finis humanorum actuum."

52 *Ibid.*, Book 1, lectio 9, 113: "Loquitur enim in hoc libro Philosophus de felicitate, qualis in hac vita potest haberi. Nam felicitas alterius vitae omnem investigationem rationis excedit."

53 Aquinas' biographer, Jean-Pierre Torrell, maintains that while Aquinas sought to restrict himself to the *intentio auctoris*, this intention is always placed within his larger apostolic purpose of seeking theological wisdom; see *Saint Thomas Aquinas*, vol. 1: *The Person and His Work*, trans. Robert Royal (Washington, DC: The Catholic University of America Press, 1996; rev. 2005), pp. 236–9.

54 Lacan, *Encore*, p. 66; trans. Fink, p. 70; Lacan derives the terminology of "physical" and "ecstatic" love from Pierre Rousselot, *Pour l'histoire du problème de l'amour au moyen âge* (Münster: Aschendorffsche Buchhandlung, 1907), translated as *The Problem of Love in the Middle Ages* by Alan Vincelette (Milwaukee, WI: Marquette University Press, 2001). For Rousselot, physical love is continuous with self-love while ecstatic love demands that the subject stand outside himself or herself.

55 Lacan, *Encore*, p. 133; trans. Fink, p. 145.

56 Paré, on the other hand, contends that Jean de Meun was in harmony with the contemporary Aristotelianism of the arts faculty at the University of Paris, especially with reference to the doctrine of carnal love espoused by Nature and Genius (which he attributes unironically to Jean); see *Les idées et les lettres*, p. 322 and *passim*.

57 Sadlek finds a "strong, coherent work ideology" in Jean's *Rose*, manifested in the discourses of Reason, Nature, and Genius (*Idleness Working*, pp. 129, 114–66 *passim*). While Sadlek reads this ideology as a valuing of primarily manual work and a critique of the mendicant orders, I see Jean's largely positive attitude toward labor as a way of experimenting with theorizations of

erotic desire, intellectual work, and art. Nicola Masciandaro places the *Rose* in a tradition of late medieval texts that associate nobility with industriousness in *The Voice of the Hammer: the Meaning of Work in Middle English Literature* (University of Notre Dame Press, 2007), p. 92.

58 Heller-Roazen marks this section of the poem as "perhaps the most extended chapter of the *Roman de la Rose* in which Jean de Meun invokes and develops a subject drawn from the faculties of theology and philosophy of his time" (*Fortune's Faces*, p. 105).

59 Alain de Lille's *De Planctu Naturae*, trans. James J. Sheridan (Toronto: Pontifical Institute of Mediaeval Studies, 1980), the main source for Jean's description of Nature and Genius, also manipulates the binary of idleness and labor. Alain begins the work by complaining of his grief in terms of the labor of childbirth, and he later (prose 5) describes the ruinous relationship between Venus and Antigenius as being the result of Venus' boredom with repetitive toil and her desire for ease.

60 Hugh White argues that Nature's engagement in the act of confession nevertheless undercuts her moral authority in *Nature, Sex, and Goodness*, p. 124.

61 Paré hazards that Nature's defense of free will is in part owing to Jean de Meun's rejection of the fatalism outlined in the condemnations issued by Étienne Tempier in 1270 and 1277 in *Les idées et les lettres*, p. 232.

62 Paul Strohm finds a similarly optimistic view of the individual's relationship to Fortune emerging in fifteenth-century England: "Fortune" begins to be understood as a collection of causes that "more fully understood, might be neutralized or even mastered altogether"; see *Politique: Languages of Statecraft between Chaucer and Shakespeare* (University of Notre Dame Press, 2005), p. 4 and *passim*.

63 Aquinas, *Summa Theologiae*, Ia IIae, q. 27, a. 2: "amor requirit aliquam apprehensionem boni quod amatur. Et propter hoc Philosophus dicit quod visio corporalis est principium amoris sensitivi. Et similiter contemplatio spiritualis pulchritudinis vel bonitatis, est principium spiritualis amoris. Sic igitur cognitio est causa amoris, ea ratione qua et bonum, quod non potest amari nisi cognitum."

64 *Ibid.*

65 In both Langlois' and Lecoy's editions of the *Rose*, the notes refer the reader to Boethius (Book II, prose 5) on man becoming bestial if deprived of self-knowledge. A closer description of animal rebellion as the result of animal reason may be found in Aelred of Rievaulx's *De Anima*, where he proves the supremacy of reason to the body: "Et ut scias in comparatione rationis quam nihil possit corpus vel sensus, quis hominum unius muscae cavere posset insidias, si ipsa, ut homo, ratione vigeret? Quis ea invita quiescere, vel tute oculos posset aperire? … Nonne congregatis in unum feris ac volucribus, totum possent humanum genus delere, si aequales essent hominibus ratione?" (And in order that you know how the body or the senses are capable of nothing in comparison with reason, what human would be able to be safe from the plots of one fly, if this fly flourished with reason as a human does? Who

could rest against the fly's will, or safely be able to open his eyes? … If they were equal to humans in reason, is it not the case that with the birds and beasts all gathered as one, they could destroy all of humankind?) (*Dialogus de Anima*, Book II.18–20, p. 713, in *Opera Omnia*). While Jean is known to have translated Aelred's *De Spirituali Amicitia*, it does not appear that his *De Anima* had any circulation on the Continent in the thirteenth century.

66 Jane Chance Nitzsche notes that art is described pejoratively throughout Jean's *Rose* (especially falsity versus the truth of Nature). She contends that "This discourse – on 'dreams', 'visions', and the artifice of mirrors – suggests obliquely that literature itself, peopled by phantoms and images, is artificial, and even deceptive" in *The Genius Figure in Antiquity and the Middle Ages* (New York: Columbia University Press, 1975), p. 124. Alan Gunn, on the other hand, interprets Jean's depictions of such delusions as an attempt to ward them off, part of his aim in creating a "true and fruitful image" reflected from the "Mind of God"; see *The Mirror of Love* (Lubbock: Texas Tech Press, 1952), pp. 270–5. My reading falls somewhere in between; Jean is not here making a pronouncement about the ultimate falsity or truth of his art, or art in general, but rather exploring the possibilities and dangers of imagination, especially when confronted with love.

67 Sarah Kay argues that the demarcation of inside and outside is one of the key concerns of Guillaume's *Rose*, where the poet problematizes the limits of the self; see *Subjectivity in Troubadour Poetry* (Cambridge University Press, 1990), pp. 179–82.

68 This distrust of contemplation may give support in a different context to Winthrop Wetherbee's claim that "Jean's Nature seems scarcely to know herself," but rather views herself through human eyes; see "The Literal and the Allegorical: Jean de Meun and the *De Planctu Naturae*," *Medieval Studies* 33 (1971): 264–91 (p. 281). Nature would be subject to the same faulty possibilities in vision and reflection as human beings.

69 Nitzsche, *The Genius Figure*, p. 97.

70 Aristotle, *Ethica Nicomachea*, x.8.18–19 (1177a19–21): "Optima et enim hec operacio; et enim intellectus eorum que in nobis et cognoscibilium circa que intellectus."

71 Gerard Paré, in *Les idées et les lettres* (p. 321, chapters 5 and 6 *passim*), takes Genius as not only a serious figure, preaching the gospel of Aristotelian "naturalism," but as the key to the entire poem. For Paré, Genius reveals Jean de Meun's affinities with "Averroists" such as Siger of Brabant and Boethius of Dacia who supposedly subscribe to notions such as the virtues of sexual procreation outside marriage and the possibility of achieving perfect happiness in this life. John Fleming takes issue with Paré's thesis, arguing for the impossibility of Jean's embracing any morality at odds with Christian ethics (*The Roman de la Rose*, pp. 214–20). Fleming cites Rosemond Tuve for support, as she argues that Genius and Nature are held up as examples of the domination of inadequate ideas concerning love and the good; see *Allegorical Imagery: Some Medieval Books and Their Posterity* (Princeton University Press,

1966), p. 262. Robertson understands Genius as "merely the inclination of created things to act naturally" (*Preface*, p. 200). Huot notes that medieval readings often revolve around the question of whether Genius' sermon can be reconciled with Christian doctrine, without recourse to satire or parody (*Medieval Readers*, p. 174).

72 Aquinas, *Ethicorum Aristotelis Expositio*, Book I, lectio I, 9.

73 This teleology leaves open the question of how we can know which pleasure is the ethical pleasure to be pursued. Jonathan Lear reads the opening of the *Ethics*, where Aristotle introduces the idea of the single ultimate good, as an "inaugural instantiation" whereby he "injects the concept of the good" into our lives; see *Happiness, Death, and the Remainder of Life* (Cambridge, MA: Harvard University Press, 2000), p. 8.

74 Aquinas, *Ethicorum Aristotelis Expositio*, Book X, lectio 9, 2072: "Vocat autem huiusmodi potentes tyrannos, quia non videntur communi utilitati intendere, sed propriae delectationi, qui in ludis conversantur ... Sic ergo felicitas in talibus consistit, propter hoc quod huiusmodi vacant illi, qui sunt in potestatibus constituti, quos homines reputant felices."

75 See Nicole Oresme, *Éthiques*, p. 517.

76 Minnis calls Jean's Pygmalion "the antithesis of Narcissus, this being part and parcel of a systematic recapitulation and redirection of Guillaume's major terms of reference" in *Magister Amoris*, p. 106. On Pygmalion, see also Roger Dragonetti, "Pygmalion ou les pièges de la fiction dans *Le Roman de la Rose*," in *La musique et les lettres: études de littérature médiévale* (Geneva: Droz, 1986), pp. 345–67; and Daniel Poirion, "Narcisse et Pygmalion dans le Roman de la Rose," in *Essays in Honour of Louis Francis Solano*, ed. Raymond J. Cormier and Urban T. Holmes (Chapel Hill: University of North Carolina Press, 1970), pp. 153–65.

77 Sylvia Huot, *From Song to Book: The Poetics of Writing in Old French Lyric and Lyrical Narrative Poetry* (Ithaca, NY: Cornell University Press, 1987), p. 98; see Brownlee, "Pygmalion," for a discussion of the Pygmalion fable as representative of "the signifying power of ART, told 'successfully' on Art's own terms as defined by Jean's *Rose*" (p. 211).

78 Kay, focusing on the role of Venus in the digression, reads the tale as a derision of "the inadequacy of masculine art, and masculine fantasy, when they join forces to confine women in the role of object" (*Rose*, p. 47).

79 The reciprocal erotic encounter between Pygmalion and Galatea is discussed by Brownlee, "Pygmalion," pp. 197–8.

80 Aristotle, *Ethica Nicomachea*, IX.7.22–3 (1168a20–1): "Superexcellentibus autem utique circa actum sequitur amare et amicabilia."

81 *Ibid.*, IX.7.4–7 (1167b34–1168a3): "omnis enim proprium opus diligit magis quam diligatur utique ab opere animato facto; maxime autem forte hoc circa poetas accidit, superdiligunt enim isti propria poemata, diligentes quemadmodum filios."

82 Aquinas, *Ethicorum Aristotelis Expositio*, Book IX, lectio 7, 1845: "Poëmata enim magis ad rationem pertinent secundum quam homo est homo, quam alia mechanica opera."

83 Douglas Kelly notes that Pygmalion's desire for his art "resembles Jean de Meun working with Guillaume's material for the *Rose*" in *Internal Differences and Meanings in the "Roman de la Rose"* (Madison: University of Wisconsin Press, 1985), p. 76.

84 References to sex as "labor" or "work" are common euphemisms in medieval Romance languages. Such euphemism is used not only by Genius, but by La Vielle, who recommends that the couple, when they "work" ("se seront mis an l'euvre," l. 14263), should work carefully so that each should have his or her pleasure and strain toward the good ("et s'antredoivent entr'atendre / por ansamble a leur bonne tendre," ll. 14269–70). The emphasis on reciprocity in both content and language (e.g., the repeated use of the prefix "-entre") prefigures the reciprocal erotic encounter between Pygmalion and Galatea. See also Dragonetti, "Pygmalion," p. 365.

85 Noah Guynn's reading of the allegory does not allow for any mitigation to the violence of the plucking ("cueillette") of the rose – it is either force or outright rape, and the violence of the poem's allegories more generally confirms the rose as a silent female object at the mercy of the elite male subject (both lover and poet). Guynn's argument is undeniably persuasive, but does not account for moments of mutuality such as are contained in the Pygmalion fable. The violence of the poem's ending may thus be read not necessarily or only as a final eruption of misogyny, but as an acknowledgment of the violence inherent in love and even in the desire for the animation of the love object and her desire. See *Allegory and Sexual Ethics in the High Middle Ages* (New York: Palgrave Macmillan, 2007), pp. 137–70.

3 METAMORPHOSES OF PLEASURE IN THE FOURTEENTH-CENTURY *DIT AMOUREUX*

1 Claire Richter Sherman, *Imaging Aristotle: Verbal and Visual Representation in Fourteenth-Century France* (Berkeley: University of California Press, 1995), p. 3.

2 Nicole Oresme, *Éthiques*, pp. 541–7; see Menut's list of coined words, pp. 79–82.

3 On the authorship, dating, and content of this treatise, see Guy Guldentops and Carlos Steel, "Vernacular Philosophy for the Nobility: *Li Ars d'Amour, de Vertu et de Boneurté*, an Old French Adaptation of Thomas Aquinas' Ethics from ca.1300," *Bulletin de Philosophie Médiévale* 45 (2003): 67–85. Guldentops and Steel note that the quotations and summaries from Aristotle and Aquinas collected together would comprise a near-complete Picardian French reconstruction of the *Ethics* along with Aquinas' commentary and sections on ethics from the *Summa Theologiae* and *Summa Contra Gentiles* (p. 72). Current scholarship identifies the author as Guy d'Avesnes, Bishop of Utrecht from 1301–17. The treatise survives in three manuscripts, one of which has been edited: *Li Ars d'Amour, de Vertu et de Boneurté*, par Jehan le Bel, publié pour la première fois d'après un manuscrit de la Bibliothèque royale de Bruxelles par Jules Petit, 2 vols. (Brussels: V. Devaux et cie, vol. I 1867; vol. II [without

reference to Jehan le Bel] 1869). The glossary is contained in vol. II, pp. xlv–lvi. Earlier, Brunetto Latini adapted and summarized the *Ethics* in his *Livres dou Tresor* (*c.*1265), working from Taddeo's translation of the *Summa Alexandrina Ethicorum*, itself translated from the Arabic by Hermannus Alemannus. See Menut's discussion in his introduction to *Le Livre de Éthiques d'Aristote*, pp. 3–4.

4 Courtenay, *Schools and Scholars*, p. 286.

5 Robert Bossuat makes this remark of Machaut in *Le Moyen Âge*, Histoire de la littérature française I (Paris: J. de Gigord, 1931), p. 237; quoted in Katherine Heinrichs, *The Myths of Love: Classical Lovers in Medieval Literature* (University Park and London: Pennsylvania State University Press, 1990), p. 225, n. 28.

6 Sylvia Huot, however, discusses Machaut's Boethianism in an expansive manner, arguing that Machaut recasts Boethian consolation as the capacity of poetry to link "love, desire, memory, and art"; see "Guillaume de Machaut and the Consolation of Poetry," *Modern Philology* 100.2 (Nov. 2002): 169–95 (p. 171). Huot argues that Machaut places hope of consolation in the replacement of the actual, individual love object with an image (of the sovereign good) that can be possessed within the imagination and thus confer joy (p. 194).

7 Kathryn Lynch, *Chaucer's Philosophical Visions* (Woodbridge: D. S. Brewer, 2000), p. 32.

8 Jacqueline Cerquiglini-Toulet, *"Un engin si soutil": Guillaume de Machaut et l'écriture au XIV siècle* (Paris: Champion, 1985), p. 165.

9 Huot, *The Romance of the Rose*, pp. 239–40.

10 Kay reads Machaut's portrayal of the virtues and happiness in the *Jugement dou roy de Navarre* as influenced by the *Nicomachean Ethics*, and argues ultimately that "In addition to taking the *Ethics* into the domain of sexual difference, Machaut moves it beyond the pleasure principle" (*The Place of Thought*, p. 118 and chapter 4 *passim*). See also Margaret Ehrhart, "Guillaume de Machaut's *Jugement dou Roy de Navarre* and Medieval Treatments of the Virtues," *Annuale Mediaevale* 19 (1979): 46–67.

11 John Fyler, *Chaucer and Ovid* (New Haven, CT: Yale University Press, 1979), p. 1.

12 Fyler discusses several fourteenth-century uses of this myth (*ibid.*, pp. 68–95).

13 Fyler notes that Ceyx and Alcyone make up one of the few "happily married" couples in the *Metamorphoses* (*ibid.*, p. 69).

14 Laurence de Looze describes the tale as one in which Ceyx, given form by Morpheus, narrates "his own" death; see "Guillaume de Machaut and the Writerly Process," *French Forum* 9.2 (May 1984): 145–161 (p. 149).

15 William H. Watts and Richard J. Utz, "Nominalist Perspectives on Chaucer's Poetry: a Bibliographical Essay," *Medievalia et Humanistica* 20 (1993): 147–73. See also the introduction to Lynch's *Chaucer's Philosophical Visions* for a useful overview (though one arguing for the relevance of

scholastic philosophy to Chaucer) of the literature on this subject, as well as Erin Labbie, *Lacan's Medievalism* (Minneapolis: University of Minnesota Press, 2006), p. 11 and p. 230, n. 1. Also Alastair Minnis, "Looking for a Sign: the Quest for Nominalism in Chaucer and Langland," in *Essays on Ricardian Literature: In Honor of J. A. Burrow*, ed. A. J. Minnis, Charlotte C. Morse, and Thorlac Turville-Petre (New York: Oxford University Press, 1997), pp. 142–78; Hugo Keiper, "A Literary 'Debate Over Universals'? New Perspectives on the Relationships between Nominalism, Realism, and Literary Discourse," in *Nominalism and Literary Discourse*, ed. Hugo Keiper, Christoph Bode, and Richard J. Utz (Atlanta, GA: Rodopi, 1997), pp. 1–85; and Richard Utz, "Negotiating the Paradigm: Literary Nominalism and the Theory of Rereading Late Medieval Texts," in *Literary Nominalism and the Theory of Rereading Late Medieval Texts*, ed. Richard Utz (Lewiston, NY: Edwin Mellen Press, 1995), pp. 1–30. Mark Miller argues for a Chaucer who is "philosophical" not only in his engagements with philosophical traditions and dialectic, but in places where his characters and concerns appear a-philosophical or even anti-philosophical. See Miller, *Philosophical Chaucer*, p. 2 and *passim*.

16 Courtenay, *Schools and Scholars*, pp. xi–xii.

17 See Robert Stepsis, "Potentia Absoluta and the Clerk's Tale," *Chaucer Review* 10 (1975): 129–46; and David Steinmetz, "Late Medieval Nominalism and the Clerk's Tale," *Chaucer Review* 12 (1977): 38–54. In his influential 1978 article, "Chaucer and the Nominalist Questions," Russell Peck begins by admitting that he could not find any evidence that Chaucer was particularly interested in nominalism per se, but does find many points of concurrence between Chaucer and Ockham on questions of language, human knowledge, and the will; see "Chaucer and the Nominalist Questions," *Speculum* 53.4 (Oct. 1978): 745–60.

18 Fradenburg discusses these debates in "Amorous Scholasticism," pp. 35–6 and again briefly in the introduction to *Sacrifice Your Love*, p. 31.

19 Aristotle, *Ethica Nicomachea*, x.5.27–8 (1174b33).

20 *Ibid.*, x.5.20–2 (1175a18–21); see Chapter 1 above, note 28.

21 See G. E. L. Owen, "Aristotelian Pleasures," in *Articles on Aristotle*, ed. Jonathan Barnes, Malcolm Schofield, and Richard Sorabji (London: Duckworth, 1975), pp. 92–103 on conflicting definitions of pleasure in the *Nicomachean Ethics*.

22 Augustine, *De Civitate Dei*, xiv.9, ll.107–8: "Potest ergo non absurde dici perfectam beatitudinem sine stimulo timoris et sine ulla tristitia futuram."

23 Albertus Magnus, *Super Ethica*, Book x, lectio 1, section 4, ll. 41–4, p. 710: see Aristotle, *Ethica Nicomachea*, ii.9 (1109b7–13) and ii.3 (1104b3–9).

24 Albertus Magnus, *Super Ethica*, Book x, lectio 1, section 4, ll. 45–9, p. 710.

25 *Ibid.*, Book x, lectio 1, section 1, ll. 72–4, p. 708: "Quod probat COMMENTATOR, quia felicitas non potest intelligi sine delectatione." References to "the Commentator" occur throughout writings on Aristotle, referring to any of the Greek commentators who were translated by Grosseteste along with the

main text, as well as to Averroes. Michael of Ephesus commented on several books of the *Nicomachean Ethics*. See Aristotle, *Ethica Nicomachea*, fasc. 3, x.8.22 (1177a23): "existimamusque oportere delectationem misceri felicitati"; in Moerbeke (fasc. 4): "Extimamusque oportere delectationem admixtam esse felicitati."

26 Michael of Ephesus, *The Greek Commentaries on the Nicomachean Ethics of Aristotle*, vol. III, ed. H. Paul F. Mercken (Leiden: Brill, 1973), Book x, chapter 8, p. 414: "Perfecta enim vita et indeficiens et per se sufficiens optima et extrema, quare et delectabilissima."

27 Thomas Aquinas, *Summa Theologiae* (*Pleasure*, IaIIae 31–9), q. 31, a. 3.

28 *Ibid.*, IaIIae, q. 34, a. 3.

29 Thomas Aquinas, *Ethicorum Aristoteles Expositio*, Book x, lectio 6, 2038: "Nam delectatio est quies appetitus in re delectante, qua quis per operationem potitur. Non autem aliquis appetit quietem in aliquo, nisi in quantum aestimat sibi conveniens. Et ideo ipsa operatio, quae delectat sicut quoddam conveniens, videtur prius appetibilis, quam delectatio."

30 Thomas Aquinas, *Summa Theologiae*, IIaIIae, q. 168, a. 2; see discussion in Olson, *Literature as Recreation*, p. 97.

31 Thomas Aquinas, *Ethicorum Aristotelis Expositio*, Book x, lectio 10, 2097: "Hoc autem apparet in sola speculatione sapientiae, quod propter seipsam diligatur et non propter aliud."

32 See Bonnie Kent, *Virtues of the Will: the Transformation of Ethics in the Late Thirteenth Century* (Washington, DC: The Catholic University of America Press, 1995), p. 82.

33 The enjoyment of the proper goal of human nature (love of God) was a prominent topic in the *Sentences* commentaries of Scotus, Ockham, Durandus of St. Pourçain, and Peter Aureoli. On the influence of these scholars throughout the fourteenth century, especially in England, see Courtenay, *Schools and Scholars*, pp. 282, 361. On the discourse surrounding enjoyment at fourteenth-century Oxford, see McGrade, "Enjoyment at Oxford."

34 Ockham discusses Aureoli's opinion along with Scotus' (implied by "argumenta aliorum") in his commentary; see *Quaestiones*, Liber I, Dist. I, q. 3, pp. 405–7.

35 *Ibid.*, Liber I, Dist. I, q. 3, p. 403: "Utrum fruitio sit qualitas realiter distincta a delectatione."

36 See McGrade, "Enjoyment at Oxford," p. 69.

37 Ockham, *Quaestiones*, Liber I, Dist. I, q. 3, p. 404: "felicitas consistit in operatione, delectatio autem non est operatio sed superveniens operationi"; see Aristotle, *Ethica Nicomachea*, x.4 (1174b31–3); translations, where possible, are from "Using and Enjoying" (from "Commentary on *Sentences*") in *Ethics and Political Philosophy*, ed. Arthur Stephen McGrade, John Kilcullen, and Matthew Kempshall, Cambridge Translations of Medieval Philosophical Texts 2 (Cambridge University Press, 2001) (p. 373).

38 Ockham, *Quaestiones*, Liber I, Dist. I, q. 3, art. 3, p. 423: "Confirmatur, quia actus amoris intensus stat cum tristitia de eodem obiecto, scilicet cum aliquis timet perdere illud quod diligit"; "Using and Enjoying," p. 386.

39 *Ibid.*, Liber I, Dist. I, q. 3, p. 409: "secundum Philosophum X *Ethicorum*, summa tristitia excludit delectationem non sibi oppositam et oppositam sibi, sicut qui summe tristatur de amissione rei temporalis non delectatur de consideratione alicuius speculabilis. Sed illa tristitia non excludit omnem amorem illius considerationis"; "Using and Enjoying," p. 377. See Aristotle, *Ethica Nicomachea*, x.5 (1175b16–24).

40 Ockham, *Quaestiones*, Liber I, Dist. I, q. 3, art. 3, p. 424: "habet dicere consequenter quod de potentia Dei absoluta actus amoris potest stare cum tristitia."

41 *Ibid.*, Liber I, Dist. I, q. 3, art. 4, p. 425: "actus amoris est simpliciter nobilior ipsa delectatione"; "Using and Enjoying," p. 388.

42 *Ibid.*, Liber I, Dist. I, q. 3, art. 4, p. 426: "amor viae est perfectior delectatione viae, ergo amor patriae est perfectior delectatione patriae, et per consequens totaliter amor est perfectior delectatione"; "Using and Enjoying," p. 388.

43 *Ibid.*, Liber I, Dist. I, q. 3, art. 4, pp. 426–7: "propter operationes et propter vivere ... si enim et quam maxime delectabiles sunt ipsae, sed non delectationis gratia studiose aguntur. Multas enim earum quae secundum virtutes operationes eligimus, quamvis tristitiae et laborum seu dolorum causas exsistentes ..."; "Using and Enjoying," p. 389.

44 See Walter Chatton, *Reportatio Super Sententias*, ed. Joseph C. Wey and Girard J. Etzkorn, 4 vols. (Toronto: Pontifical Institute for Mediaeval Studies, 2002), Dist. I, q. 2, art. 2, vol. I, pp. 39–43.

45 Adam Wodeham, *Lectura Secunda In Librum Primum Sententiarum*, ed. Rega Wood, assisted by Gedeon Gál, 3 vols. (St. Bonaventure, NY: St. Bonaventure University Press, 1990), vol. I, Dist. I, q. 6: "Utrum Fruitio Realiter Distinguatur a Delectatione."

46 *Ibid.*, Dist. I, q. 6, section I, ll. 22–4.

47 *Ibid.*, Dist. I, q. 6, section 3, ll. 61–4.

48 Buridan, *Quaestiones super Decem Libros Ethicorum*, Book x, q. 4, section 1b, p. 209[r], col. b: "Sed arguitur quod hoc sit impossibile quemcunque illorum dicas. Quia si dicas quod actus nobilissimus qui potest homini inesse sit clara dei visio, tunc probo quod ille non esset essentialiter felicitas. Quia si esset essentialiter felicitas tunc ipso manente, aliis actibus ablatis sicut auferri possunt per potentiam dei absolutam (ut aliqui theologi dicunt) adhuc homo esset felix, sicut lapis esset albus manente in eo albedine omnibus aliis accidentibus remotis; et tamen illud consequens est falsum, scilicet quod homo clare videns deum sine alia delectatione et sine amore dei diceretur beatus. Oportet enim felicitatem esse delectabilissimam, ut dicit Aristoteles. Ergo, etc. Et confirmatur fortius, quia dicunt illi theologi quod in anima Sortis cum clara dei visione posset deus formare intensam tristitiam sine delectatione, et odium dei sine amore; an igitur esset felix? Constat mihi quod ego non vellem talem felicitatem"; "Questions on Book X of the Ethics," p. 541. See Wieland, "Happiness," p. 684.

49 Buridan, *Quaestiones super Decem Libros Ethicorum*, Book x, q. 4, section 1b, p. 209[r], col. b: "felicitas ponitur consistere in perfecta dei contemplatione

que nec est dei cognitio sine amore, nec amor sine cognitione, sed ex ambobus constituta"; "Questions," p. 542.

50 *Ibid.*, Book x, q. 4, section 2b, p. 210^{r}, col. b: "nomen contemplationis connotat, sicut nomen felicitatis, adiacentiam amoris et delectationis naturaliter connexorum illi speculationi vel visioni"; "Questions," p. 547.

51 *Ibid.*, Book x, q. 4, section 2a, p. 210^{r}, col. a; "Questions," p. 546.

52 *Ibid.*, Book x, q. 5, section 2a, p. 212^{r}, col. b: "Idem est ergo actus noster optimus et actus noster delectabilissimus"; section 2b, thesis 3, p. 212^{v}, col. b: "principali seu primaria intentione delectatio est pro[p]ter operationem"; "Questions," pp. 562, 565.

53 *Ibid.*, Book x, q. 5, section 2b, thesis 3, p. 213^{r}, col. a: "beatus non solum intelligit et amat deum: sed reflexive potest intelligere et intelligit se intelligere et amare et delectari"; "Questions," p. 567.

54 *Ibid.*, Book x, q. 5, section 2b, thesis 4, p. 213^{r}, col. b: "objecti sub ratione boni presentis et obtenti"; "Questions," p. 568.

55 McGrade argues for the importance of psychology to fourteenth-century ethics in "Enjoyment at Oxford," especially pp. 69, 86.

56 Guillaume de Machaut, *Prologue*, in *Œuvres*, ed. Ernest Hoepffner, 3 vols. (Paris: Librairie de Firmin-Didot et Cie, 1908), vol. 1. Translations are from *"The Fountain of Love" and Two Other Love Vision Poems*, ed. and trans. R. Barton Palmer (New York: Garland Publishing, Inc., 1993); all poems in this section will be cited first in footnotes and subsequently by line and/or page number within the text. See discussion of Machaut's *Prologue* in Ardis Butterfield, *Poetry and Music in Medieval France* (Cambridge University Press, 2002), pp. 292–5; and Cerquiglini-Toulet, *"Un engin si soutil"*, pp. 17–21.

57 Deborah McGrady explores the way that Machaut made reading a subject of romance in *Controlling Readers: Guillaume de Machaut and his Late Medieval audience* (University of Toronto Press, 2006), pp. 45, 46, and chapter 2, *passim*. She argues that, from Machaut's perspective, individual, private reading creates the conditions for greater authorial control (p. 74).

58 *Le Livre du Voir Dit*, ed. Paul Imbs, revised and coordinated with an introduction by Jacqueline Cerquiglini-Toulet, index of proper names and glossary by Noël Musso (Paris: Librairie Générale Française, 1999); translation from *Le Livre dou Voir Dit*, ed. Daniel Leech-Wilkinson, trans. R. Barton Palmer (New York: Garland, 1998).

59 Aquinas states that hope and memory cause pleasure by rendering the loved object present according to apprehension and possibility of attainment; see *Summa Theologiae*, IaIIae, q. 32, a. 3.

60 Brownlee observes that the "love experience is, as it were, transformed into poetry before the reader's eyes" in *Poetic Identity in Guillaume de Machaut* (Madison: University of Wisconsin Press, 1984), p. 121. Critics own differing opinions as to whether any physical consummation takes place between the narrator and Toute-Belle. Brownlee maintains that the poem leaves this question deliberately obscure, while William Calin concludes that Toute-Belle

has not lost her virginity, in *A Poet at the Fountain: Essays on the Narrative Verse of Guillaume de Machaut* (Lexington: University Press of Kentucky, 1974), pp. 190–1. Daniel Poirion reads the scene in terms of an elevation of physical pleasure, and a fourteenth-century optimism about grounding spirituality in sense experience, in *Le poète et le prince: l'évolution du lyrisme courtois de Guillaume de Machaut à Charles de Orléans* (Paris: Presses Universitaires de France, 1965), pp. 529–30.

61 Guillaume de Machaut, *Fonteinne Amoureuse*, in *Œuvres*, vol. III; translations from *"The Fountain of Love."*

62 McGrady reads Froissart as celebrating the idea that poetry both incites and results from a "vibrant and vital exchange between authors and readers" – a positive valuation that marks a conscious critique of Machaut (*Controlling Readers*, p. 171).

63 Douglas Kelly reads Machaut's Lover as a Pygmalion *in bono*, reconciled to his adoration of an image; see *Medieval Imagination: Rhetoric and the Poetry of Courtly Love* (Madison: Wisconsin University Press, 1978), p. 130.

64 In the *Voir Dit*, Machaut refers several times to the *Fonteinne Amoureuse*, typically as *Le Livre de Morpheus*; see, for example, the fourth letter to his lady where he promises to copy "l'un de mes livres que j'ai fait darreinnement, que on apelle *Morpheus*" (4.f, pp. 124–6) and tenth letter where he sends "mon livre de *Morpheus*, que on appelle *La Fonteinne Amoureuse*" (10.b, p. 186). In Ovid's *Metamorphoses* (Book XI), Morpheus is the son of the god of sleep; his talent is for taking on human shapes in dreams. He comes to take the place of the god of sleep himself in late medieval poetry.

65 Ovid, *Metamorphoses*, ed. and trans. Frank Justus Miller, 2 vols. (Cambridge, MA and London: Harvard University Press and W. Heinemann, 1977–84), XI.634.

66 Calin reads the exemplum of Paris and the golden apple as a meditation on the choice between love and wisdom in *A Poet at the Fountain*, p. 165. R. Barton Palmer similarly reads Paris' choice as demonstrating the dominance of love, but also reads Venus as a bestower of both *clergie* and *chevalrie*; see "*The Book of the Duchess* and *Fonteinne Amoureuse*: Chaucer and Machaut Reconsidered," *Canadian Review of Comparative Literature* 7 (Fall 1980): 380–93 (pp. 383, 391). Margaret Ehrhart reads the entire poem as an exemplum for rulers (though not specifically directed at Machaut's patron, Jean, Duc de Berry) and the myth of Paris as a critique of the "vie voluptueuse"; see "Machaut's *Dit de la Fonteinne Amoureuse*, the Choice of Paris, and the Duties of Rulers," *Philological Quarterly* 59.2 (Spring 1980): 119–39 (p. 130 and *passim*).

67 Calin reads the end of the *dit* as demonstrating the artistry of the Lover: "Love has made a poet of him (and of the Lady too, for that matter), so that, in the course of the narrative, he also becomes a master of *sapientia*, a devotee of Pallas as well as of Venus" (*A Poet at the Fountain*, p. 165).

68 On the points of contact between the two poets, see John Fyler, "Froissart and Chaucer," in *Froissart across the Genres*, ed. Donald Maddox and Sara

Sturm-Maddox (Gainesville: University Press of Florida, 1998), pp. 195–218 (p. 195).

69 Jean Froissart, *L'Espinette Amoureuse*, ed. Anthime Fourrier (Paris: Éditions Klincksieck, 1963); translations are from *An Anthology of Narrative and Lyric Poetry*, ed. and trans. Kristen M. Figg and R. Barton Palmer (New York: Routledge, 2001).

70 Huot reads the narrator's wish in terms of the "writerly" qualities of Froissart's poem; scc *From Song to Book*, pp. 307–9.

71 Douglas Kelly reads Froissart's representations of such "images" in terms of his evolving relationship to the imagination itself; see *Medieval Imagination*, pp. 155–76. Huot reads Froissart's continual exchange of real women for images in his poetry (culminating in his mythography of the marguerite) as his comment on the power and limitations of poetry: it can commemorate beauty and desire, but will always embody absence and loss; see Huot, "The Daisy and the Laurel: Myths of Desire and Creativity in the Poetry of Jean Froissart," *Yale French Studies* 80 (1991): 240–51 (p. 246).

72 Jean Froissart, *Le Paradis D'Amour, L'Orloge Amoureus*, ed. Peter F. Dembowski (Geneva: Droz, 1986); translations are from *An Anthology of Narrative and Lyric Poetry*.

73 Jean Froissart, *La Prison Amoureuse*, ed. Anthime Fourrier (Paris: Éditions Klincksieck, 1974); translations are from *La Prison Amoureuse*, ed. and trans. Laurence de Looze (New York and London: Garland, 1994).

74 In *From Song to Book*, Huot discusses the wide range of Ovidian references in this tale – not just Pyramus and Thisbe, but Orpheus, Apollo, Leucothoë, Coronis, and Aesculapius (p. 312).

75 Mary Wack, *Lovesickness in the Middle Ages: the Viaticum and its Commentaries* (Philadelphia: University of Pennsylvania Press, 1990); see pp. 146–76 on the cultural and literary reception of lovesickness.

76 *Ibid.*, p. 72. See also Alastair Minnis on the physician Évrart de Conty's commentary on the *Eschez Amoureux*, a poem heavily indebted to the *Roman de la Rose*; Évrart brings Aristotle to bear on his ethical advice regarding passion, love, and marriage, directed toward a courtly audience (Minnis, *Magister Amoris*, p. 56, n. 61, pp. 282–96).

77 Wack, *Lovesickness*, p. 56.

78 Peter of Spain, *Questions on the Viaticum* (Version B), in Wack, *Lovesickness*, pp. 236–7.

79 Claire Nouvet, "Pour une économie de la dé-limitation: la *Prison Amoureuse* de Jean Froissart," *Neophilologus* 70 (1986): 341–56 (pp. 349–50).

80 Nouvet, *ibid.*, argues that the status of the "reality" of the metamorphosis remains unresolved by the poem (p. 351).

81 Brooke Heidenreich Findley reads Neptisphelé's awakening as an instance of female agency that threatens the autonomous creativity of the poet; see "Deadly Words, Captive Imaginations: Women and Poetic Creation in Jean Froissart's *Prison Amoureuse*," *French Forum* 32.3 (Fall 2007): 1–21 (pp. 15–16).

82 The dream is a fairly general lament for a society in which the virtues have been wronged. Scholars have argued that "Rose" should be identified as Wenceslas of Brabant, Froissart's patron, and a prisoner captured at the battle of Baesweiler; some have further claimed that Wenceslas in fact wrote the poems and letters attributed to Rose in the manuscripts, though Froissart is now generally accepted as the author of the entire poem. See Kelly, *Medieval Imagination*, p. 162. On the relationship between the tale of Pynoteüs and Rose's dream, see Kelly, "Imitation, Metamorphosis, and Froissart's Use of the Exemplary *Modus Tractandi*," in *Froissart Across the Genres* (Gainesville: University Press of Florida, 1998), pp. 101–18 (pp. 110–11).

83 On the French inheritance of *The Book of the Duchess* in particular and Chaucer's poetry more generally, see James I. Wimsatt, *Chaucer and His French Contemporaries: Natural Music in the Fourteenth Century* (University of Toronto Press, 1991), and *Chaucer and the French Love Poets: The Literary Background of "The Book of the Duchess"* (Chapel Hill: University of North Carolina Press, 1968).

84 The corresponding lines in Froissart, *Le Paradis d'Amour*, are: "Je sui de moi en grant mervelle / Coument tant vifs, car moult je velle, / Et on ne poroit en vellant / Trouver de moi plus travellant, / Car bien sachiés que par vellier / Me viennent souvent travellier / Pensees et merancolies / Qui me sont ens on coer liies. / Et pas ne les puis desliier, / Car ne voel la belle oubliier / Pour quelle amour en ce travel" (ll. 1–11) (I marvel greatly at how I stay alive, / For I lie awake so many nights / And one could not find any man / More tormented in his sleepless plight; / For, you see, as I lie awake / There often come to worry me / Heavy thoughts and melancholies / That are shackles on my heart. / And I cannot undo them, / For I don't wish to forget the beautiful one / For whose love I began this suffering").

85 The cause of what the narrator further on describes as his "eight-year" illness has been the subject of much discussion, as has his invocation of an unspecified "phisicien" who can cure him; rather than pointing to Christ, a paradigmatic courtly lady, or any other coded meaning, I would argue that Chaucer here is invoking a purposely generalized ethical lovesickness. David Lawton refers to the opening of the poem as a "portrait of general numbness" in *Chaucer's Narrators* (Cambridge: D. S. Brewer, 1985), p. 53. See explanatory note to ll. 30–43 in *Riverside Chaucer* for a survey of scholarly solutions to the identity of the illness and physician (God, sleep, Joan of Kent, Christ, etc.).

86 Johannes Afflacius in his *Liber de Heros Morbo* differed, arguing that the pathology of love proceeds from the choice of object, rather than from the intensity of pleasure: loyalty is immoderate love for one's lord, while *heros* is immoderate love for those one desires to possess sexually. See Wack, *Lovesickness*, pp. 47, 186.

87 Aristotle, *Ethica Nicomachea*, VII.13.17–18 (1152b16–18): "Nullum enim utique posse intelligere aliquid in ipsa."

88 Aquinas, *Ethicorum Aristotelis Expositio*, Book VII, lectio 11, 1477: "nullus in ipsa delectatione actuali potest aliquid actu intelligere."

89 Aristotle, *Politics*, Book 1, lectio 11 (1253a14–18): "sermo autem est ad manifestandum iam expediens et nocivum, quare et iustum et iniustum. Hoc enim est preter alia animalia hominibus proprium solum, boni et mali, iusti et iniusti et aliorum sensum habere; horum autem communitas facit domum et civitatem." As Trevor Saunders notes in his comment on these lines in *Politics: Books I and II* (Oxford: Clarendon Press, 1995), pp. 69–70, Aristotle seems to overstate the case for difference between animals and humans; animals too can make distinctions between benefit and harm and communicate them, and the philosopher attributes a kind of practical wisdom to animals in the *Ethics* and elsewhere. In John Trevisa's translation of Giles of Rome's *De Regimine Principum*, these lines are quoted and commented on in the context of a discussion of the "comynte" (community) of house and city; see Trevisa, *The Governance of Kings and Princes*, ed. David C. Fowler, Charles F. Briggs, and Paul G. Remley (New York: Garland Publications, 1997).

90 In Chaucer's *Legend of Good Women*, he refers to a poem he wrote titled "The Deeth of Blaunche the Duchesse," allying the *Book* with the death of John of Gaunt's wife in 1368. Internal evidence also suggests that the poem is dedicated to John of Gaunt; lines 1318–19, which mention "A long castel with walles white, / Be Seynt Johan, on a ryche hil" are generally taken to refer to Lancaster, Blanche, John of Gaunt, and Richmond (of which he was Earl).

91 For a survey of readings of the *Book* that focus on the issue of consolation, see Richard Rambuss, "Process of Tyme: History, Consolation, and Apocalypse in *The Book of the Duchess*," *Exemplaria* 2.2 (Fall 1990): 659–83, where Rambuss summarizes the debate between "consolationist" and "anti-consolationist" critics. In *Sacrifice Your Love*, Fradenburg reads the narrator and knight as performing "for each other the role of the other through whom one can recognize oneself" (p. 99); Bernard Huppé and D. W. Robertson, "The Book of the Duchess," in *Chaucer's Dream Visions and Shorter Poems*, ed. William A. Quinn (New York: Garland, 1963), pp. 131–82, argue for the Black Knight's learning a moral lesson – that he should appreciate White's enduring virtues rather than her temporal physical presence. See also Robert Hanning, "Chaucer's First Ovid: Metamorphosis and Poetic Tradition in *The Book of the Duchess* and *The House of Fame*," in *Chaucer and the Craft of Fiction*, ed. Leigh Arrathoon (Rochester, MI: Solaris Press, 1986), pp. 121–63, on the poem's transformation of grief into poetry (pp. 122–41).

92 On the consolation and education of the narrator, see Lawton, *Chaucer's Narrators*, pp. 53–6. Peter Travis, "White," *Studies in the Age of Chaucer* 22 (2000): 1–66, reads the entire poem as a work of mourning, and as a salutary movement from depression to mourning for the dreaming narrator.

93 The narrator's apparent obtuseness – and its possible offensiveness – in regard to the nature of the Black Knight's loss has long been a critical crux in discussions of the poem. The problem of the narrator's disregard in relation to the

poem's status as a possible offering to the mourning John of Gaunt and as an elegy is discussed in Ardis Butterfield, "Lyric and Elegy in the Book of the Duchess," *Medium Aevum* 60.1 (1991): 33–60; and Steven Davis, "Guillaume de Machaut, Chaucer's *Book of the Duchess*, and the Chaucer Tradition," *Chaucer Review* 364 (2002): 391–405. Both critics discuss this problem in the context of Chaucer's relationship to his French contemporaries.

94 *MED* cônnen (v.)

95 For a reading of *The Book of the Duchess* in terms of idleness and work, see also Lisa Kiser, "Sleep, Dreams, and Poetry in Chaucer's *Book of the Duchess*," *Papers on Language and Literature* 19.1 (1983): 3–11. She discusses the hunt as an antidote to idleness and notes that hunting manuals in the late Middle Ages often endorse the sport as offering productive focus for the mind, relieving it from idle tendencies to imagine fleshly lusts and pleasures.

96 These lines are likely adapted from Machaut's *Le Jugement du Roy de Behaigne* (*Œuvres*, vol. 1), in which a lady whose lover has died laments that her "pleasures have become grief-filled toils and [her] joys are bitter grief" ("mes douceurs sont dolereus labours / Et mes joies sont ameres dolours," ll. 178–9); see *"Le Jugement dou Roy de Behaigne" and "Remede de Fortune"*, ed. and trans. James I. Wimsatt and William W. Kibler (Athens: University of Georgia Press, 1988).

97 See J. Stephen Russell, *The English Dream Vision* (Columbus: Ohio State University Press, 1988) for a reading of the *Book* that claims its subject to be "routhe."

98 Alastair Minnis' claim that Chaucer "ignored" the moralization of Ovid's fable is certainly true in that Chaucer does not adopt the lesson that we should take no regard for vain, earthly pleasures. But the fleetingness of earthly joys is certainly a subject that *The Book of the Duchess* meditates upon. See *Chaucer and Pagan Antiquity* (Woodbridge, Suffolk: D. S. Brewer, 1982), pp. 16–18.

99 *Ovide Moralisé*, ed. C. de Boer, 5 vols. (Amsterdam: J. Müller, 1915–38), Tome IV, XI.3884. Translations are my own.

100 Heinrichs also notes a parallel between Ceyx's statement and the concerns of the *Ovide Moralisé* (*The Myths of Love*, p. 221).

101 Fradenburg discusses Alcyone's death (in exchange for the narrator's life) as a symptom of "elegiac misogyny" in "'Voice Memorial': Loss and Reparation in Chaucer's Poetry," *Exemplaria* 2.1 (March 1990): 169–202.

102 The lady of Machaut's *Le Jugement dou Roy de Behaigne* also recalls that her heart and her lover's were of one accord, alike in will and desire: "they felt as one each good, each trial, each joy" ("Un bien, un mal, une joie sentoient / Conjointement," ll. 171–2).

103 Travis, "White," pp. 61–2.

104 See de Looze, "Guillaume de Machaut and the Writerly Process," p. 157: "I might add that in the *Fonteinne amoureuse* to ask whether life is a dream is tantamount to asking also whether life might be a poem."

4 LOVE'S KNOWLEDGE: FABLIAU, ALLEGORY, AND FOURTEENTH-CENTURY ANTI-INTELLECTUALISM

1 The condemnations have long played a central role in the intellectual history of the late thirteenth and early fourteenth centuries, though their unified effects have begun to be questioned, along with Étienne Gilson's narrative of a "golden age" of confidence in the tools of philosophy as a means to gain metaphysical truths giving way to suspicion; see *The History of Christian Philosophy in the Middle Ages* (New York: Random House, 1955), pp. 402–27. Gordon Leff similarly argues for the chilling effect of the 1277 condemnations in *Medieval Thought: St. Augustine to Ockham* (Harmondsworth, Middlesex: Penguin, 1958), p. 234; Bonnie Kent discusses the dominance of this narrative of conservative, anti-Aristotelian reaction in *Virtues of the Will*, pp. 5–6. With Fernand van Steenberghen, she challenges the idea that the doctrinal conflicts of the late thirteenth century pitted Augustinians against Aristotelians, and argues that they are better understood as struggles between different forms of Aristotelianism (p. 12). See Courtenay, *Schools and Scholars*, pp. 282–4 on the specific rejection of the Thomist view that enjoyment is an intellectual act; see Wieland, "Happiness," pp. 682–5 on debates regarding the active and contemplative paths to happiness and the role of the will versus the intellect. For recent scholarship on the condemnations and their immediate effects, see Jan A. Aertsen, Kent Emery, Jr., and Andreas Speer (eds.), *After the Condemnation of 1277 (Nach der Verurteilung von 1277)* (Berlin and New York: Walter de Gruyter, 2001).

2 Kempshall, *The Common Good*, p. 205.

3 See Kent, *Virtues of the Will*, chapter 2; and Steenberghen, *Aristotle in the West*, p. 130.

4 Kempshall, *The Common Good*, p. 151. Giles notes that Aristotle seems to present two types of felicity, but simply makes note of this interpretive difficulty and avers that it is not for his treatise to determine whether the philosopher ultimately has a unified position.

5 Giles of Rome, *De Regimine Principum Librum III* (Rome, 1556), Book 1, Part 1, chapter 4, p. 8v: "Posuerunt etiam vitam contemplativam esse in pura speculatione, quod est falsum. Nunquam enim quis in tali vita perficitur, nisi sit in eo amor dei, sive dilectio charitatis."

6 Plato, *Theaetetus*, 174a–175b.

7 Aesop, "The Astronomer," in *Fables*, trans. Olivia and Robert Temple (New York: Penguin, 1998).

8 Christine de Pizan, *The Vision of Christine de Pizan*, trans. Glenda McLeod and Charity Cannon Willard (Cambridge: D. S. Brewer, 2005), II.6, p. 62. The old woman also appears in Diogenes Laertius' life of Thales.

9 Michel de Montaigne, *Apology for Raymond Sebond* (Indianapolis, IN: Hackett, 2003), p. 99. For an antique Greek comic perspective, see Aristophanes' *The Clouds*; a student at Socrates' school relates a story in which the philosopher was gazing openmouthed at the stars at night when a gecko defecated on him. Other references to the stargazing philosopher include Cicero, *De Divinatione*,

II.13.30, and *De Republica*, I.30; *Cento Novelle Antiche*, 38; and Philip Sidney, *Astrophil and Stella*, 19.

10 For a discussion of Montaigne's claim in relation to late medieval optical and epistemological theory, see Dallas G. Denery II, *Seeing and Being Seen in the Later Medieval World: Optics, Theology, and Religious Life* (Cambridge University Press, 2005), pp. 1–3.

11 Karma Lochrie reads the Miller's pun on "pryvetee" as a means to equate women "with their genitals, their privacy, and all that is secret, and then to expose them to public laughter"; see *Covert Operations: the Medieval Uses of Secrecy* (Philadelphia: University of Pennsylvania Press, 1999), p. 169.

12 E. D. Blodgett observes succinctly that "pryvetee, like cupiditas, is wanting what we cannot have and receiving what we do not want" in "Chaucerian Pryvetee and the Opposition to Time," *Speculum* 51.3 (July 1976): 477–93 (p. 484). In Lacanian terms, "pryvetee" might be understood as both the deferred enjoyment of desire and the inescapable obscene enjoyment of the drives. See also Mark Miller's reading of Alison as the tale's "perfect exemplar of the human" who never erects artificial barriers to pleasure (*Philosophical Chaucer*, pp. 57–8).

13 Alastair Minnis notes that the pseudo-Aristotelian *Problemata* contains the assertions that "all men who have become outstanding in philosophy, statesmanship, poetry or the arts are melancholic" and further that "the melancholic are usually lustful." He concludes that it "requires little inference to produce the proposition that the cleverest men have the strongest sex drives" (*Magister Amoris*, p. 303, n. 137).

14 Aristotle entered vernacular literature in the twelfth-century tradition of the *Roman d'Alexander*. In the romances that adhere to the narratives available in Latin (such as the Anglo-Norman romance by Thomas of Kent, *c.*1175), Aristotle is a relatively minor character, but in the vulgate version by Alexandre de Paris (*c.*1180), Aristotle plays a larger role as Alexander's childhood teacher and continuing mentor, advising him on his political campaigns. Catherine Gaullier-Bougassas argues that in Alexandre de Paris' romance, Aristotle is presented in ambiguous terms, and that one can detect a critique of the vanity of pagan philosophy, possibly in response to the dissemination of Aristotelian texts in the Parisian schools where Alexandre may have studied; see "Alexander and Aristotle in the French Alexander Romances," in *The Medieval French Alexander*, ed. Donald Maddox and Sara Sturm-Maddox (Albany: State University of New York Press, 2002), pp. 57–74 (p. 65).

15 John Gower, *Confessio Amantis*, in *The English Works of John Gower*, vol. 1, ed. G. C. Macauley, 2 vols. (London: for The Early English Text Society by K. Paul, Trench, Trübner & Co., 1900–1), VIII.2705–9.

16 The editor of the standard edition of the poem, Maurice Delbouille, dates the poem to before 1230, possibly before 1225; see his introduction to *Le Lai d'Aristote de Henri D'Andeli* (Paris: Société d'Édition "Les Belles Lettres," 1951), p. 29. Recent editor Alain Corbellari proposes a date of *c.*1235 in his

introduction to *Les Dits d'Henri d'Andeli* (Paris: Éditions Champion, 2003), p. 22, partially in order to place Henri's *œuvre* in relation to the rising dominance of Aristotelian philosophy in the university.

17 See *Le Lai*, ed. Corbellari, p. 25; *Le Lai*, ed. Delbouille, pp. 20, 58; Susan L. Smith, *The Power of Women: a Topos in Medieval Art and Literature* (Philadelphia: University of Pennsylvania Press, 1995), p. 69; Michel Zink, "De Jean Le Teinturier à Jean Bras-de-Fer: le triomphe des cuistres," in *Les voix de la conscience: parole du poète et parole de Dieu dans la littérature médiévale* (Caen: Paradigme, 1992), pp. 261–74, repr. from *Milieux universitaires et mentalités urbaines au Moyen Age*, ed. Daniel Poirion (Paris: Presses de l'Université de Paris-Sorbonne, 1987), pp. 157–70; and George Sarton, *Aristotle and Phyllis*, *ISIS* 14.1 (May 1930): 8–19 (repr. Bruges: St. Catherine Press, 1930), p. 11.

18 On the origins of the Aristotle tale, see *Le Lai*, ed. Delbouille, pp. 35–61; for analogues of tales of the seduction of a wise man in the Eastern tradition, see Joseph Bédier, *Les Fabliaux* (Paris: Librairie Honoré Champion, 1964), pp. 204–12.

19 For an excellent discussion of the origins of the tale and its legacy, see Smith, *The Power of Women*, pp. 67–8 and throughout her third chapter, "Tales of the Mounted Aristotle."

20 All citations of *Le Lai d'Aristote* are from Delbouille's edition, cited above. Translations are my own.

21 Anne Ladd, "Attitude toward Lyric in the *Lai d'Aristote* and Some Later Fictional Narratives," *Romania* 96 (1975): 194–208 (p. 197). Gregory Stone remarks that "it is song's specularity that enchants Aristotle" (p. 37) and offers an acute reading of the multiplicity of mirrors in the tale; see *The Death of the Troubadour: the Late Medieval Resistance to the Renaissance* (Philadelphia: University of Pennsylvania Press, 1994), pp. 33–42. Maureen Bolton observes Aristotle's misrecognition of himself in the girl's later *chanson de toile*, a misrecognition that recalls the dreamer's encounter with the Narcissus myth in the *Roman de la Rose*; see *The Song in the Story: Lyric Insertions in French Narrative Fiction, 1200–1400* (Philadelphia: University of Pennsylvania Press, 1993), pp. 279–80.

22 On the ethical ambiguity of the tale's ending, see Barbara Nolan, "Promiscuous Fictions: Medieval Bawdy Tales and their Textual Liaisons," in *The Body and the Soul in Medieval Literature*, ed. Piero Boitani and Anna Torti (Cambridge: D. S. Brewer, 1999), pp. 79–105 (p. 87).

23 Smith, *The Power of Women*, p. 81.

24 An illustrative example is a fourteenth-century ivory box at the Metropolitan Museum of Art in which a frame containing Aristotle and Alexander reading together is juxtaposed with an image of the maiden "riding" Aristotle, with Alexander looking on. See "Box with Aristotle and Phyllis [French] (17.190.173ab,1988.16)," in *Heilbrunn Timeline of Art History* (New York: The Metropolitan Museum of Art, 2000), www.metmuseum.org/toah/hd/anti/ho_17.190.173ab,1988.16.htm (October 2006). For a reading of the casket as a

whole, and the Aristotle and maiden compartments in particular, see Paula Mae Carns, "Compilatio in Ivory: the Composite Casket in the Metropolitan Museum," *Gesta* 44 (2005): 69–88 (pp. 71–2).

25 Joachim Storost suggests that certain general aspects of the story were perhaps inspired by the *Nicomachean Ethics*, especially Book VII on the problem of passion overcoming reason, in "Femme chevalchat Aristotte," *Zeitschrift für französische Sprache und Literatur* 66 (1956): 186–201 (p. 195). As Storost acknowledges, however, the dating of the poem makes it unlikely that Henri would have had any direct knowledge of the *Ethics* aside from the first three books.

26 Jacques de Vitry's sermon is dated *c.*1228–40. Bédier argues for the priority of Henri's version in *Les Fabliaux*, pp. 204–12. Smith narrates the history of source study for the Western "mounted Aristotle" tales (*The Power of Women*, pp. 68–72); she herself argues persuasively for the influence of a group of twelfth-century poems (e.g., "Altercatio Phyllidis et Florae") that debate the greater suitability of knights or clerks as lovers.

27 Jacques de Vitry, *Die Exempla aus den Sermones Feriales et Communes*, ed. Joseph Greven (Heidelberg: Carl Winter, 1914), sermon 15.

28 On the sermon staging a conflict between two different orders of men – the clerical and the knightly – see Smith, *The Power of Women*, p. 74.

29 The original Latin poem was written by Mathieu of Boulogne around 1295; Le Fèvre popularized the Latin poem, which also remained in circulation at least through the fifteenth century.

30 Jehan Le Fèvre, *Les Lamentations de Matheolus et le Livre de Leesce de Jehan Le Fèvre, de Resson*, ed. A.-G. van Hamel, 2 vols. (Paris: É. Bouillon, 1892–1905), ll. 1143–5: "que dira philosophie, / Quant figure d'amphibolie / A le grant maistre deceü?"; ll. 495–6: "Quid dicet philosophia / Cum sibi doctorem deceperit amphibolia?"

31 Jehan Le Fèvre, *Lamentations*, ll. 1150–2: "est advenue / Aux arciens continuele / Confusion perpetuele"; l. 499: "Pro quibus artistis confusion perpetuator."

32 Smith notes in *The Power of Women* that the tale "resisted permanent inscription within the discourse of the preacher" (p. 81) and further that "Different interpretations of the Aristotle tale coexisted at the same time, within the same linguistic boundaries, and even within the confines of the same text" (p. 93). On the tale's inscription in discourses of erotic violence and mastery, see Marilynn Desmond, *Ovid's Art and the Wife of Bath: the Ethics of Erotic Violence* (Ithaca, NY: Cornell University Press, 2006), pp. 13–27.

33 Kent, *Virtues of the Will*, p. 96.

34 *Ibid.*, p. 113.

35 Kent specifically discusses the works of Peter Olivi (pp. 130–1), Walter of Bruges (p. 175), and Richard of Middleton (p. 189) in this context and discusses voluntarism generally in chapter 4 of her book.

36 *Ibid.*, p. 198.

37 Bonaventure, *Itinerarium Mentis in Deum*, in *The works of Saint Bonaventure*, vol. II, ed. Philotheus Boehner and Sr. M. Frances Laughlin, 2 vols. (Saint Bonaventure, NY: The Franciscan Institute, Saint Bonaventure University, 1955–6), VII.4; translation from *The Mind's Road to God*, trans. George Boas (Indianapolis, IN: Bobbs-Merrill, 1953).
38 *Ibid.*, VII.5.
39 *Ibid.*, VII.6.
40 John Duns Scotus, *Ordinatio* IV., suppl. dist. 49, qq. 9–10 ("Beatitudo") in *Duns Scotus on the Will and Morality*, ed. and trans. Allan B. Wolter (Washington, DC: The Catholic University of America Press, 1986), pp. 184–97 (pp. 186–7); see also Wieland, "Happiness," p. 683.
41 Duns Scotus, *Ordinatio*, IV, pp. 188–9.
42 See McGrade, "Enjoyment at Oxford," p. 69.
43 Ockham, *Quaestiones*, Liber I, Dist. I, q. 2, p. 394: "fruitio est formaliter beatitudo, quia dicitur a fructu quod est ultimum, cuiusmodi est beatitudo. Sed beatitudo est operatio intellectus, secundum Philosophum X et I *Ethicorum*. Ergo fruitio erit operatio intellectus"; "Using and Enjoying," p. 367.
44 *Ibid.*, Liber I, Dist. I, q. 2, art. 2a, p. 396: "Tamen intelligendum est quod quando dicitur quod fruitio est actus solius voluntatis, non intendo negare quod proprie et de virtute sermonis loquendo fruitio non sit actus intellectus, quia, sicut alias ostendetur, intellectus et voluntas sunt omnino idem, et ideo quidquid est in intellectu est in voluntate et e converso"; "Using and Enjoying," p. 368.
45 *Ibid.*, Liber I, Dist. I, q. 2, art. 2b, p. 397; "Using and Enjoying," p. 369.
46 *Ibid.*, Liber I, Dist. I, q. 2, art. 2bii, p. 400: "solus Deus est causa effectiva, et hoc propter nobilitatem ipsius beatitudinis"; "Using and Enjoying," p. 370.
47 Buridan, *Quaestiones super Decem Libros Ethicorum*, Book X, q. 4, sect. 1b, p. 209r, col. b.
48 *Ibid.*, Book X, q. 4, sect. 1b, p. 209r, col. b: "Item, felicitas ponitur consistere in perfecta dei contemplatione que nec est dei cognitio sine amore, nec amor sine cognitione: sed ex ambobus constituta"; "Questions on Book X of the Ethics," p. 542.
49 *Ibid.*, Book X, q. 4, sect. 2a, p. 210r, col. a: "quod illud sic optimum sit actus speculationis circa divinam essentiam"; "Questions," p. 546.
50 *Ibid.*, Book X, q. 5, sect. 2b, thesis 3, p. 213r, col. a: "beatus non solum intelligit et amat deum: sed reflexive potest intelligere et intelligit se intelligere et amare et delectari"; "Questions," p. 567.
51 See *ibid.*, Book X, q. 5, sect. 1a, p. 211v, col. b, on the love of an old woman pleasing God more than the knowledge of the cleric; "Questions," p. 559; see Wieland, "Happiness," p. 686.
52 Nicole Oresme, *Éthiques*, p. 520, n. 19.
53 *Ibid.*, p. 523, n. 3.
54 On curiosity as a sin, see Richard Newhauser, "Augustinian 'vitium curiositatis' and its Reception," in *Saint Augustine and his Influence in the Middle Ages*, ed. Edward B. King and Jacqueline T. Schaefer, Sewanee Mediaeval

Studies 3 (Sewanee, TN: The Press of the University of the South, 1988), pp. 99–124.

55 *The Conflict of Wit and Will*, ed. Bruce Dickins (Leeds: Kendal, printed by T. Wilson for members of the school for English language in the University of Leeds, 1937), p. 19.

56 On the relationship between the two poems, see Steven Wright, "Deguileville's *Pèlerinage de Vie Humaine* as 'contrepartie edifiante' of the *Roman de la Rose*," *Philological Quarterly* 68.4 (1989): 399–422; and Sylvia Huot, *Medieval Readers*, chapter 6, "'Exposé sur le Roman de la Rose': rewriting the Rose in the Pèlerinage de vie humaine."

57 Guillaume de Deguileville, *Le Pèlerinage de Vie Humaine*, ed. J. J. Sturzinger (London: Nichols and Sons, printed for the Roxburghe Club, 1893), l. 3; all subsequent references to the poem will be parenthetical.

58 Wright observes that allusions to the garden of the *Rose* are also present in Deguileville's description of the tonsured head of a monk (ll. 889–902); see Wright, "Contrepartie Edifiante," p. 405.

59 Kay, *The Place of Thought*, p. 74. She contends that the notion of place developed by Deguileville is ultimately intellectual rather than physical.

60 Kay notes that in this answer Aristotle shifts from the *Physics* to the *Ethics*, a shift which "confirms that the concept of place is now topological and moral, rather than plotted with reference to physical location" (*The Place of Thought*, p. 78).

61 Aristotle's other works are also referred to as repositories of knowledge, as at the very end of the poem, where Aristotle provides an explanation for the way that blood is changed into milk through decoction – giving a scientific rationale both for the breast milk offered to the dreamer by Mercy and for the nourishing nature of the blood of Christ (ll. 13334–8).

62 Chaucer leaves off the final stanzas in his translation; see "An ABC" in *Riverside Chaucer*.

63 John Burrow has argued for the direct influence of Deguileville's pilgrimage trilogy on Langland; see *Langland's Fictions* (Oxford University Press, 1993). On the influence of Deguileville's trilogy on medieval English literature, as well as on Langland in particular, see Emily Steiner, *Documentary Culture and the Making of Medieval English Literature* (Cambridge University Press, 2003), pp. 29–31, 48–9.

64 On the possibilities for Will as a personification of "the will," see John Bowers, *The Crisis of Will in "Piers Plowman"* (Washington, DC: The Catholic University of America Press, 1986). David Lawton reviews critical interpretations of Will in "The Subject of Piers Plowman," *Yearbook of Langland Studies* 1 (1987): 1–30, and proposes a new approach based on modern theories of the subject. See also Anne Middleton, "William Langland's *Kynde Name*: Authorial Signature and Social Identity in Late Fourteenth-Century England," in *Literary Practice and Social Change in Britain, 1380–1530*, ed. Lee Patterson (Berkeley: University of California Press, 1993), pp. 15–82.

65 On the representation of faculty psychology in the poem, see Joseph Wittig, "'Piers Plowman' B, Passus IX–XII: Elements in the Design of the Inward Journey," *Traditio* 28 (1972): 211–80; and A. V. C. Schmidt, "Langland and Scholastic Philosophy," *Medium Aevum* 38 (1969): 134–56. Wittig focuses on the monastic, Schmidt on the scholastic, contexts of the poem's psychological models. For a sustained treatment of fourteenth-century thought on the will in relation to the poem, see Bowers, *The Crisis of Will*, especially pp. 41–60. See also Zeeman, *Medieval Discourse of Desire*, pp. 64–108.

66 James Simpson argues that Langland conceives of theology in the "sapiential" tradition, a tradition in which the affective, the good, and the voluntary are prioritized over the speculative, the true, and the intellectual; see "From Reason to Affective Knowledge: Modes of Thought and Poetic Form in *Piers Plowman*," *Medium Aevum* 55.1 (1986): 1–23 (p. 4). Simpson claims straightforwardly that Langland's theology is voluntarist (p. 7). Elsewhere, he observes that the poem appears "conservative," in that "Will moves from scholastic to monastic habits of reading"; see Simpson, "Desire and the Scriptural Text: Will as Reader in *Piers Plowman*," in *Criticism and Dissent in the Middle Ages*, ed. Rita Copeland (Cambridge University Press, 1996), pp. 215–43 (p. 234).

67 Simpson, "From Reason to Affective Knowledge," p. 7. He describes the voluntarist tradition as eschewing Aristotelian logic in favor of movement through example: scriptural literary metaphor, symbol, and parable.

68 References cited in-text are to William Langland, *The Vision of Piers Plowman: a Critical Edition of the B-Text Based on Trinity College Cambridge MS B.15.17*, ed. A. V. C. Schmidt, 2nd edn. (London: J. M. Dent, 1995) and to *Piers Plowman: the C-Text*, ed. Derek Pearsall (Exeter: University of Exeter Press, 1994).

69 Zeeman, *Medieval Discourse of Desire*, argues that Will's intellectual "failures" should not be read as rebukes to the intellect itself, but as integral human experiences, part of a spiritual and ethical education (pp. 21–2 and *passim*); see also Michelle Karnes, "Will's Imagination in *Piers Plowman*," *Journal of English and Germanic Philology* 108 (Jan. 2009): 27–58. Daniel Murtaugh earlier judged that the poem's attitude toward "Intellectualism, pro- and anti-, is thus basically ambivalent" in *Piers Plowman and the Image of God* (Gainesville: University Press of Florida, 1978), p. 65. He observes also that grace and learning are stated by the poem to have the same source – Christ's love (p. 94).

70 Masha Raskolnikov, "Promising the Female, Delivering the Male," *Yearbook of Langland Studies* 19 (2005): 81–105 (p. 101); and Britton Harwood, *"Piers Plowman" and the Problem of Belief* (Toronto and London: University of Toronto Press, 1992), p. 105. See also Schmidt, "Langland and Scholastic Philosophy," pp. 140–1.

71 Andrew Galloway, "*Piers Plowman* and the Schools," *Yearbook of Langland Studies*, 6 (1992): 89–107 (p. 97).

72 James Paxson, "Inventing the Subject and the Personification of Will in *Piers Plowman*: Rhetorical, Erotic, and Ideological Origins and Limits in Langland's Allegorical Poetics," in *William Langland's "Piers Plowman": a Book of Essays*, ed. Kathleen Hewett-Smith (New York: Routledge, 2001), pp. 195–231 (p. 196).

73 See Mary Clemente Davlin, "Kynde Knowyng as a Major Theme in Piers Plowman B," *The Review of English Studies*, n.s. 22.85 (Feb. 1971): 1–19 (p. 5).

74 See Zeeman, *Medieval Discourse of Desire*, pp. 9, 160–1.

75 Nature is imagined as "devouring" knowledge in Henri's *Lai d'Aristote*; Aristotle defends himself by claiming that because he was in love, nature bereft him of all knowledge gained from a life of learning and reading.

76 M. Teresa Tavormina observes that in attributing knowledge of the divine mystery of sexuality to Kynde, an authoritative figure, the poem acknowledges the importance of the sexual dimension of experience; see *Kindly Similitude: Marriage and Family in "Piers Plowman"* (Cambridge: D. S. Brewer, 1995), p. 184. In the C-version of the poem, however, the sexual content of natural knowledge is excised. The mystery of Adam and Eve's shame over their "privy members" is replaced with the more abstract, though clearly related, problem of why Kynde willed that evil should exist in the world (C.XIV.164–7).

77 This passage is complicated by its possible allusion to the second recension of Deguileville's poem, in which Grace Dieu advises the pilgrim to remove his eyes and place them in his ears so that he will be able to "see" his staff and scrip. Under Grace Dieu's logic, true understanding comes only through a mode of vision that is mediated by what one has heard and learned; Studie's wish might then be read as a recommendation that the curious soul should seek knowledge humbly through all possible senses and with all resources, rather than solely through the eyes. As Karnes notes, "Perceiving the spiritual significance of the natural world … takes all the resources of the intellect and the will" ("Will's Imagination," p. 30). See John Lydgate's translation, *The Pilgrimage of the Life of Man*, ed. Frederick J. Furnivall, EETS e.s. 77, 83, 92 (London: Kegan Paul, Trench, Trübner & Co., 1899–1904), ll. 6241–58; discussed in Susan Hagen, *Allegorical Remembrance: a Study of "The Pilgrimage of the Life of Man" as a Medieval Treatise on Seeing and Remembering* (Athens: University of Georgia Press, 1990), p. 49.

78 But see Zeeman's argument that intellectual suffering is productive, natural, and even ethical in the poem. She discusses suffering and deprivation as an integral aspect of 'kynde' itself in her fifth chapter, "Seeing and Suffering in Nature," in *Medieval Discourse of Desire*.

79 Fradenburg discusses the heroization of "suffering for" as devalorizing actual suffering in "'Our owen wo to drynke': Loss, Gender and Chivalry in *Troilus and Criseyde*," in *"And subgit be to alle poesie": Essays on Troilus and Criseyde*, ed. R. A. Shoaf (Binghamton, NY: Medieval and Renaissance Texts & Studies, 1992), pp. 88–106 (p. 89).

80 On learning/loving through suffering in *Piers Plowman*, see Harwood, "*Piers Plowman*, Fourteenth-Century Skepticism, and the Theology of Suffering," *Bucknell Review* 19.3 (1971): 119–36 (p. 135); and Davlin, "Major Theme," p. 8.

81 See, for example, Bruce Harbert, "Langland's Easter," in *Langland, the Mystics and the Medieval English Religious Tradition*, ed. Helen Phillips (Cambridge: D. S. Brewer, 1990), pp. 57–70; David Aers, "Christ's Humanity and *Piers Plowman*: Contexts and Political Implications," *Yearbook of Langland Studies* 8 (1994): 107 25; and Mary Clemente Davlin, "Devotional Postures in *Piers Plowman*, with an Appendix on Divine Postures," *Chaucer Review* 42.2 (2007): 161–79.

82 Davlin comments on the originality of this idea in Langland ("Major Theme," p. 13), as does Elizabeth Kirk, "Langland's Narrative Christology," in *Art and Context in Late Medieval English Narrative*, ed. Robert R. Edwards (Cambridge: D. S. Brewer, 1994), pp. 17–35; see also Kirk, "'Who Suffreth More Than God?': Narrative Redefinition of Patience in *Patience* and *Piers Plowman*," in *The Triumph of Patience*, ed. Gerald J. Schiffhorst (Orlando: University Presses of Florida, 1978), pp. 88–104 (pp. 90–1, 98) on patience as an *imitatio Christi* that is active, part of a "comic" vision of the human predicament.

83 Lacan, *Encore*, pp. 82, 90; trans. Fink, pp. 89, 98. Lacan discusses the divinization of suffering in *L'éthique*, p. 304; trans. Porter, p. 262.

84 Amy Hollywood, "Suffering Transformed: Marguerite Porète, Meister Eckhart, and the Problem of Women's Spirituality," in *Meister Eckhart and the Beguine Mystics*, ed. Bernard McGinn (New York: Continuum, 1994), pp. 87–113.

5 ON HUMAN HAPPINESS: DANTE, CHAUCER, AND THE FELICITY OF FRIENDSHIP

1 I take this bliss literally, as a means of thinking about the relationship between erotic and philosophical discussions of happiness, but I do not want to deny that it is also circumscribed and complicated. David Aers reads Book III as a depiction of mutual love and happiness in "Criseyde: Woman in Medieval Society," *Chaucer Review* 13 (1979): 177–200, but see Elaine Tuttle Hansen's critique in *Chaucer and the Fictions of Gender* (Berkeley: University of California Press, 1992), pp. 141–87.

2 *MED* lust (n.). In Chaucer's closest source for the poem, *Il Filostrato*, Boccaccio speaks of ineffable delight at the moment of the lovers' consummation, but this bliss is not linked to the lovers' mutuality. See Barry Windeatt's parallel text edition of *Il Filostrato* and Chaucer's poem: *Troilus and Criseyde: a New Edition of "The Book of Troilus"* (London and New York: Longman, 1984).

3 J. Allan Mitchell argues that the narrative and moral shape of *Troilus and Criseyde* is analogous to the wheel of Fortune, and considers the poem as an erotic "adventure" of fortune that is also an ethical adventure; see *Ethics and Eventfulness*, pp. 28–9 and chapter 2 *passim*.

4 My question echoes the query made by Simon Gaunt with reference to courtly interest in religion: "Why is love in courtly texts made analogous to a religion? Does this not imply a 'serious' as well as an ironic mind-set? What is the import of the use of Christian imagery in erotic contexts, and what is its affective value?" (*Love and Death*, p. 7). With respect to *Troilus and Criseyde*, David Wallace explores the juxtaposition of pagan and Christian morality and beliefs, contending that Chaucer (with Boccaccio) seeks neither to integrate them nor to produce an ironic effect, but rather to "explore the uncertain space between them"; see *Chaucer and the Early Writings of Boccaccio* (Woodbridge, Suffolk: D. S. Brewer, 1985), pp. 70–2.

5 Martin Camargo, "The Consolation of Pandarus," *Chaucer Review* 25.3 (1991): 214–28 (p. 221). See also Alan Gaylord, "Friendship in Chaucer's *Troilus*," *Chaucer Review* 3.4 (1969): 239–64.

6 Bernard Jefferson, *Chaucer and the Consolation of Philosophy of Boethius* (Princeton University Press, 1917), p. 81.

7 *Riverside Chaucer*, p. 396.

8 Other recent scholarship that questions ideas of the "Boethian" includes Jennifer Arch, "The Boethian *Testament of Love*," *Studies in Philology* 105.4 (Fall 2008): 448–62; and J. Allan Mitchell, "Romancing Ethics in Boethius, Chaucer, and Levinas: Fortune, Moral Luck, and Erotic Adventure," *Comparative Literature* 57.2 (Spring 2005): 102–16. Scholars who consider the possibilities for an ironic Boethius in the context of Menippean satire include Anne F. Payne, *Chaucer and Menippean Satire* (Madison: University of Wisconsin Press, 1981); Peter Dronke, *Verse with Prose from Petronius to Dante: the art and scope of the mixed form* (Cambridge, MA: Harvard University Press, 1994); and Joel Relihan, *The Prisoner's Philosophy: Life and Death in Boethius' Consolation*, with a contribution by William E. Heise (University of Notre Dame Press, 2007).

9 Miller, *Philosophical Chaucer*, p. 111; on the resistance to Philosophia's perspective, Camargo remarks that "Lady Philosophy must always convert the particular and unique into the general and typical, and that move is always a reduction" ("The Consolation of Pandarus," p. 226). Frank Grady reads the poem as a series of dialogic situations in which the reader is positioned both as a lover and as God/Lady Philosophy, and in which the foreknowledge of the reader regarding the end of the narrative mimics the foreknowledge of God; see "The Boethian Reader of *Troilus and Criseyde*," *Chaucer Review* 33.3 (1999): 231–51.

10 Miller, *Philosophical Chaucer*, p. 149.

11 David Aers, *Chaucer, Langland, and the Creative Imagination* (London: Routledge, 1979), p. 142.

12 Alastair Minnis and Lodi Nauta, "*More Platonico loquitur*: What Nicholas Trevet really did to William of Conches," in *Chaucer's Boece and the Medieval Tradition of Boethius*, ed. Alastair Minnis (Cambridge: D. S. Brewer, 1993), pp. 1–33. See also Lodi Nauta, "The Scholastic Context of the Boethius Commentary by Nicholas Trevet," in *Boethius in the Middle Ages*, ed.

Maarten Hoenen and Lodi Nauta (New York: Brill, 1997), pp. 41–67; and Mark Gleason, "Clearing the Fields: Towards a Reassessment of Chaucer's Use of Trevet in the 'Boece,'" in *The Medieval Boethius: Studies in the Vernacular Translations of "De Consolatione Philosophiae"*, ed. Alastair Minnis (Cambridge: D. S. Brewer, 1987), pp. 89–105. For a discussion of Trevet's supposed radical Aristotelianism, see Pierre Courcelle, *La Consolation de philosophie dans la tradition littéraire: antécédents et postérité de Boèce* (Paris: Études augustiniennes, 1967), pp. 318–19.

13 Joseph Owens, "Faith, Ideas, Illumination, and Experience," in *The Cambridge History of Later Medieval Philosophy*, pp. 440–59.

14 Lodi Nauta, "'*Magis sit Platonicus quam Aristotelicus*': Interpretations of Boethius' Platonism in the *Consolatio Philosophiae* from the Twelfth to the Seventeenth Century," in *The Platonic Tradition in the Middle Ages* (Berlin: Walter de Gruyter, 2002), pp. 165–204.

15 Aristotle, *Ethica Nicomachea*, IX.12.10–11 (1171a24–6): "Necessarium magis quidem enim utique in infortuniis … Melius autem in bonis fortunis."

16 *Ibid.*, IX.13.1–2 (1172a1–3): "et quod aliquando est singulis esse vel cuius gratia eligunt vivere, in hoc cum amicis volunt conversari."

17 Jacques Derrida, *The Politics of Friendship*, trans. George Collins (London: Verso, 1997; repr. 2005), p. 29.

18 Aristotle, *Ethica Nicomachea*, VIII.4.29 (1158b9): "inpermutabilem et mansivam."

19 Derrida, *The Politics of Friendship*, p. 37; Derrida cites Nietzsche, "Mitfreude, nicht Mitleiden, macht den Freund" (*Human, All Too Human*, para. 499: "Fellow rejoicing, not fellow suffering, makes the friend").

20 Grady notes that "future tyme" is a Chaucerian neologism, and that Chaucer is often cited as having introduced the word "future" into English in *Boece* ("Boethian Reader," p. 242).

21 Minnis and Nauta, "*More Platonico loquitur*," p. 33; see also Nauta, "*Magis sit Platonicus quam Aristotelicus*," pp. 189–204.

22 Nauta, "*Magis sit Platonicus quam Aristotelicus*," p. 192.

23 Minnis speculates that Jean was attracted to this text (while using a commentary by William of Conches in the body of his translation) because of its apparent status on the cutting edge of Parisian scholasticism, in "Aspects of the Medieval French and English Traditions," pp. 323–4.

24 *Ibid.*, p. 314; and Copeland, *Rhetoric, Hermeneutics and Translation*, pp. 140–1.

25 William of Aragon, "Omnia appetunt bonum" (Terbille, "William of Aragon's Commentary," p. 1; Scott, "William of Aragon," p. 328). William of Aragon's commentary is not currently available in a complete published edition, though Carmen Olmedilla Herrero has an edition forthcoming in the series Corpus Christianorum. Citations are of the most readily available versions of the commentary: Charles Terbille, "William of Aragon's Commentary on Boethius' 'De Consolatione Philosophiae,'" unpublished Ph.D. thesis (University of Michigan, 1972); and Carmen Olmedilla Herrero,

"Commentaire de Guillaume d'Aragon sur 'De Consolatione Philosophiae' de Boèce" in *L' "Orphee" de Boèce au Moyen Âge: traductions françaises et commentaires latins, XIIe–XVe siècles*, ed. J. K. Atkinson and A. M. Babbi (Verona: Fiorini, 2000) (Book III, meter 12 only). The prologue and commentary on Book III, meter 12 are translated by A. B. Scott, "William of Aragon, Commentary on Boethius, The Consolation of Philosophy: Prologue and Exposition of Book III, metre xii," in *Medieval Literary Theory and Criticism, c.1100–1375*, ed. A. J. Minnis and A. B. Scott, with the assistance of David Wallace (Oxford: Clarendon Press, 1988), pp. 328–36. Where possible, I use Scott's translation; unmarked translations are my own.

26 Scott, "William of Aragon," p. 329; "Unde inter alia entia solus homo indiget exercitio in agendo et doctrina in eligendo ut directe et sine errore in bonum proprium moveatur" (Terbille, "William of Aragon's Commentary," p. 2).

27 *Ibid.*, p. 329; "... bonum hominis ... primo venit homo per sensum" (Terbille, "William of Aragon's Commentary," p. 2).

28 *Ibid.*, p. 331; Terbille, "William of Aragon's Commentary," p. 5.

29 *Ibid.*, p. 331; "unde humanum est valde sentire et dolere de infortuniis contingentibus circa ipsa" (Terbille, "William of Aragon's Commentary," p. 5).

30 Aristotle, *Ethica Nicomachea*, VII.14.12–13 (1153b19–21).

31 Happiness proceeding from knowledge of the "causes of things" echoes Virgil, *Georgics*, II.490: "felix qui potuit rerum cognoscere causas."

32 Scott, "William of Aragon," p. 332; "Felix quem faciunt aliena pericula cautum" (Olmedilla Herrero, "Commentaire de Guillaume d'Aragon," p. 187).

33 Aristotle, *Ethica Nicomachea*, IX.9.25–6 (1169b33–4): "speculari autem magis proximos possumus quam nosmet ipsos et illorum acciones quam proprias."

34 Minnis and Nauta, "*More Platonico loquitur*," p. 3 and *passim*.

35 Tim William Machan (ed., with the assistance of A. J. Minnis), *Sources of the Boece* (Athens: University of Georgia Press, 2005).

36 Nicholas Trevet, "Exposicio Fratris Nicolai Trevethi Anglici Ordinis Predicatorum Super Boecio 'De Consolatione,'" ed. Edmund T. Silk, unpublished edition (MS 1614, Sterling Memorial Library Manuscripts and Archives, Yale University), p. 10: "... tum quia incipit a planctu quo intendit animum audientis movere ad compassionem. Musica autem, cuius proprietas in metro et non in prosa observatur, est maxime motiva affectus, ut patet per Boecium istum in prologo Musice."

37 Mark Gleason, "Nicholas Trevet, Boethius, Boccaccio: Contexts of Cosmic Love in Troilus, Book III," *Medievalia et Humanistica* 15 (1987): 161–88.

38 *Ibid.*, p. 168.

39 *Ibid.*, p. 179.

40 Bruce Holsinger, "Lyrics and Short Poems," in *The Yale Companion to Chaucer*, ed. Seth Lerer (New Haven, CT: Yale University Press, 2006), pp. 179–212 (p. 203).

41 Dante Alighieri, *Il Convivio*, ed. G. Busnelli and G. Vandelli, 2 vols. (Firenze: Felice le Monnier, 1934), IV.6.16; *Dante's Il Convivio*, trans. Richard H. Lansing (New York: Garland, 1990).

42 Dante, *Monarchia*, ed. Pier Giorgio Ricci (Milan: Arnoldo Mondadori [Società Dantesca Italiana Edizione Nazionale], 1965), I.I, ll. 13–14; *Monarchia*, trans. Prue Shaw (Cambridge University Press, 1996).
43 Lerner, "Petrarch's Coolness," p. 217.
44 Dante, *Monarchia*, III.15, ll. 26–32 (III.16 in Shaw's translation); see discussion in Peter Dronke, *Dante's Second Love: The Originality and Contexts of the "Convivio"* (Exeter: Society for Italian Studies, 1997), p. 40.
45 Lerner, "Petrarch's Coolness," p. 219.
46 *Ibid.*, p. 221.
47 Olivia Holmes, *Dante's Two Beloveds: Ethics and Erotics in the "Divine Comedy"* (New Haven, CT: Yale University Press, 2008), p. 42.
48 Dronke, *Dante's Second Love*, p. 44.
49 Alastair Minnis, "'Dante in Inglissh': What *Il Convivio* really did for Chaucer," *Essays in Criticism* 55:2 (April 2005): 97–116 (p. 109). John Livingston Lowes argued for Chaucer's knowledge of the full *Convivio* in "Chaucer and Dante's *Convivio*," *Modern Philology* 13.1 (May 1915): 19–33.
50 Lerner argues that the *Convivio*, as opposed to the *Monarchia*, is "basically Thomistic," and that the two felicities of the former treatise are transformed here into the active life and contemplative life, both subordinated to otherworldly felicity ("Petrarch's Coolness," p. 219, n. 50). I am less interested in proving that the *Convivio* is radically Aristotelian than in showing that it harmonizes Boethian and Aristotelian ideas about philosophy, friendship, and happiness.
51 Dronke, *Dante's Second Love*, p. 29.
52 Joel Relihan rightly cautions that, in its original context, Boethius' *Consolation* does not portray a courtly milieu, and thus we should not anachronistically read Boethius' Philosophia as a courtly lady or translate her name as "Lady Philosophy" (*The Prisoner's Philosophy*, p. xiv). Yet Dante's emphasis on *philia* picks up on a submerged strand in Boethius – the association of love of wisdom with human models of friendship and love – that is not simply a late medieval imposition.
53 Joseph E. Grennen, "Aristotelian Ideas in Chaucer's Troilus: a Preliminary Study," *Medievalia et Humanistica* 14 (1986): 125–38. Grennen argues that Aristotle's *Nicomachean Ethics* was more influential on Chaucer than has been recognized, but he makes a disabling distinction between the "new" scholastic learning (Aristotle) and old-fashioned Boethianism.
54 He would also have found a model for the assimilation of Boethius' *Consolation* to the world of courtly love in Machaut's *Remede de Fortune*. There, the lover is instructed by Esperence rather than Philosophia, and she teaches him that in order to salve the stings of fortune and find sovereign happiness ("beneürté souveraine," l. 2467), he must love loyally – and love in hope rather than in desire. On Machaut's recasting of the *Consolation* in the *Remede* and the *Confort d'Ami*, see Sarah Kay, "Touching Singularity: Consolation, Philosophy, and Poetry in the *Dit*," in *The Erotics of Consolation: Desire and Distance in the Late Middle Ages*, ed. Catherine E. Léglu and Stephen J. Milner (New York: Palgrave Macmillan, 2008), pp. 21–38.

55 See Patricia Margaret Kean, *Chaucer and the Making of English Poetry* (London: Routledge, 1972), p. 129; and Ida Gordon, *The Double Sorrow of Troilus: a Study of Ambiguities in "Troilus and Criseyde"* (Oxford: Clarendon Press, 1970), p. 29.
56 *Fasciculus Morum: a Fourteenth-Century Preacher's Handbook*, ed. and trans. Siegfried Wenzel (University Park: Pennsylvania State University Press, 1989), III.1, l. 13.
57 A. C. Spearing, *The Medieval Poet as Voyeur* (Cambridge University Press, 1993), p. 136. Carolyn Dinshaw discusses the relationship between voyeurism and "masculine reading" in *Chaucer's Sexual Poetics* (Madison: University of Wisconsin Press, 1989), p. 31.
58 Lee Patterson, *Chaucer and the Subject of History* (Madison: University of Wisconsin Press, 1991), p. 107.
59 Boethius, *Consolation*, Book III, meter 12, ll.16–7: "Nec qui cuncta subegerant / Mulcerent dominum modi."
60 Albertus Magnus, *Super Ethica*, Book X, lectio 1, section 842, p. 708.
61 See Monica McAlpine, "Criseyde's Prudence," *Studies in the Age of Chaucer* 25 (2003): 199–224 for a different reading of Criseyde as an ethical subject.
62 *Ovide Moralisé*, XI.3884.
63 Fradenburg, *Sacrifice Your Love*, pp. 225–30. Jill Mann's reading of Pandarus' coercive intent is also relevant here, yet Pandarus' attitude toward Criseyde may also mark the dangers of too narrow identification with the desire of another; see Mann, *Feminizing Chaucer* (Woodbridge, Suffolk and Rochester, NY: D. S. Brewer, 2002), pp. 83–7. While acknowledging Criseyde's subjection to late medieval courtly ideology, Mitchell argues that she illustrates the Levinasian idea that "ethical choices can be as much a matter of passive discovery and acceptance as of positive self-determination" (*Ethics and Eventfulness*, p. 42).
64 Aristotle, *Politics*, III.4.2 (1278b21–2).
65 *Ovide Moralisé*, XI.168–76: "En la piteuse compaignie / Trouva sa compaigne et s'amie ... Or la resgarde il asseür / Sans doute de nul mal eür ... Sans doute et sans perte et sans paine."
66 Aers, *Chaucer, Langland, and the Creative Imagination*, p. 139.
67 Camargo, "The Consolation of Pandarus," p. 226. More strongly, Patterson reads the poem as "fending off a culturally prescribed transcendentalism," ultimately sending a message of "bafflement" in the face of a world beyond either comprehension or consolation (*Chaucer and the Subject of History*, pp. 155, 163). Richard Cook, "Chaucer's Pandarus and the Medieval Ideal of Friendship," *Journal of English and Germanic Philology* 69 (1970): 407–24, describes the poem as dramatizing "how one lives and loves in a world one must ultimately come to hate" (p. 423). See also E. T. Donaldson, "The Ending of Chaucer's *Troilus*," in *Early English and Norse Studies Presented to Hugh Smith*, ed. Arthur Brown and Peter Foote (London: Methuen, 1963), pp. 26–45.
68 Relihan, *The Prisoner's Philosophy*, p. 67.

CODA: CHAUCER'S PHILOSOPHICAL WOMEN

1 E. Jane Burns, "Courtly Love: Who Needs It? Recent Feminist Work in the Medieval French Tradition," *Signs* 27.1 (2001): 23–57 (p. 48).
2 *Ibid.*, p. 50.
3 See Badiou, "What is Love?" in *Sexuation*, ed. Renata Salecl (Durham, NC and London: Duke University Press, 2000), pp. 263–81 (p. 279), as well as Kenneth Reinhard's discussion in "Toward a Political Theology of the Neighbor," in *The Neighbor: Three Inquiries in Political Theology*, by Slavoj Žižek, Eric L. Santer, and Kenneth Reinhard (Chicago University Press, 2005), pp. 11–75 (pp. 61–5). In Badiou's *Logics of Worlds: Being and Event 2*, trans. Alberto Toscano (London and New York: Continuum, 2009), love does not have such a privileged status, but is presented as one truth among several (math, politics, art) in the preface (pp. 1–40).
4 Alain Badiou, "What is Love?" p. 279.
5 Lacan, *L'éthique*, p. 14; trans. Porter, p. 5. In the same seminar, Lacan will characterize Aristotle's morality as founded on a "tidied-up, ideal order" (p. 363; p. 315).
6 *Ibid.*, p. 22; trans. Porter, p. 13.
7 See Pierre-Christophe Cathelineau, *Lacan, lecteur d'Aristote: politique, métaphysique, logique* (Paris: Association Freudienne Internationale, 2001).
8 In *The Politics of Friendship*, Derrida addresses the problem of the classical legacy that situates *philia* between men; he proposes a "love *in* friendship" ("aimance") that might go "beyond the homo-fraternal and phallogocentric schema" (p. 306). Lacan insists that both men and women are subjects of *philia*, though this love is often described as "hommosexual" – a play on "homme" and "homosexual."
9 Lacan, *Encore*, p. 49; trans. Fink, p. 51.
10 *Ibid.*, p. 50; trans. Fink, p. 52.
11 *Ibid.*, p. 51; trans. Fink, p. 53.
12 *Ibid.*, p. 65; trans. Fink, p. 69.
13 *Les Chansons de Jaufré Rudel*, ed. Alfred Jeanroy (Paris: Librairie Ancienne Honoré Champion, 1924), p. 21.
14 Erin Labbie discusses this shift from courtly love to Aristotle in *Lacan's Medievalism*, pp. 100–1, glossing Aristotle's idea of the obstacle as "inaction or the performance of activities that are not inherently good." While Aristotle does discuss fatigue and inaction as a barrier to continuous pleasure (*Ethica Nicomachea*, x.5 [1175a4ff]), I read Lacan as more interested in Aristotle's use of *ĕnstasis* as a logical objection. Lacan goes on to argue that by positing an infinite set, one can maintain both that all jouissance is phallic and that woman as "not-whole" (*pas-toute*) can enjoy a radically other *jouissance* that is not phallic, and that is nevertheless not an exception to that rule; this feminine enjoyment is elsewhere akin to Aristotle's idea of a pursuit of the good by "being the most being they can be" (*Encore*, pp. 94, 77; trans. Fink, pp. 103, 82).

15 Lacan, *Encore*, p. 66; trans. Fink, p. 70. Lacan's four formulas may be found on p. 78 of the translated seminar, and had been presented earlier in Seminars 18 and 19. They signify the possible subject positions of a speaking being and the logical categories into which these positions fall ("all," or "not all"): two masculine positions ("all jouissance is phallic"; "there exists a jouissance that is not phallic") and two feminine ("not all jouissance is phallic"; and "there is not jouissance that is not phallic"). The formulas are glossed helpfully by Bruce Fink in *Lacan to the Letter: Reading Écrits Closely* (Minneapolis: University of Minnesota Press, 2004), pp. 160–4. See the discussion of Lacan's use of Aristotelian logic in Cathelineau, *Lacan, lecteur d'Aristote*, pp. 287–319.

16 Sarah Kay remarks that medieval love poetry "obligingly performs the analysis that Lacan himself is promoting, because it demystifies law and desire in favor of what lies beyond the pleasure principle" (*Courtly Contradictions*, p. 311). See Bruce Holsinger, *The Premodern Condition: Medievalism and the Making of Theory* (Chicago: University of Chicago Press, 2005), pp. 83–7 for a discussion of Lacan's reading of Arnaut's poem.

17 Lacan, *Encore*, p. 131–2; trans. Fink, p. 144.

18 In French the linguistic, punning connection between "le nécessaire" and the act that "ne cesse pas de s'écrire" (doesn't stop being written) is much clearer.

19 It is one of Lacan's famous gnomic pronouncements that "the sexual relationship does not exist," meaning both that the "real" of sexual difference is never fully symbolized within language and that the subject's narcissistic experience of sexual desire can never place him in a fully symmetrical relationship to another person.

20 Lacan, *Encore*, p. 78; trans. Fink, p. 85.

21 For a discussion of the contingent and impossible as being on the side of feminine logic, see Ellie Ragland, *The Logic of Sexuation: from Aristotle to Lacan* (Albany, NY: State University of New York Press, 2004), p. 106.

22 Slavoj Žižek, *The Metastases of Enjoyment: Six Essays on Women and Causality* (London and New York: Verso, 1994), p. 153. On love as an experience of truth and contingency, see Jean-Michel Rabaté, *Jacques Lacan: Psychoanalysis and the Subject of Literature* (New York: Palgrave, 2001); Rabaté discusses Alain Badiou's reading of Lacanian love as aiming "at pure being, at the surprise of an event, be it provided by a sudden passion or a renewed daily occurrence" (p. 138).

23 Badiou, "What is Love?" p. 274.

24 *Ibid.*, pp. 267, 275. Badiou describes the impossibility of speaking from an external third position which would pronounce upon the disjunction between the sexes; rather than fabricating an "angelic" imaginary outside position, he theorizes love as an encounter that produces "truth from the point of the unknown" (pp. 276–7). For Badiou, desire is inherently "homosexual" (because narcissistic and thus desiring the "same"), while love – even love between two people of the same sex – is "principally heterosexual,"

acknowledging difference (p. 279). Love consists in two subjects who take a logical (masculine) and ontological (feminine) perspective on truth. Lacan claims that love "beyondsex" is "hommosexual" and that a woman who loves must take up a masculine position; yet in the formulations discussed above, the sexual relationship can come into existence via love, in an encounter with "everything that marks in each of us the trace of his exile – not as subject but as speaking – his exile from the sexual relationship"; in such an encounter "lies the point of suspension to which all love is attached" (*Encore*, p. 132; trans Fink, p. 145).

25 On the subject of Lacan's Thomism, see Julia Kristeva, *Tales of Love*, trans. Leon S. Rudiez (New York: Columbia University Press, 1987), p. 183. On Lacan's relationship to medieval literature and philosophy more generally, see Labbie, *Lacan's Medievalism*; Holsinger, *The Premodern Condition*, pp. 57–93; and Kay, *Courtly Contradictions.*

26 Lacan, *Encore*, p. 102; trans. Fink, p. 112.

27 *Ibid.*, p. 103; trans. Fink, p. 114.

28 Lacan, *Seminar XXI: Les non-dupes errent* (1973–1974), unpublished typescript, January 8, 1974. See discussion in Ellie Ragland, "Psychoanalysis and Courtly Love," *Arthuriana* 5.1 (1995): 1–20 (p. 16).

29 Aristotle, *Ethica Nicomachea*, IX.13.1–2 (1172a1–3): "et quod aliquando est in singulis esse vel cuius gratia eligunt vivere, in hoc cum amicis volunt conversari."

30 Lacan, *Encore*, p. 48; trans. Fink, p. 50.

31 Badiou, "The Scene of Two," trans. Barbara P. Fulks, *Lacanian Ink* 21 (2003): 42–55.

32 Burns, "Courtly Love," p. 49.

33 *Ibid.*, p. 47.

34 The Aristotelian dictum that "God and Nature make nothing in vain" is found in the *Politics*, Book 1, chapter 1.9 (1253a9), and *De Caelo* Book 1, chapter 4 (271a33) ("Deus autem et natura nichil frustra faciunt") and is quoted in a variety of medieval meteorological tracts and florilegia; see Edward Wilson, "An Aristotelian Commonplace in Chaucer's 'Franklin's Tale,'" *Notes and Queries* 230 (1985): 303–5. Wilson refers to H. Bonitz, *Index Aristotelicus*, ed. O. Gignon, 2nd edn. (Berlin, 1961), 836 col. b/28–37.

35 Mann, *Feminizing Chaucer*, p. 92 (emphasis original).

36 Susan Crane, "The Franklin as Dorigen," *Chaucer Review* 24.3 (1990): 236–52 (p. 248).

37 Badiou, "What Is Love?" p. 276.

38 Lacan, *L'éthique*, p. 231; trans. Porter, pp. 196–7.

39 Mitchell, "Romancing Ethics," p. 112.

Bibliography

Abelard, Peter. *Dialogus inter Philosophum, Judaeum et Christianum*, ed. Rudolf Thomas (Stuttgart-Bad Cannstatt: Friedrich Frommann Verlag, 1970).

Ethical Writings: "Ethics" and "Dialogue Between a Philosopher, a Jew, and a Christian", ed. and trans. Paul Vincent Spade and Marilyn McCord Adams (Indianapolis, IN: Hackett Publishing Co., 1995).

Ackrill, J. L. "Aristotle on *Eudaimonia*," in *Aristotle's Ethics: Critical Essays*, ed. Nancy Sherman (Lanham, MD: Rowman and Littlefield, 1999), pp. 57–78.

Adams, Don. "Aquinas on Aristotle on Happiness," *Medieval Philosophy and Theology* 1 (1991): 98–118.

Aelred of Rievaulx. *Opera Omnia*, ed. A. Hoste and Charles H. Talbot, CCCM 1 (Turnhout: Brepols, 1971).

Aers, David. *Chaucer, Langland, and the Creative Imagination* (London: Routledge, 1979).

"Christ's Humanity and Piers Plowman: Contexts and Political Implications," *Yearbook of Langland Studies* 8 (1994): 107–25.

"Criseyde: Woman in Medieval Society," *Chaucer Review* 13 (1979): 177–200.

Aertsen, Jan A., Kent Emery, Jr., and Andreas Speer (eds.). *After the Condemnation of 1277 (Nach der Verurteilung von 1277)* (Berlin and New York: Walter de Gruyter, 2001).

Aesop, *Fables*, trans. Olivia and Robert Temple (New York: Penguin, 1998).

Agamben, Giorgio. *Stanzas: Word and Phantasm in Western Culture*, trans. Ronald L. Martinez (Minneapolis: University of Minnesota Press, 1993).

Akbari, Suzanne. *Seeing through the Veil: Optical Theory and Medieval Allegory* (University of Toronto Press, 2004).

Alain de Lille. *De Planctu Naturae*, trans. James J. Sheridan (Toronto: Pontifical Institute of Mediaeval Studies, 1980).

Albertus Magnus. *Ethicorum Libri X*, in *Opera Omnia*, vol. VII, ed. Auguste Borgnet (Paris: Vivés, 1891).

"Questions on Book x of the Ethics," in *Ethics and Political Philosophy*, ed. Arthur Stephen McGrade, John Kilcullen, and Matthew Kempshall, Cambridge Translations of Medieval Philosophical Texts 2 (Cambridge University Press, 2001), pp. 12–168.

Super Ethica, 2 vols., in *Opera Omnia,* ed. Wilhelm Kübel, tome XIV (Monasterii Westfalorum: Aschendorff, 1968–87).

Alexander de Paris. *The Medieval French "Roman d'Alexandre"*, ed. E. C. Armstrong, D. L. Buffum, Bateman Edwards, and L. F. H. Lowe, 7 vols., Elliott Monographs 37 (Princeton University Press, 1937).

Allen, Judson. *The Ethical Poetic of the Later Middle Ages: a Decorum of Convenient Distinction* (University of Toronto Press, 1982).

Ambrose. *De Officiis*, ed. and trans. Ivor J. Davidson (Oxford University Press, 2001).

Annas, Julia. *Platonic Ethics, Old and New* (Ithaca, NY: Cornell University Press, 1999).

Aquinas, Thomas. *Commentary on Aristotle's Nicomachean Ethics,* trans. C. I. Litzinger (Notre Dame, IN: Dumb Ox Books, 1993).

In Decem Libros Ethicorum Aristotelis Ad Nicomachum Expositio, ed. Raymund Spiazzi (Taurini: Marietti, 1964).

Summa Theologiae, vol. XIX (*The Emotions*, Ia IIae 22–30), vol. XX (*Pleasure*, Ia IIae 31–9), ed. E. 'Arcy (Blackfriars and New York: McGraw-Hill, 1972).

Arch, Jennifer. "The Boethian Testament of Love," *Studies in Philology* 105.4 (Fall 2008): 448–62.

Aristotle. *Aristotelis Politicorum Libri Octo cum Vetusta Translatione Guilelmi de Moerbeka*, ed. Franz Susemihl (Leipzig: Teubner, 1872).

Ethica Nicomachea: Praefatio, Ethica Vetus, Ethica Nova, Liber Ethicorum (Recensio Pura et Recensio Recognita), in *Arisoteles Latinus*, vol. XXVI, parts 1–3, fasc. 1–5, ed. R. A. Gauthier (Leiden and Brussels: Brill and Desclée De Brouwer, 1972–4).

Ethics, trans. Terence Irwin (Indianapolis, IN: Hackett Publishing Co., 1985).

L'Éthique à Nicomaque, ed. R. A. Gauthier and J. Y. Jolif, 3 vols., 2nd edn. (Louvain: Publications Universitaires, 1958–9).

Metaphysics, Oeconomica, and Magna Moralia, trans. G. Cyril Armstrong (Cambridge, MA: Harvard University Press, 1936).

Politica I–II: Translatio Prior Imperfecta, in *Aristoteles Latinus,* vol. XXIX, part 1, ed. P. Michaud-Quantin (Bruges: Desclée de Brouwer, 1961).

Politics, trans. H. Rackham (Cambridge, MA: Harvard University Press, 1932).

Politics: Books I and II, ed. and trans. Trevor Saunders (Oxford: Clarendon Press, 1995).

Armstrong, A. H. "The One and Intellect," in *The Cambridge History of Later Greek and Early Medieval Philosophy*, ed. A. H. Armstrong (Cambridge University Press, 1970).

Asztalos, Monika. "The Faculty of Theology," in *A History of the University in Europe*, vol. 1: *Universities in the Middle Ages*, ed. Hilde de Ridder-Symoens (Cambridge University Press, 1992), pp. 409–41.

Augustine. *Concerning the City of God against the Pagans,* trans. Henry Bettenson (New York: Penguin, 1972).

Confessionem Libri XIII, ed. Lucas, Verheijen CCSL 27 (Turnhout: Brepols, 1981).

Confessions, trans. Edward Pusey (New York: Collier Books, 1961).
De Civitate Dei, ed. Bernard Dombart and Alphonse Kalb, CCSL 47–8 (Turnhout: Brepols, 1955).
De Doctrina Christiana, ed. Joseph Martin, CCSL 32 (Turnhout: Brepols, 1962).
De Trinitate, ed. W. J. Mountain, CCSL 50 (Turnhout: Brepols, 1968).
Badiou, Alain. *Logics of Worlds: Being and Event 2*, trans. Alberto Toscano (London and New York: Continuum, 2009).
"The Scene of Two," trans. Barbara P. Fulks, *Lacanian Ink* 21 (2003): 42–55.
"What is Love?" in *Sexuation*, ed. Renata Salecl (Durham, NC and London: Duke University Press, 2000), pp. 263–81.
Bédier, Joseph. *Les Fabliaux* (Paris: Librairie Honoré Champion, 1964).
Bernart de Ventadorn. *The Songs of Bernart de Ventadorn*, ed. and trans. Stephen Nichols, John Galm, and A. Bartlett Giamatti, with Roger Porter, Seth Wolitz, and Claudette Charbonneau (Chapel Hill: University of North Carolina Press, 1962; rev. 1965).
Blamires, Alcuin. *Chaucer, Ethics, and Gender* (Oxford University Press, 2006).
Blodgett, E. D. "Chaucerian Pryvetee and the Opposition to Time," *Speculum* 51.3 (July 1976): 477–93.
Boethius. *The Theological Tractates and "The Consolation of Philosophy"*, ed. and trans. Stephen Tester (Cambridge, MA: Harvard University Press, 1973).
Boethius of Dacia. *De Summo Bono*, in *Topica – Opuscula*, pars. 2, ed. Niels Jørgen Green-Pederson, in *Boethii Daci Opera*, Corpus philosophorum Danicorum Medii Aevi 6 (Hauniae: G. E. C. Gad, 1976).
On the Supreme Good; On the Eternity of the World; On Dreams, trans. John F. Wippel (Toronto: Pontifical Institute of Mediaeval Studies, 1987).
Boland, Vivian. "Thinking about Good: Thomas Aquinas on Nicomachean Ethics I, Divine Names IV–V and De Ebdomadibus," *New Blackfriars* 83.979 (2002): 384–400.
Bonaventure. *Itinerarium Mentis in Deum*, in *The Works of Saint Bonaventure*, vol. II, ed. Philotheus Boehner and Sr. M. Frances Laughlin, 2 vols. (Saint Bonaventure, NY: The Franciscan Institute, Saint Bonaventure University, 1955–6).
The Mind's Road to God, trans. George Boas (Indianapolis, IN: Bobbs-Merrill, 1953).
Bond, Gerald. *The Loving Subject: Desire, Eloquence, and Power in Romanesque France* (Philadelphia: University of Pennsylvania Press, 1995).
Bossuat, Robert. *Le Moyen Âge, Histoire de la littérature française* 1 (Paris: J. de Gigord, 1931).
Boulton, Maureen Barry McCann. *The Song in the Story: Lyric Insertions in French Narrative Fiction, 1200–1400* (Philadelphia: University of Pennsylvania Press, 1993).
Bowers, John. *The Crisis of Will in "Piers Plowman"* (Washington, DC: The Catholic University of America Press, 1986).

Brams, Jozef. "The Revised Version of Grosseteste's Translation of the Nicomachean Ethics," *Bulletin de Philosophie Médiévale* 36 (1994): 45–55.

Brownlee, Kevin. *Poetic Identity in Guillaume de Machaut* (Madison: University of Wisconsin Press, 1984).

"Pygmalion, Mimesis, and the Multiple Endings of the Roman de la Rose," *Yale French Studies* 95 (1999): 193–211.

Brownlee, Kevin and Sylvia Huot (eds.). *Rethinking the Romance of the Rose: Text, Image, Reception* (Philadelphia: University of Pennsylvania Press, 1992).

Buridan, John. "Questions on Book X of the Ethics," in *Ethics and Political Philosophy*, ed. Arthur Stephen McGrade, John Kilcullen, and Matthew Kempshall, Cambridge Translations of Medieval Philosophical Texts 2 (Cambridge University Press, 2001), pp. 498–586.

Quaestiones super Decem Libros Ethicorum (Frankfurt: Minerva, 1968; facs. Paris 1513 edition).

Burns, E. Jane. "Courtly Love: Who Needs It? Recent Feminist Work in the Medieval French Tradition," *Signs* 27.1 (2001): 23–57.

Burrow, John. *Langland's Fictions* (Oxford University Press, 1993).

Butterfield, Ardis. "Lyric and Elegy in the Book of the Duchess," *Medium Aevum* 60.1 (1991): 33–60.

Poetry and Music in Medieval France (Cambridge University Press, 2002).

Calin, William. *A Poet at the Fountain: Essays on the Narrative Verse of Guillaume de Machaut* (Lexington: University Press of Kentucky, 1974).

Callus, D. A. "Introduction of Aristotelian Learning at Oxford," *Proceedings of the British Academy* 29 (Nov. 1943): 229–81.

Camargo, Martin. "The Consolation of Pandarus," *Chaucer Review* 25.3 (1991): 214–28.

The Cambridge History of Later Medieval Philosophy: from the Rediscovery of Aristotle to the Disintegration of Scholasticism, 1100–1600, ed. Norman Kretzmann, Anthony Kenny, and Jan Pinborg, assoc. ed. Eleonore Stump (Cambridge University Press, 1982).

Carns, Paula Mae. "Compilatio in Ivory: the Composite Casket in the Metropolitan Museum," *Gesta* 44 (2005): 69–88.

Cathelineau, Pierre-Christophe. *Lacan, lecteur d'Aristote: politique, métaphysique, logique* (Paris: Association Freudienne Internationale, 2001).

Celano, Anthony. "The Understanding of the Concept of Felicitas in the Pre-1250 Commentaries on the Ethica Nicomachea," *Medioevo* 12 (1986): 29–53.

Cerquiglini-Toulet, Jacqueline. *"Un engin si soutil": Guillaume de Machaut et l'écriture au XIV siècle* (Paris: Champion, 1985).

Chadwick, Henry. "Philo," in *The Cambridge History of Later Greek and Early Medieval Philosophy*, ed. A. H. Armstrong (Cambridge University Press, 1970).

Chartularium Universitatis Parisiensis, ed. Émile Chatelain and Heinrich Denifle (Paris: Fratrum Delalain, 1889–97).

Chatton, Walter. *Reportatio super Sententias*, ed. Joseph C. Wey and Girard J. Etzkorn, 4 vols. (Toronto: Pontifical Institute for Mediaeval Studies, 2002).

Chaucer, Geoffrey. *The Riverside Chaucer*, gen. ed. Larry D. Benson, 3rd edn. (Boston, MA: Houghton Mifflin, 1987).

Troilus and Criseyde: a New Edition of "The Book of Troilus", ed. Barry Windeatt (London and New York: Longman, 1984).

Chenu, M.-D. *Nature, Man, and Society in the Twelfth Century: Essays on New Theological Perspectives in the Latin West*, trans. J. Taylor and L. K. Little (University of Chicago Press, 1960).

Christine de Pizan. *The Vision of Christine de Pizan*, trans. Glenda McLeod and Charity Cannon Willard (Cambridge: D. S. Brewer, 2005).

Cicero, Marcus Tullius. *Tusculan Disputations*, trans. J. E. King (Cambridge, MA and London: Harvard University Press and W. Heinemann, 1945).

Colish, Marcia. *Peter Lombard* (Leiden and New York: Brill, 1994).

The Stoic Tradition from Antiquity to the Early Middle Ages, 2 vols. (Leiden: Brill, 1985).

"Condemnation of 219 Propositions," ed. and trans. Ernest L. Fortin and Peter D. O'Neill, in *Medieval Political Philosophy: a Sourcebook*, ed. Ralph Lerner and Muhsin Mahdi (New York: Free Press of Glencoe, 1963).

The Conflict of Wit and Will, ed. Bruce Dickins (Leeds: Kendal, printed by T. Wilson for members of the school for English language in the University of Leeds, 1937).

Cook, Richard. "Chaucer's Pandarus and the Medieval Ideal of Friendship," *Journal of English and Germanic Philology* 69 (1970): 407–24.

Cooper, John M. *Reason and Emotion: Essays on Ancient Moral Psychology and Ethical Theory* (Princeton University Press, 1998).

Copeland, Rita. *Rhetoric, Hermeneutics and Translation in the Middle Ages: Academic Traditions and Vernacular Texts* (Cambridge University Press, 1991).

Courcelle, Pierre. *La Consolation de philosophie dans la tradition littéraire: antécédents et postérité de Boèce* (Paris: Études augustiniennes, 1967).

Courtenay, William. *Adam Wodeham: an Introduction to His Life and Writings, Studies in Medieval and Reformation Thought 21* (Leiden: Brill, 1978).

"Between Despair and Love: Some Late Medieval Modifications of Augustine's Teaching on Fruition and Psychic States," in *Augustine, the Harvest, and Theology (1300–1650): Essays Dedicated to Heiko Augustinus Oberman in Honor of his Sixtieth Birthday*, ed. Kenneth Hagen (Leiden: Brill, 1990), pp. 5–20.

Schools and Scholars in Fourteenth-Century England (Princeton University Press, 1987).

Crane, Susan. "The Franklin as Dorigen," *Chaucer Review* 24.3 (1990): 236–52.

Dagenais, John. *The Ethics of Reading in Manuscript Culture: Glossing the "Libro de Buen Amor"* (Princeton University Press, 1994).

Dante Alighieri. *Il Convivio*, ed. G. Busnelli and G. Vandelli, 2 vols. (Firenze: Felice le Monnier, 1934).

Dante's Il Convivio, trans. Richard H. Lansing (New York: Garland, 1990).

Monarchia, ed. Pier Giorgio Ricci (Milan: Arnoldo Mondadori [Società Dantesca Italiana Edizione Nazionale], 1965).

Monarchia, trans. Prue Shaw (Cambridge University Press, 1996).

Davis, Steven. "Guillaume de Machaut, Chaucer's Book of the Duchess, and the Chaucer Tradition," *Chaucer Review* 36.4 (2002): 391–405.

Davlin, Mary Clemente. "Devotional Postures in Piers Plowman, with an Appendix on Divine Postures," *Chaucer Review* 42.2 (2007): 161–79.

"Kynde Knowyng as a Major Theme in Piers Plowman B," *The Review of English Studies*, n.s. 22.85 (Feb. 1971): 1–19.

de Looze, Laurence. "Guillaume de Machaut and the Writerly Process," *French Forum* 9.2 (May 1984): 145–61.

Denery II, Dallas G. *Seeing and Being Seen in the Later Medieval World: Optics, Theology, and Religious Life* (Cambridge University Press, 2005).

Derrida, Jacques. *The Politics of Friendship*, trans. George Collins (London: Verso, 1997; repr. 2005).

Desmond, Marilynn. *Ovid's Art and the Wife of Bath: the Ethics of Erotic Violence* (Ithaca, NY: Cornell University Press, 2006).

Dinshaw, Carolyn. *Chaucer's Sexual Poetics* (Madison: University of Wisconsin Press, 1989).

Dod, Bernard G. "Aristoteles Latinus," in *The Cambridge History of Later Medieval Philosophy*, pp. 45–79.

Donaldson, E. T. "The Ending of Chaucer's *Troilus*," in *Early English and Norse Studies Presented to Hugh Smith*, ed. Arthur Brown and Peter Foote (London: Methuen, 1963).

Dragonetti, Roger. "Pygmalion ou les pièges de la fiction dans *Le Roman de la Rose*," in *La musique et les lettres: études de littérature médiévale* (Geneva: Droz, 1986), pp. 345–67.

Dronke, Peter. *Dante's Second Love: the Originality and Contexts of the "Convivio"* (Exeter: Society for Italian Studies, 1997).

Verse with Prose from Petronius to Dante: the art and scope of the mixed form (Cambridge, MA: Harvard University Press, 1994).

Duns Scotus, John. *Duns Scotus on the Will and Morality*, ed. and trans. Allan B. Wolter (Washington, DC: The Catholic University of America Press, 1986).

Ehrhart, Margaret. "Guillaume de Machaut's Jugement dou Roy de Navarre and Medieval Treatments of the Virtues," *Annuale Mediaevale* 19 (1979): 46–67.

"Machaut's Dit de la Fonteinne Amoureuse, the Choice of Paris, and the Duties of Rulers," *Philological Quarterly* 59.2 (Spring 1980): 119–39.

Fasciculus Morum: a Fourteenth-Century Preacher's Handbook, ed. and trans. Siegfried Wenzel (University Park: Pennsylvania State University Press, 1989).

Le felicità nel medioevo. Atti del convegno della Società Italiana per lo studio del pensiero medievale (S.I.S.P.M.), Lecce, 12–13 settembre 2003, ed. Maria Bettetini and Francesco D. Paparella, Textes et études du Moyen

Âge 31 (Louvain-la-Neuve: Fédération International des Instituts d'Études Médiévales, 2005).

Filosofia in volgare nel medioevo. Atti del convegno della Società Italiana per lo studio del pensiero medievale (S.I.S.P.M.), Lecce, 27–29 settembre 2002, ed. Nadia Bray and Loris Sturlese, Textes et études du Moyen Âge 21 (Louvain-la-Neuve: Fédération International des Instituts d'Études Médiévales, 2003).

Findley, Brooke Heidenreich. "Deadly Words, Captive Imaginations: Women and Poetic Creation in Jean Froissart's Prison Amoureuse," *French Forum* 32.2 (Fall 2007): 1–21.

Fink, Bruce. *Lacan to the Letter: Reading Écrits Closely* (Minneapolis: University of Minnesota Press, 2004).

Fleming, John. *The Roman de la Rose: a Study in Allegory and Iconography* (Princeton University Press, 1969).

Fradenburg, L. O. Aranye. "Amorous Scholasticism," in *Speaking Images: Essays in Honor of V. A. Kolve*, ed. R. F. Yeager and Charlotte C. Morse (Ashville, NC: Pegasus Press, 2001), pp. 27–53.

"'Our owen wo to drynke': Loss, Gender and Chivalry in Troilus and Criseyde," in *"And subgit be to alle poesie": Essays on Troilus and Criseyde*, ed. R. A. Shoaf (Binghamton, NY: Medieval and Renaissance Texts and Studies, 1992), pp. 88–106.

Sacrifice Your Love: Psychoanalysis, Historicism, Chaucer (Minneapolis: University of Minnesota Press, 2002).

"'Voice Memorial': Loss and Reparation in Chaucer's Poetry," *Exemplaria* 2.1 (March 1990): 169–202.

Froissart, Jean. *An Anthology of Narrative and Lyric Poetry*, ed. and trans. Kristen M. Figg and R. Barton Palmer (New York: Routledge, 2001).

L'Espinette Amoureuse, ed. Anthime Fourrier (Paris: Éditions Klincksieck, 1963).

Le Paradis d'Amour, L'Orloge Amoureus, ed. Peter F. Dembowski (Geneva: Droz, 1986).

La Prison Amoureuse, ed. Anthime Fourrier (Paris: Éditions Klincksieck, 1974).

La Prison Amoureuse, ed. and trans. Laurence de Looze (New York and London: Garland, 1994).

Fyler, John. *Chaucer and Ovid* (New Haven, CT: Yale University Press, 1979).

"Froissart and Chaucer," in *Froissart across the Genres*, ed. Donald Maddox and Sara Sturm-Maddox (Gainesville: University Press of Florida, 1998), pp. 195–218.

Galloway, Andrew. "Piers Plowman and the Schools," *Yearbook of Langland Studies* 6 (1992): 89–107.

Gaullier-Bougassas, Catherine. "Alexander and Aristotle in the French Alexander Romances," in *The Medieval French Alexander*, ed. Donald Maddox and Sara Sturm-Maddox (Albany: State University of New York Press, 2002), pp. 57–74.

Gaunt, Simon. *Love and Death in Medieval French and Occitan Courtly Literature: Martyrs to Love* (Oxford University Press, 2006).

Gaylord, Alan. "Friendship in Chaucer's Troilus," *Chaucer Review* 3.4 (1969): 239–64.

Gentili, Sonia. *L'uomo Aristotelico alle origini della letteratura italiana* (Rome: Carocci and Università degli Studi di Roma "La Sapienza," 2005).

Gersh, Stephen. *Middle Platonism and Neoplatonism: the Latin Tradition* (University of Notre Dame Press, 1986).

Giles of Rome. *De Regimine Principum Libri III* (Rome, 1556).

Gilson, Étienne. *History of Christian Philosophy in the Middle Ages* (New York: Random House, 1955).

Gleason, Mark. "Clearing the Fields: Towards a Reassessment of Chaucer's Use of Trevet in the 'Boece,'" in *The Medieval Boethius: Studies in the Vernacular Translations of "De Consolatione Philosophiae"*, ed. Alastair Minnis (Cambridge: D. S. Brewer, 1987), pp. 89–105.

"Nicholas Trevet, Boethius, Boccaccio: Contexts of Cosmic Love in Troilus, Book III," *Medievalia et Humanistica* 15 (1987): 161–88.

Godefroy, Frédéric. *Dictionnaire de l'ancienne langue française* (Paris: F. Vieweg, 1881–1902).

Godman, Peter. *Paradoxes of Conscience in the High Middle Ages: Abelard, Heloise and the Archpoet* (Cambridge University Press, 2009).

Goldin, Frederick. *The Mirror of Narcissus in the Courtly Love Lyric* (Ithaca, NY: Cornell University Press, 1967).

Gordon, Ida. *The Double Sorrow of Troilus: a Study of Ambiguities in "Troilus and Criseyde"* (Oxford: Clarendon Press, 1970).

Gosling, J. C. B. and C. C. W. Taylor. *The Greeks on Pleasure* (Oxford: Clarendon Press, 1982).

Gower, John. *Confessio Amantis*, in *The English Works of John Gower, vol. i*, ed. G. C. Macauley, 2 vols. (London: for The Early English Text Society by K. Paul, Trench, Trübner & Co., 1900–1).

Grabmann, Martin. *Methoden und Hilfsmittel des Aristotelesstudiums im Mittelalter* (Munich: Verlag der Bayerischen Akademie der Wissenschaften, 1939).

Grady, Frank. "The Boethian Reader of Troilus and Criseyde," *Chaucer Review* 33.3 (1999): 231–51.

Grennen, Joseph E. "Aristotelian Ideas in Chaucer's Troilus: A Preliminary Study," *Medievalia et Humanistica* 14 (1986): 125–38.

Guilhem IX, Duke of Aquitaine. *Poesie*, ed. Nicolò Pasero (Modena: STEM, 1973).

The Poetry of William VII, Count of Poitiers, IX Duke of Aquitaine, ed. and trans. Gerald A. Bond (New York and London: Garland Publishing Co., 1982).

Guillaume de Deguileville. *Le Pèlerinage de Vie Humaine*, ed. J. J. Sturzinger (London: Nichols and Sons, printed for the Roxburghe Club, 1893).

Guillaume de Lorris and Jean de Meun. *Le Roman de La Rose*, ed. Félix Lecoy (Paris: Honoré Champion, 1965–70).

Le Roman de la Rose, ed. Ernest Langlois (Paris: Firmin-Didot, 1914–24).

The Romance of the Rose, trans. Charles Dahlberg (Princeton University Press, 1971).

Guldentops, Guy and Carlos Steel. "Vernacular Philosophy for the Nobility: Li Ars d'Amour, de Vertu et de Boneurté, an Old French Adaptation of Thomas Aquinas' Ethics from ca.1300," *Bulletin de Philosophie Médiévale* 45 (2003): 67–85.

Gunn, Alan. *The Mirror of Love* (Lubbock: Texas Tech Press, 1952).

Guynn, Noah. *Allegory and Sexual Ethics in the High Middle Ages* (New York: Palgrave Macmillan, 2007).

Hagen, Susan. *Allegorical Remembrance: a Study of "The Pilgrimage of the Life of Man" as a Medieval Treatise on Seeing and Remembering* (Athens: University of Georgia Press, 1990).

Hanning, Robert. "Chaucer's First Ovid: Metamorphosis and Poetic Tradition in *The Book of the Duchess* and *The House of Fame*," in *Chaucer and the Craft of Fiction*, ed. Leigh Arrathoon (Rochester, MI: Solaris Press, 1986), pp. 121–63.

Hansen, Elaine Tuttle. *Chaucer and the Fictions of Gender* (Berkeley: University of California Press, 1992).

Harbert, Bruce. "Langland's Easter," in *Langland, the Mystics and the Medieval English Religious Tradition*, ed. Helen Phillips (Cambridge: D. S. Brewer, 1990), pp. 57–70.

Harwood, Britton. *"Piers Plowman" and the Problem of Belief* (Toronto and London: University of Toronto Press, 1992).

"Piers Plowman, Fourteenth-Century Skepticism, and the Theology of Suffering," *Bucknell Review* 19.3 (1971): 119–36.

Heilbrunn Timeline of Art History (New York: The Metropolitan Museum of Art, 2000–), www.metmuseum.org/toah/hd/anti/ho_17.190.173ab,1988.16.htm (October 2006).

Heinrichs, Katherine. *The Myths of Love: Classical Lovers in Medieval Literature* (University Park and London: Pennsylvania State University Press, 1990).

Heller-Roazen, Daniel. *Fortune's Faces: The "Roman de la Rose" and the Poetics of Contingency* (Baltimore, MD: The Johns Hopkins University Press, 2003).

Henri d'Andeli. *Les Dits d'Henri d'Andeli*, ed. Alain Corbellari (Paris: Éditions Champion, 2003).

Le Lai d'Aristote de Henri D'Andeli, ed. Maurice Delbouille (Paris: Société d'Édition "Les Belles Lettres," 1951).

Hissette, Roland. *Enquête sur les 219 articles condamnés à Paris le 7 Mars 1277* (Louvain: Publications Universitaires, 1977).

Hollywood, Amy. "Suffering Transformed: Marguerite Porète, Meister Eckhart, and the Problem of Women's Spirituality," in *Meister Eckhart and the Beguine Mystics*, ed. Bernard McGinn (New York: Continuum, 1994), pp. 87–113.

Holmes, Olivia. *Dante's Two Beloveds: Ethics and Erotics in the "Divine Comedy"* (New Haven, CT: Yale University Press, 2008).

Holsinger, Bruce. "Lyrics and Short Poems," in *The Yale Companion to Chaucer*, ed. Seth Lerer (New Haven, CT: Yale University Press, 2006), pp. 179–212.

The Premodern Condition: Medievalism and the Making of Theory (University of Chicago Press, 2005).

Hult, David. *Self-fulfilling Prophecies: Readership and Authority in the first Roman de la Rose* (Cambridge University Press, 1986).

Huot, Sylvia. "The Daisy and the Laurel: Myths of Desire and Creativity in the Poetry of Jean Froissart," *Yale French Studies* 80 (1991): 240–51.

From Song to Book: The Poetics of Writing in Old French Lyric and Lyrical Narrative Poetry (Ithaca, NY: Cornell University Press, 1987).

"Guillaume de Machaut and the Consolation of Poetry," *Modern Philology* 100.2 (Nov. 2002): 169–95.

The Romance of the Rose and its Medieval Readers (Cambridge University Press, 1993).

Huppé, Bernard and D. W. Robertson. "The Book of the Duchess," in *Chaucer's Dream Visions and Shorter Poems*, ed. William A. Quinn (New York: Garland, 1963), pp. 131–82.

Irwin, Terence. *The Development of Ethics: from Socrates to the Reformation*, 3 vols. (Oxford University Press, 2007–9).

Isidore of Seville. *Sententiae*, ed. Pierre Cazier, CCSL 111 (Turnhout: Brepols, 1998).

Jacques de Vitry. *Die Exempla aus den Sermones Feriales et Communes*, ed. Joseph Greven (Heidelberg: Carl Winter, 1914).

Jaufré Rudel. *Les Chansons de Jaufré Rudel*, ed. Alfred Jeanroy (Paris: Librairie Ancienne Honoré Champion, 1924).

The Songs of Jaufré Rudel, ed. Rupert T. Pickens (Toronto: Pontifical Institute of Mediaeval Studies, 1978).

Jefferson, Bernard. *Chaucer and the Consolation of Philosophy of Boethius* (Princeton University Press, 1917).

Karnes, Michelle. "Will's Imagination in Piers Plowman," *Journal of English and Germanic Philology* 108 (Jan. 2009): 27–58.

Kay, Sarah. *Courtly Contradictions: the Emergence of the Literary Object in the Twelfth Century* (Stanford, CA: Stanford University Press, 2001).

The Place of Thought: the Complexity of One in Late Medieval French Didactic Poetry (Philadelphia: University of Pennsylvania Press, 2007).

The Romance of the Rose (London: Grant & Cutler, Ltd., 1995).

Subjectivity in Troubadour Poetry (Cambridge University Press, 1990).

"Touching Singularity: Consolation, Philosophy, and Poetry in the *Dit*," in *The Erotics of Consolation: Desire and Distance in the Late Middle Ages*, ed. Catherine E. Léglu and Stephen J. Milner (New York: Palgrave Macmillan, 2008), pp. 21–38.

Kean, Patricia Margaret. *Chaucer and the Making of English Poetry* (London: Routledge, 1972).

Keiper, Hugo. "A Literary 'Debate Over Universals'? New Perspectives on the Relationships between Nominalism, Realism, and Literary Discourse," in

Nominalism and Literary Discourse, ed. Hugo Keiper, Christoph Bode, and Richard J. Utz (Atlanta, GA: Rodopi, 1997), pp. 1–85.

Kelly, Douglas. "Imitation, Metamorphosis, and Froissart's Use of the Exemplary *Modus Tractandi*," in *Froissart Across the Genres* (Gainesville: University Press of Florida, 1998), pp. 101–18.

Internal Differences and Meanings in the "Roman de la Rose" (Madison: University of Wisconsin Press, 1985).

Medieval Imagination: Rhetoric and the Poetry of Courtly Love (Madison: University of Wisconsin Press, 1978).

Kempshall, Matthew S. *The Common Good in Late Medieval Political Thought* (Oxford: Clarendon Press, 1999).

Kendrick, Laura. *The Game of Love: Troubadour Wordplay* (Berkeley: University of California Press, 1988).

Kent, Bonnie. *Virtues of the Will: the Transformation of Ethics in the Late Thirteenth Century* (Washington, DC: The Catholic University of America Press, 1995).

Keys, Mary M. *Aquinas, Aristotle, and the Promise of the Common Good* (Cambridge University Press, 2006).

Keyt, David. "Intellectualism in Aristotle," in *Essays in Ancient Greek Philosophy*, vol. II, ed. J. P. Anton, George L. Kustas, and A. Preus (Albany: State University of New York Press, 1983).

Kirk, Elizabeth. "Langland's Narrative Christology," in *Art and Context in Late Medieval English Narrative*, ed. Robert R. Edwards (Cambridge: D. S. Brewer, 1994), pp. 17–35.

"'Who Suffreth More Than God?': Narrative Redefinition of Patience in *Patience* and *Piers Plowman*," in *The Triumph of Patience*, ed. Gerald J. Schiffhorst (Orlando: University Presses of Florida, 1978), pp. 88–104.

Kiser, Lisa. "Sleep, Dreams, and Poetry in Chaucer's Book of the Duchess," *Papers on Language and Literature* 19.1 (1983): 3–11.

Konstan, David. *On Aristotle's Nicomachean Ethics 8 and 9: Aspasius, Anonymous, Michael of Ephesus* (Ithaca, NY: Cornell University Press, 2001).

Kristeva, Julia. *Tales of Love*, trans. Leon S. Rudiez (New York: Columbia University Press, 1987).

Labbie, Erin. *Lacan's Medievalism* (Minneapolis: University of Minnesota Press, 2006).

Lacan, Jacques. *Encore*, ed. Jacques-Alain Miller (Paris: Seuil, 1999).

The Ethics of Psychoanalysis, 1959–1960, trans. Dennis Porter (New York: Norton, 1997).

L'éthique de la psychanalyse, ed. Jacques-Alain Miller (Paris: Seuil, 1986).

On Feminine Sexuality: the Limits of Love and Knowledge (Encore), 1972–3, trans. Bruce Fink (New York: Norton, 1998).

Seminar XXI: Les non-dupes errent (1973–4), January 8, 1974, unpublished typescript.

Ladd, Anne. "Attitude toward Lyric in the Lai d'Aristote and Some Later Fictional Narratives," *Romania* 96 (1975): 194–208.

Langland, William. *Piers Plowman: The B Version*, ed. George Kane and E. Talbot Donaldson (London: The Athlone Press, 1975).

Piers Plowman: the C-Text, ed. Derek Pearsall (University of Exeter Press, 1994).

Piers Plowman: The C Version, ed. George Russell and George Kane (London and Berkeley: The Athlone Press and University of California Press, 1997).

The Vision of Piers Plowman: a Critical Edition of the B-Text Based on Trinity College Cambridge MS B.15.17, ed. A. V. C. Schmidt, 2nd edn. (London: J. M. Dent, 1995).

Latini, Brunetto. *Li Livres dou Tresor*, ed. Spurgeon Baldwin and Paul Barrette (Tempe: Arizona Center for Medieval and Renaissance Studies, 2003).

Lawlor, John. "The Pattern of Consolation in The Book of the Duchess," *Speculum* 31.4 (1956): 626–48.

Lawton, David. *Chaucer's Narrators* (Cambridge: D. S. Brewer, 1985).

"The Subject of Piers Plowman," *Yearbook of Langland Studies* 1 (1987): 1–30.

Lazar, Moshe. "Fin'Amor," in *Handbook of the Troubadours*, ed. F. Akehurst and Judith Davis (Berkeley: University of California Press, 1995), pp. 61–100.

Lear, Jonathan. *Happiness, Death, and the Remainder of Life* (Cambridge, MA: Harvard University Press, 2000).

Le Fèvre, Jehan. *Les Lamentations de Matheolus et le Livre de Leesce de Jehan Le Fèvre, de Resson*, ed. A.-G. van Hamel, 2 vols. (Paris: É. Bouillon, 1892–1905).

Leff, Gordon. *Medieval Thought: St. Augustine to Ockham* (Harmondsworth, Middlesex: Penguin, 1958).

Lerner, Robert. "Petrarch's Coolness Toward Dante: A Conflict of 'Humanisms,'" in *Intellectuals and Writers in Fourteenth-Century Europe*, ed. Piero Boitani and Anna Torti (Tübingen and Cambridge: Gunter Narr Verlag and D. S. Brewer, 1986), pp. 204–25.

Lewis, C. S. *The Allegory of Love* (London: Oxford University Press, 1938).

Lewry, P. Osmund. "Robert Kilwardby's commentary on the *Ethica Noua* and *Vetus*," in *L'homme et son univers au Moyen Âge: actes du septième congrès international de philosophie médiévale*, ed. C., Wenin Philosophes médiévaux 27 (Louvain-la-Neuve: L'Institut supérieur de philosophie, 1986), pp. 799–807.

Li Ars d'Amour, de Vertu et de Boneurté, par Jehan le Bel, publié pour la première fois d'après un manuscrit de la Bibliothèque royale de Bruxelles par Jules Petit, 2 vols. (Brussels: V. Devaux et cie, vol. I 1867; vol. II [without reference to Jehan le Bel], 1869).

Liddell, Henry George and Robert Scott. *A Greek–English Lexicon*, revised and augmented throughout by Sir Henry Stuart Jones with the assistance of Roderick McKenzie (Oxford: Clarendon Press, 1996).

Lochrie, Karma. *Covert Operations: the Medieval Uses of Secrecy* (Philadelphia: University of Pennsylvania Press, 1999).

Lottin, C. O. *Psychologie et Morale aux XIIe et XIIIe Siècles*, 6 vols. (Louvain and Gembloux: Abbaye du Mont César, 1942–60).

Lowes, John Livingston. "Chaucer and Dante's Convivio," *Modern Philology* 13.1 (May 1915): 19–33.

Lydgate, John. *The Pilgrimage of the Life of Man*, ed. Frederick J. Furnivall, EETS e.s. 77, 83, 92 (London: Kegan Paul, Trench, Trübner & Co., 1899–1904).

Lynch, Kathryn. *Chaucer's Philosophical Visions* (Woodbridge: D. S. Brewer, 2000).

Machan, Tim William (ed., with the assistance of A. J. Minnis). *Sources of the Boece* (Athens: University of Georgia Press, 2005).

Machaut, Guillaume de. *"The Fountain of Love" and Two Other Love Vision Poems*, ed. and trans. R. Barton Palmer (New York: Garland, 1993).

"Le Jugement du Roy de Behaigne" and "Remede de Fortune", ed. and trans. James I. Wimsatt and William W. Kibler; music ed. Rebecca A. Baltzer (Athens: University of Georgia Press, 1988).

Le Livre dou Voir Dit, ed. Daniel Leech-Wilkinson, trans. R. Barton Palmer (New York: Garland, 1998).

Le Livre du Voir Dit, ed. Paul Imbs, revised and coordinated with an introduction by Jacqueline Cerquiglini-Toulet, index of proper names and glossary by Noël Musso (Paris: Librairie générale française, 1999).

Œuvres, ed. Ernest Hoepffner, 3 vols. (Paris: Librairie de Firmin-Didot et Cie, 1908).

Mann, Jill. *Feminizing Chaucer* (Woodbridge, Suffolk and Rochester, New York: D. S. Brewer, 2002).

Marenbon, John. *Early Medieval Philosophy (480–1150): an Introduction*, 2nd edn. (London and New York: Routledge, 1988).

Masciandaro, Nicola. *The Voice of the Hammer: the Meaning of Work in Middle English Literature* (University of Notre Dame Press, 2007).

McAlpine, Monica. "Criseyde's Prudence," *Studies in the Age of Chaucer* 25 (2003): 199–224.

McEvoy, James. "Ultimate Goods: Happiness, Friendship, and Bliss," in *The Cambridge Companion to Medieval Philosophy*, ed. A. S. McGrade (Cambridge University Press, 2003), pp. 254–75.

McGrade, Arthur S. "Enjoyment at Oxford after Ockham: Philosophy, Psychology, and the Love of God," in *From Ockham to Wyclif*, ed. Anne Hudson and Michael Wilks, Studies in Church History, Subsidia, 5 (London: Blackwell, 1987), pp. 63–88.

"Ockham on Enjoyment – Towards an Understanding of Fourteenth-Century Philosophy and Psychology," *Review of Metaphysics* 34.4, issue 136 (June 1981): 706–28.

McGrady, Deborah. *Controlling Readers: Guillaume de Machaut and his Late Medieval Audience* (University of Toronto Press, 2006).

Michael of Ephesus. *The Greek Commentaries on the Nicomachean Ethics of Aristotle*, vol. III, ed. H. Paul F. Mercken (Leiden: Brill, 1973).

Middleton, Anne. "William Langland's *Kynde Name*: Authorial Signature and Social Identity in Late Fourteenth-Century England," in *Literary Practice and Social Change in Britain, 1380–1530*, ed. Lee Patterson (Berkeley: University of California Press, 1993), pp. 15–82.

Miller, Mark. *Philosophical Chaucer: Love, Sex, and Agency in the Canterbury Tales* (Cambridge University Press, 2004).
Minnis, Alastair. "Aspects of the Medieval French and English Traditions of the *De Consolatione Philosophiae*," in *Boethius: His Life, Thought, and Influence*, ed. Margaret Gibson (Oxford: Blackwell, 1981), pp. 312–61.
"The Biennial Chaucer Lecture: 'I speke of folk in seculer estaat': Vernacularity and Secularity in the Age of Chaucer," *Studies in the Age of Chaucer* 27 (2005): 25–58.
Chaucer and Pagan Antiquity (Woodbridge, Suffolk: D. S. Brewer, 1982).
"'Dante in Inglissh': What *Il Convivio* Really Did for Chaucer," *Essays in Criticism* 55.2 (April 2005): 97–116.
"Looking for a Sign: the Quest for Nominalism in Chaucer and Langland," in *Essays on Ricardian Literature: in Honor of J. A. Burrow*, ed. A. J. Minnis, Charlotte C. Morse, and Thorlac Turville-Petre (New York: Oxford University Press, 1997), pp. 142–78.
Magister Amoris: the Roman de la Rose and Vernacular Hermeneutics (Oxford University Press, 2001).
"*More Platonico loquitur*: What Nicholas Trevet Really Did to William of Conches," in *Chaucer's Boece and the Medieval Tradition of Boethius*, ed. Alastair Minnis (Cambridge: D. S. Brewer, 1993), pp. 1–33.
Mitchell, J. Allan. *Ethics and Eventfulness in Middle English Literature* (New York: Palgrave Macmillan, 2009).
Ethics and Exemplary Narrative in Chaucer and Gower (Cambridge: Boydell and Brewer, 2004).
"Romancing Ethics in Boethius, Chaucer, and Levinas: Fortune, Moral Luck, and Erotic Adventure," *Comparative Literature* 57.2 (Spring 2005): 102–16.
Montaigne, Michel de. *Apology for Raymond Sebond* (Indianapolis, IN: Hackett, 2003).
Murphy, J. J. "Aristotle's Rhetoric in the Middle Ages," *Quarterly Journal of Speech* 52 (1966): 109–15.
Murtaugh, Daniel. *Piers Plowman and the Image of God* (Gainesville: University Presses of Florida, 1978).
Nauta, Lodi. "'*Magis sit Platonicus quam Aristotelicus*': Interpretations of Boethius's Platonism in the *Consolatio Philosophiae* from the Twelfth to the Seventeenth Century," in *The Platonic Tradition in the Middle Ages* (Berlin: Walter de Gruyter, 2002), pp. 165–204.
"The Scholastic Context of the Boethius Commentary by Nicholas Trevet," in *Boethius in the Middle Ages*, ed. Maarten Hoenen and Lodi Nauta (New York: Brill, 1997), pp. 41–67.
Nederman, Cary J. "Aristotelian Ethics before the Nicomachean Ethics: Alternate Sources of Aristotle's Concept of Virtue in the Twelfth Century," *Parergon* 7 (1989): 55–75.
"Nature, Ethics, and the Doctrine of 'Habitus': Aristotelian Moral Psychology in the Twelfth Century," *Traditio* 45 (1989–90): 87–110.

Newhauser, Richard. "Augustinian 'vitium curiositatis' and its Reception," in *Saint Augustine and his Influence in the Middle Ages*, ed. Edward B. King and Jacqueline T. Schaefer, Sewanee Mediaeval Studies 3 (Sewanee, TN: The Press of the University of the South, 1988), pp. 99–124.

Nicole Oresme, *Le Livre de Éthiques d'Aristote published from the text of MS 2902, Bibliothèque Royale de Belgique*, ed. Albert Menut (New York: G. E. Stechert & Co., 1940).

"Maistre Nicole Oresme: Le Livre de Yconomique D'Aristote, Critical Edition of the French Text from the Avranches Manuscript with the Original Latin Version, Introduction, and Translation," ed. Albert Douglas Menut, *Transactions of the American Philosophical Society*, n.s. 47.5 (1957): 783–853.

Nitzsche, Jane Chance. *The Genius Figure in Antiquity and the Middle Ages* (New York: Columbia University Press, 1975).

Nolan, Barbara. "Promiscuous Fictions: Medieval Bawdy Tales and their Textual Liaisons," in *The Body and the Soul in Medieval Literature*, ed. Piero Boitani and Anna Torti (Cambridge: D. S. Brewer, 1999), pp. 79–105.

Nouvet, Claire. "An Allegorical Mirror: The Pool of Narcissus in Guillaume de Lorris' Romance of the Rose," *The Romanic Review* 91.4 (Nov. 2000): 353–74.

"Pour une économie de la dé-limitation: la Prison Amoureuse de Jean Froissart," *Neophilologus* 70 (1986): 341–56.

Ockham, William. *Quaestiones in Librum Quartum Sententiarum*, in *Opera Philosophica et Theologica*, ed. Rega Wood and Gedeon Gal (Bonaventure, NY: St. Bonaventure University, 1984).

"Using and Enjoying" (from "Commentary on *Sentences*"), in *Ethics and Political Philosophy*, ed. Arthur Stephen McGrade, John Kilcullen, and Matthew Kempshall, *Cambridge Translations of Medieval Philosophical Texts* 2 (Cambridge University Press, 2001).

Olmedilla Herrero, Carmen. "Commentaire de Guillaume d'Aragon sur 'De Consolatione Philosophiae' de Boèce," in *L' "Orphee" de Boèce au Moyen Âge: traductions françaises et commentaires latins, XIIe–XVe siècles*, ed. J. K. Atkinson and A. M. Babbi (Verona: Fiorini, 2000).

Olson, Glending. *Literature as Recreation in the Later Middle Ages* (Ithaca, NY: Cornell University Press, 1982).

Osborne, Catherine. *Eros Unveiled: Plato and the God of Love* (Oxford: Clarendon Press, 1994).

Ovid. *Metamorphoses*, ed. and trans. Frank Justus Miller, 2 vols. (Cambridge, MA and London: Harvard University Press and W. Heinemann, 1977–84).

Ovide Moralisé, ed. C. de Boer, 5 vols. (Amsterdam: J. Müller, 1915–38).

Owen, G. E. L. "Aristotelian Pleasures," in *Articles on Aristotle*, ed. Jonathan Barnes, Malcolm Schofield, and Richard Sorabji (London: Duckworth, 1975), pp. 92–103.

Owens, Joseph. "Faith, Ideas, Illumination, and Experience," in *The Cambridge History of Later Medieval Philosophy*, pp. 440–59.

Palmer, R. Barton. "The Book of the Duchess and Fonteinne Amoureuse: Chaucer and Machaut Reconsidered," *Canadian Review of Comparative Literature* 7 (Fall 1980): 380–93.

Paré, Gérard. *Les idées et les lettres au XIIIe Siècle: "Le Roman de la Rose"* (Montréal: Centre de Psychologie et de Pédagogie, 1947).

Le "Roman de la Rose" et la scholastique courtoise (Paris and Ottawa: Publications de l'Institut d'Études Médiévales d'Ottawa, 1941).

Patterson, Lee. *Chaucer and the Subject of History* (Madison: University of Wisconsin Press, 1991).

Paxson, James. "Inventing the Subject and the Personification of Will in *Piers Plowman*: Rhetorical, Erotic, and Ideological Origins and Limits in Langland's Allegorical Poetics," in *William Langland's "Piers Plowman": a Book of Essays*, ed. Kathleen Hewett-Smith (New York: Routledge, 2001), pp. 195–231.

Payne, Anne F. *Chaucer and Menippean Satire* (Madison: University of Wisconsin Press, 1981).

Peck, Russell. "Chaucer and the Nominalist Questions," *Speculum* 53.4 (Oct. 1978): 745–60.

Peter Lombard. *Sententiae in IV Libris Distinctae*, tome I, part 2, Books I and II (Grottaferrata: Editiones Collegii S. Bonaventura ad Claras Aquas, 1971).

The Sentences, Book I: The Mystery of the Trinity, trans. Giulio Solano (Toronto: Pontifical Institute of Mediaeval Studies, 2007).

Phillips, Adam. *Going Sane: Maps of Happiness* (New York: Fourth Estate, 2005).

Philo of Alexandria. *De Fuga et Inventione*, in *The Works of Philo: Complete and Unabridged*, trans. C. D. Yonge (Peabody, MA: Hendrickson Publishing, 1993).

Plato, *Laws*, trans. A. E. Taylor (London: Dent, 1960).

Meno, ed. Victor Kordeuter, *Plato Latinus* I (London: Warburg Institute, 1940; repr. Nendeln, Liechtenstein: Kraus, 1973).

Phaedo, trans. David Gallop (Oxford: Clarendon Press, 1975).

Phaedo, ed. Laurence Minio-Paluello, *Plato Latinus* 2 (London: Warburg Institute, 1950).

Protagoras, trans. C. C. W. Taylor (Oxford: Clarendon Press, 1991).

Theaetetus, trans. M. J. Levett (Indianapolis, IN: Hackett Publishing Co., 1992).

Timaeus: a Calcidio Translatus Commentarioque Instructis, ed. J. H. Waszink (London and Leiden: Warburg Institute and Brill, 1975).

Plotinus, *Enneads*, trans. Stephen MacKenna (Burdett, NY: Larson Publications, 1992).

Poirion, Daniel. "Narcisse et Pygmalion dans le Roman de la Rose," in *Essays in Honour of Louis Francis Solano*, ed. Raymond J. Cormier and Urban T. Holmes (Chapel Hill: University of North Carolina Press, 1970), pp. 153–65.

Le poète et le prince: l'évolution du lyrisme courtois de Guillaume de Machaut à Charles de Orléans (Paris: Presses Universitaires de France, 1965).

Potkay, Adam. *The Story of Joy* (Cambridge University Press, 2007).

Rabaté, Jean-Michel. *Jacques Lacan: Psychoanalysis and the Subject of Literature* (New York: Palgrave, 2001).

Ragland, Ellie. *The Logic of Sexuation: from Aristotle to Lacan* (Albany: State University of New York Press, 2004).

"Psychoanalysis and Courtly Love," *Arthuriana* 5.1 (1995): 1–20.

Rambuss, Richard. "'Process of Tyme': History, Consolation, and Apocalypse in *The Book of the Duchess*," *Exemplaria* 2.2 (Fall 1990): 659–83.

Raskolnikov, Masha. "Promising the Female, Delivering the Male," *Yearbook of Langland Studies* 19 (2005): 81–105.

Reinhard, Kenneth. "Toward a Political Theology of the Neighbor," in *The Neighbor: Three Inquiries in Political Theology*, by Slavoj Žižek, Eric L. Santer, and Kenneth Reinhard (University of Chicago Press, 2005), pp. 11–75.

Relihan, Joel. *The Prisoner's Philosophy: Life and Death in Boethius' Consolation*, with a contribution by William E. Heise (University of Notre Dame Press, 2007).

Richards, Earl Jeffrey. "Reflections on Oiseuse's Mirror: Iconographic Tradition, Luxuria, and the Roman de la Rose," *Zeitschrift für romanische Philologie* 98.3–4 (1982): 296–311.

Rigby, Steven. *Wisdom and Chivalry: Chaucer's Knight's Tale and Medieval Political Theory* (Leiden: Brill, 2009).

Rissanen, Matti. "In search of Happiness: Felicitas and Beatitudo in Early English Boethius Translations," *Studia Anglica Posnaniensa* 31 (1997): 237–48.

Robertson, D. W. *A Preface to Chaucer* (Princeton University Press, 1962).

Rosemann, Philipp. *Peter Lombard* (Oxford University Press, 2004).

Roudinesco, Elisabeth. *Jacques Lacan*, trans. Barbara Bray (New York: Columbia University Press, 1997).

Rousselot, Pierre. *Pour l'histoire du problème de l'amour au moyen âge* (Münster: Aschendorffsche Buchhandlung, 1907).

The Problem of Love in the Middle Ages, trans. Alan Vincelette (Milwaukee, WI: Marquette University Press, 2001).

Russell, J. Stephen. *The English Dream Vision* (Columbus: Ohio State University Press, 1988).

Sadlek, Gregory. *Idleness Working: the Discourse of Love's Labor from Ovid through Chaucer and Gower* (Washington, DC: The Catholic University of America Press, 2004).

Sarton, George. *Aristotle and Phyllis, ISIS* 14.1 (May 1930): 8–19 (repr. Bruge: St. Catherine Press, 1930).

Schmidt, A. V. C. "Langland and Scholastic Philosophy," *Medium Aevum* 38 (1969): 134–56.

Scott, A. B. "William of Aragon, Commentary on Boethius, The Consolation of Philosophy: Prologue and Exposition of Book III, meter xii," in *Medieval Literary Theory and Criticism, c.1100–1375*, ed. A. J. Minnis and A. B. Scott, with the assistance of David Wallace (Oxford: Clarendon Press, 1988), pp. 328–36.

Sherman, Claire Richter. *Imaging Aristotle: Verbal and Visual Representation in Fourteenth-Century France* (Berkeley: University of California Press, 1995).

Siger of Brabant. *Quaestiones Morales*, in *Écrits de logique, de morale et de physique*, ed. Bernardo Bazán (Louvain: Publications Universitaires, 1974).

Simpson, James. "Desire and the Scriptural Text: Will as Reader in *Piers Plowman*," in *Criticism and Dissent in the Middle Ages,* ed. Rita Copeland (Cambridge University Press, 1996), pp. 215–43.

"From Reason to Affective Knowledge: Modes of Thought and Poetic Form in Piers Plowman," *Medium Aevum* 55.1 (1986): 1–23.

Smith, D. Vance. *Arts of Possession: the Middle English Household Imaginary* (Minneapolis: University of Minnesota Press, 2003).

Smith, Susan L. *The Power of Women: a Topos in Medieval Art and Literature* (Philadelphia: University of Pennsylvania Press, 1995).

Sorabji, Richard (ed.). *Aristotle Transformed: the Ancient Commentaries and their Influence* (Ithaca, NY: Cornell University Press, 1990).

Spearing, A. C. *The Medieval Poet as Voyeur* (Cambridge University Press, 1993).

Steenberghen, Fernand van. *Aristotle in the West: the Origins of Latin Aristotelianism,* trans. Leonard Johnston (Louvain: E. Nauwelaerts, 1955).

La Philosophie au XIIIe Siècle, 2nd edn., Philosophes médiévaux 28 (Louvain: Peeters, 1991).

Steiner, Emily. *Documentary Culture and the Making of Medieval English Literature* (Cambridge University Press, 2003).

Steinmetz, David. "Late Medieval Nominalism and the Clerk's Tale," *Chaucer Review* 12 (1977): 38–54.

Stepsis, Robert. "Potentia Absoluta and the Clerk's Tale," *Chaucer Review* 10 (1975): 129–46.

Stone, Gregory. *The Death of the Troubadour: the Late Medieval Resistance to the Renaissance* (Philadelphia: University of Pennsylvania Press, 1994).

Storost, Joachim. "Femme chevalchat Aristotte," *Zeitschrift für französische Sprache und Literatur* 66 (1956): 186–201.

Strohm, Paul. *Politique: Languages of Statecraft between Chaucer and Shakespeare* (University of Notre Dame Press, 2005).

Tavormina, Teresa. *Kindly Similitude: Marriage and Family in "Piers Plowman"* (Cambridge: D. S. Brewer, 1995).

Terbille, Charles. "*William of Aragon's Commentary on Boethius*'De Consolatione Philosophiae,'" unpublished Ph.D. thesis (University of Michigan, 1972).

Tilmouth, Christopher. *Passion's Triumph Over Reason: a History of the Moral Imagination from Spenser to Rochester* (Oxford University Press, 2007).

Topsfield, Leslie. *Troubadours and Love* (New York: Cambridge University Press, 1975).

Torrell, Jean-Pierre. *Saint Thomas Aquinas*, vol. 1: *The Person and His Work*, trans. Robert Royal (Washington, DC: The Catholic University of America Press, 1996; rev. 2005).

Travis, Peter. "White," *Studies in the Age of Chaucer* 22 (2000): 1–66.

Trevet, Nicholas. "*Exposicio Fratris Nicolai Trevethi Anglici Ordinis Predicatorum Super Boecio* 'De Consolatione,'" ed. Edmund T. Silk, unpublished edition (MS 1614, Sterling Memorial Library Manuscripts and Archives, Yale University).

Trevisa, John. *The Governance of Kings and Princes*, ed. David C. Fowler, Charles F. Briggs, and Paul G. Remley (New York: Garland Publications, 1997).

Tuve, Rosemond. *Allegorical Imagery: Some Medieval Books and Their Posterity* (Princeton University Press, 1966).

Utz, Richard. "Negotiating the Paradigm: Literary Nominalism and the Theory of Rereading Late Medieval Texts," *Literary Nominalism and the Theory of Rereading Late Medieval Texts*, ed. Richard Utz (Lewiston, NY: Edwin Mellen Press, 1995), pp. 1–30.

Vlastos, Gregory. "The Individual as Object of Love in Plato," in *Platonic Studies* (Princeton University Press, 1973).

Wack, Mary. *Lovesickness in the Middle Ages: the Viaticum and its Commentaries* (Philadelphia: University of Pennsylvania Press, 1990).

Wallace, David. *Chaucer and the Early Writings of Boccaccio* (Woodbridge, Suffolk: D. S. Brewer, 1985).

Walsh, James J. "Nominalism and Ethics: Some Remarks about Buridan's Commentary," *Journal of the History of Philosophy* 4.1 (Jan. 1966): 1–13.

Watts, William H. and Richard J. Utz. "Nominalist Perspectives on Chaucer's Poetry: a Bibliographical Essay," *Medievalia et Humanistica* 20 (1993): 147–73.

Wetherbee, Winthrop. "The Literal and the Allegorical: Jean de Meun and the De Planctu Naturae," *Medieval Studies* 33 (1971): 264–91.

Platonism and Poetry in the Twelfth Century (Princeton University Press, 1972).

White, Hugh. *Nature, Sex, and Goodness in a Medieval Literary Tradition* (Oxford University Press, 2000).

Wieland, Georg. *Ethica, scientia practica: die Anfänge der philosophischen Ethik im 13.* Jahrhundert (Münster Westfalen: Aschendorff, 1981).

"Happiness: the Perfection of Man," in *The Cambridge History of Later Medieval Philosophy*, pp. 673–86.

"The Reception and Interpretation of Aristotle's *Ethics*," in *The Cambridge History of Later Medieval Philosophy*, pp. 657–72.

Wilson, Edward. "An Aristotelian Commonplace in Chaucer's 'Franklin's Tale,'" *Notes and Queries* 230 (1985): 303–5.

Wimsatt, James I. *Chaucer and His French Contemporaries: Natural Music in the Fourteenth Century* (University of Toronto Press, 1991).

Chaucer and the French Love Poets: the Literary Background of "The Book of the Duchess" (Chapel Hill: University of North Carolina Press, 1968).

Wittig, Joseph. "'Piers Plowman' B, Passus IX–XII: Elements in the Design of the Inward Journey," *Traditio* 28 (1972): 211–80.

Wodeham, Adam. *Lectura Secunda in Librum Primum Sententiarum*, ed. Rega Wood, assisted by Gedeon Gál, 3 vols. (St. Bonaventure, NY: St. Bonaventure University Press, 1990).

Wright, Steven. "Deguileville's Pèlerinage de Vie Humaine as 'contrepartie edifiante' of the Roman de la Rose," *Philological Quarterly* 68.4 (1989): 399–422.

Wulf, Maurice de. *History of Mediaeval Philosophy*, trans. Ernest C. Messenger (New York: Dover, 1952; trans. of 6th edn., 1934–7).

Zavattero, Irene. "Moral and Intellectual Virtues in the Earliest Latin Commentaries on the *Nicomachean Ethics*," in *Virtue Ethics in the Middle Ages: Commentaries on Aristotle's Nicomachean Ethics, 1200–1500*, ed. István P. Bejczy (Leiden: Brill, 2008), pp. 31–54.

Zeeman, Nicolette. *"Piers Plowman" and the Medieval Discourse of Desire* (Cambridge University Press, 2006).

Zink, Michel. "De Jean Le Teinturier à Jean Bras-de-Fer: le triomphe des cuistres," in *Les voix de la conscience: parole du poète et parole de Dieu dans la littérature médiévale* (Caen: Paradigme, 1992), pp. 261–74; reprinted from *Milieux universitaires et mentalités urbaines au Moyen Age*, ed. Daniel Poirion (Paris: Presses de l'Université de Paris-Sorbonne, 1987), pp. 157–70.

Žižek, Slavoj. *The Metastases of Enjoyment: Six Essays on Women and Causality* (London and New York: Verso, 1994).

Zupancic, Alenka. *Ethics of the Real: Kant, Lacan* (London and New York: Verso, 2000).

Index

CAMBRIDGE STUDIES IN MEDIEVAL LITERATURE

1 Robin Kirkpatrick *Dante's Inferno: Difficulty and Dead Poetry*
2 Jeremy Tambling *Dante and Difference: Writing in the "Commedia"*
3 Simon Gaunt *Troubadours and Irony*
4 Wendy Scase *"Piers Plowman" and the New Anticlericalism*
5 Joseph Duggan *The "Cantar De Mio Cid": Poetic Creation in its Economic and Social Contexts*
6 Roderick Beaton *The Medieval Greek Romance*
7 Kathryn Kerby-Fulton *Reformist Apocalypticism and "Piers Plowman"*
8 Alison Morgan *Dante and the Medieval Other World*
9 Eckehard Simon (ed.) *The Theatre of Medieval Europe: New Research in Early Drama*
10 Mary Carruthers *The Book of Memory: A Study of Memory in Medieval Culture*
11 Rita Copeland *Rhetoric, Hermeneutics and Translation in the Middle Ages: Academic Traditions and Vernacular Texts*
12 Donald Maddox *The Arthurian Romances of Chrétien de Troyes: Once and Future Fictions*
13 Nicholas Watson *Richard Rolle and the Invention of Authority*
14 Steven F. Kruger *Dreaming in the Middle Ages*
15 Barbara Nolan *Chaucer and the Tradition of the "Roman Antique"*
16 Sylvia Huot *The "Romance of the Rose" and its Medieval Readers: Interpretations, Reception, Manuscript Transmission*
17 Carol M. Meale (ed.) *Women and Literature in Britain, 1150–1500*
18 Henry Ansgar Kelly *Ideas and Forms of Tragedy from Aristotle to the Middle Ages*
19 Martin Irvine *The Making of Textual Culture: Grammatica and Literary Theory, 350–1100*
20 Larry Scanlon *Narrative, Authority and Power: The Medieval Exemplum and the Chaucerian Tradition*
21 Erik Kooper *Medieval Dutch Literature in its European Context*
22 Steven Botterill *Dante and the Mystical Tradition: Bernard of Clairvaux in the "Commedia"*
23 Peter Biller and Anne Hudson (eds) *Heresy and Literacy, 1000–1530*
24 Christopher Baswell *Virgil in Medieval England: Figuring the "Aeneid" from the Twelfth Century to Chaucer*
25 James Simpson *Sciences and Self in Medieval Poetry: Alan of Lille's "Anticlaudianus" and John Gower's "Confessio Amantis"*
26 Joyce Coleman *Public Reading and the Reading Public in Late Medieval England and France*
27 Suzanne Reynolds *Medieval Reading: Grammar, Rhetoric and the Classical Text*

28 Charlotte Brewer *Editing "Piers Plowman": the Evolution of the Text*
29 Walter Haug *Vernacular Literary Theory in the Middle Ages: The German Tradition in its European Context*
30 Sarah Spence *Texts and the Self in the Twelfth Century*
31 Edwin Craun *Lies, Slander and Obscenity in Medieval English Literature: Pastoral Rhetoric and the Deviant Speaker*
32 Patricia E. Grieve *"Floire and Blancheflor" and the European Romance*
33 Huw Pryce (ed.) *Literacy in Medieval Celtic Societies*
34 Mary Carruthers *The Craft of Thought: Meditation, Rhetoric, and the Making of Images, 400–1200*
35 Beate Schmolke-Hasselman *The Evolution of Arthurian Romance: The Verse Tradition from Chrétien to Froissart*
36 Siân Echard *Arthurian Narrative in the Latin Tradition*
37 Fiona Somerset *Clerical Discourse and Lay Audience in Late Medieval England*
38 Florence Percival *Chaucer's Legendary Good Women*
39 Christopher Cannon *The Making of Chaucer's English: A Study of Words*
40 Rosalind Brown-Grant *Christine de Pizan and the Moral Defence of Women: Reading Beyond Gender*
41 Richard Newhauser *The Early History of Greed: the Sin of Avarice in Early Medieval Thought and Literature*
42 Margaret Clunies Ross *Old Icelandic Literature and Society*
43 Donald Maddox *Fictions of Identity in Medieval France*
44 Rita Copeland *Pedagogy, Intellectuals, and Dissent in the Later Middle Ages: Lollardy and Ideas of Learning*
45 Kantik Ghosh *The Wycliffite Heresy: Authority and the Interpretation of Texts*
46 Mary C. Erler *Women, Reading, and Piety in Late Medieval England*
47 D. H. Green *The Beginnings of Medieval Romance: Fact and Fiction 1150–1220*
48 J. A. Burrow *Gestures and Looks in Medieval Narrative*
49 Ardis Butterfield *Poetry and Music in Medieval France: From Jean Renart to Guillaume de Machaut*
50 Emily Steiner *Documentary Culture and the Making of Medieval English Literature*
51 William E. Burgwinkle *Sodomy, Masculinity, and Law in Medieval Literature*
52 Nick Havely *Dante and the Franciscans: Poverty and the Papacy in the "Commedia"*
53 Siegfried Wenzel *Latin Sermon Collections from Later Medieval England*
54 Ananya Jahanara Kabir and Deanne Williams (eds) *Postcolonial Approaches to the European Middle Ages: Translating Cultures*
55 Mark Miller *Philosophical Chaucer: Love, Sex, and Agency in the "Canterbury Tales"*
56 Simon Gilson *Dante and Renaissance Florence*
57 Ralph Hanna *London Literature, 1300–1380*
58 Maura Nolan *John Lydgate and the Making of Public Culture*

59 Nicolette Zeeman *"Piers Plowman" and the Medieval Discourse of Desire*
60 Anthony Bale *The Jew in the Medieval Book: English Antisemitisms 1350–1500*
61 Robert J. Meyer-Lee *Poets and Power from Chaucer to Wyatt*
62 Isabel Davis *Writing Masculinity in the Later Middle Ages*
63 John M. Fyler *Language and the Declining World in Chaucer, Dante and Jean de Meun*
64 Matthew Giancarlo *Parliament and Literature in Late Medieval England*
65 D. H. Green *Women Readers in the Middle Ages*
66 Mary Dove *The First English Bible: The Text and Context of the Wycliffite Versions*
67 Jenni Nuttall *The Creation of Lancastrian Kingship: Literature, Language and Politics in Late Medieval England*
68 Laura Ashe *Fiction and History in England, 1066–1200*
69 J. A. Burrow *The Poetry of Praise*
70 Mary Carruthers *The Book of Memory: A Study of Memory in Medieval Culture*
71 Andrew Cole *Literature and Heresy in the Age of Chaucer*
72 Suzanne M. Yeager *Jerusalem in Medieval Narrative*
73 Nicole R. Rice *Lay Piety and Religious Discipline in Middle English Literature*
74 D. H. Green *Women and Marriage in German Medieval Romance*
75 Peter Godman *Paradoxes of Conscience in the High Middle Ages: Abelard, Heloise and the Archpoet*
76 Edwin D. Craun *Ethics and Power in Medieval English Reformist Writing*
77 David Matthews *Writing to the King: Nation, Kingship, and Literature in England, 1250–1350*
78 Mary Carruthers (ed) *Rhetoric Beyond Words: Delight and Persuasion in the Arts of the Middle Ages*
79 Katharine Breen *Imagining an English Reading Public, 1150–1400*
80 Antony J. Hasler *Court Poetry in Late Medieval England and Scotland: Allegories of Authority*
81 Shannon Gayk *Image, Text, and Religious Reform in Fifteenth-Century England*
82 Lisa H. Cooper *Artisans and Narrative Craft in Late-Medieval England*
83 Alison Cornish *Vernacular Translation in Dante's Italy: Illiterate Literature*
84 Jane Gilbert *Living Death in Medieval French and English Literature*
85 Jessica Rosenfeld *Ethics and Enjoyment in Late Medieval Poetry: Love after Aristotle*